Success in
PRINCIPLES OF CATERING

Success Studybooks

Accounting and Costing
Accounting and Costing: Problems and Projects
Book-keeping and Accounts
British History 1760–1914
British History since 1914
Business Calculations
Chemistry
Commerce
Commerce: West African Edition
Communication
Economic Geography
Economics
Economics: West African Edition
Electronics
Elements of Banking
European History 1815–1941
Geography: Human and Regional
Geography: Physical and Mapwork
Information Processing
Insurance
Investment
Law
Management: Personnel
Nutrition
Office Practice
Organic Chemistry
Physics
Principles of Accounting
Principles of Accounting: Answer Book
Statistics
Twentieth Century World Affairs
World History since 1945

Success in
PRINCIPLES OF CATERING

Michael Colleer, MPhil FHCIMA MRPharmS
Colin Sussams, BEd
Colchester Institute

John Murray

© Michael Colleer and Colin Sussams 1990

First published 1990

All rights reserved. No part of this publication may be reproduced, copied or transmitted save with the written permission of John Murray (Publishers) Ltd, 50 Albemarle Street, London W1X 4BD, or in accordance with the provisions of the Copyright Act 1956 (as amended), or under the terms of any licence permitting limited copying issued by The Copyright Licensing Agency, 33-34 Alfred Place, London WC1E 7DP.

Any person who does any unauthorised act in relation to this publication may be liable to criminal prosecution and civil claims for damages.

Typeset in 11/12 pt Compugraphic English Times
by Colset Private Ltd, Singapore
Printed in Great Britain by Richard Clay Ltd, Bungay, Suffolk.

British Library Cataloguing in Publication Data

Colleer, Michael
   Success in principles of catering.
   1. Catering
   I. Title   II. Sussams, Colin   III. Series
   642'.4

ISBN 0-7195-4771-7

Contents

Foreword xiii

Acknowledgements xiv

Part 1   Working in the catering industry   1

1 **Industrial studies**   2
    1.1   The main services provided by the catering industry   2
    1.2   Sectors of the industry   2
    1.3   Employment in the industry   5
    1.4   Qualifications   7
    1.5   Useful addresses   8

2 **Health and safety**   9
    2.1   Main regulations and responsibilities   9
    2.2   Writing a health-and-safety policy   10
    2.3   Creating a safe workplace   10
    2.4   Care for your own health and safety   11
    2.5   Accidents   11
    2.6   First aid   14
    2.7   Fires and fire prevention   15

Part 2   Commodities   19

3 **Cereals and pasta**   20
    3.1   Wheat   20
    3.2   Barley   22
    3.3   Maize   22
    3.4   Oats   22
    3.5   Rice   23
    3.6   Semolina   23
    3.7   Rye   24
    3.8   Millet   24
    3.9   Other starch products   24
    3.10 Storage of cereals   24
    3.11 Pasta   24

4 **Meat**   26

5 Poultry 27
- 5.1 Choosing and buying for value 27
- 5.2 Thawing frozen poultry 27
- 5.3 Chicken 27
- 5.4 Duck 31
- 5.5 Goose 32
- 5.6 Turkey 32
- 5.7 Guinea-fowl 32
- 5.8 Quail 33

6 Beef and veal 34
- 6.1 Types of beef 34
- 6.2 Maturing and tenderising beef 34
- 6.3 Purchasing and storing beef 35
- 6.4 Larger cuts of beef 36
- 6.5 Small cuts of beef 41
- 6.6 Methods of cooking used for beef 42
- 6.7 Veal 42
- 6.8 Purchasing and storing veal 42
- 6.9 Cuts of veal 43
- 6.10 Methods of cooking used for veal 45

7 Lamb 46
- 7.1 Types of lamb 46
- 7.2 Purchasing and storing lamb 47
- 7.3 Cuts of lamb 47
- 7.4 Methods of cooking used for lamb 50

8 Pork and bacon 51
- 8.1 Porkers and baconers 51
- 8.2 Types of porker 51
- 8.3 Purchasing and storing pork 51
- 8.4 Cuts of pork 52
- 8.5 Uses of pork 54
- 8.6 Bacon 54
- 8.7 Joints of bacon 55
- 8.8 Purchasing and storing bacon 56
- 8.9 Uses of bacon 56
- 8.10 Ham 57

9 Game 58
- 9.1 The supply of game 58
- 9.2 Quality purchasing points for young game 58
- 9.3 Uses of game 59

10 Fish and shellfish 63
- 10.1 The supply of fish 63
- 10.2 Classification of fish 63
- 10.3 Purchasing and storing fish 64
- 10.4 Cuts of fish 66

　　　　10.5　Identification and uses of fish　68
　　　　10.6　Preserved and processed fish　72
　　　　10.7　Caviar　74
　　　　10.8　Classification of shellfish　75
　　　　10.9　Purchasing and storing shellfish　76
　　　　10.10　Uses of shellfish　76
　　　　10.11　Other commodities classed as seafood　80

11　Eggs　81
　　　　11.1　Composition and structure　81
　　　　11.2　Quality points for fresh eggs　81
　　　　11.3　Purchasing and storing eggs　82
　　　　11.4　Spoilage of eggs　83
　　　　11.5　Uses and properties of eggs　83
　　　　11.6　Methods of cooking eggs　85

12　Milk and milk products　86
　　　　12.1　Milk　86
　　　　12.2　Cream　87
　　　　12.3　Yoghurt and fermented milk　88
　　　　12.4　Cheese　88
　　　　12.5　Butter　93

13　Fats and oils　94
　　　　13.1　Uses of fats and oils　94
　　　　13.2　Types of fat and oil　94

14　Vegetables, salads, and pulses　97
　　　　14.1　Classification of vegetables　97
　　　　14.2　Purchasing and storing vegetables　98
　　　　14.3　Vegetables and their uses　100
　　　　14.4　Dried pulses　107

15　Fruit and nuts　110
　　　　15.1　Classification of fruit　110
　　　　15.2　Purchasing and storing fruit　110
　　　　15.3　Fruit and their uses　111
　　　　15.4　Nuts　114

16　Sugars and syrups　116
　　　　16.1　Sugars　116
　　　　16.2　Syrups　117

17　Non-alcoholic beverages　118
　　　　17.1　Tea　118
　　　　17.2　Herb teas　118
　　　　17.3　Coffee　119

18　Herbs and spices　123
　　　　18.1　Herbs　123

18.2 Spices 124
18.3 Uses of herbs and spices 126

19 Condiments 127
19.1 Salt 127
19.2 Pepper 127
19.3 Monosodium glutamate (MSG) 128
19.4 Vinegar 128
19.5 Mustard 128
19.6 Bottled sauces 129

20 Pickles and chutneys 130
20.1 Pickles 130
20.2 Chutneys 130

21 Essences, flavourings, and colourings 131

22 Convenience foods 132
22.1 When convenience foods might be used 132
22.2 Labour and food costs 133
22.3 Special points concerning convenience foods 133

23 Food additives 134

Part 3 Catering and food science 135

24 Nutrition 137
24.1 Components of food 137
24.2 Digestion 138
24.3 Absorption 139
24.4 Functions of nutrients 139
24.5 The body's need for nutrients 145
24.6 A balanced diet 148
24.7 Contribution of foods to a diet 149
24.8 The effect of cooking processes on nutrients 153
24.9 The effect of storage and preparation on nutrients in food 154
24.10 Nutritional value of convenience foods 154
24.11 Antinutritional food components 155

25 Food science 156
25.1 Why food is cooked 156
25.2 Substances in food affected by cooking 157
25.3 Cooking by heat – heat transfer 159
25.4 Substances used to transfer heat 163
25.5 Other methods of cooking 164
25.6 Energy in cooking 166
25.7 Refrigeration 169

26 Microbiology and hygiene 170
26.1 Types of micro-organism 170
26.2 Bacteria 170
26.3 Moulds 172
26.4 Yeasts 173
26.5 Conditions needed for the growth of micro-organisms 173
26.6 Useful micro-organisms 175
26.7 Food spoilage and food preservation 176
26.8 Food poisoning 178
26.9 Personal hygiene 180
26.10 Kitchen hygiene 181
26.11 Hygienic work practices 182
26.12 Pests 187

Part 4 Food preparation and cooking 189

27 Introduction to food preparation and cooking 190
27.1 Methods of cooking 190
27.2 Basic preparatory tasks 191
27.3 Basic procedures and equipment 192

28 Boiling 193
28.1 General principles 193
28.2 Boiling vegetables 194
28.3 Boiling fish 196
28.4 Boiling meats and poultry 197
28.5 Boiling eggs 197
28.6 Boiling rice 198
28.7 Boiling pulses 198
28.8 Boiling pasta 198
28.9 Some points to be observed when boiling 198
28.10 Equipment used for boiling 199

29 Poaching 202
29.1 General principles 202
29.2 Poaching fish 203
29.3 Poaching meats 204
29.4 Poaching fruit 204
29.5 Poaching eggs 205
29.6 Some points to be observed when poaching 205
29.7 Equipment used for poaching 205

30 Stewing 206
30.1 General principles 206
30.2 Types of stew 207
30.3 Some points to be observed when stewing 207
30.4 Equipment used for stewing 207

31 Braising 209
31.1 General principles 209

    31.2   Braising meat   209
    31.3   Braising vegetables   210
    31.4   Some points to be observed when braising   210
    31.5   Equipment used for braising   211

32 Steaming   212
    32.1   General principles   212
    32.2   Steaming sweet and savoury puddings   213
    32.3   Steaming vegetables   213
    32.4   Steaming fish and poultry   213
    32.5   Some points to be observed when steaming   213
    32.6   Equipment used for steaming   213

33 Deep frying   215
    33.1   General principles   215
    33.2   Suitable frying fats or oils   216
    33.3   Selection of foods for deep frying   217
    33.4   Presentation of deep-fried foods   217
    33.5   Some points to be observed when deep frying   218
    33.6   Equipment used for deep frying   218

34 Shallow frying   221
    34.1   General principles   221
    34.2   Shallow-fried-fish – meunière   222
    34.3   Stir-frying   222
    34.4   Flambé method   222
    34.5   Commodities suitable for shallow frying   223
    34.6   Some points to be observed when shallow frying   223
    34.7   Equipment used for shallow frying   224

35 Baking   226
    35.1   General principles   226
    35.2   Baking cakes, pastries, and bread   226
    35.3   Cooking in a bain-marie in an oven   227
    35.4   Baking fish   227
    35.5   Baking en croûte   227
    35.6   Baking vegetables   227
    35.7   Baking fruit   228
    35.8   Some points to be observed when baking   228
    35.9   Equipment used for baking   228

36 Grilling   230
    36.1   General principles   230
    36.2   Commodities suitable for grilling   231
    36.3   Degree of cooking for grilled foods   232
    36.4   Some points to be observed when grilling   233
    36.5   Equipment used for grilling   233

37 Sautéing 237
    37.1   General principles 237
    37.2   Commodities suitable for sautéing 237
    37.3   Special points to be observed when sautéing 238
    37.4   Equipment used for sautéing 238

38 Roasting 239
    38.1   General principles 239
    38.2   Roasting meat, poultry, and game 239
    38.3   Roasting vegetables 241
    38.4   Some points to be observed when roasting 241
    38.5   Equipment used for roasting 241

39 Poêlé cooking 244
    39.1   General principles 244
    39.2   Items suitable for poêlé cooking 244
    39.3   Equipment used for poêlé cooking 244

40 Cold preparations 245
    40.1   Decorated cold-buffet dishes 245
    40.2   Hors-d'oeuvres 246
    40.3   Salads 246
    40.4   Sandwiches and filled rolls 247
    40.5   Some points to be observed when making cold preparations 247

41 Microwave cooking 248
    41.1   General principles 248
    41.2   Points to be observed when cooking by microwave 248

42 Batch cooking 250
    42.1   General principles 250
    42.2   Equipment used for batch cooking 251

43 Sous-vide cooking 257
    43.1   General principles 257
    43.2   Some points about sous-vide cooking 258
    43.3   Vacuum packing 258

44 Centralised production 259
    44.1   General principles 259
    44.2   Cook-chill operation 259
    44.3   Cook-freeze operation 262

45 Stocks, thickening agents, and sauces 263
    45.1   Stocks 263
    45.2   Glazes 263
    45.3   Thickening agents 264
    45.4   Sauces 267

46 Cooking utensils and small equipment 269
- 46.1 Materials used in cooking equipment 269
- 46.2 Small items of kitchen equipment 272
- 46.3 Pots and pans 274
- 46.4 Professional cooks' knives 274
- 46.5 Electrical food-preparation equipment 276
- 46.6 Dishwashers 283
- 46.7 Hotplates and heated cupboards 284

Part 5 The business of catering 287

47 The menu and the organisation 288
- 47.1 Types of menu 288
- 47.2 Course content of different menus 289
- 47.3 Factors to be taken into account in compiling a menu 291
- 47.4 The use of computers in menu planning 292
- 47.5 Examples of menus for a variety of operations and customer requirements 293
- 47.6 Presenting and selling the menu 296
- 47.7 The language of the menu 300
- 47.8 Producing new dishes 300
- 47.9 Design of the premises in relation to the menu 301
- 47.10 Kitchen organisation 307
- 47.11 Professional attitudes and behaviour of staff 309

48 Catering calculations and costing 311
- 48.1 Measurement systems 311
- 48.2 Applied calculations 314
- 48.3 Food costing 318
- 48.4 Standard recipes 320
- 48.5 The cost of sales 320
- 48.6 Gross profit and net profit 322
- 48.7 Value added tax 323
- 48.8 Business documents 324
- 48.9 Stock control 326
- 48.10 Food control 329
- 48.11 Computers and food control 331

Index 337

Foreword

The constantly changing approaches to the provision of food and drink mean that people working in the industry, or thinking about working in the industry, need to have a fund of skills and knowledge which can be applied in almost any situation which is likely to arise. This also means that any work leading to qualifications must take account of this flexible approach which is so important for a successful career in the catering industry.

This book, as its title implies, concentrates on principles which can be applied in a variety of situations. It is not a practical cookery book and you are strongly advised to use it in conjunction with your practical work and possibly a practical cookery book. For this reason you will not find many recipes, and the commodities selected for study are those in most common use. Similarly, the equipment illustrated and discussed is limited to that which you could find in many trade production kitchens.

It is hoped that you will find the book both readable and useful and that it will contribute to some extent to a successful and enjoyable career for you in the catering industry.

Acknowledgements

The wide spread of information contained in such a book as this has necessitated help and advice from many people. Mention cannot be made of everyone who has assisted us at some time, but special thanks are due to Dorothy Slyfield and Wilf Hudson for their contributions in the early stages; to Richard Warner and Ivor Mounteney who were responsible for the business calculations and French respectively; to Sandra Fairbairn for secretarial support; and to Bob Ball for some of the photographs.

We are grateful to Bill Farnsworth of Cantlow Software for permission to use material.

Thanks must go to the Success team at John Murray, especially to Bob Davenport for his unfailing support and constant encouragement in his editorial role.

Our thanks are also due to the very large number of catering students – past and present – who made the book both necessary and possible.

MICHAEL COLLEER AND COLIN SUSSAMS

The authors and publishers wish to thank the following for permission to reproduce the illustrations indicated:

British Standards Institution   figs 2.1, 2.2, and 2.3 – extracts from BS 5378: *Safety Signs and Colours, Part 1* (1980)
Bob Ball, Colchester Institute   cover, figs 46.1, 46.2, 46.3, 48.8, 48.9, and 48.13
G. G. E. Bartlett and Son Ltd   figs 28.2 and 42.3
Beecham Pharmaceuticals, Research Division   fig. 26.3
British Gas plc   fig. 47.7, from *A Student's Guide to Gas Catering* (1987)
Cona Ltd   fig. 17.1
Falcon Catering Equipment   figs 28.1, 28.3, 33.1, 34.1, 34.2, 35.1, and 42.1
HMSO   figs 46.5 46.6, 46.7, 46.8, and 46.9 – diagrams reproduced from *Food Preparation Machinery* (Health and Safety Executive) with the permission of the Controller, Her Majesty's Stationery Office
Happy Eater Restaurants   fig. 47.6
Hobart Manufacturing Co. Ltd   fig. 47.8
Hotel Inter-Continental, London   fig. 47.5
Don Mackean   figs 3.1, 4.1(a), and 11.1 – taken from *Success in Nutrition*
Meat and Livestock Commission   fig. 4.1(b)
North-East Essex Area Health Authority   fig. 47.3
Stratford Catering Equipment Manufacturing Ltd   figs 47.9 and 47.10

PART ONE
Working in the catering industry

The first part of this book is intended to introduce you to the idea of working in the catering industry. All industries have their own special features, and the catering industry is no exception.

One of the peculiarities of the catering industry is the immense range and variety of services that it offers. Chapter 1 looks at many of these and explains briefly what their role is. It also examines career patterns and opportunities to acquire appropriate qualifications to enable you to progress within the industry.

Chapter 2 considers the problems of health and safety relating to the catering industry. It outlines most of the legal requirements with regard to health and safety and also points out the commoner hazards associated with the use of catering equipment. This chapter should not be regarded as containing all that there is to know about health and safety, however. Other chapters in this book include references to health and safety – either yours, your colleagues', or your customers' – for example, chapters 27–46 on cooking processes and chapter 26 on microbiology and hygiene.

The very diverse nature of the catering industry means that these chapters which are concerned with 'working in the catering industry' cannot possibly cover all aspects of working or of health and safety. You are strongly recommended to bear health and safety in mind throughout all your study of this book and your work in the industry.

1 Industrial studies

Welcome to the catering industry!

In this chapter we shall explore the industry and show what a wide range of activities the term 'catering' covers. The large range of activities means that the variety of employment available for suitably qualified people is tremendous. It is the purpose of this book to help you to gain a qualification and to give you sufficient knowledge to progress within the industry.

It must be remembered that the catering industry is constantly changing to meet the demands of customers, and you must have sufficient skills, knowledge, and understanding to adapt to these changes as they come.

1.1 The main services provided by the catering industry

Catering is a 'service' industry – that is to say, it provides a service to customers in return for payment. Some jobs within the industry do not involve contact with the customer or with cash, but whatever position you eventually hold will have at least an indirect effect on the customer and your wages will depend on the fact that the customer will pay for a service, either directly or indirectly.

The services provided can be separated into four areas and, except in very small operations, the tasks in each will be undertaken by different groups of people:

- *Food* This may be provided by establishments ranging from a modest sandwich-bar to a large high-class hotel restaurant.
- *Drink* The type of operation may demand little knowledge of beverages or considerable expertise with alcoholic beverages.
- *Accommodation* This normally means the provision of somewhere to sleep, but of course it may include many additional services, such as laundry and shoe-cleaning.
- *Reception* Reception will involve welcoming prospective customers and making sure that they are able to get any or all of the other services which they may require, such as booking theatre tickets and changing foreign currency.

These four types of service provided by the industry can be and are applied in a number of different situations which are referred to as *sectors* of the industry. It is unlikely that you will ever work in all of these sectors, but you should at least know of their existence.

1.2 Sectors of the industry

(Remember that any of these can involve any of the four services mentioned above.)

It is useful to divide the sectors of the industry into two main groups:

- those that aim to make a profit by providing a service (*commercial*);

- those that provide a service without necessarily setting out to make a profit (*non-commercial*).

This distinction is becoming slightly blurred, however – for example, private hospitals are set up to make a profit, but not necessarily from the provision of food, drink, and accommodation.

Commercial catering operations

HOTELS

Hotels offer food, drink, and accommodation. The standard of these will vary according to the type of hotel and the type of customer that the hotel is trying to attract. Many hotels offer additional facilities for their guests, such as office services. Although many hotels are members of large hotel groups, many are not. Probably nearly half of the hotels in the United Kingdom have fewer than ten bedrooms.

MOTELS

It is characteristic of motels that the customers stay only for a night or two. The motel may provide meals in a restaurant attached to the operation and/or supply self-catering facilities.

GUEST HOUSES, BED AND BREAKFAST, AND FARMHOUSES

These tend to cater for much smaller numbers of people than hotels, and the services they provide are likely to be somewhat limited. This is not to say that the standard may not be first-class.

HOLIDAY CAMPS

Many holiday camps are only open for part of the year, usually the 'summer season'. Their customers often stay for set periods such as a week or a fortnight. The type of accommodation may range from 'basic' to good. The food is often self-service or cafeteria-style.

PUBLIC HOUSES

Licensed houses and inns are all licensed to sell alcoholic beverages within the law. There are at least 40 000 of them in the UK. Very many of them now sell food and operate restaurants within the premises. Some licensed houses offer accommodation.

RESTAURANTS

The aim of a restaurant is to sell food and drink. Many restaurants are licensed to sell alcoholic beverages. Some restaurants limit their opening hours to coincide with 'meal-times', while others are 'open all hours'. A restaurant may be a member of a chain of restaurants owned by the same company.

FAST-FOOD OUTLETS

It is common for these to have a very restricted menu, to enable the food to be dispensed quickly. If they form part of a chain, they are likely to have the same menu and the same decor and restaurant layout as the other members of the chain. Some of them have take-away facilities.

WINE AND COCKTAIL BARS

These tend to sell a wide range of alcoholic beverages, but most of them do also provide food, although the choice may be limited.

TRANSPORT CATERING

Food and drink may be provided while the customer is on the move – as on trains, boats, or aeroplanes – or at appropriate stopping points such as stations, ports, or airline terminals.

CONFERENCE CENTRES

Conference centres provide the space and facilities for addressing large numbers of people and/or a number of small groups of people at the same time. Food and drink are usually provided, and many of the purpose-built centres are also able to offer residential accommodation.

CLUBS

The main purpose of clubs is to provide sporting or social facilities and/or entertainment to those who have paid a membership fee. In addition, most clubs provide drink. Some will provide food as well, and a few provide accommodation.

LEISURE COMPLEXES

As with clubs, their main aim is to offer a variety of leisure activities, but membership is not usually required. They may also supply food and drink to their patrons.

CONTRACT CATERING

This is a service in which a contractor agrees to undertake the catering for another company which is not a caterer, such as providing staff meals. The contractor has to operate within the terms of the agreement.

Non-commercial catering operations

HOSPITAL AND WELFARE CATERING

Hospitals have to provide food, drink, and accommodation for a constantly changing range of people, within a strictly controlled budget. Day centres may just provide food. Residential homes provide accommodation and food and drink and cater for people who are resident over a long period of time.

HALLS OF RESIDENCE AND HOSTELS

These provide accommodation for people living away from home for educational or training purposes. Food and drink may be available, or self-catering facilities may be provided. Residential training centres may be run by companies for their own employees.

EDUCATION ESTABLISHMENTS

The school meals service is the responsibility of the local education authority and is responsible for supplying reasonably priced lunches in schools.

INDUSTRIAL CATERING

This sector provides food and drink to employees while they are at work. This service may be operated by the employers themselves or be handed over to contract caterers (see page 4).

THE ARMED SERVICES

Her Majesty's Forces need to be catered for both in the UK and overseas. The services have their own catering organisations which are largely staffed by services personnel.

The lists above could be extended (we haven't included prisons, for example!). You have probably had experience of several of the sectors mentioned and you must have begun to realise what a vast amount of trade comes under the heading of 'catering'. As a result of this, catering is one of the largest employers of labour in the United Kingdom and contributes very substantially to the economy, through its earnings both from UK residents and from overseas visitors.

1.3 Employment in the industry

If you want to find out about the opportunities within the catering industry, there are a number of people who will be happy to help you. If you are unsure of the precise area of the industry in which you wish to work, a tutor at your local college of further education will probably be pleased to advise. Many companies supply material about their operations and career prospects, and local members of the industry are usually willing to chat. Other organisations listed at the end of this section may also be useful contacts. Your local careers service will be able to help you find suitable employment.

In all sectors of the industry, how well you progress will to a large extent depend on you. Of course your technical skills are of great importance, and the more you can develop them the better, but you will be unlikely to work in isolation, so a lot of other attributes which relate to working with people will be just as important. You probably know what some of them are, and we shall look at them in section 47.11. All this can be summed up in one word: 'professionalism'. Your aim should be to be a *professional* caterer.

Career opportunities within the industry can be divided into four areas –

food preparation, food and beverage service, housekeeping, and reception. As you progress within an organisation, these areas may become less well-defined, however, and at certain levels of supervision and management your responsibility may be for more than one area.

Most organisations will usually require you to have an appropriate qualification from those listed in section 1.4, and there will also normally be an induction period of training and getting used to the organisation in which you are to work. This may vary from a few hours to several days, depending on the complexity of your employer's business set-up.

Food preparation

The career opportunities in food preparation are best considered as you read chapter 47. The way in which food-preparation staff are organised in a kitchen will depend on the type of operation. Progress within this staff structure will depend on how you have performed.

Food and beverage service

In a traditional hotel or restaurant, a trainee or commis waiter would assist a station waiter, who is responsible for the food service in part of the restaurant. After a period spent as a station waiter you might be promoted to head waiter if you had done your job well.

As a supervisor in a mass-market food restaurant you need to know about all aspects of the work. Many supervisors have worked their way up through the company, having first gained experience in taking orders and serving customers.

Housekeeping

A new entrant to this area of work might begin by doing some housekeeping and general cleaning duties. The next stage could be that of floor housekeeper, who is responsible for the whole of one section of the accommodation, supervising staff and maintaining standards for that area. The head housekeeper is responsible for the accommodation of the whole operation and may have an assistant head housekeeper. In the case of a large hotel group, an executive housekeeper may be employed to look after the housekeeping in a number of hotels.

Reception

The work of the reception desk and front office will vary with the size of the operation. A trainee receptionist might begin by dealing with advance reservations and simple clerical tasks. This might be followed by duties at the reception desk itself, which may involve attending to customers' needs and dealing with cash and billing. The next stage could be that of shift leader, where responsibility is taken for a period of the day. A reception manager is responsible for the whole of the reception operation.

In addition to these fairly clear-cut positions in the different areas of the catering industry – which of course may be in any sector of the industry –

there are other areas that are common to many industries. Personnel and training and sales and marketing are important aspects of the catering industry which present opportunities for suitably qualified people with experience of the industry.

1.4 Qualifications

The catering industry places great emphasis on appropriate qualifications. These are obtainable by a number of methods such as full-time or part-time college courses and training schemes organised by the Training Agency or the Hotel and Catering Training Board and other training organisations.

The National Council for Vocational Qualifications (NCVQ) is coordinating work on establishing National Vocational Qualifications (NVQs) in various aspects of hotel and catering work. NVQs will certify competence in appropriate tasks and can be obtained by successful performance in relevant City and Guilds or BTEC examinations and in practical assessment in the Hotel and Catering Training Board 'Caterbase' programme (see below). Employees within the catering industry sometimes need to gain additional or updated qualifications to further their career prospects. It is usually possible to do this, and the NVQ system will allow credits towards additional qualifications to be accumulated at the employee's own pace.

Examining and validating bodies

- *The City and Guilds of London Institute*   There are City and Guilds examinations in General catering, Cookery (basic, intermediate, and advanced), and specialist types of cookery; Food service (basic and advanced); Reception studies; Accommodation studies; and Alcoholic beverages. Successful performance in these may count towards a National Vocational Qualification (NVQ).
- *The Business & Technician Education Council*   BTEC validates First, National, and Higher National certificates and diplomas in hotel and catering studies. These certificates and diplomas may also count towards a National Vocational Qualification.
- *The Hotel and Catering Training Board*   The HCTB organises the 'Caterbase' programme for assessing practical performance in catering skills. Successful performance in this and appropriate City and Guilds or BTEC awards may count towards a National Vocational Qualification.
- *The Wine and Spirit Education Trust* offers a range of qualifications involving expertise in many aspects of alcoholic beverages.
- *The Royal Society of Health* sets examinations in food hygiene and nutrition.
- *The Royal Institute of Public Health and Hygiene* awards qualifications in hygienic food handling.

The awards of the above organisations are designed to be obtained as a result of following courses of study that include practical work, by full-time, part-time, or day-release methods.

Working in the catering industry

Professional and technical associations

A number of professional and technical associations and institutions exist to encourage and help caterers to develop and maintain the highest standards within the industry. Among these are:

- *The Hotel, Catering and Institutional Management Association* The HCIMA aims to set and maintain standards of catering management to benefit the industry, its staff, and its customers. Membership is only available to employees in the industry who can meet the educational and industrial standards required. It is also an examining body.
- *The Cookery and Food Association* The Association is open to people in the industry who wish to further their professionalism. It produces a magazine and organises meetings and competitions to encourage the maintenance of the highest standards of craft skills.

Other professional associations exist which encourage membership from those employed in specific sectors of the industry. Their aim is usually to support and inform those who work in that particular sector.

You could well benefit by joining an appropriate association at some stage in your career, as it will keep you up to date with developments and new ideas and bring you into contact with other members of the industry working in your area.

1.5 Useful addresses

- Business & Technician Education Council, Central House, Upper Woburn Place, London WC1H 0HH
- City and Guilds of London Institute, 76 Portland Place, London W1N 4AA
- Cookery and Food Association, 1 Victoria Parade, 331 Sandycombe Road, Richmond, Surrey TW9 3NB
- Hotel, Catering and Institutional Management Association, 191 Trinity Road, London SW17 7HN
- Hotel and Catering Training Board, International House, High Street, Ealing, London W5 5DB
- Royal Institute of Public Health and Hygiene, 28 Portland Place, London W1N 4DE
- Royal Society of Health, RSH House, 38a St George's Drive, London SW1V 4BH
- Wine and Spirit Education Trust Ltd, Five Kings House, Kennet Wharf Lane, Upper Thames Street, London EC4V 3AJ

2 Health and safety

(The Hotel and Catering Training Board (HCTB) publishes some very useful material that will help you to put into practice much of the rather complicated legislation discussed below. The HCTB's address is given in section 1.5.)

Everyone at work is responsible for behaving in a safe and hygienic manner so that we do not place ourselves, our colleagues, or our customers at risk. Employers must maintain a safe working environment, and employees must co-operate with management in carrying out the firm's safety policy.

2.1 Main regulations and responsibilities

The Health and Safety at Work Act 1974 is one of a number of regulations which are designed to protect people while at work. The Offices, Shops and Railway Premises Act 1963 also relates to working conditions. The Food Hygiene Regulations 1970 and The Food Act 1984 are particularly concerned with conditions under which food is prepared and served (see chapter 26). The environmental health officer (EHO) employed by the local authority is responsible for enforcing the regulations.

As is mentioned in chapter 26, EHOs are only too pleased to advise you on any problems and should be regarded as a source of information and help, rather than as law enforcement officers. However, EHOs do have responsibilities to the local authority and can enter premises at any reasonable time to carry out an inspection. They also have the power to remove, destroy, or make harmless anything that they consider to be a danger or to present a risk of personal injury. If the law is not being complied with, EHOs may give advice on how to improve matters. If this advice is not taken, they may serve a *prohibition order* which prevents the problem continuing or an *improvement notice* which requires that action to remedy the fault is taken within a certain time-limit. If no notice is taken of either of these, they may issue a *prosecution notice* which may result in a fine, imprisonment, or both. Such action will badly damage the reputation of the business and its staff.

Employers have particular responsibilities under the Health and Safety at Work Act. They should

- provide safe equipment and safe working methods;
- ensure that the use, handling, storage, and transport of everything are safe and without risk to health;
- provide information, instruction, training, and supervision to ensure health and safety;
- provide a safe workplace, including safe access to the workplace;
- provide a safe working environment with adequate facilities;

- produce a written safety policy.

Employees also have responsibilities under the Health and Safety at Work Act. They should

- take reasonable care for their own health and safety;
- ensure that colleagues and other people are not adversely affected by their behaviour;
- co-operate with employers to meet health-and-safety requirements;
- ensure that there is no misuse of or interference with anything provided for health and safety.

2.2 Writing a health-and-safety policy

All employers who employ five or more employees must produce a written statement about their health-and-safety policies. The policies should be brought to the notice of all employees, either in an induction package or on notice-boards or by individual communication. The information should include details of any particular hazards or danger areas that are of special importance within a particular job or workplace. It may be particularly important to point out to new staff in a kitchen the need for tidiness and for wearing protective clothing and footwear. The health-and-safety policy may also include items that relate to the company's policies, such as periodic training in safety or the use of updated machinery as well as who to get in touch with about any aspect of health and safety.

Companies must set up joint employer–employee safety committees if requested to by safety representatives (who are employees), to make sure that health-and-safety policies are kept up-to-date and relevant to the operations for which they were originally designed. Since both employers and employees have responsibilities under the regulations, this would seem to be a very appropriate move.

2.3 Creating a safe workplace

Various regulations require that the premises are safe and that the level of lighting, ventilation, heating, and noise are acceptable. Many of these present problems in a busy kitchen.

Lighting should be sufficient without producing a glare. Frequently, stairways and corridors are poorly lighted. This makes it difficult to see if they are clean and clear of obstruction.

Poor ventilation makes working conditions difficult and can lead to tiredness and headaches. Ventilation systems that remove much of the heat and steam and fumes produced by cooking should be installed.

Since it is essential to keep all parts of the kitchen clean for hygiene reasons, the walls and floors should be made of material which is hard-wearing and easy to clean. Similarly, equipment should be maintained in good condition as it will then be both safer to use and easier to clean.

Facilities for employees need also to be considered. The provision of somewhere to store outdoor clothing and toilet and washing facilities is required by The Food Hygiene Regulations, but many employers provide more than the bare minimum required by the law and have rest-rooms and shower facilities for their staff.

Health and safety

2.4 Care for your own health and safety

Health and safety at work and food hygiene are both affected by how you look after yourself. Your diet, your personal cleanliness, your clothing, and your life-style can all influence both your own health and safety and that of others. Because you will be breaking the law if you work with food if you have certain illnesses, you should always notify your employer or supervisor when you are ill or have been ill.

2.5 Accidents

Reporting accidents

All businesses should keep records of accidents. Many firms have special accident report forms or accident books. The local authority has to be notified of an accident which causes death or serious injury. In addition it must be told about 'dangerous notifiable occurrences' such as an explosion. Accidents at work which result in three or more days' absence from work must be notified to the Department of Social Security, in accordance with the Reporting of Injuries, Diseases, and Dangerous Occurrences Regulations 1985 ('RIDDOR').

Apart from complying with the law, it makes good sense for both you and your employer to make a note of all accidents, however trivial they appear at the time, in case they may be relevant in some future dispute and also so that safety performance can be monitored.

Preventing accidents

The prevention of accidents is very much tied up with the methods of working. If you can arrange your tasks for a particular working period into a logical order – for example, washing all the produce required before processing any of it further – you should be able to avoid panic, which is frequently a cause of accidents. Untidiness can also cause accidents. Equipment left about which you are not using and spilled food which has not been cleaned up can be hazards that are quite unnecessary. If you keep your equipment in good working order – for example, keep your knives sharp – it will be much easier to use and less likely to be the cause of an accident.

However well-organised and methodical you are in your work, it is necessary for you to be aware that some equipment and situations have particular hazards associated with them.

To draw attention quickly to potentially hazardous equipment and situations, safety signs and safety colours may be used. To satisfy the Safety Signs Regulations 1980, all safety signs must comply with the recommendations of British Standard BS 5378: 1976 – even if the signs are required only temporarily.

There are four categories of sign, each with a distinctive shape and colour that have been standardised throughout the European Community:

- *Prohibition signs* These have a red outline circle with a red cross-bar and indicate either 'Stop' or that something must not be done – for example that smoking is prohibited or that water is unsuitable for drinking (see fig. 2.1).

12 Working in the catering industry

Fig. 2.1 Prohibition signs (Red, Not drinking water)

Fig. 2.2 Warning signs (Black, Yellow, CAUTION risk of fire)

Fig. 2.3 Safe condition signs (Green, First aid)

- *Warning signs*   These have a yellow triangle with a black outline and are used to indicate hazards – such as risk of fire or of tripping over thresholds (see fig. 2.2).
- *Mandatory-action signs*   These have a solid blue circle and indicate something that must be done – such as washing hands or using an adjustable guard on a machine.
- *Safe-condition signs*   These have a green rectangle and indicate safety in an emergency – such as first-aid facilities or the location of an emergency-stop button (see fig. 2.3).

Notices for fire equipment, such as a fire-phone, a fire-alarm, or a hose reel, should feature a red rectangle as recommended by BS 5499.

It should be noted that the use of safety signs does not replace the need for other accident-prevention measures.

It is illegal for anyone to operate certain machines unless they have been properly trained or are in the process of being trained and are using the machine under supervision. The types of machine are mechanical mixers, mincers, slicers, cutters, saws, and chippers. The Prescribed Dangerous Machines Order 1964 prohibits anyone under the age of 18 from using some mechanical equipment unless they are fully instructed and trained, or being trained and using it under supervision. The list of equipment includes worm-type mincers and dough mixers.

Table 2.1 lists some of the commoner possibilities of causing accidents in a kitchen. (Some of the equipment is dealt with in more detail in the chapters on particular cooking methods.)

Table 2.1   Hazards in the kitchen

Hazard	Possible dangers	Precautionary action
Ovens	High temperatures and exposed flames	Always: • open doors fully; • remove hot trays and dishes with a thick dry oven-cloth; • avoid overfilling roasting-trays and baking-sheets; • warn others that hot trays and dishes have just been removed from the oven.

Table 2.1 Hazards in the kitchen (*continued*)

Hazard	Possible dangers	Precautionary action
Boiling tables	High temperatures and exposed flames	Always: • keep the centre ring (bull's-eye) in position on solid-top stoves; • ensure that open flames are covered with cooking utensils; • reduce the heat to prevent liquids boiling over; • place saucepan handles in a safe direction; • avoid placing containers of hot liquids on a rack above the stove.
Deep-fat fryers	High temperature of frying oil	Always: • avoid overfilling with oil – follow the manufacturer's recommendation; • avoid adding wet food items; • avoid overloading with food items; • roll down sleeves to protect your arms; • carefully lower food items into the oil; • mop up any spilt oil immediately.
Grills and salamanders	High cooking temperatures	Always: • roll down sleeves to protect your arms; • use a thick dry cloth to hold grill bars and trays; • be careful when turning cooked foods.
Steamers	Sudden escape of steam from opened door	Always: • allow pressure to reduce before fully opening the door; • stand away from the door when opening; • use a thick dry cloth when handling hot trays – change it when wet.
Hot plates/cupboards and bains-marie	Hot surfaces and objects	Always: • check the water level in bains-marie at regular intervals; • stack plates carefully to allow easy removal; • check doors for easy opening.
Storage cupboards	Danger from falling objects	Always: • store heavy items on lower shelves, lighter items on higher shelves; • place cupboards to provide easy access, not so high that you cannot easily reach them.
Mechanical equipment	Risk of cuts and electric shocks	Always: • maintain equipment in good working order; • fully understand the operating instructions – these should be displayed nearby;

Table 2.1 Hazards in the kitchen (*continued*)

Hazard	Possible dangers	Precautionary action
		• locate equipment for easy access; • ensure adequate lighting; • dismantle and clean after use, having first switched off electrical equipment; • report any faults to your supervisor immediately; • observe safety regulations – particularly those relating to your age (see page 12).
Chefs' hand tools used for cutting and chopping	Risk of cuts	Always: • keep knives sharp and in good condition; • use the most suitable knife for the task being completed; • work hard at using knives competently; • clean and put away knives after use.
Floors	Falling on dirty, wet, or greasy floors	Always: • keep all floors clean and free of rubbish; • mop up any spilt water or fat immediately; • report any chipped or broken floor tiles to your supervisor; • place out of bounds those areas of the kitchen where the floor is being washed, using the appropriate prohibition sign (see pages 11–12)

2.6 First aid

There are some special regulations that employers must obey concerning the provision of first aid for employees while they are at work (the Health and Safety (First Aid) Regulations 1981). These regulations require

- adequate first-aid provision for employees who fall ill or are injured while at work,
- trained first-aiders (or someone to take charge of an incident if no first-aider is available).

The first-aid provision will depend on the number of employees and the particular hazards involved. Catering kitchens are considered to be a high-risk area, whereas other areas in a hotel are reckoned to be low or medium risk. Your local environmental health officer will advise you as to how many first-aid boxes you should have, what they should contain, and how many trained first-aiders would be suitable for your size of operation. (You should seriously consider becoming a trained first-aider by qualifying for a first-aid certificate from the St John Ambulance Association, the British Red Cross Society, or some other approved organisation.)

2.7 Fires and fire prevention

Catering kitchens carry a greater risk of fire than many other employment situations. Your friture is more likely to catch fire than an office worker's wordprocessor!

The Fire Precautions Act 1971 lays down regulations, some of which will apply only to larger operations. Hotels and employers with more than a certain number of employees have to obtain a fire certificate, but applying for this is not likely to be your responsibility until much later in your career.

Employers have certain responsibilities which will affect you at all stages of your career. One of these is to provide fire training. As an employee you should receive

- a personal written copy of fire instructions;
- two half-hour talks by a competent person, and these talks should be repeated every six months (unless you work at night, when they should be repeated every three months);
- fire drills at least every six months.

The fire training should make sure that

- you are familiar with the layout of the premises;
- you know where the emergency exits and assembly points are and how to get to them;
- you know where the fire-fighting equipment is;
- you know where the fire-alarms and warning systems are;
- you know what to do and what not to do if you discover a fire;
- you know what to do if someone else discovers a fire.

What to do if you discover a fire

- Raise the alarm.
- Call for help.
- Close doors and windows. (Fire-doors should never be left open!)
- Evacuate the building.
- Carry out any special duties which have been allocated to you – for example, checking staff at the assembly point.

If you can do so without risk to yourself or others,

- switch off power supplies;
- attack the blaze with suitable extinguishers (*but no heroics*).

Since guests or customers cannot be expected to attend fire-drill, notices must be available which tell them what to do if the fire-alarm sounds and what to do if they discover a fire.

Fire prevention

It is a good idea to have a fire-prevention checklist which suits your particular operation. This should include regular inspection of the alarm system and fire-fighting equipment, and making sure that combustible rubbish is not stored near central-heating boilers, that emergency exits are kept clear, and so on.

Fire extinguishers

Fires occur when something burns. When something burns, a number of things happen. It gets hot; it uses oxygen (from the air); it may produce flames. This means that if we can cool it down, cut off the air supply, and restrain the flames, the fire will be extinguished. Unfortunately it is not usually as easy as that, but the principles of putting out fires make use of some or all of these ideas.

Fires are classified into different groups, and extinguishers are classified into certain types. It is then possible to match the best type of extinguisher with the fire that you are tackling (Table 2.2).

Table 2.2 The choice of fire extinguishers

Type of fire	Type of extinguisher recommended
Class A (wood, paper)	Water, foam, powder, halon (fire blanket for very small fires)
Class B (fat, oil)	Foam, carbon dioxide, powder, halon, fire blanket
Class C (gas)	Foam, carbon dioxide, powder, halon
Class E (electrical)	Powder, carbon dioxide, halon

Types of fire

- *Class A* Fires where solid organic materials (wood, paper, textiles, etc.) burn and produce flames and glowing embers.
- *Class B* Fires where liquids such as fat or paint burn.
- *Class C* Fires where gas burns.
- *Class E* Fires involving electrical equipment.

(Class D involves some metals, and you are not likely to come across one of these fires in a kitchen.)

Types of fire extinguisher

- *Fire blanket* Made of heat-resistant and flame-retardant material. Used to exclude air and for personal protection.
- *Water* Used for cooling and extinguishing flames.
- *Foam* The effect is to exclude the air and retard the flame.
- *Carbon dioxide* Excludes the air.
- *Dry powders* These inhibit the flame and exclude the air.
- *Halon* Excludes the air by forming a heavy gas. Must not be used in confined spaces.

Fire extinguishers are now colour-coded to indicate the contents:

- *blue* – dry powder;

- *black* – carbon dioxide;
- *cream* – foam;
- *red* – water;
- *green* – halon.

The colour may be indicated by the label, a coloured band, or a coloured spot.

It is very important to note that

- you should not use water to try to put out fires caused by burning fat, oil, or gas or by an electrical fault;
- halon extinguishers should not be used in confined spaces if an operator is present.

PART TWO
Commodities

Commodities are groups of food items that are used for the preparation of dishes. This part of the book explains the origin and characteristics of these items, describes how to recognise good-quality material, and provides some buying hints. Storage requirements and typical uses are also considered. The list of commodities is not absolutely complete, but we have tried to include everything that you are likely to come across in your first few years in the kitchen. Similarly, we have not been able to list all the possible menu items. You should also have a look at specialist books on commodities and practical cookery books as you proceed with your studies.

You must constantly bear in mind how important it is to buy material which is appropriate for the proposed menu items in terms of both customer satisfaction and selling price (see page 319).

The commodities are discussed in the following groups:

- cereals and pasta (chapter 3);
- meat – poultry, beef and veal, lamb, pork and bacon, game (chapters 4–9);
- fish and shellfish (chapter 10);
- eggs (chapter 11);
- milk and milk products (chapter 12);
- fats and oils (chapter 13);
- vegetables, salads, and pulses (chapter 14);
- fruit and nuts (chapter 15);
- sugar and syrup (chapter 16);
- non-alcoholic beverages (chapter 17);
- herbs and spices (chapter 18);
- condiments (chapter 19);
- pickles and chutneys (chapter 20);
- essences, flavourings, and colourings (chapter 21);
- convenience foods (chapter 22);
- additives (chapter 23).

Where metric and imperial weights are quoted, these are only approximately equivalent – based on 450 grams = 1 pound.

The French names for items likely to be mentioned on a menu are given in *italics*, followed by '(m)' or '(f)' to indicate whether the item is masculine or feminine in French.

3 Cereals and pasta

Cereals are the edible seeds of cultivated grasses: wheat, maize, rice, barley, oats, rye, and millet. The type of cereal grown will depend on the soil and the climate. Every cuisine in the world has a variety of starchy dishes based on cereals – tortillas from Mexico, pasta from Italy, egg and rice noodles from China, and so on. Cereals are an important energy source in many people's diet – rice is the staple food for half of the world's population.

Cereals are important in the diet for the following reasons:

- Cereal crops grow in most parts of the world, and many regions can support more than one type of cereal.
- They are pleasant to eat and have no dominant or unpleasant flavour.
- They can easily be prepared into a wide variety of products – flour, biscuits, breakfast cereals, pasta, noodles, etc.
- They are inexpensive when compared with foods of animal origin.
- Ripened grain is easily preserved and transported, keeping in good condition for many months.
- As well as starch, cereals contain protein, mineral substances, and vitamins (see chapter 24).

Figure 3.1 shows the structure of a cereal grain.

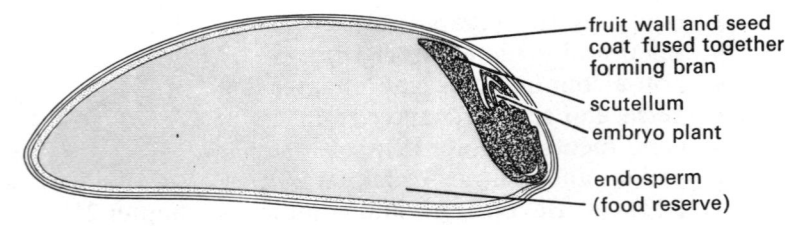

Fig. 3.1 Section through a cereal grain

3.1 Wheat

Wheat is grown for milling into flour. The character of the flour depends on how the wheat is grown and is referred to as being strong, medium, or weak – each of these types of flour having particular uses.

Strong flour is used to make bread. Due to its climate, the United Kingdom is unable to grow the best bread-making wheats. These require the type of climate found in the wheat-growing belt of North America and Canada, where the winters are severe and the summers are dry and hot. These wheats are sown in the autumn for harvesting the following summer.

In climates where the contrast between winter and summer temperatures is not so marked, the wheat grown will produce flour that is not so strong and is more suited to the production of items such as buns and scones.

All wheat flours contain the proteins glutenin and gliadin which join together when water is added to form a tough rubbery substance called gluten. The gluten formed from strong flours is tough, resistant to stretching, and can be kneaded, rolled, and pounded without breaking down. Weak flour produces less gluten (has a lower gluten potential) and the gluten is not suitable for stretching or prolonged fermentation.

Gluten is very important in baking: without it the air beaten in or the gas generated by yeast or baking powder would escape from the dough and there would be no aeration (see page 159). The structure of a loaf of bread, a cake, aerated buns, etc. is achieved when the gluten coagulates at approximately 60°C (140°F), leaving the baked product with a rigid shape.

Gluten has the ability to absorb nearly twice its own weight of water. This means that the higher the gluten potential of the flour the greater the volume of water that can be added, resulting in a larger yield of cooked products.

The milling process

There are two different methods of milling: stone milling and roller milling.

Stone milling is mainly used for the production of wholemeal flour. A stone mill has two circular stones lying one on top of the other. The bottom stone remains stationary while the one on top revolves. The faces of the stones are roughened and grooved so that wheat fed into a hole in the centre of the top stone trickles down and finds its way outward between the stones. In the process the grain is crushed into a fine powder – wholemeal flour.

Roller milling is the modern method of producing flour. This involves three distinct processes:

- cleaning to remove soil, stones, weed seeds, straw, etc.;
- conditioning – raising the moisture content of the grain and toughening the bran so that it does not break up so easily during milling, which would make separation more difficult;
- separation of flour from the bran – achieved by a series of rollers and sieves.

Extraction rate of flour

The extraction rate is the proportion of the original whole grains that ends up in the finished flour. An extraction rate of approximately 70% of the whole wheat will produce flour of a good white colour. With roller milling it is possible to produce flour of any extraction rate, and some typical values are

- wholemeal   100% extraction rate
- white straight-run 70–72% extraction rate
- white patent   25–40% extraction rate

In the UK, white flour must by law be fortified with the following nutrients to replace some of those lost by removing the bran and germ during milling:

- calcium carbonate (chalk),
- vitamin B1 (thiamin),
- nicotinic acid,
- iron.

Advantages of white flour

- It has a longer shelf life than wholemeal flour.
- The removal of the germ (which contains a natural oil) means that the flour is less likely to go rancid during storage.
- White flour finds greater acceptance with the general public for the production of cakes, pastries, etc.

Disadvantages of white flour

- It lacks the flavour of wholemeal flour.
- Wholemeal flour is a good source of the fibre essential for a balanced diet (see chapter 24).

Types of white flour available for general use

- *Strong flour* Milled from imported hard Canadian and North American wheat, this contains 10–15% protein and is suitable for the production of bread dough and puff pastry.
- *Medium-strength flour* Milled from a blend of imported hard wheat and English wheat, this has a protein content of 8–10% and is suitable for the preparation of scones and short-crust pastry.
- *Weak flour* Milled from English wheat or imported wheat of similar strength, such as Australian, this has a protein content of up to 8% and is used for cakes and sponges.
- *Self-raising flour* This is a blend of white flour of medium strength with a slow-acting chemical raising agent. It is convenient to use but has the disadvantage of having a fixed quantity of raising agent, so the amount of aeration that takes place cannot be controlled.
- *Plain flour* A blend of white flour of medium strength with no raising agent.

3.2 Barley

Barley is now mainly grown for the making of malt for the production of beer and whisky. (It was formerly milled to make bread.) Pearl barley is barley with the husk and germ removed and the endosperm polished. It is used in the preparation of soups and stews.

3.3 Maize

When young and tender, maize is eaten as a vegetable (sweetcorn (*maïs* (m))). Fully ripened maize is ground into flour for use mainly as a thickening agent (cornflour) or to be processed into custard and blancmange powder. Whole endosperms are used to produce breakfast cereals.

3.4 Oats

Oats have a high protein and fat content compared with other cereals, but no gluten, so oatmeal flour is unsuitable for bread-making. It is used in

Scotland for the making of biscuits, cakes, porridge, and haggis. Other uses include the coating of fish before frying.

Oatmeal is available in three grades: coarse, pinhead, and fine. It is used for the making of parkins, gingerbread, and oatcakes.

Oatflakes (or rolled oats) are husked grains rolled into flakes, mainly used for the making of porridge.

3.5 Rice

Rice (*riz* (m)) is the least nutritious of the cereals, containing more starch and less protein, fat, and minerals than the others. Much rice is eaten white, after the removal (pearling) of the bran and germ. If only the outer husk is removed, the rice is sold as brown rice.

Rice eaten in the UK is mainly imported from North America, Italy, South America, or the Far East.

Types of rice

- *American long-grained rice*   A long-grained rice with a hard outer structure, this is chiefly used for savoury dishes which require the individual grains to remain firm, fluffy, and separate when cooked. It is available as either brown or white rice.
- *Basmati*   A long-grained rice with a good flavour – ideal for serving with curry.
- *Avirio and arborio* (Italian or crystal rice)   The rice grains are rounder and plumper than American long-grained rice. These are mainly used for risotto and are available as brown or white rice.
- *Short-grain, pudding, or Carolina rice*   Short, plump grains of polished rice which become soft and sticky, clinging together when cooked. Used for a variety of rice dishes, including puddings and condés.
- *Brown rice*   The whole grain of the rice, with only the outer husk removed. Brown rice contains much more fibre and B-group vitamins and is more nutritious than white polished rice (see chapter 24). It is used mainly for the preparation of savoury dishes. It absorbs more water than polished rice and requires a longer period of cooking.
- *Wild rice*   The grains of wild rice are long and thin and are very dark brown or black. Wild rice is used cooked as a garnish for savoury meat dishes, either on its own or mixed with other rice.

Other rice products

- *Rice cones* }   Hard, gluten-free granules of rice used in the making of
- *Ground rice* }   rice cakes and shortbread.
- *Rice flour*   Used in puddings and cakes and as a thickening agent.
- *Rice flakes*   Used in puddings and cakes.
- *Rice paper*   Used to line baking-sheets before piping macaroons, almond biscuits, etc.

3.6 Semolina

This is the crushed (not rolled) endosperm of wheat, the best quality being manufactured from a variety known as durum wheat. It is used for milk puddings, for gnocchi, for thickening soups, and in the preparation of pasta.

3.7 Rye Rye is used for bread-making in some countries – rye bread is dark in colour and close in texture. Probably the best-known rye bread is the German pumpernickel.

3.8 Millet Millet is rarely used in European cooking but can be used to make flat bread and griddle cakes.

3.9 Other starch products
- *Arrowroot* A fine pure-white flour popular as a thickening agent, produced from the West Indian tuber *Maranta arundinacea*.
- *Potato flour* Processed from cooked potatoes and used as a thickening agent.
- *Sago* Processed from the pith of the sago palm grown in the Far East, this is mainly used in milk puddings.
- *Tapioca* Granules processed from the starch of the cassava or manioc root, mainly used in milk puddings.

3.10 Storage of cereals Opened bags of flour are best emptied into mobile bins with tightly fitting lids and stored in cool, very dry conditions. Smaller quantities of flour and cereal products are best stored in tightly lidded containers on shelving units. Whole unopened bags of flour should be stored off the floor, on slatted shelves.

3.11 Pasta Traditionally associated with Italy, the term 'pasta' is used to describe a variety of fresh and dried dough products available in many shapes and sizes. Pasta products are popular for the preparation of a wide range of dishes – either as the main ingredient or as part of the garnish – and they are usually purchased dried.

The type of pasta selected for use will normally depend on the requirements of the finished dish. Fresh pasta must be used within 2–3 days of making or purchase.

A good-quality dried pasta should normally be a translucent amber colour, without blemishes or discoloration. When stored in an airtight container, good-quality dried pasta will have a long shelf life without loss of quality or flavour.

The best pasta products are manufactured from durum-wheat semolina (hard wheat with a high gluten potential), the other basic ingredients being water, eggs, oil, and, for some pasta products (such as green lasagne), vegetable colours.

Types of pasta

Pasta can be divided into two main groups:

- large types mainly used in dishes where the pasta will be the main ingredient, including filled-pasta dishes;
- small types used mainly for garnishing.

Cereals and pasta

Large types/shapes

- *Spaghetti*   Solid threads of pasta – probably the most popular of all the pasta products.
- *Macaroni*   Hollow rods – larger than spaghetti.
- *Lasagne*   Large oblong sheets.
- *Lasagne verdi*   Lasagne coloured and flavoured with spinach.
- *Farfalle*   Large butterfly shapes.
- *Conchiglie rigate*   Sea-shells.
- *Noodles, tagliatelli, fettucini*   Ribbons, 5 mm (¼ inch) wide.
- *Ravioli*   Stuffed envelopes of pasta.
- *Canneloni*   Large hollow tubes, for stuffing.

Ravioli and canneloni are similar in several respects but are, however, prepared and cooked differently. You can make both of them by using fresh noodle paste. Sauces, stuffings, and garnishes are the same for both dishes.

Small types/shapes

- *Vermicelli, capellini*   The finest/thinnest ribbon pasta.
- *Farfalli*   Small butterflies.
- *Alfabetti*   Letters.
- *Ruotini*   Small wheels

The above are just a few of the many shapes available, some of which are shown in fig. 3.2.

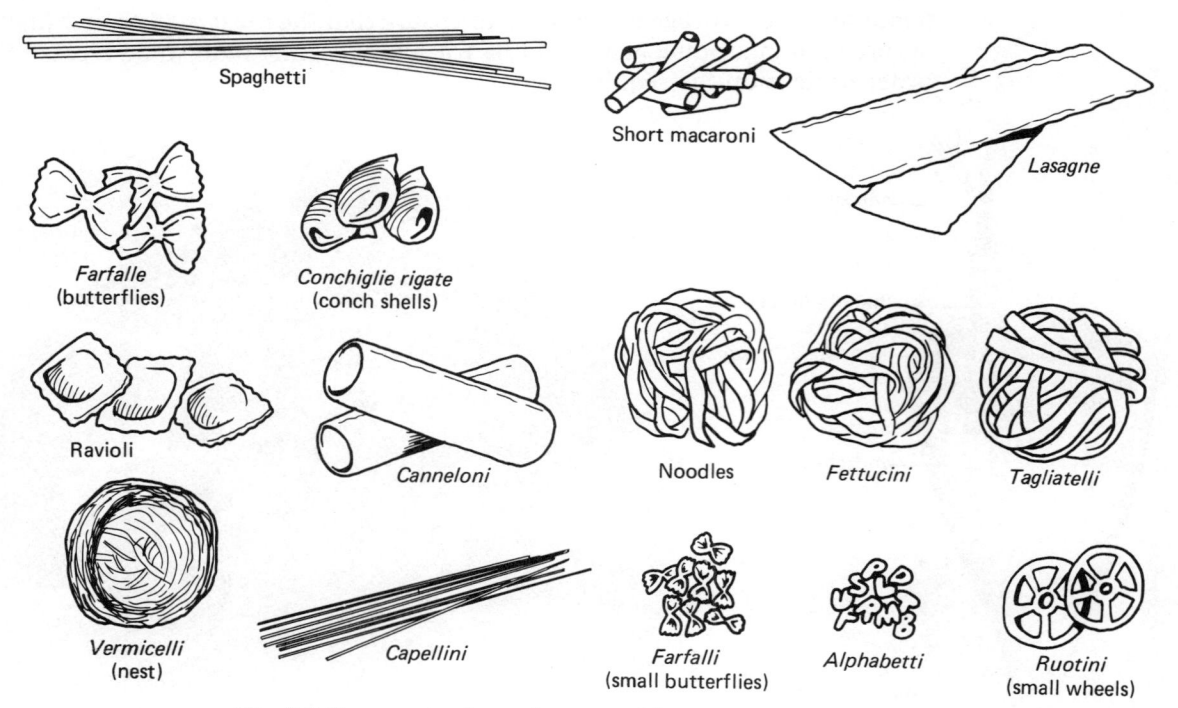

Fig. 3.2 Some pasta shapes (not to scale)

4 Meat

Before the following chapters look in detail at poultry, beef and veal, lamb, pork and bacon, and game, this chapter considers a few general points about all meats.

Meat (*viande* (f)) comes, of course, from animals or birds. Most of what we call meat is muscle; any other edible part of the animal may be referred to as offal.

The structure of meat is outlined in fig. 4.1. The quality of the meat is affected by the amount of connective tissue in the muscle and the amount of fat. The proportion of connective tissue will depend on the age of the animal and the part of the animal from which the meat has been taken. Meat taken from a shin, for example, will contain much more connective tissue than a fillet taken from the lower back, because the shin contains lots of active muscles whereas the fillet consists of a single muscle which does not get much use.

Another factor which affects the eating quality of meat is how it has been treated after the animal has been slaughtered. When meat is 'hung', some very complicated changes take place which affect both the tenderness and the flavour. These changes are affected by temperature, so the time and temperature of storage can be used to ensure that the meat is at its best just before cooking. Some game is hung for a longer time than some meats in order to develop the required flavour.

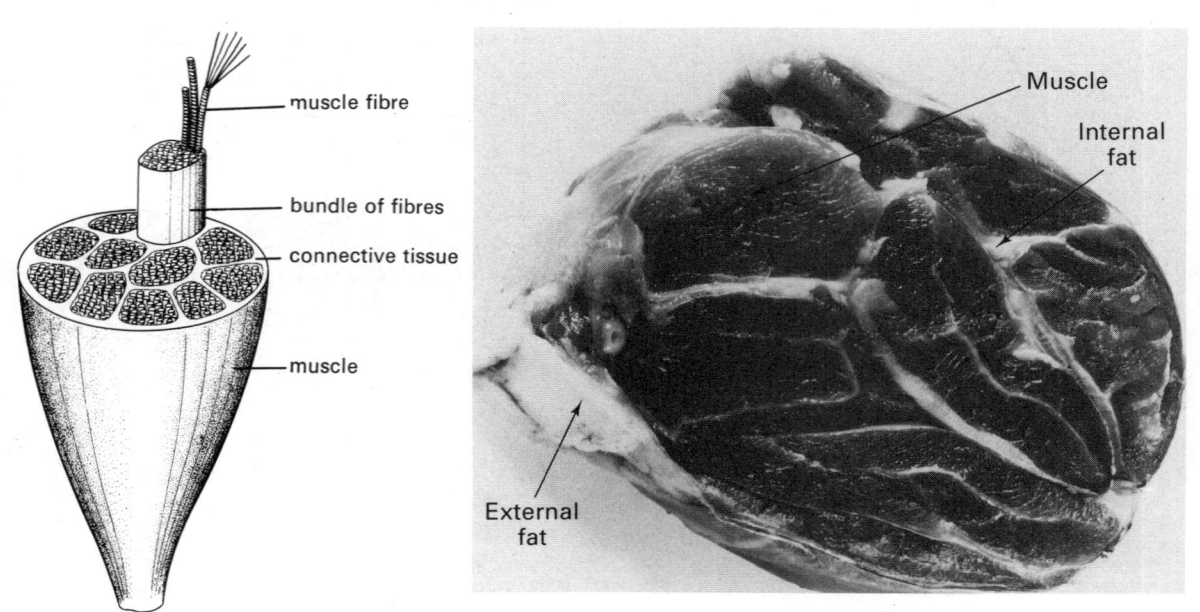

Fig. 4.1 *Left* The structure of muscle, with fat dispersed among the bundles of muscle fibres (not to scale). *Right* The structure of meat

5 Poultry

'Poultry' is the term used to refer to domesticated birds that are reared under controlled conditions for human consumption. Wild birds used for food are referred to as 'game' and are discussed in chapter 9.

This chapter will deal with six types of poultry (*volaille* (f)): chicken, duck, goose, turkey, guinea-fowl, and quail. First, however, we will look at some points that are relevant to them all.

5.1 Choosing and buying for value

Your purchase should depend on the use you are going to make of the poultry and the selling price of the finished dish (see page 319).

Frozen poultry is readily available and is cheaper and more standard than fresh. Some weight loss occurs on thawing. Fresh poultry is considered to be of a better quality and should be used if your customers are prepared to pay a little more for the dish. Fresh poultry must be used within 3 or 4 days of being purchased.

With frozen and oven-ready fresh poultry the giblets (neck, heart, liver, and gizzard) are often sold with the bird, usually packed into the cavity of the bird in polythene bags. These must be removed before you cook the bird. The giblets can be used to make gravy; the liver can be used for stuffing or pâté.

Quality purchasing points for fresh poultry

The following points should enable you to identify poultry in good condition for cooking:

- *Skin*   Unbroken with no bruising or discolouration.
- *Smell*   Pleasant and fresh.
- *Breastbone*   Fine and flexible at the vent end.
- *Breast*   Plump, not bruised or discoloured.
- *Spurs*   Showing no signs of development.
- *Scales on legs*   Tight, fine, and even.

A sticky skin with a bluish-grey tinge and an unpleasant smell indicate that the bird is deteriorating in quality.

5.2 Thawing frozen poultry

A frozen bird should be thawed slowly, and well before you need to start preparing it for cooking. It is best thawed in a refrigerator on a rack with a tray underneath to catch the drips. A very large bird may take up to 48 hours to thaw completely. The bird must be completely thawed before you start cooking – and don't forget to remove the bag of giblets!

5.3 Chicken

Chickens are domesticated birds that may be reared for meat and egg production.

Chicken is readily available whole or jointed, fresh or frozen. For a number of reasons to do with new breeds and farming methods, chicken is now much cheaper than popular butchers' meat such as lamb, beef, or pork.

A number of different grades of chicken are available. Some of these are more suitable for certain catering uses than others – see Table 5.1.

Table 5.1 Grades of chicken and their uses

Grade of chicken	Description	Catering uses*
Baby/spring chicken (*poussin* (m))	3–4 weeks old. Available all the year. Weight 340–450 grams (¾–1 lb)	Roasting. Poêlé cooking. Split spatchcock-style and grilled.
Double poussin	Older and larger than poussin (560–675 grams (1¼–1½ lb)). Available all the year.	As for poussin.
Broiler chicken (*poulet reine* (m))	Plump, tender birds (age 5–7 weeks) available all the year. Weight up to 2.75 kg (6 lb), with the 1.25–1.75 kg (3–4 lb) the most popular.	Roasting. Poêlé cooking. Grilling. Deep poaching. Sautéing. Shallow frying.
Boiling fowl (*poule* (f))	Laying hens from battery cages at 18 months. Often poorly fleshed, tough, and stringy. Weight 2–2.25 kg (4½–5 lb).	Boiling. Soups. Stocks.
Capon (castrated cockerel) (*chapon* (m))	Traditional caponised birds are no longer available. Modern broiler hybrids can reach a similar weight in a shorter time, but lack the flavour of true capons. Weight 3.6–5.5 kg (8–12 lb).	Roasting.
Free range	A plump tender bird with good flavour. Traditionally reared.	As for broiler chickens.

* For more details of catering uses, refer to the appropriate cookery methods.

Chickens are available either fresh or frozen as oven-ready whole birds, individual portions (legs, wings, thighs, drumsticks), halves, quarters, and suprêmes. Some specialist suppliers offer complete chicken dishes for sale – for example suprême of chicken Kiev.

For the preparation of suprêmes and cutting for sauté, a 1.25–1.5 kg (3–3½ lb) oven-ready bird will provide good value. If you want to roast your chicken and divide it into quarters then the same sort of bird will do. If you want a chicken to carve into slices then a larger one will be more suitable, as it will have a higher ratio of meat to bone.

Boiling fowl require long, slow, moist cooking to make them tender.

Cutting chicken for sauté

Before starting you will need to collect the following:

- a chopping board,
- a large cook's knife,
- a boning knife,
- a waste-bowl,
- a storage tray,
- a 1.25–1.5 kg (3–3½ lb) chicken (four portions).

Stage 1

- Remove any giblets from inside the chicken.
- Trim off the shank at the first leg joint.
- Pull one of the legs away from the body and cut through the skin.
- Dislocate the thigh bone where it joins the body.
- Place the chicken on its side. Using the boning knife, cut from the neck end towards the parson's nose, removing the whole leg from the carcass.

   Repeat for the other leg.

- Place the legs on the chopping board, skin side down. Cut down through the cartilage of the joint, dividing the leg into two (fig. 5.1).

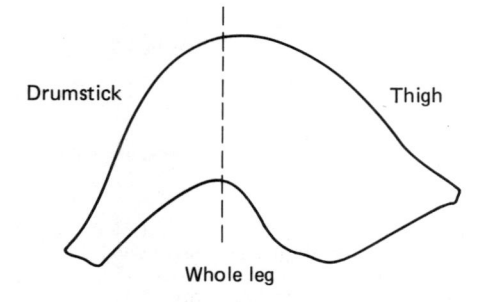

Fig. 5.1 Dividing a chicken leg

Fig. 5.2 A rolled-up chicken thigh (*gras de cuisse* (m))

- *Thigh* Using the cook's knife, trim off the joints from both ends of the thigh bone. Remove any excess fat and roll up the thigh with the skin side facing outwards (fig. 5.2).
- *Drumstick* Trim away the joint from the end of the bone. From the same end, push the bone down until it protrudes (fig. 5.3). Fold any loose skin over the exposed flesh.

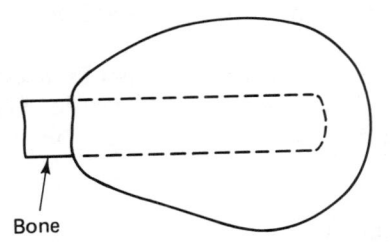

Fig. 5.3 A prepared chicken drumstick (*pilon de cuisse* (m))

- Place the prepared leg pieces on to a storage tray.

Stage 2

- Pull the loose neck skin back over the breast and remove the wishbone.
- Hold up the chicken and, still using the large cook's knife, cut down to and around the bone of the wing immediately against the breast.
- Place the heel of the knife on the wing in front of the first joint and cut through.
- Scrape away the loose flesh, leaving a clean bone.

Repeat for the other wing.

- Cut away the back of the carcass, leaving the white breast meat and the underlying bone.
- Cut the breast into four pieces (fig. 5.4).
- Trim the wings to leave only the middle section (fig. 5.5)

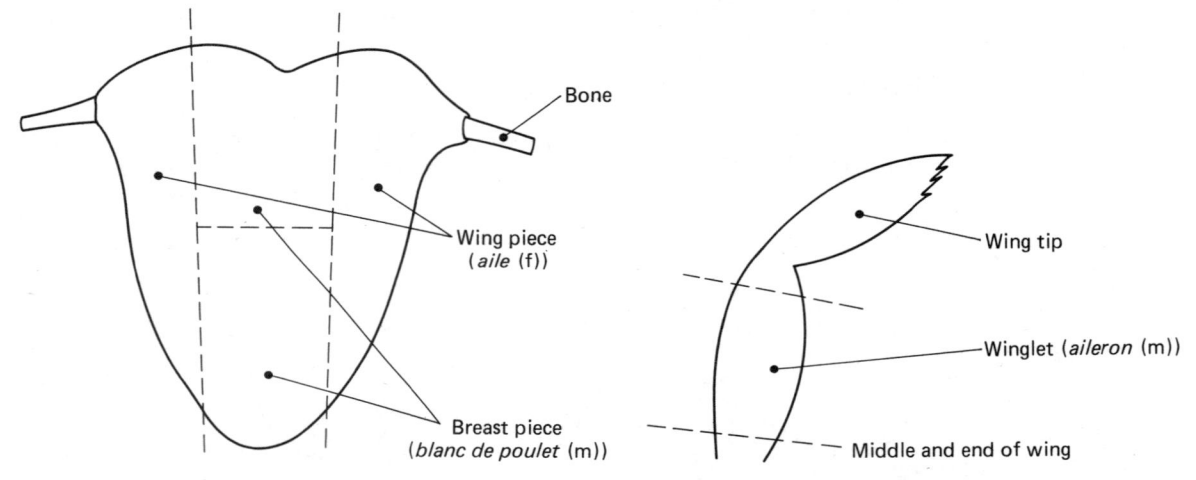

Fig. 5.4 A whole chicken breast

Fig. 5.5 Trimming a chicken wing

You will now have the following:

- two drumsticks ⎫ four pieces of brown
- two thighs ⎭ leg meat
- two wing pieces ⎫ four pieces of white
- two breast pieces ⎭ breast meat
- two winglets
- carcass, bones, and trimmings

Each portion should consist of one piece of brown and one piece of white meat.

The above method of cutting chicken can also be used when preparing chicken for pies, casseroles, blanquette, and fricassée. The winglets can be used to garnish soup and rice dishes. Stock can be prepared from the bones.

Preparing suprêmes of chicken

- For two portions, use a 1.25–1.5 kg (3–3½ lb) chicken and proceed as for cutting chicken for sauté to the end of stage 1, but leaving the legs whole for later use.

- Place the chicken on its back on the chopping board. Hold the skin firmly and pull from the vent end of the breastbone to the neck end. The skin should come off in one piece.
- Using the boning knife, cut down one side of the breastbone, starting at the vent.
- Continue cutting down the front of the carcass and through the wing joint.
- Place the chicken on its side (opposite to the side from which the suprême is being cut). Pull the suprême from the carcass, using the knife only when necessary.

Repeat for the second suprême.

- Turn the suprêmes over and trim away the sinew from the fillet.
- Shape and trim each suprême as necessary (fig. 5.6).

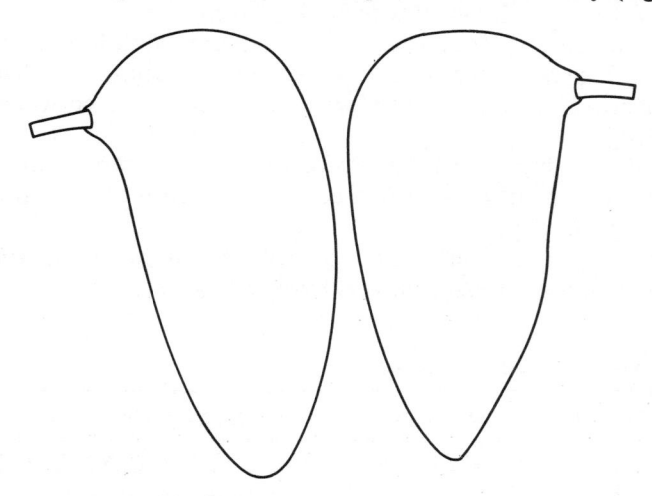

Fig. 5.6 Suprêmes of chicken

5.4 Duck

Table 5.2 describes the grades of duck used.

The high fat content of both duck and duckling means that they lose more weight in cooking than chicken, due to the fat rendering – that is, melting and running out (see page 158).

Table 5.2 Grades of duck

Grade of duck	Description	Catering uses
Duck (*canard* (*m*))	Mature birds, often fatty and tough.	Stocks. Soups. Braising.
Duckling (*caneton* (*m*))	Tender, well-flavoured flesh, dark in colour and not so meaty as chicken. Usually killed at 10–16 weeks. Available all the year, fresh and frozen. Oven-ready birds weigh 1.5–2.75 kg (3½–6 lb).	Roasting. Sautéing.

5.5 Goose

Goose (Table 5.3) is expensive to buy and is usually available only during the autumn and early winter. As with duck, there is a considerable weight loss in cooking due to the fat rendering.

Table 5.3 Grades of goose

Grade of goose	Description	Catering uses
Goose (*oie* (f))	Mature birds up to 9 kg (20 lb) in weight.	Confit d'oie.
Gosling (*oison* (m))	Young birds weighing 3.5–4.5 kg (8–10 lb) when dressed.	Roasting.

5.6 Turkey

Table 5.4 shows the grades of turkey used.

Hens are smaller than the males. Both are available throughout the year, fresh or frozen. Turkeys are usually killed at about 5 to 6 months, and the most useful sizes for most catering operations are between 11 and 13.5 kg (24–30 lb).

There is a high ratio of white meat to brown meat. When roasting turkey, you should baste it frequently to prevent the breast meat from becoming too dry.

In addition to whole turkeys, jointed birds are available as well as escalopes, cubes, sausages, turkey-burgers, etc.

Table 5.4 Grades of turkey

Grade of turkey	Description	Catering uses
Cock/stag (*dindon* (m)/ *dindonneau* (m))	Male turkey	Roasting. Poêlé cooking. Shallow frying. Stewing. Pies.
Hen (*dinde* (f))	Female turkey.	As for male.

5.7 Guinea-fowl

Guinea-fowl (Table 5.5) have a stronger flavour than chicken, somewhat more like pheasant. The bones are small and fine, giving the bird a high proportion of flesh to bone.

Table 5.5 Guinea-fowl

Type	Description	Catering uses
Guinea-fowl (*pintade* (f)/ *pintadeau* (m))	Farmed extensively in France. Usually killed at 4–6 months, when they produce a dressed weight of 800–1125 grams (1¾–2½ lb).	Roasting, Poêlé cooking. Shallow frying.

5.8 Quail

Quail (Table 5.6) are normally available as oven-ready birds, fresh or frozen, in graded sizes ranging from 90 g to 200 g. (110–140 g is the most usual size.)

Table 5.6 Quail

Type	Description	Catering uses
Quail (*caille* (f))	A small bird with plump breasts. The skin has a reddish tinge. Normally two per portion.	Roasting. Poêlé cooking. Soup. Cold, decorated and masked with aspic jelly.

6 Beef and veal

6.1 Types of beef

Beef (*boeuf* (m)) is the meat obtained from domesticated cattle. New breeds that have been introduced tend to have less fat than their predecessors, since this is what most customers require. The emphasis on reducing fat in the diet for health reasons (see pages 142–3) seems to have got through to most of us.

The main types of carcasses available are as follows:

- *Bobby calves*   Animals up to 6 weeks old, poorly fleshed with little or no fat.
- *Veal*   Calves specially reared to produce animals with tender, pale-coloured flesh – see section 6.7.
- *Steers/bullocks*   Male cattle that have been castrated at an early age. They may have a higher lean-to-fat ratio than heifer beef.
- *Bull beef*   Uncastrated male animals that are brought to a marketable size in about 15 months, before the meat becomes tainted due to changes occuring at maturity.
- *Heifers*   Female animals that have not produced a calf. They are considered to mature more quickly and to have smaller bones than steers or bullocks.
- *Cow beef*   Female animals that have been used for breeding. These are older animals with poor muscle (meat) development and a high proportion of bone. The flesh is dry and the fat has a yellow colour.
- *Mature bull beef*   Uncastrated male animals that have been used for breeding. The flesh is dark in colour, strong-flavoured, and very tough.

(The meat from mature bulls and cows is used only for manufacturing purposes and would not normally be found in a catering kitchen.)

6.2 Maturing and tenderising beef

Tenderness in beef is probably the most important factor taken into account when judging quality, especially if you are going to cook the meat by a dry-heat method (roasting, grilling, etc.). The tenderness depends on the carcass being matured by hanging for up to 14 days under the right conditions before being cut and jointed.

Beef can be tenderised by adding an enzyme that breaks down the protein (see page 141) in the meat to some extent. One of the enzymes used is papain, which is injected into the bloodstream of the animal immediately before it is killed. This makes sure that the enzyme is distributed throughout the body of the animal. (Papain occurs in the leaves of the papaw tree, and South American natives used to wrap their killed animals in these leaves to tenderise them long before we knew anything about enzymes.)

Beef and veal 35

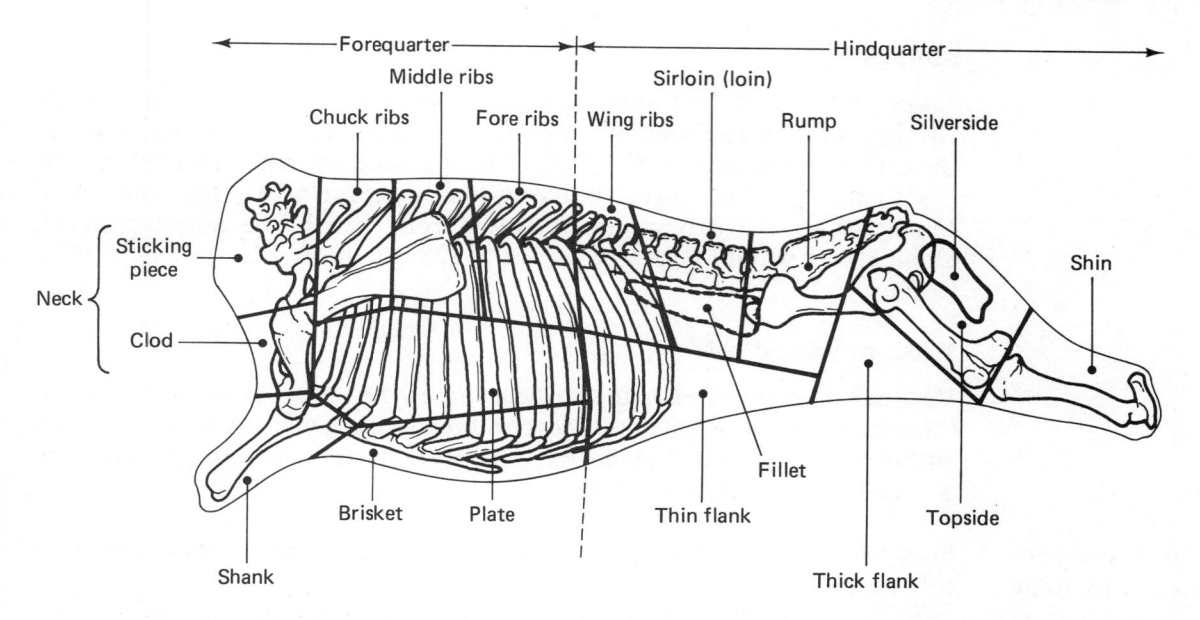

Fig. 6.1 A side of beef. The forequarter and hindquarter are usually separated from each other between the 10th and 11th rib bones, counting from the head.

6.3 Purchasing and storing beef

Beef can be purchased as a whole forequarter or hindquarter (see fig. 6.1), or jointed, boned and rolled, diced for stewing or for pies, minced, or butchered into steaks etc. The hindquarter provides most of the best-quality meat for roasting, grilling, or frying, whereas the meat from the forequarter is more suitable for stewing or braising. Most establishments purchase only those joints that they require – rumps, striploins, and fillets rather than whole forequarters or hindquarters, for example.

Beef is available all the year, and the quality remains constant thoughout.

Quality purchasing points for fresh beef

- *Fat* This should be firm, brittle in texture, and creamy white. Older animals and dairy cattle have fat that is soft and deep yellow.
- *Marbling* in lean meat is formed by small areas of fat which should be evenly distributed, especially in sirloin and wing and fore ribs.
- *Colour* The colour of the lean meat should be bright red. Cut surfaces that are dull and sticky have been exposed to the air for some time.
- *Touch* The lean meat should be firm and elastic to the touch.
- *Fluid* Any moisture on the cut surfaces should be watery, not thick and sticky to the touch.

In the United Kingdom, fresh home-produced (TK) beef – particularly Scotch beef – is considered by many caterers and customers to be of a better quality than imported, chilled, or frozen carcasses.

Storage

Large sections of beef such as sides, forequarters, hindquarters, whole sirloins, and rumps should be suspended on meat hooks from racks fixed to the ceiling of the cold-room. Cuts of beef should be stored on trays at 2°C (36°F) and covered to prevent drying-out of cut surfaces. These trays need to be changed daily to prevent the meat from lying in the collected blood. Chilled beef should be stored at −2°C (28°F) and frozen beef at −18°C (0°F).

Vacuum-packed beef

Vacuum-packing extends the storage life of the boned joint or cut and at the same time allows the maturing and tenderising processes to take place within the pack. Only the more expensive items are vacuum-packed, such as striploins, fillets, and rumps.

6.4 Larger cuts of beef

Figure 6.1 shows the usual cutting lines and terminology of the cuts from a side of beef.

Tables 6.1 to 6.5 describe the uses of the various cuts and offal.

Table 6.1 Joints/cuts from a hindquarter of beef (H¼), 63.5–91 kg (140–200 lb)

Joint/cut	Description	Typical weight	Catering uses
Shin (*jambe* (f)/*jarret* (m))	The meat from below the kneecap, boned and trimmed before use. When cracked open the bone provides marrow, used as a garnish for other dishes – entrécôte bordelaise, for example.	5.5–7.25 kg (12–16 lb)	Consommé. Stewing – ragôut. Steak-and-kidney or beef pudding.
Topside (*tranche tendre* (f))	Usually rolled and tied for roasting and braising, after trimming to remove all gristle. Additional fat is often added before rolling.	7.25–11 kg (16–25 lb)	Second-class/slow roasting. Stewing – ragôut, carbonnade, curry, etc. Braising – whole/jointed, steaks.
Silverside (*gîte à la noix* (m))	Rolled and tied after trimming away the thick, tough, silver-coloured skin (silverskin) on the surface of the joint.	10–13.5 kg (22–30 lb)	Boiling (fresh or pickled), served with carrots and dumplings. Cold salt beef – salads and sandwiches.
Thick flank (*tranche grasse* (f))	Trimmed and rolled for braising whole. A prime-quality braising/stewing joint.	5.5–8 kg (12–18 lb)	Braising – whole/jointed, steaks. Stewing – carbonnade, ragôut, goulash, curry, etc.

Beef and veal 37

Table 6.1 Joints/cuts from a hindquarter of beef (H¼), 63.5–91 kg (140–200 lb) *(continued)*

Joint/cut	Description	Typical weight	Catering uses
Rump (*culotte* (f))	The whole rump is supplied with the head/rump fillet still attached. It is also available boned without the fillet and part of the fatty flap (the skirt).	9–13.5 kg (20–30 lb)	Grilling, frying – as steaks. Occasionally braised (whole/jointed).
Sirloin (*aloyau* (m))	Supplied with the loin fillet still attached (fig. 6.2), but without the suet and kidney knob.	11.25–16.75 kg (25–37 lb)	Grilling – T-bone/porterhouse steaks.

Fig. 6.2 Cross-section of a whole sirloin

Joint/cut	Description	Typical weight	Catering uses
Striploin (*contrefilet* (m))	The completely boned loin that has been trimmed of excess fat. The strip of muscle running the length of the striploin (chain muscle) and part of the surface layer of fat and the thick leathery silver-coloured skin (backstrap gristle) covering the oval-shaped eye-meat are cut away before butchering into steaks.	4.5–8 kg (10–18 lb)	Roasting – prime quality. Grilling, frying – as steaks.
Wing ribs (*côte d'aloyau* (f))	The forward portions of the sirloin, consisting of the eye-meat between the 11th and 13th rib bones. They are often supplied attached to the sirloin.	5–7.75 kg (11–17 lb)	Roasting – prime quality, Grilling, frying – as steaks.
Fillet (whole/long fillet) (*filet* (m))	Located on the underside of the rump and sirloin. It is supplied trimmed of excess surface fat, but with the chain muscle (see under 'Striploin') still attached to one side of the fillet.	1.75–2.75 kg (4–6 lb)	Poêlé cooking – prime quality requires larding before cooking. Roasting. Grilling, frying. Baking – e.g. Beef Wellington.
Thin flank (*bavette d'aloyau* (f))	The hindquarter skirt (the fatty stomach flap) requires careful trimming before use. Rolled and tied before boiling.	6.5–8 kg (14–18 lb)	Boiling. Stewing – ragoût. Beef sausages. Minced beef. Steak-and-kidney pie.

Table 6.2 Joints/cuts from a forequarter of beef (F¼), 59–86 kg (130–190 lb)

Joint/cut	Description	Typical weight	Catering uses
Forerib (*côte première* (f))	For roasting, the rib bones and skirt should be trimmed back to approximately the diameter of the eye-meat. The spine bones (chine bones) should be removed together with the thick yellow band of gristle (paddywax gristle) found under the surface fat near the chine bones.	5.5–8 kg (12–18 lb)	Roasting – traditional British dish served with Yorkshire pudding and horseradish sauce.
Middle rib (*côte dé couverte* (f))	This may be roasted either on the bone or after boning, trimming, and rolling. When braised whole, the meat benefits from larding and marinading.	9–13.5 kg (20–30 lb)	Roasting – second-class/slow roast. Braising – whole, steaks.
Chuck rib (*côte du collier* (f))	When braised whole, the meat benefits from larding and marinading.	11.25–16 kg (25–35 lb)	Stewing – ragôut, curry, goulash. Braising – jointed, steaks. Steak-and-kidney pudding.
Clod and sticking (*collier* (m))	For stewing, the meat is boned out completely and carefully trimmed.	9–13.5 kg (20–30 lb)	Stewing, Pudding meat. Mince. Sausages.
Plate (*plate de côte* (f))	This is the forequarter flank. It is boned out and carefully trimmed for stewing.	5.5–8 kg (12–18 lb)	Stewing – ragôut. Sausages. Mince.
Brisket (*poitrine* (f))	This is boned, rolled, and tied before boiling, or carefully trimmed before stewing.	9–13.25 kg (20–30 lb)	Pickled and boiled. Pressed beef. Stewing – ragôut. Pudding beef.
Leg-of-mutton cut (*talon du collier* (m))	Part of the upper foreleg, boned and trimmed. The meat benefits from larding and marinading before braising.	7.25–11 kg (16–24 lb)	Braising – jointed, steaks. Stewing – ragôut, curry, goulash.
Shank (*jambe* (f))	The meat from below the elbow joint of the foreleg, boned and trimmed of all fat, skin, and sinew before mincing.	4.5–6.5 kg (10–14 lb)	Consommé. Mince.

Table 6.3 Small cuts of beef

Small cut/steak	Joint	Description	Typical weight	Serving suggestion
Chateaubriand (*chateaubriand* (m))	Fillet	Cut from the large head end or rump end of the fillet, slightly flattened before cooking. Served to a minimum of two people.	380–450 g (12–16 oz)	Grilled, garnished with a bouquetière of fresh vegetables, and accompanied by a sauce-boat of béarnaise sauce.
Fillet steak (*filet* (m))	Fillet	Cut from the middle section of the fillet, with the underside fat and chain muscle still attached.	175–225 g (6–8 oz)	Grilled and served with a suitable garnish.
Tournedos (*tournedos* (m))	Fillet	Cut from the lower middle section of the fillet, with the fat and chain muscle trimmed away. Tied before cooking, to keep the round shape.	175 g (6 oz)	Grilled, garnished and served with béarnaise sauce. Sautéed served with a suitable sauce and garnish, such as chasseur, fleuriste, Rossini.
Fillet mignon (*filet mignon* (m))	Fillet	Cut from the tail section of the fillet – two small, slightly flattened, steaks for each portion.	2 × 85 g (2 × 3 oz)	As for tournedos.
Steak tartare (*steak tartare* (m))	Fillet	The tail section of the fillet, finely chopped using a large cooks' knife and eaten raw.	120–175 g (4–6 oz)	Presented at the table for the final mixing with flavourings and garnishings in front of the customer.
Fingers/strips of beef	Fillet	Cut from the tail section of the fillet into strips 5 cm × 1 cm (2 inch × ½ inch).	150–175 g (5–6 oz)	Often used for restaurant flambé dishes, such as filet de boeuf Stroganoff (beef Stroganoff).
Fillet minute steaks (*filet minute* (m))	Fillet	Carefully flattened steaks cut from the middle section of the fillet.	175 g (6 oz)	Normally used for restaurant flambé dishes, such as steak Diane.
Porterhouse/ T-bone steak	Whole sirloin	Both these names are now used to describe the same steak. It is prepared from the whole sirloin, cutting down through the skirt, sirloin eye, fillet, and chine bone.	Single portion 340–400 g (12–14 oz); double portion (for two people) 650–750 g (22–26 oz)	Grilled and served with a bouquetière of vegetables or an alternative vegetable garnish.
Sirloin steak (*entrecôte* (f))	Boned trimmed sirloin (contrefilet/striploin)	Cut into slices 1.5–2 cm (½–¾ inch) thick from the striploin previously trimmed of excess fat and sinew.	175–225 g (6–8 oz)	Grilled or sautéed, served with an appropriate garnish/sauce.
Double sirloin steak (*entrecote double* (f))	Contrefilet/striploin	Double-size sirloin steaks served to two persons.	340–450 g (12–16 oz)	Usually grilled and served with an appropriate vegetable garnish.
Minute steak (*entrecote minute* (f))	Contrefilet/striploin	A small sirloin steak, well flattened with the aid of a cutlet bat and trimmed of excess fat.	175 g (6 oz)	Grilled – garnished as for a grilled sirloin. Toasted steak sandwich, e.g. bookmaker's.
Rump steak	Rump	Cut from a slice taken from the whole rump 1.5–2 cm (½–¾ inch) thick.	225 g (8 oz)	Grilled.
Point steak	Rump	Cut from the triangular-shaped end of the rump slice, hence the name 'point steak'.	225 g (8 oz)	Grilled.

Table 6.3 Small cuts of beef (*continued*)

Small cut/steak	Joint	Description	Typical weight	Serving suggestion
Beef olives (*paupiettes* (f))	Thick flank/topside	Before cooking, the thin slices of beef are flattened between two sheets of clear polythene. They are then stuffed, rolled, and loosely tied. Depending on size, a portion will consist of one or two paupiettes.	120–150 g (4–5 oz) plus stuffing	Braised – served with an appropriate garnish.
Rib steaks, bone-in	Wing or fore rib	The chine bone, surface fat, and paddywax gristle are trimmed away and the flank/skirt is trimmed to within 6–8 cm (2½–3 inches) of the eye-meat. Usually served to two persons.	560–675 g (20–24 oz)	Grilled – garnish as for double sirloin.
Braising steaks	Chuck ribs/middle rib/thick flank	Cut across the grain, ensuring that each steak is of an even thickness with the minimum of surface fat.	175–225 g (6–8 oz)	Braised.

Table 6.4 Special or alternative cuts of beef

Cut	Description
Baron – full	A pair of rumps, sirloins, and wing ribs joined together into one large piece.
Baron – short	A pair of rumps and sirloins joined together in one piece.
Baron – double sirloin	A pair of sirloins joined together.
Roasting – rump and loin	One half of a full baron – that is, one rump, sirloin, and wing rib joined together.
Top piece	The hindquarter minus the rump, loin (sirloin and wing rib), and thin flank.
Round/buttock	The top piece minus the shin.
Short forequarter	The forequarter minus the fore rib and plate.
Pony	The chuck rib and middle rib joined together.

Table 6.5 Beef offal

Type	Description	Catering uses
Oxtail (*queue de boeuf* (f))	Trimmed of surface fat and cut through the cartilage of the tail vertebrae into short sections. With care, the sections can be boned and stuffed before cooking.	Braising. Grilling – rolled in English mustard and breadcrumbs after first braising. Soup – thick; clear (prepared as for consommé).
Ox tongue (*langue de boeuf* (f))	Available fresh, salted or pickled in brine. The tongue must be skinned and the root end trimmed after cooking. Ox tongue can also be purchase tinned for salads and sandwiches.	Braising – au madère (madeira sauce); aux épinards (madeira sauce and leaf spinach). Boiling – cold for salads, sandwiches, etc.

Table 6.5 Beef offal (*continued*)

Type	Description	Catering uses
Kidney (*rognon de boeuf* (m))	Skinned, trimmed, diced, or sliced before use.	Puddings/pies. Stewing. Soup.
Heart (*coeur de boeuf* (m))	Requires long, slow cooking after either slicing or trimming, stuffing, and loose tying to retain the shape.	Braising.
Ox liver (*foie de boeuf* (m))	Skinned and trimmed before slicing, ox liver is inclined to be dry when cooked.	Braising. Occasionally fried as a cheaper alternative to lambs' and calves' liver.
Tripe (*tripes* (plural) (f))	The lining of the cow's stomach, blanched before being sold.	Stewing – with milk and onion, for example. Boiling. Braising.
Sweetbreads (*ris de boeuf* (m))	Inferior in quality to those of lambs and calves.	Braising. Frying – after first braising.

6.5 Small cuts of beef

The smaller cuts of beef commonly used are obtained from three of the top-quality joints: the fillet, the rump, and the sirloin (Table 6.3).

- *The fillet* (fig. 6.3) provides the tenderest steaks, but these may lack the flavour of those obtained from the rump.

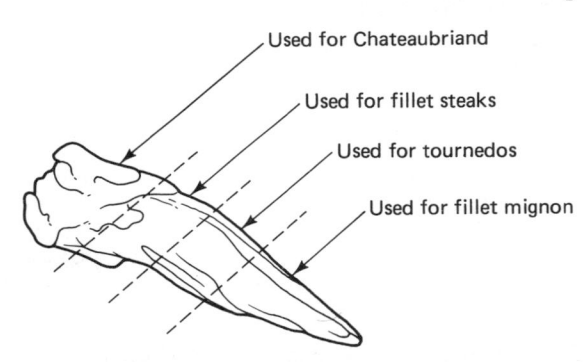

Fig. 6.3 Cuts from the fillet

- *Rump steaks* are likely to be less tender than fillet steaks.
- *Sirloin steaks* are a compromise between those from the tender fillet and the flavoursome rump.

Frozen steaks

These are available ready-prepared and in a variety of weights. They offer the following advantages to the caterer:

- *Value for money* They are fully prepared, with no waste.
- *Ordering* Over-ordering does not result in loss, since they do not deteriorate if stored correctly.
- *Cost* Cheaper than fresh steaks (and little seasonal price variation).
- *Labour-saving* Ready-prepared, making little or no demand for skilled labour.

6.6 Methods of cooking used for beef

Table 6.6 summarises the cuts of beef most suitable for particular cooking processes.

Table 6.6 Methods of cooking used for beef

Method	Joint or cut	Method	Joint or cut
Roasting	Topside (slow roasting). Striploin. Wing rib. Whole fillet (after larding). Fore rib. Middle rib (slow roasting).	Stewing	Shin. Topside. Thick flank. Thin flank. Chuck rib. Clod and sticking. Plate. Brisket. Leg-of-mutton cut. Kidneys. Tripe.
Poêlé cooking	Fillet. Striploin.		
Grilling	Rump – point and rump steak. Whole sirloin – T-bone and porterhouse steaks. Striploin – sirloin and minute steaks. Fillet – chateaubriand, fillet steak, tournedos. Wing ribs – rib steaks. Fore rib – rib steaks.	Sautéing	Fillet. Striploin.
		Braising	Topside. Thick flank. Middle rib. Chunk rib. Leg-of-mutton cut. Oxtail. Ox tongue. Ox heart. Ox liver. Tripe. Sweetbreads.
Shallow frying	As for grilling.		
Boiling	Silverside. Thin flank. Brisket. Ox tongue. Tripe.		

6.7 Veal

Veal (*veau* (m)) comes from specially reared calves which are intensively reared and killed at 3 to 4 months with a weight of about 100 kg (220 lb). To produce lightly coloured flesh, the calves are fed only on milk and milk substitutes.

6.8 Purchasing and storing veal

Veal is not normally purchased as a whole side or a carcass, because there is little demand for the poorer-quality meat, which is suitable only for stewing or making puddings. You will probably buy just the joints or cuts that you actually can use.

Veal is available fresh or frozen. In addition, frozen breaded escalopes, re-formed cutlets, and escalopes can be purchased.

The low demand for good-quality fresh veal from the housewife means that you may have to obtain your supplies from butchers who deal largely with the catering industry.

Quality purchasing points for fresh veal

- *Flesh* Pale pink, firm, resilient, and smooth to the touch. It should be

free from marbling. The cut surface should be moist, with a pleasant milky smell.
- *Fat* Firm and pinkish-white, with only a thin covering over the top of the leg, back, and shoulders. The kidneys should be well covered with a smooth white fat.
- *Bones* Heavy in relation to the thickness of the meat. They should be pinkish-white and show signs of blood in their structure. The ends of the rib bones should be soft and bendy (cartilaginous).

Storage

Fresh veal should be stored in a refrigerator or cold-room at 2–3°C (36–37°F). Large joints should be suspended on meat hooks attached to bars in the ceiling of the cold-room. Small cuts should be stored on clean trays and covered. The trays need to be changed daily to prevent the meat from lying in the collected blood.

6.9 Cuts of veal

Table 6.7 shows the joints that can be obtained from a carcass of veal (see fig. 6.4). Small cuts are shown in Table 6.8.

Table 6.7 Joints of veal

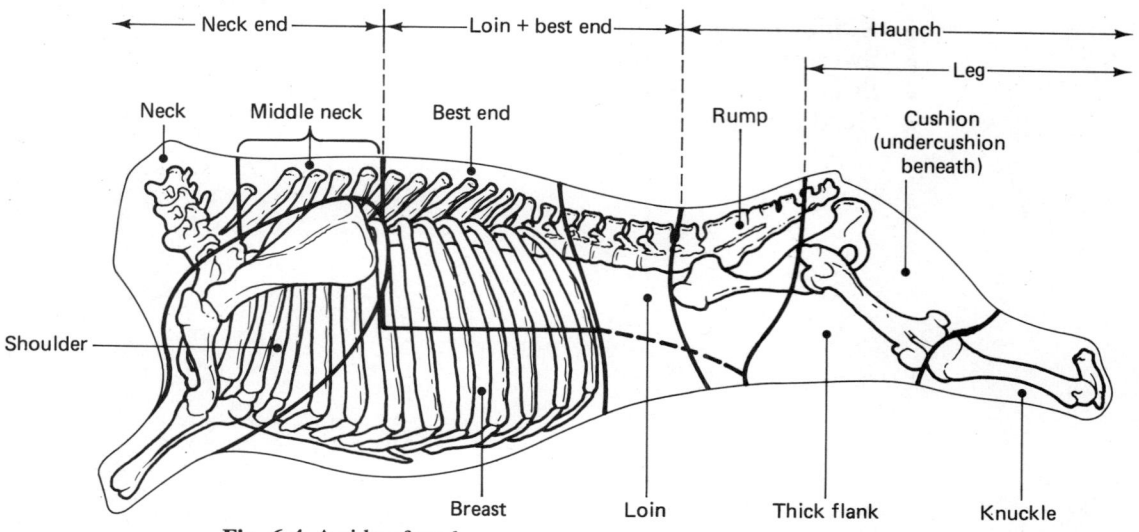

Joint	Typical weight
Knuckle (*jarret* (m))	2.25 kg (5 lb)
Cushion (*noix* (m))	
Undercushion (*sous-noix* (m))	11.25 kg (25 lb)
Thick flank (*noix patissière* (m))	
Rump or chump end (*quasi* (m))	2.75 kg (6 lb)
Loin (*longe* (f))	4.5 kg (10 lb)
Best end (*carré* (m))	3.6 kg (8 lb)
Breast (*poitrine* (f))	2.75 kg (6 lb)
Middle neck (*basses côtes* (f))	2.75 kg (6 lb)
Neck or scrag (*cou* (m))	3.6 kg (8 lb)
Shoulder (*épaule* (f))	8.0 kg (18 lb)

Fig. 6.4 A side of veal

Table 6.8 Small cuts of veal (usually grilled or shallow-fried)

Cut	Description	Typical weight
Veal cutlet (*côtelette de veau* (f))	Cut from the chined, trimmed best end. The bone is cleaned for presentation.	225–275 g (8–10 oz), one per portion
Veal chop (*côte de veau* (f))	Prepared by cutting across the trimmed loin through the eye-meat, backbone, and fillet.	225–275 g (8–10 oz), one per portion.
Veal escalope (*escalope de veau* (f))	A thin slice of veal cut from the cushion and thick flank and trimmed of all fat and sinew; can also be prepared from the rump or the loin. Flattened using a cutlet bat and clear polythene.	120–150 g (4–5 oz), one per portion
Veal escalopine (*escalopine de veau* (f))	Prepared as for escalopes.	40–60 g (1½–2 oz) each, two or three per portion.
Veal medallion (*médaillon de veau* (m))	A thick round slice cut from the fillet, slightly flattened.	60–75 g (2–2½ oz) each, two per portion
Veal grenadin (*grenadin de veau* (m))	A thick oval-shaped slice of veal, larded with bacon or pork fat and braised.	60–75 g (2–2½ oz) each, two per portion
Veal osso-bucco (*osso-bucco de veau* (m))	Prepared from a knuckle of veal by cutting through the meat and bone into thick slices.	225–275 g (8–10 oz) (including the bone), one per portion
Veal paupiette (*paupiette de veau* (f))	A thin slice of veal cut from the thick flank or under-cushion and flattened as for escalopes. The slices are stuffed with forcemeat, rolled, loosely tied, and braised.	100–135 g (3½–4½ oz), one or two per portion

The following offal can be obtained from veal:

- Kidney (*rognon* (m))
- Sweetbread (*ris* (m))
- Brain (*cervelle* (f))
- Head (*tête* (f))

6.10 Methods of cooking used for veal

Table 6.9 summarises the cuts of veal most suitable for particular cooking processes.

Table 6.9 Methods of cooking used for veal

Method	Joint or cut
Roasting	Leg – whole or jointed. Rump – boned and tied. Loin – on or off the bone. Best end. Breast (second-quality roast, usully stuffed and rolled).
Poêlé cooking	Leg – jointed. Rump – boned and tied. Loin – on or off the bone. Best end.
Shallow frying	Cushion and thick flank – escalopes, escalopines. Loin – escalopes, escalopines. Fillet – medallions. Loin – chops. Best end – cutlets. Brains – blanched. Kidneys – sliced or diced. Sweetbreads – blanched and sliced.
Grilling	Cushion and thick flank – escalopes, escalopines. Loin – chops. Best end – cutlets.
Stewing	Knuckle – osso-bucco. Neck, middle neck. Shoulder. Breast.
Braising	Leg – whole or jointed. Rump. Shoulder. Sweetbreads.
Pies and puddings	Neck, middle neck. Breast.
Mincing	Neck, middle neck. Breast.
Deep poaching	Brains.
Boiling	Head.
Stock, jus-lié	Bones.

7 Lamb

7.1 Types of lamb

Lamb (*agneau* (m)) is the meat of sheep that are assumed to be under one year old when slaughtered. The UK market has two main supplies: imported New Zealand lamb (NZ) and home-produced lamb from UK farmers (TK).

Mutton is the meat of mature sheep and is now sold mainly for manufacturing purposes. It has virtually disappeared from the menu in catering outlets. Mutton has a stronger flavour than lamb and is less tender, darker in colour, and has a higher proportion of fat.

Pré-salé or salt-marsh lamb is provided by animals that have grazed on the coastal pastures. The meat has extra flavour, with a salty tang.

A small market exists for milk-fed baby lambs. These are small and naturally very tender, with a delicate flavour.

Home-produced lamb

Home-produced lamb falls into two main groups:

- mountain and hill breeds – these provide fresh lamb carcasses for the autumn and winter markets;
- lowland or Downs breeds – these provide fresh lamb carcasses for the spring and summer markets.

Home-produced lamb – particularly the smaller carcasses – is scarce in late winter and early spring before the new season's lamb comes in in May.

New Zealand lamb

Frozen lamb imported from New Zealand is of a consistently high quality and is competitively priced, with little seasonal fluctuation. The animals are normally killed between 4 and 6 months old and are generally smaller than UK-produced carcasses, which are usually somewhat older.

New Zealand lamb is available in the following grades:

- *P grade* – prime-quality carcasses with excellent conformation and an even, though not excessive, surface layer of fat.
- *Y grade* – good-quality carcasses with good conformation, slightly longer than P grade, with a moderate covering of surface fat.
- *O grade* – similar to a P-grade carcass, but with longer legs.

Carcass weights range from 8 to 25 kg (18–55 lb) and are indicated by the letters L, M, H (light, medium, heavy).

7.2 Purchasing and storing lamb

Lamb can be purchased whole, jointed, butchered into cutlets and chops, or as one of the special catering cuts such as baron or crown roast. When purchasing whole carcasses, the menu must be carefully planned to make use of the less tender joints that are suitable only for stewing. Most establishments purchase only those joints that they require – for example, legs for roasting, best ends for the cutting of cutlets for grilling, etc.

Quality purchasing points for fresh lamb

- *Carcass conformation* Compact, evenly fleshed, feeling heavy for its size. The legs and shoulders should be plump and well-filled, the back broad and well-developed.
- *Flesh* Light pinky-red in colour, firm to the touch with a fine close grain.
- *Bones* Small, pinkish in colour, porous, with blood still showing when cut. In older animals the bones are white and splinter when chopped.
- *Fat* White, brittle, very little in relation to the thickness of the meat. The saddle and best end should be covered with a thin unbroken layer of fat.

Storage

Where possible, whole carcasses should be suspended by meat hooks from racks fixed to the ceiling of the cold-room. Joints and small cuts should be stored on clean stainless-steel trays at a temperature of 2–3°C (36–37°F). The trays must be changed daily to prevent the meat from lying in the collected blood.

Frozen lamb should be stored at a temperature of −18°C (0°F) until required.

7.3 Cuts of lamb

Table 7.1 shows the joints that can be obtained from a carcass of lamb (see fig. 7.1) Small cuts and offal are described in Tables 7.2 and 7.3

Table 7.1 Joints of lamb

Joint	Typical weight
Leg (2) (*gigot* (m))	2 kg (4½ lb) each
Saddle (*selle* (f))	3.5 kg (7¾ lb)
Best end (2) (*carré* (m))	1 kg (2 lb) each
Middle neck (*côte découverte* (f))	1.5 kg (3½ lb)
Neck and scrag (*cou* (m))	0.5 kg (1 lb)
Shoulder (2) (*épaule* (f))	1.5 kg (3½ lb) each
Breast (2) (*poitrine* (f))	0.75 kg (1½ lb) each

Table 7.2 Small cuts of lamb

Cut	Description	Typical weight	Catering uses
Cutlet (côtelette d'agneau (f))	Butchered from the skinned, trimmed, unscored best end by cutting down between the rib bones. Six cutlets are obtained from a best end. They are served with a cutlet frill placed over the end of each bared rib bone.	85–120 g (3–4 oz), two per portion	Grilling. Shallow frying – breaded or plain. As part of a mixed grill.
Double cutlet (côtelette d'agneau double (f))	Prepared as for lamb cutlets, but cutting down only between every other rib bone. Three double cutlets are obtained from a best end.	175–225 g (6–8 oz), one per portion	Grilling.
Crown chop/ Barnsley chop	Butchered from the skinned, trimmed, short saddle by cutting across, leaving the two loin chops joined together by the chine bone. Half a lamb's kidney is rolled inside each flap and skewered in place.	275–340 g (10–12 oz), one per portion	Grilling.
Loin/lamb chop (côte d'agneau (f))	Butchered from the skinned, trimmed, short loin, cutting down through the nut of meat, bone, and fillet into slices 25 mm (1 inch) thick. If long, the flap should be shortened.	200–225 g (7–8 oz), one per portion	Grilling. Braising.
Chump chop	Butchered from the skinned chump end of the loin (leg end), cutting down through the meat and bone into slices about 2 cm (¾ inch). Each chump end will normally yield two chops.	200–225 g (7–8 oz), one per portion	Grilling
Rosette (rosette d'agneau (f))	Butchered from the boned, skinned, trimmed, short loin, shortening the flap before rolling and tying. (When rolled, the loin nut should be covered by the fat of the flap.) Cut through the rolled loin between the strings into the required size.	85g (3 oz), two per portion	Shallow frying. Braising.
Noisette (noisette d'agneau (f))	Butchered either from the boned, skinned, trimmed, short loin (laying the meat fat down to the board) or from a boned best end. Cut into thick slices on the slant, lightly flattening and trimming into cutlet shape.	85 g (3 oz), two per portion	Sauté. Grilling. Shallow frying.

Lamb 49

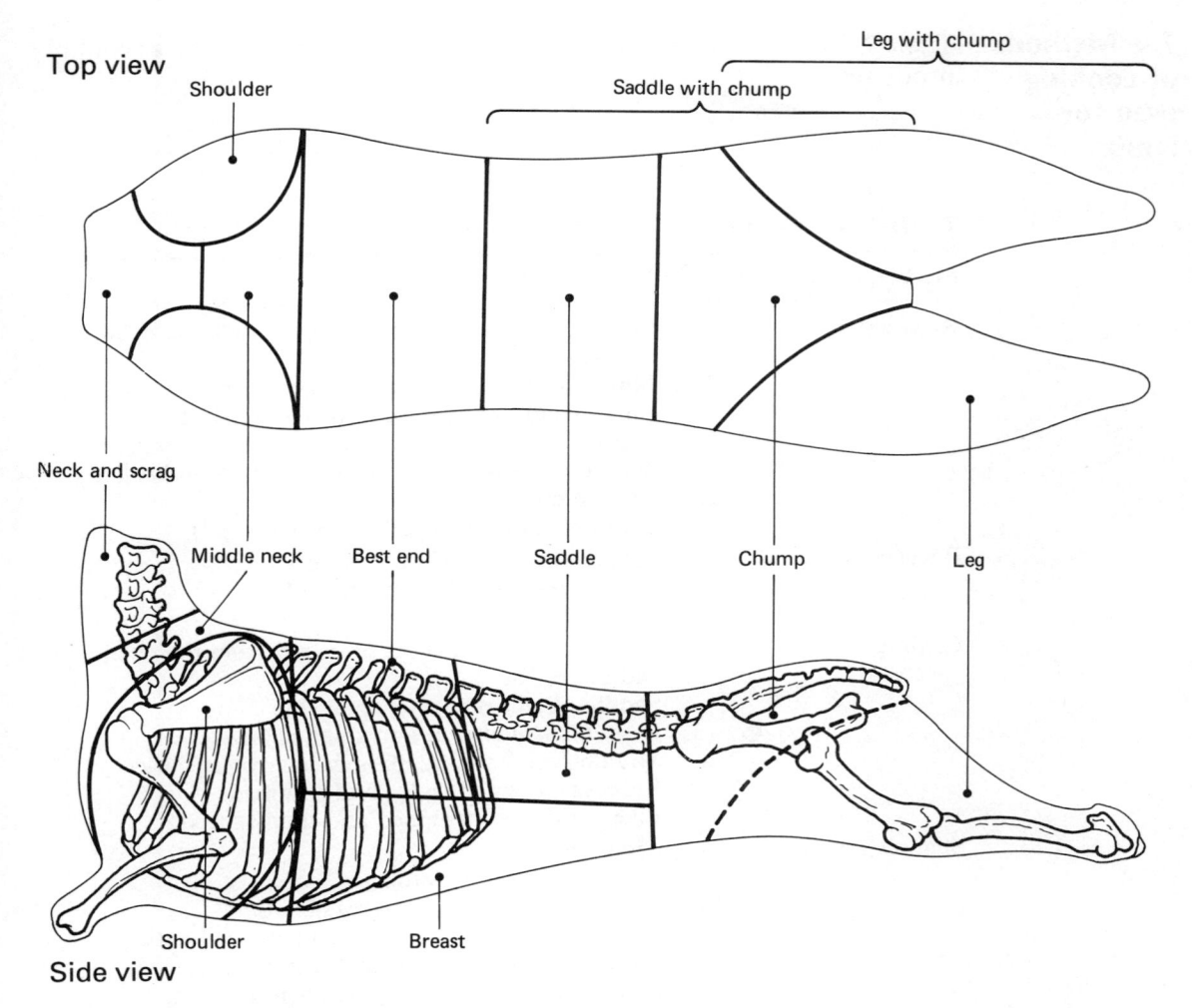

Fig. 7.1 A carcass of lamb

Table 7.3 Lamb offal

Type	Description and preparation for cooking
Kidney (*rognon d'agneau* (m))	Attached to the underside of the saddle. Skinned, the hard fatty core removed, and cut as required.
Liver (*foie d'agneau* (m))	Skinned, the tubes and fatty deposits trimmed away, and cut into thin slices on the slant.
Sweetbreads (*ris d'agneau* (m))	Smaller in size than calves' sweetbreads. Soaked, blanched, and trimmed before final cooking.
Tongue (*langue d'agneau* (f))	Available fresh or pickled in brine. Skinned and the root end trimmed after cooking. Can also be purchased tinned for salads and sandwiches.
Heart (*coeur d'agneau* (m))	Trimmed of tubes and excess fat, stuffed, and loosely tied to retain the shape before cooking. Usually sliced after cooking to improve the presentation. Serve a whole heart for each portion.

7.4 Methods of cooking used for lamb

Table 7.4 summarises the cuts of lamb most suitable for particular cooking processes.

Table 7.4 Methods of cooking used for lamb

Method of cooking	Joint or cut
Roasting	Leg – bone in (whole or half) or boned and rolled. Saddle – bone in, whole. Loin (the saddle split into two equal halves down the chine bone) – bone in or boned and rolled. Best end – rack, guard of honour, crown roast. Shoulder – boned and rolled or stuffed and rolled (second-class). Breast – stuffed and rolled (second-class).
Poêlé cooking	Saddle – bone in, whole. Loin – bone in or boned and rolled. Best end.
Grilling	Gigot chop – thick slices prepared from the chump end of the leg. Saddle – butchered into small cuts. Best end – butchered into small cuts. Middle neck – second-class or uncovered cutlets. Kidneys – skinned, split, and trimmed. Liver – skinned, trimmed and thinly sliced.
Shallow frying	Gigot chops. Saddle – butchered into small cuts. Best end – butchered into small cuts. Middle neck – second-class or uncovered cutlets. Kidneys – skinned, split, and trimmed. Liver – skinned, trimmed, and thinly sliced. Sweetbreads – soaked, blanched, and trimmed before cooking.
Stewing	Shoulder – navarin, curry, ragoût. Breast – ragoût. Middle neck – Irish stew, hotpot. Neck and scrag – Irish stew, hotpot.
Boiling	Tongue – cold sliced, – ingredient for pancake and vol-au-vent filling.
Sauté	Kidneys – skinned, split in half, trimmed, and sliced.
Braising	Sweetbreads – soaked, blanched, and trimmed before braising. Tongue. Heart – stuffed.

8 Pork and bacon

8.1 Porkers and baconers

The meat obtained from pigs falls into two distinct categories: that obtained from pigs reared to provide fresh pig meat (porkers) and that from pigs reared for processing into bacon (baconers). With modern farming methods, pigs of all types are ready for slaughter by 30 weeks at the latest. Porkers are slaughtered at 3½–4 months with an average weight range of 45–50 kg (100–110 lb); baconers at 5–6 months, weighing 85–90 kg (185–200 lb).

As with sheep and cattle, much cross-breeding has occurred in recent years to develop an animal that matures early and produces a high-quality carcass of good conformation. Compared with the traditional breeds, new breeds are able to convert relatively little food into lean meat.

Most pig farming today is done in factory-type, intensive systems, where the temperature and humidity can be controlled.

8.2 Types of porker

- *Sucking or suckling pig* A young pig, purchased whole with the head on, slaughtered at 6–8 weeks old, weighing 4–6.5 kg (9–14 lb). In practice, however, many exceed these weights by several kilos.
- *Gilt* A young female pig that has not been used for breeding, providing a well-fleshed carcass of good conformation.
- *Hog meat* Meat from a well-fleshed young castrated male pig. The rind and part of the back fat (to leave a maximum thickness of 1 cm (½ inch)) are trimmed off the loin before selling.
- *Stag* A castrated older male pig, providing a larger carcass with heavier deposits of fat.
- *Sow* An older female pig used for breeding. The carcass is mainly used for manufacturing purposes.
- *Boar* An uncastrated male pig used for breeding. The flesh is tough, with a thick layer of surface fat, and is used exclusively for manufacturing purposes.

8.3 Purchasing and storing pork

Pork (*porc* (m)) is available fresh and frozen, as whole sides, joints, pre-cut chops, etc. The UK market is mainly supplied by home-produced pork.

Quality purchasing points for fresh pork

- *Flesh* Pale pink in colour, with a fine even grain; firm and resilient to the touch.
- *Fat* Smooth, firm, and white in colour with an even but not excessive covering, particularly over the loins.
- *Skin/rind* Smooth, unbroken, a light pinkish-brown colour.
- *Bones* Small in size, low in proportion to the lean, pinkish in colour.

52 Commodities

- *Smell* Pork deteriorates quicker than other types of meat. The cut surface should be free from stickiness, discolouration, and unpleasant smells.

Storage

Pork does not improve with hanging after purchase, so it is best used without delay. Whole sides and joints are suspended by hooks from racks fixed to the ceiling of the cold-room. Small cuts are placed into trays, covered to prevent drying, and stored at a temperature of 2°C (36°F). The trays must be emptied and changed daily, to prevent the meat from lying in the collected blood.

8.4 Cuts of pork

Table 8.1 shows the joints that can be obtained from a carcass of pork (see fig. 8.1). Small cuts and offal are shown in Tables 8.2 and 8.3, and alternative cuts in Table 8.4.

Table 8.1 Joints of pork

Joint	Typical weight
Leg (*cuissot* (m))	5.5 kg (12 lb)
Loin (*longe* (f))	6.5 kg (14 lb)
Belly (*poitrine* (f))	2.25 kg (5 lb)
Spare-rib (*basse-côte* (f))	2.25 kg (5 lb)
Shoulder/hand and spring (*épaule* (f))	3.25 kg (7 lb)

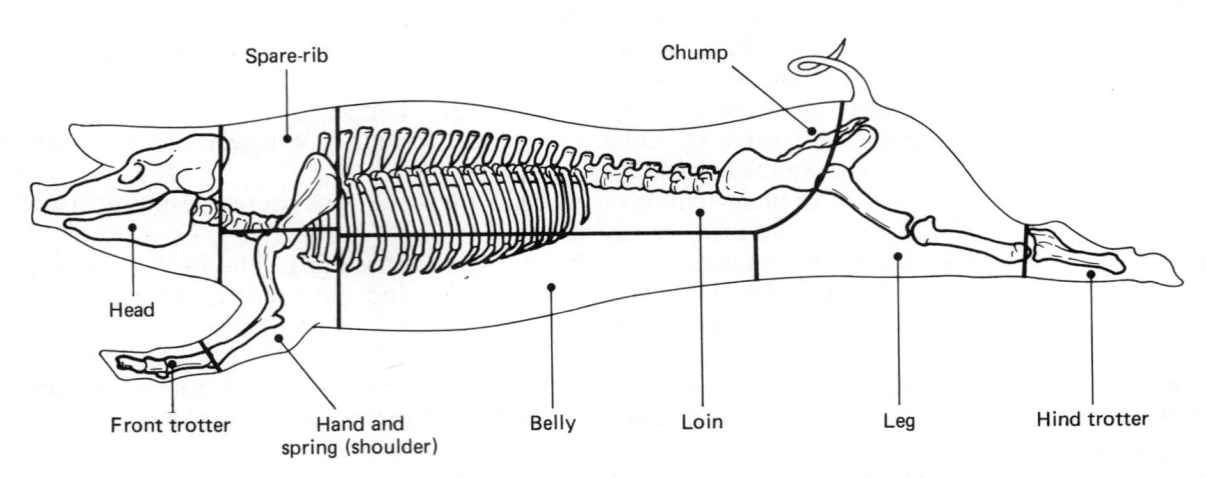

Fig. 8.1 Joints of pork

Table 8.2 Small cuts of pork

Cut	Description	Typical weight	Catering uses
Chop (*côte* (f))	Chops are prepared from the short loin by cutting down through the rind, fat, eye-meat, bone, and fillet. Those butchered from the eye-meat and fat covering the rib bones are correctly termed cutlets. If long, the bone is trimmed back to within 50 mm (2 inches) of the eye-meat. Chops or cutlets can also be prepared from a hogmeat short loin.	175–200 g (6–7 oz), one per portion	Grilling – garnished with an appropriate vegetable and accompanied by a suitable sauce. Shallow frying – breaded and garnished or plain
Escalope (*escalope* (f))	Slices of trimmed pork fillet flattened between two sheets of clear polythene before cooking. Prepared from a trimmed fillet or occasionally a boned, trimmed loin.	120–150 g (4–5 oz), one per portion	Shallow frying as for escalope of veal.
Escalopine (*escalopine* (f))	Prepared as for escalopes.	40–60 g (1½–2 oz), two or three per portion	Shallow frying
Spare-ribs – barbecue style	Not to be confused with the spare-rib joint (fig. 8.1) – these are the rib bones with the accompanying meat after removal from the belly. Sometimes the sternum (breastbone) is also included. They are usually marinaded before cooking.		Shallow frying. Grilling.

Table 8.3 Pork offal

Type	Preparation for cooking
Kidney (*rognon* (m))	Skinned, the hard fatty core removed, and cut as required.
Liver (*foie* (m))	Skinned, the fatty deposits and tubes removed, then cut into thin slices on the slant.
Head (*tête* (f))	Washed and cleaned before boiling with aromatic vegetables to make brawn.
Trotter (*pied* (m))	Washed, blanched, and scraped before being used to make aspic or before being stuffed and braised.

Table 8.4 Alternative cuts of pork

Cut	Description
Carcass	The whole body, including the head, tail, and kidneys.
Side	One half of the carcass after splitting lengthways down the chine bone.
Long loin	The loin including the chump end, blade bone, and spare-rib.
Short loin	The loin including the chump end only.
Fillet	This is removed whole from the pork loin or hogmeat loin and trimmed of all surface fat and silverskin. It can be cooked whole in puff pastry, stuffed and roasted, or cut into escalopes.

8.5 Uses of pork

Table 8.5 summarises the cuts of pork most suitable for particular uses.

Table 8.5 Uses of pork

Use	Joint or cut
Roasting	Leg – bone in or boned, whole or half. Loin – bone in, whole or half, boned and rolled. Belly – second-class roast, boned, stuffed, and rolled. Spare-rib – second-class roast.
Boiling/pickled and boiled	Head – preparation of brawn. Belly. Trotters – washed, blanched, and scraped before final cooking.
Grilling	Loin – chops, cutlets. Belly – cut into thick slices. Spare-rib – cut into spare-rib chops. Trotters – boiled first before grilling. Kidneys – skinned, split into two, and trimmed. Liver – skinned, trimmed, and finely sliced. Spare-rib – barbecue style.
Shallow frying	Loin – chops, cutlets. Belly – cut into thick slices. Spare-rib – cut into spare-rib chops. Kidneys – skinned, split into two, trimmed, and sliced. Liver – skinned, trimmed, and finely sliced. Spare-ribs – barbecue style.
Pies	Spare-rib. Shoulder and hand.
Sausages and forcemeat	Shoulder and hand. Trimmings from other joints.

8.6 Bacon

Bacon (*lard* (m)) is produced by curing or curing and smoking a side of pork (minus the head, kidney, fillet, chine bone, sternum, trotters, and tail) from specially reared pigs called baconers (see section 8.1). Curing is the process of using salt to preserve meat for future use. All meats have a high water content, but applying salt (either dry or in the form of a pickle or brine) will remove part of this moisture content and prevent the growth of micro-organisms (see section 26.7).

Using salt alone tends to dry the meat, leaving it hard and salty. Sugar can be added to counteract the saltiness. Saltpetre, which is sometimes used as a preservative, provides the characteristic pinkish-red colour of cured meats. When these ingredients are rubbed into the cut surface the process is known as dry-curing. When they are mixed with water, a brine or pickle is produced in which the meat is immersed. This method is considerably quicker than dry-curing and produces a milder, less salty product.

Bacon cured by either method is matured under cool conditions for up to two weeks to allow the salt, saltpetre, and sugar to become more evenly distributed – improving both the eating qualities and the flavour. In recent years a number of new techniques have been developed to speed up the slower traditional methods of curing.

If the bacon is to be smoked, the cured sides are first washed in cold water, before cold-smoking at a temperature between 21 and 32°C (70–90°F). This type of produce is known as smoked bacon. Bacon that is not smoked is known as green bacon.

8.7 Joints of bacon

Table 8.6 shows the joints that can be obtained from a side of bacon (see fig. 8.2).

Table 8.6 Joints of bacon from a baconer pig

Joint	Typical weight
Gammon (*jambon* (m))	8 kg (18 lb)
Back	10 kg (22 lb)
Streaky (*lard de poitrine* (m))	5 kg (11 lb)
Collar (*collet* (m))	5 kg (11 lb)
Hock (*jarret* (m))	5 kg (11 lb)

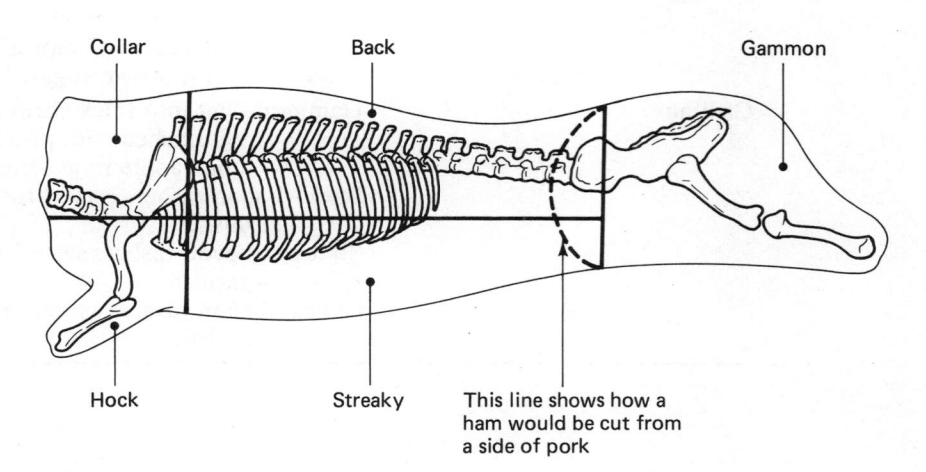

Fig. 8.2 A side of bacon

8.8 Purchasing and storing bacon

Bacon rashers are usually purchased by the caterer pre-sliced, either loose-wrapped or vacuum-packed. If a whole back or streaky is preferred, the bones, cartilage, and rind are cut away before slicing.

Quality purchasing points for bacon

- *Smell* Pleasant, with no signs of rancidity.
- *Fat* Smooth, white. There should not be excess fat.
- *Flesh* An even pinkish colour, resilient to the touch, free from stickiness.
- *Rind* Thin, smooth, free from blemishes.

Storage

Vacuum packs can be stored either deep-frozen or under normal refrigeration. Once open, the contents must be used within 2–3 days. Whole sides, gammons, etc. should be suspended on meat hooks from bars attached to the ceiling of the cold-room.

8.9 Uses of bacon

Table 8.7 summarises the cuts of bacon most suitable for particular uses.

Table 8.7 Uses of bacon

Use	Joint or cut
Boiling	Gammon – hot: thinly sliced and served with a suitable sauce. – cold: thinly sliced and served with a salad and a selection of mustards and pickles. Collar – served hot with pease pudding. – cold as for gammon. Hock – served hot with pease pudding.
Baking	Gammon – wrapped in common paste (flour, salt, and water). – studded with cloves and sprinkled with brown sugar.
Grilling	Gammon – cut into thick slices (steaks), garnished with peach halves, pineapple rings, fried egg, etc. Back – bacon rashers served for breakfast. – garnish. Streaky – bacon rashers served for breakfast. – garnish. Collar – bacon rashers served for breakfast. – garnish.

Table 8.7 Uses of bacon (*continued*)

Use	Joint or cut
Shallow-frying	Back – bacon rashers served for breakfast. 　　　 – garnish. Streaky – bacon rashers served for breakfast. 　　　 – garnish. Collar – bacon rashers served for breakfast. 　　　 – garnish.
Pies, flavouring, mincing, etc.	Hock. Collar. Trimmings from other joints.

8.10 Ham

Originally the term 'ham' (*jambon* (m)) was applied only to the cured and smoked hind leg of a baconer pig that had been removed from the fresh side and processed separately. Today, however, the term is also used to describe the shoulder joint that is processed in a similar way. Subtle changes in flavour can be produced by varying the method of preparation, for example by dry-curing, brining, smoking or not smoking, adding sugar and spices, or feeding the pigs on a certain type of food.

Hams are either thinly sliced and eaten raw or cooked by a variety of methods including boiling, baking, braising, and shallow frying.

- Hams eaten raw include Parma ham, Bayonne ham, Toulouse ham, Mainz ham, and Westphalian ham.
- Hams eaten cooked include York ham, Suffolk ham, and Virginian ham.

Pre-cooked, boneless hams

Pre-cooked, boneless shoulder hams are available either tinned or vacuum-packed and are used extensively in the catering industry for the preparation of sandwiches, salads, and garnishes. This type of product is popular because of its comparatively low purchase price.

9 Game

9.1 The supply of game

Game (*gibier* (m)) is the flesh of wild birds and animals that have been hunted and killed with the intention of being eaten by humans. Game has a stronger flavour than that associated with domestically reared birds and animals. This is mainly due to a 'natural' diet of grasses, grubs, berries, leaves, etc. The flesh is lean with little fat covering, except for wild duck. Only young game birds or animals have tender flesh suitable for roasting – older examples are more suitable for stewing.

Some types of game (pheasants, for example) are reared artificially and released into the wild to increase the stock, and the farming of deer has proved profitable in some regions of Great Britain.

All game is normally hung for a time in a cool, dry, well-ventilated room before cooking (see page 26). The length of time depends on the type of game and the preference of the consumer. Hanging allows the flesh to tenderise and develop the characteristic 'gamey' flavour. In recent years the demand has been for game with a milder flavour, which results from a shorter hanging period. The ultimate result of excessive hanging is rotten flesh which may be infested with maggots.

The sale of most fresh game is controlled by the shooting season, which allows a safe period each year when the young replacement stock can be reared. Frozen game – particularly the more popular types – is usually available all the year, provided it was shot during the permitted season. Both fresh and frozen game can be purchased only from licensed game wholesalers and retailers.

9.2 Quality purchasing points for young game

Feathered game – pheasants, partridges, wild duck, grouse, etc.

- *Breast* Plump, well-fleshed with a pliable breastbone.
- *Bruising* Minimal.
- *Legs* Smooth.
- *Bleeding* Not excessive.
- *Smell* Gamey without being unpleasant.

Avoid birds that have been poorly shot and are showing extensive damage from lead shot, and also cock pheasants with long sharp spurs.

Furred game – hares, rabbits

- *Claws* These should be long and sharp.
- *Ears* The tips should tear easily.
- *Flesh* Plump, well-fleshed, free from excessive bleeding and bruising.
- *Jaw-bones* The lower jaw-bones should break easily.

Venison

- *Flesh* Dark reddish-brown in colour, free from any signs of blood

clots and excessive bleeding and bruising.
- *Age* Young animals up to 4 years in age – older animals will only provide dry, tough flesh.
- *Smell* Gamey without being unpleasant.

9.3 Uses of game

Tables 9.1 and 9.2 describe the principal types of game and their catering uses.

Table 9.1 Uses of feathered game (weights quoted are for the average, undressed, fully grown adult birds)

Type	Description	Typical weight	Catering uses
Grouse/red grouse (this variety of grouse is found only in the UK). Male – *lagopède* (m) *rouge à l'Écosse*. Female – *poule* (f) *lagopède a l'Écosse*	The grouse is a smallish bird, renowned for its flavour. It has dark reddish-brown plumage, except for soft, white leg feathers. The female is slightly smaller than the male bird. When roasted, the best results are obtained when cooked underdone. One bird per portion.	560 g (20 oz)	Roasting–young birds. Game pie, soup, terrines, pâté – older, mature birds.
Partridge (*perdrix* (f)) Red-legged/French partridge Grey-legged/common partridge	The two varieties of partridge found in the UK are easily distinguished from each other. In both sexes the red-legged have black and white eye-stripes with rich chestnut barring on grey flanks. The grey-legged has a distinctive dark horseshoe pattern on its breast and is smaller in size.	340 g (12 oz)	Roasting – young birds, one per portion. Stewing, soup, terrine, pâté, pie – older, mature birds. As part of a decorated cold buffet. Bones – stock.
Pheasant (*faissan* (m))	Pheasant is the most common and easily recognised of all the game birds in the UK. The male pheasant has a long tail of barred feathers, copper body plumage, and a richly coloured head. The female is less brightly coloured with a shorter tail. A brace of pheasants consists of a male and a female bird. The hen bird is considered by many to provide more tender and better-tasting flesh than the cock bird. When used for roasting and sauté, the meat is less dry when cooked underdone. Each bird provides 2–4 portions, depending on size.	Male/cock 1.25–1.5 kg (3–3½ lb). Female/hen 1–1.25 kg (2–2½ lb)	Roasting – young birds Sauté – suprêmes from young birds. Stewing, soup, terrine, pâté, pie – older, mature birds. As part of a decorated cold buffet. Bones – stock.

Table 9.1 Uses of feathered game (weights quoted are for the average, undressed, fully grown adult birds) (*continued*)

Type	Description	Typical weight	Catering uses
Snipe (*becassine* (f))	The common snipe is the variety usually eaten. The plumage is patterned with various shades of dark and light brown, and the head is marked with dark stripes. For roasting, the snipe is often left undrawn, with only the gizzard and vent removed. The head and neck are skinned, the eyes are removed, and the long beak is twisted round and pushed through its legs, trussing the bird into shape.	90–120 g (3½–4½ oz)	Roasting – young birds. Stewing, pâté, terrines – older mature birds.
Wild duck (*canard sauvage* (m))	The mallard, widgeon, and teal are the main types of wild duck usually available to the caterer, the mallard being more popular than the other two. The mallard and widgeon are similar in size, but the teal is much smaller. The mallard and widgeon will yield two portions from each bird and the teal only one.	Mallard 1.25 kg (2¾ lb). Widgeon 1 kg (2 lb). Teal 340 g (12 oz).	Roasting, à la presse – young birds. Salmis, braising – older, mature birds.
Woodcock (*bécasse* (f))	A small bird, with a boldly striped head, a long thin beak, and brown patterned plumage. It is prepared for roasting as for snipe. Usually one bird for each portion.	225–340 g (8–12 oz)	Roasting – young birds. Stewing, pâté, terrines – older, mature birds.
Wood-pigeon (*pigeon* (m))	This is not to be confused with the domestic pigeon, which may be reared to provide squabs (which are classified as poultry). The wood-pigeon is easily recognised by its grey plumage, white wing bar, and purple-green neck patch. A portion usually consists of one pigeon. When used for roasting and sauté, best results are obtained when cooked underdone.	450–675 g (1–1½ lb)	Roasting, sauté (breasts only) – young birds. Stewing, braising, pie, terrine, pâté, soup – older, mature birds.

Other game birds occasionally available to the caterer include the black grouse or black game, capercaillie, and ptarmigan.

Table 9.2 Uses of furred game

Type	Description	Typical weight	Catering uses
Hares – brown or common hare; mountain, blue, or Scottish hare (*lièvre* (m))	Hares are larger than rabbits and can be distinguished by their heavier build; longer, more powerful hind legs; and the two large incisor teeth set in the upper jaw. All hares are tender up to one year old, after which the flesh becomes dry and tough. After killing, fresh hares are suspended by their hind legs to allow the blood to collect in the chest cavity. This blood is used to thicken and provide the distinctive flavour to the sauce of jugged hare. Hares should be hung for only 2–3 days before cooking. The râble or baron – the whole body of the hare from the base of the neck to the stump of the tail, minus the fore and hind legs, rib ends, and belly flaps – is often used for roasting, after larding with strips of fat bacon or pork fat. Usually, however, only the eye-meat covering the lower back (lumbar vertebrae) is used. The flesh of hares is dark reddish-brown in colour with a strong flavour. Hares are available frozen, whole, fully dressed, jointed, râbles only, or fresh skinned or unskinned with only the intestine and stomach removed (paunched).	Mountain hare 2.25–2.75 kg (5–6 lb). Brown hare 3–3.25 kg (6½–7 lb).	Roasting – râble. (Young hares (leverets) can however be roasted whole.) Jugged hare. Pâté, terrine, pie.
Rabbit/coney (*lapin* (m))	The flavour of the flesh can be affected by the rabbit's diet. The flesh is a pale whitish-brown colour. Young immature rabbits up to 4 months old are best, the flesh of older animals being rather dry and stringy and requiring long cooking. Available fresh or frozen, skinned or unskinned, whole or jointed, Wild rabbits only rarely appear on the menu. Fresh rabbits require hanging for only 2–3 days.	1.25–1.5 kg (2½–3½ lb)	Sauté, roasting, grilling – young animals only. Pie, pâté, terrines, soup, stewing (curry, fricassée, ragoût) – older animals.

Table 9.2 Uses of furred game (*continued*)

Type	Description	Typical weight	Catering uses
Venison (*venaison* (f))	In the UK, venison is provided by the roebuck, red deer, and fallow deer. The roebuck is considered to be superior. Meat from young wild animals up to 4 years old is best. The flesh of older animals will be dry and coarse. Venison is dark reddish-brown in colour, with a distinctive 'sweetish' flavour. The carcass is gutted and skinned shortly after killing, then hung for 2–3 weeks to tenderise the meat and develop the gamey flavour. Wild and farmed venison is available fresh or frozen, butchered into joints such as haunch (hind leg), saddle, loin, shoulder, etc.	Weights of the various joints vary widely.	Roasting – saddle, haunch. Stewing – shoulder, neck, breast. Shallow frying or grilling – venison sausages, liver. Sauté – cutlets/chops, medallions, fillet. Pâté, pies, terrines, soup.

10 Fish and shellfish

10.1 The supply of fish

Because great Britain is an island, fish (*poisson* (m)) has always featured in the British diet, providing protein and some minerals and vitamins. In the last few years, however, fish prices have increased dramatically, and even the once less popular fish such as coalfish (coley), pollock, dogfish (huss, rock salmon), and monkfish can now demand high prices when purchased by the caterer.

In the past, the plentiful supply of fresh salt-water fish led to most freshwater fish being given less prominence on the menu. Salmon, salmon trout, and trout are popular types of freshwater fish, but others, such as carp, pike, and eels rarely appear except on special menus. Trout farming has made rainbow trout plentiful, readily available and competitively priced. Salmon farming – a more recent development – has also become a viable commercial proposition. Fish farming is not new, however – oysters and carp have been farmed for centuries.

The White Fish Authority and the Ministry of Agriculture for Scotland have investigated the possibilities of unfamiliar deep-sea varieties of fish. As yet the general public, unfamiliar with the appearance and names of these new varieties, has been slow to purchase them.

Fish is an important alternative to meat in the provision of high-biological-value proteins (see page 141) and it appears on the menu at all times of day. Fish can be deep-fried or shallow-fried, grilled, poached, baked, steamed, etc. in the preparation of a large variety of dishes.

10.2 Classification of fish

For catering purposes fresh fish, both salt-water and freshwater fish, are divided into two main groups, oily and white, with the white types being subdivided into round and flat. The method of cooking will often depend on whether the fish is oily or white. Oily fish, except for whitebait and possibly sprats, are not deep-fried but are usually shallow-fried or grilled. The fat can then render during cooking, making the flesh more palatable.

Table 10.1 compares the general features of white fish and oily fish.

Table 10.1 A comparison of white fish and oily fish

White fish	Oily fish
The flesh is always white in colour when cooked.	Darker flesh, ranging from light brown to deep pink.
The oil is stored in the liver and may be extracted and sold as vitamin-rich fish oil, for example cod-liver oil.	The oil is distributed throughout the flesh.
Can be round or flat.	Always round in shape.

Table 10.1 A comparison of white fish and oily fish (*continued*)

White fish	Oily fish
Fat-soluble vitamins A and D found in the liver.	Vitamins A and D dispersed throughout the flesh.
Easily digested – suitable for young children, invalids, and those on a restricted diet.	Richer, less easy to digest, therefore less suitable for these groups of people.
Many types of white fish – cod, plaice, haddock, whiting, etc. – are popular deep-fried.	Except for whitebait, these are not normally deep-fried.
Delicate flavour.	Stronger, more pronounced flavour.

The following features can be used to aid identification:

- *Fins* Shape and position.
- *Colour/markings* Barred/striped, mottled, speckled, blotched.
- *Scales* Large, small, abundance.
- *Size* Varies with each species.
- *Shape* Round, flat, compact, elongated.

10.3 Purchasing and storing fish

Prices of fresh fish vary according to the season and the weather conditions. Prices increase during long periods of high wind which makes fishing difficult, resulting in the supply not being able to meet the market demands. Fish which live near the surface of the water and migrate around the shores of the UK are more plentiful at certain periods of the year.

The supply of wild salmon is controlled by legislation that permits salmon fishing only between February and August, However, farmed salmon is available all the year round at a lower price.

Frozen fish is unaffected by season and weather conditions and is available all the year. Prices of frozen fish are stable, because they are not affected so directly by the laws of supply and demand. Considerable quantities of frozen fish are imported from other countries, increasing the availability of many unusual and less common types.

Quality purchasing points

Whole fresh fish

- *Smell* Wholesome, pleasant.
- *Scales* (if any) Plentiful and firmly attached.
- *Eyes* Bright, prominent, not sunken.
- *Gills* Bright, pinkish-red colour.
- *Flesh* Firm, springs back into shape when pressed.
- *Skin* Covered with a fresh sea-slime, undamaged, and free from bruising and discolouration.

An unpleasant smell of ammonia; sunken eyes; dull, darkly coloured gills; and soft flabby flesh indicate a fish that has deteriorated in quality.

Cuts of fish – fresh

- Good colour without discolouration.
- Firm to the touch.
- Free from stickiness.
- Pleasant smell.

Frozen fish

- No signs of thawing when delivered.
- Encased in a coating of ice (glace).
- No sign of dryness or discolouration.

The flesh of white fish discolours and turns yellow when stored frozen for a long time.

Points to note when purchasing fresh fish

- Whenever possible, purchase daily.
- Purchase either direct from a wholesale fish market or from a local wholesale or retail fish merchant.
- Check all fish on arrival for quality, returning any that are damaged or unsatisfactory.
- Fish should arrive packed in layers of ice, especially in periods of warm weather.
- Medium-sized fish (in relation to their maximum size) will provide the best value. Large examples may be tough and coarse. Small examples lack flavour.
- All types of fish should be well-fleshed and feel heavy for their size.
- Avoid purchasing fish when out of season and not in peak condition – for example, flat fish immediately after spawning.
- Freshly caught fish can be purchased by the stone direct from the fish market or in smaller quantities and by the number from a fish merchant.

Storage of fresh fish

- Use a separate fish refrigerator or a part of a refrigerator especially reserved for the storage of wet fish (fresh fish).
- Store all wet fish between layers of ice. The surface of fish stored in this way in direct contact with the ice will remain at freezing point until all the ice melts.
- Empty the fish boxes or trays daily, wash them out, and repack the fish with fresh ice.
- Practice good stock rotation – ensure that the old stock is placed in front of the new, ready to be used first.
- Empty, defrost, and thoroughly clean all surfaces of the fish refrigerator regularly – weekly is best.
- Don't over-order.

Storage of smoked fish

Smoked fish is stored dry on trays in a normal refrigerator.

Storage of frozen fish

Frozen fish is stored in a deep freeze at a maximum temperature of $-18°C$ ($0°F$). Defrosting is best carried out slowly on trays in the refrigerator. Once thawed, even if only partly, deep-frozen fish must not be returned to the deep freeze.

Storage of live fish

Trout, eels, and carp purchased live should be placed into a clean, well-aerated freshwater tank as soon as possible after delivery. They should be fed as required with a proprietary brand of fish pellets.

10.4 Cuts of fish

Table 10.2 describes the main cuts of fish, which are illustrated in figs 10.1 to 10.7.

Table 10.2 Cuts of fish

Type	Description
Fillet (*filet* (m))	A cut of fish free from all skin and bone, prepared from either a round or a flat fish (fig. 10.1). Fillets of fish can be poached, grilled, deep-fried, shallow-fried, or cooked au gratin or en papillote. Flat fish – plaice, dover and lemon sole, flounders, etc. – yield four fillets from a fish weighting 560–675 g (1¼–1½ lb). Cross-cut fillets, two from each fish, can be prepared from smaller fish. Round fish – trout, mackerel, whiting, small haddock, etc. – yield two fillets from a fish weighing 340–500 g (12–18 oz).
Goujon (*goujon* (m))	A long, thin strip of fish cut from a prepared fillet, approximately 6 cm × 0.5 cm (2½ inch × ¼ inch) (fig. 10.2). Goujons are often egg-and-breadcrumbed and deep-fried, but can also be shallow-fried or sautéed.
Délice (*délice* (m))	Not a cut of fish but a menu term indicating a neatly folded fillet (fig. 10.3).
Paupiette (*paupiette* (f))	A neatly rolled fillet, stuffed with either a fish farce, shellfish, vegetables, or a mixture of vegetables and shellfish (fig. 10.4). The fillet is rolled from the tapered tail to the wider head end, and poached.
Suprême (*suprême* (m))	A thick slice of fish cut on the slant from a fillet prepared from a large fish such as salmon, halibut, and turbot (fig. 10.5). (Cutting on the slant increases the surface area for heat to penetrate and improves presentation). Suprêmes are usually poached, shallow-fried, or cooked en papillote.
Darne (*darne* (f))	A thick slice of fish on the bone, prepared by cutting across a large round fish such as salmon, cod, hake, etc. (fig. 10.6). The tapered tail end of the fish is unsuitable for cutting darnes. The term 'cutlet' is sometimes used by fishmongers. Depending on the type of fish, darnes are suitable for grilling, shallow frying, and deep poaching.

Table 10.2 Cuts of fish (*continued*)

Type	Description
Tronçon (*tronçon* (m))	A thick slice of fish on the bone, prepared from a large flat fish such as turbot, brill, and halibut (fig. 10.7). The fish is split into two by chopping down the backbone from the tail end. Cutting across the fish, the best tronçons are prepared from the long side not containing the gut cavity. They are usually deep-poached.

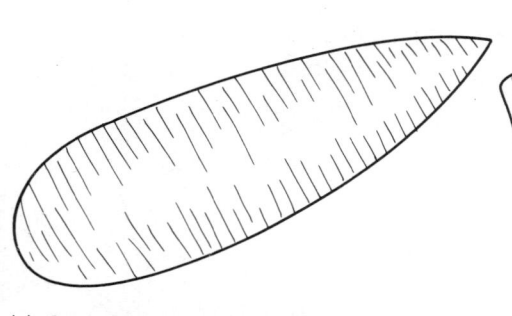

(a) Quarter-cut – four per fish from flat fish weighing 560–675 g (1¼–1½ lb)

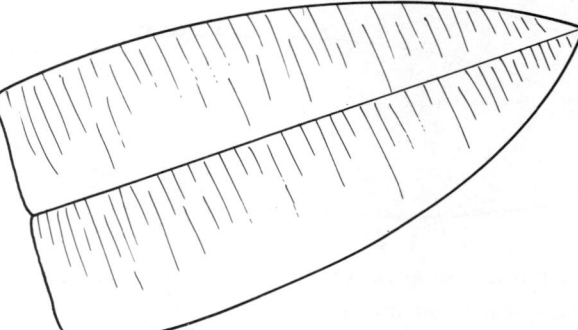

(b) Cross-cut – two per fish from round or flat fish weighing 340–500 g (12–18 oz)

Fig. 10.1 A fillet of fish

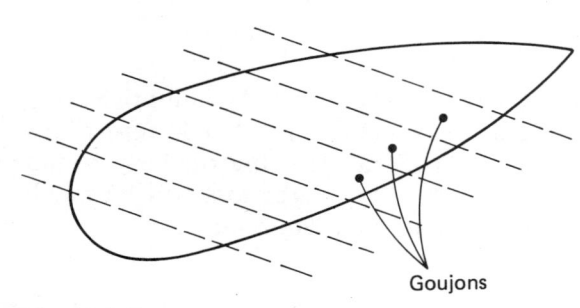

Fig. 10.2 Goujons – thin strips cut from a quarter-fillet

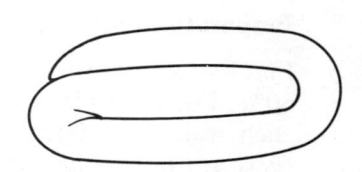

Fig. 10.3 A délice of fish – a neatly rolled fillet

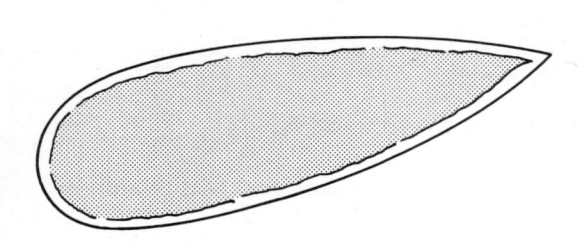

Fig. 10.4 A paupiette – a fillet spread with stuffing and rolled up

68 Commodities

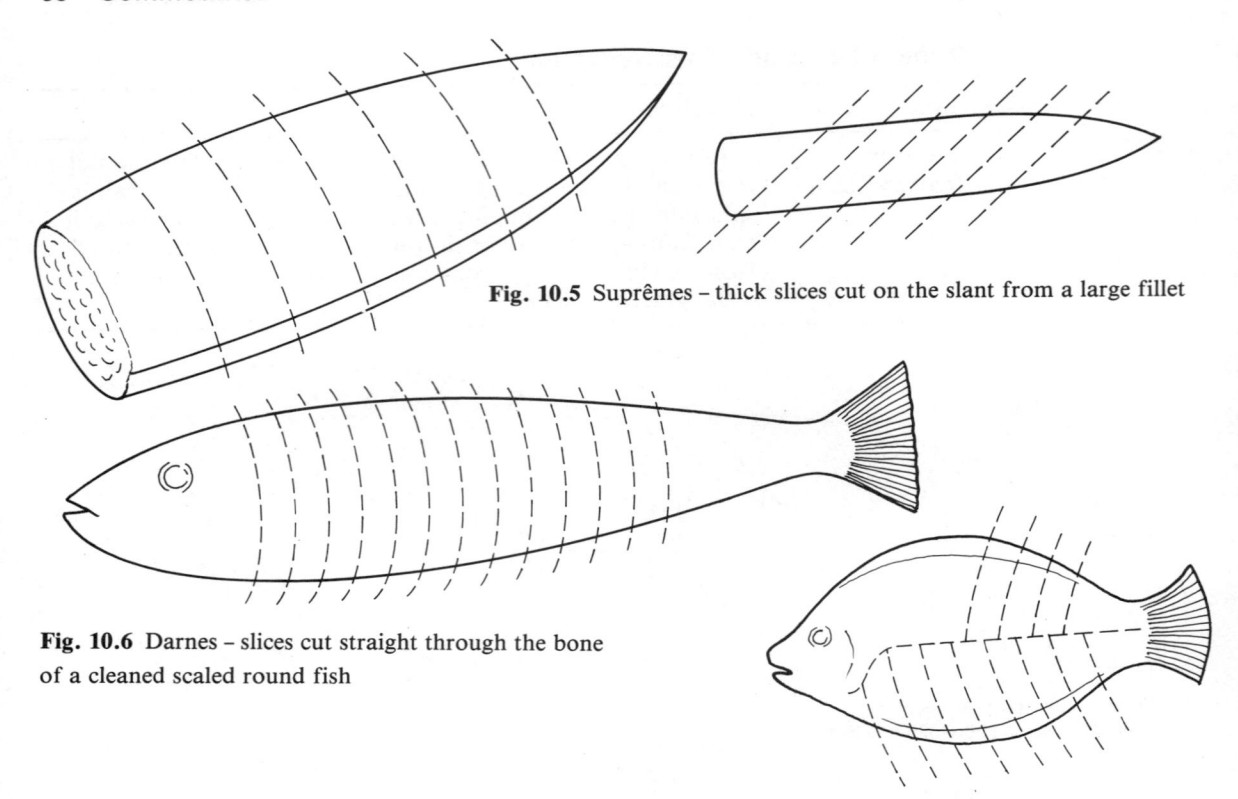

Fig. 10.5 Suprêmes – thick slices cut on the slant from a large fillet

Fig. 10.6 Darnes – slices cut straight through the bone of a cleaned scaled round fish

Fig. 10.7 Tronçons – slices cut through the bone of a cleaned large flat fish

Preparation loss

Flat fish lose up to 50% of their total weight when filleted, round fish up to 60%. For example, a flat fish weighing 675 g (1½ lb) will yield four fillets each weighing approximately 85 g (3 oz). Small fish (particularly round fish) are normally served whole, and here the weight loss will be much smaller – only 5–10% after gutting, scaling, and trimming.

Portion size

For normal table d'hôte service the following average raw weight of fish per portion is suitable:

- Fillet, goujon, suprême   120–150 g (4–5 oz)
- Darne, tronçon   150–200 g (5–7 oz)
- Small whole fish   175–225 g (6–8 oz)

For some menus, increase these weights by up to 50%.

10.5 Identification and uses of fish

Tables 10.3 and 10.4 describe the principal salt-water and freshwater fish and their catering uses.

Table 10.3   Identification and uses of salt-water fish

Type	Classification	Description	Best size	Catering uses
Bass (*bar* (m))	Round, white	A medium to large fish, uniform silver-grey in colour, with a large mouth, a spiny dorsal fin, and large scales. The flesh is firm, slightly pink in colour, and of a good flavour.	School bass 1–2.25 kg (2–5 lb). Bass 2.25–4.5 kg (5–10 lb).	Fillets, suprêmes, whole (stuffed). Suprêmes, darnes.
Brill (*barbue* (f))	Flat, white	The brownish upper side is covered with small scales; the underside is an opaque white. The flesh is firm but fairly flaky, with a good flavour similar to turbot.	2.75–3.6 kg (6–8 lb)	Suprêmes, tronçons, whole (cold buffet), poaching, shallow frying, deep poaching.
Cod (*cabillaud* (m))	Round, white	A large fish, with a mottled greenish-grey colour, shading to a white belly. The flesh has a loose texture with large flakes of a moderate to good flavour, especially when very fresh.	Codling 1–2.25 kg (2–5 lb). Cod 2.25–5.5 kg (5–12 lb).	Fillets. Suprêmes, darnes, deep poaching, deep frying, shallow frying, grilling.
Coalfish/coley (*colin* (m))	Round, white	Coley is cheaper than many fish. It is dark bottle-green, shading to a dull silver belly. The flesh is fairly firm in texture, greyish in colour, and lacking in flavour. The flesh whitens when cooked.	2.75–3.6 kg (6–8 lb)	Fillets, suprêmes, darnes, shallow frying, deep frying, grilling, fish pies, fish cakes.
Dover sole (*sole* (f))	Flat, white	An oval-shape, medium-sized fish, with a brownish-grey upper side and a white underside. The skin is rough and scaly. The flesh is firm with a close texture, and the flavour is excellent.	340–450 g (12–16 oz) served whole; or 560–675 g (1¼–1½ lb) whole fish for fillets	Fillets, goujons, paupiettes, poaching, shallow frying, deep frying, grilling.
Lemon sole	Flat, white	This is broader than the Dover sole, with a brownish-yellow upper side and a white underside. The skin is covered in thick slime when fresh and has no scales. The flesh is less firm than that of the Dover sole and the flavour is considered to be inferior.	340–400 g (12–14 oz) whole; 560–675 g (1¼–1½ lb) whole fish for fillets	Fillets, goujons, paupiettes, poaching, shallow frying, deep frying, grilling.
Grey mullet (*muge capiton* (m))	Round, white	A medium-size fish, uniform silver-grey colour, with large, easily detached scales. It is covered in a thick sea slime when fresh. The flesh is firm with large flakes and a pleasant distinctive taste.	450g–1.1 kg (1–2½ lb)	Whole (stuffed), fillets, baking, grilling, stewing, shallow frying, en papillote.
Haddock (*aiglefin* (m))	Round, white	A medium-size fish, similar in appearance to cod. Brownish olive-green back, shading to a silver belly, with a distinctive dark 'thumb mark' on each shoulder. The flesh, eaten fresh or smoked, has a flaky texture with a delicate taste.	450g–1.25kg (1–3 lb)	Whole, fillets, goujons, shallow frying, deep frying, grilling, poaching, deep poaching.

Table 10.3 Identification and uses of salt-water fish (*continued*)

Type	Classification	Description	Best size	Catering uses
Halibut (*flétan* (m))	Flat, white	An extremely large, flat fish. It has an olive-green upper side and a greyish-white belly. The flesh of small halibut is firm and flaky in texture, with a good flavour. Large fish are inclined to be coarse, tough, and dry.	2.75–5.5 kg (6–12 lb)	Suprêmes, tronçons, shallow frying, poaching, deep poaching, grilling.
Herring (*hareng* (m))	Round, oily	These are small to medium-sized, dark greenish-grey shading to silver, scaly, with a small mouth. They are eaten fresh, smoked, pickled, or salted and the flesh has a distinctive flavour	200–340 g (7–12 oz)	Whole, fillets, shallow frying, grilling, baking, poaching (sousing).
Huss (rock salmon) (*chien de mer* (m)/*aiguillat* (m))	Round, oily	A collective name for the dogfish family. All are shark-like in appearance, with an extremely rough skin. The flesh is rather soft, closely textured, with a pinkish-brown colour and a pleasant flavour.	Normally gutted, skinned, and split when purchased.	Shallow frying, deep frying.
Mackerel (*maquereau* (m))	Round, oily	A small to medium-sized fish, streamlined in shape, brilliant dark blue and green, shading to silver when first caught. The flesh is firm and flaky when fresh, with a distinctive flavour.	340–560 g (12 oz–1¼ lb)	Whole, fillets, shallow frying, grilling, deep poaching, baking, sousing.
Monkfish (*baudroie* (f)/ *lotte de mer* (f))	Flat, white	An extremely ugly fish with a large mouth and a head that quickly tapers to the tail. Only the tail is edible, being skinned and sold by weight. The flesh is firm, slightly rubbery, with an excellent flavour.	Tail only	Shallow frying, deep frying, poaching, grilling.
Plaice (*plie* (f))	Flat, white	A popular medium-sized flat fish. The upper side is brown with orange/red spots, the underside white. The flesh is soft, close-textured, and of a good flavour.	340–400 g (12–14 oz) whole; 560–675 g (1¼–1½ lb) whole fish for fillets.	Whole, fillets, goujons, shallow frying, deep frying, poaching, grilling.
Red mullet (*rouget* (m))	Oily	A small to medium-sized fish, brilliant red in colour. The flesh is firm and flaky, and has an excellent flavour.	200–340 g (7–12 oz)	Whole, fillets, shallow frying, grilling, baking, en papillote
Sardine (*sardine* (f))	Oily	A small, round, torpedo-shaped fish, dark greenish-blue shading to silvery sides and belly. The flesh is fairly firm and flaky in texture, with an excellent distinctive flavour. Enormous quantities are caught and canned in olive oil.	10–15 cm (4–6 inches) in length	Whole with head on, shallow frying, grilling.

Table 10.3 Identification and uses of salt-water fish (*continued*)

Type	Classification	Description	Best size	Catering uses
Skate (*raie* (f))	Flat, white	A medium to large fish with a flattened body, long tail, and greatly enlarged pectoral fins. Only the triangular wings are eaten, which are skinned but not filleted. The flesh is soft, with long ribs of a good flavour.	Wings only	Shallow frying, deep frying, deep poaching.
Sprat (*esprot* (m)/*sprat* (m))	Oily	The smallest member of the herring family, greenish-blue shading to silvery sides and belly. The flesh has a firm flaky texture, slightly translucent, with a good distinctive flavour.	7.5–12.5 cm (3–5 inches)	Whole, shallow frying, grilling, occasionally deep-fried.
Turbot (*turbot* (m))	Flat, white	These are medium to large diamond-shaped flat fish, upper side mottled light to medium brown, underside white. Distinguished from brill by the numerous lumps on the upper skin. The flesh has a firm white flaky texture of excellent flavour.	3.6–5.5 kg (8–12 lb)	Suprêmes, tronçons, whole (cold buffet), shallow frying, grilling, poaching, deep poaching.
Whitebait (*blanchaille* (f))	Oily	Thought to be the fry of herrings and sprats, these small, silvery fish are caught in large numbers. They have a crisp, distinctive texture and flavour when deep-fried.	Per 500 g (lb)	Whole (ungutted), deep-fried.
Whiting (*merlan* (m))	Round, white	A medium-sized fish of the cod family, with a slender body, a pronounced jaw, and an olive-green back shading to a silvery green belly. The flesh is rather soft and flaky, with a delicate flavour when fresh.	340–675 g (12 oz–1½ lb)	Whole, fillets, goujons, shallow frying, deep frying, grilling, poaching, baking.

Table 10.4 Identification and uses of freshwater fish

Type	Classification	Description	Best size	Catering uses
Carp (*carpe* (f)) Young carp (*carpeau* (m))	Round, white	A medium to large fish. The skin is olive-brown in colour, shading to a yellow-brown belly. The flesh is firm, flaky, and of good, mud-free flavour.	1.25–2.25 kg (3–5 lb)	Whole (stuffed), fillets, shallow frying, baking, steaming.
Eel (*anguille* (f))	Oily	Eels have a long, snake-like appearance. The skin is greenish-brown, shading to an off-white belly. They are skinned before cooking. The flesh is firm, closely textured, with a good distinctive flavour.	340 g–1 kg (¾–2 lb)	Shallow frying, poaching, stewing.

Table 10.4 Identification and uses of freshwater fish (*continued*)

Type	Classification	Description	Best size	Catering uses
Pike (*brochet* (m))	Round, white	This has an elongated, distinctive appearance and a prominent jaw. The skin is olive-green on the back and sides with yellow-green markings. The flesh is firm and flaky but inclined to be dry and coarse. Moderate to good flavour.	Jack pike 1.25–2.25 kg (3–5 lb). Pike 2.25–4.5 kg (5–10 lb).	Whole (stuffed), processed into quenelles, fillets, suprêmes, poaching, baking, steaming.
Salmon (*saumon* (m))	Oily	These are medium to large, steely-blue shading to a silver belly, with distinctive pinky-red flesh of a firm texture and an excellent flavour.	2.25–5.5 kg (5–12 lb)	Suprêmes, darnes, whole (cold buffet), shallow frying, grilling, poaching, deep poaching, en papillote.
Salmon trout (*truite saumonée* (f))	Oily	These are halfway between the salmon and the trout, larger than trout, with pink-coloured flesh. The flesh is firm, flaky, with a delicate flavour.	1–1.75 kg (2–4 lb)	Fillets, suprêmes, whole (cold buffet), shallow frying, grilling, poaching, deep poaching.
Trout (*truite* (f))	Oily	These are small to medium-sized fish. Rainbow trout are extensively farmed. They have an attractive speckled blue-green colour, shading to a silver belly. The flesh is firm, with small flakes of a good distinctive flavour.	175–275 g (6–10 oz)	Whole, fillets, shallow frying, grilling, poaching, deep poaching.

10.6 Preserved and processed fish

Smoked fish

At one time smoking was an important method of preserving fish. It is today mainly used to increase the range of available fish products (Table 10.5) – smoking provides a pleasant taste and a pleasing aroma. Both white and oily fish are smoked, by either cold smoking or hot smoking, after a short period of salting to lower the water content.

Dried fish

Fish can be dried either without or after salting. The fish are hung in pairs and dried in a dry, warm air current for up to 6 weeks. Machine drying provides an alternative method. Heavily salted dried fish require prolonged soaking in several changes of water before cooking. See Table 10.5.

Table 10.5 Preserved fish

Type of fish	Product	Description	Catering uses
Smoked fish			
Cod	Individual fillets	Brined and dyed before cold smoking. Sold as a lightly smoked alternative to smoked haddock.	Kedgeree. Poached and served as a dish for breakfast, luncheon, or high tea. Filling for savoury flans.
	Roe	Roe of the female cod, dry-salted and dyed before cold smoking. Also available uncooked and boiled.	Processed into pâté – taramasalata. Hors-d'oeuvre.

Table 10.5 Preserved fish (*continued*)

Type of fish	Product	Description	Catering uses
Eel	Whole	Gutted whole eels with the head on, dry-salted and brined before hot smoking.	Hors-d'oeuvre.
Haddock	Individual fillets	Brined and dyed before lightly cold smoking.	As for smoked cod fillets.
	Arbroath smokies	Small haddock gutted and cleaned, brined, and hot-smoked.	Hors-d'oeuvre.
	Finnan	Gutted whole haddock, headed and split open to lie flat, brined, and cold-smoked.	Poached and served at breakfast or high tea. Filling for omelette Arnold Bennett.
Herring	Buckling	Whole ungutted herrings, dry-salted before hot smoking.	Hors-d'oeuvre, salads.
	Kippers	Gutted whole herrings, split open to lie flat, brined, and dyed before cold smoking. Boned fillets also available.	Grilled or poached as a breakfast dish. Processed into kipper pâté.
Mackerel	Whole or fillets	Gutted, dry-salted, or brined before hot smoking.	Hors-d'oeuvre, salads, processed into pâté.
Salmon	Sides (individual fillets)	Headed, gutted, filleted salmon, dry-salted before cold smoking.	Hors-d'oeuvre, salads, sandwiches, canapés.
Trout	Whole	Whole, gutted trout with the head on, dry-salted or brined before hot smoking.	Hors-d'oeuvre.

Other types of smoked fish include sturgeon fillets, sprats, and bloaters.

Pickled fish

Herrings	Bismarck	Filleted herrings, marinaded in vinegar and sliced onions.	Hors-d'oeuvre.
	Rollmops	Gutted, headed whole herrings, boned out, rolled up (usually with slices of onion), skewered with a wooden pin, and marinaded in spiced vinegar.	Hors-d'oeuvre.

Dried fish

Bummaloe	Bombay duck	Wind-dried fillets with a distinctive flavour.	Accompaniment to curry.
Cod	Whole	Gutted, headed, boned and laid flat, dry-salted to remove most of the water content. Wind-dried – requires long soaking in cold water before use.	Traditional Portuguese/Spanish fish dishes.

Pickled fish

Pickling is a popular method of preserving oily fish, particularly herrings (Table 10.5). The raw fish are marinaded in vinegar or wine with various flavourings. Pickled herrings are usually sold in glass or earthenware containers.

Canned fish

Many of the oily fish are canned, frequently in oil, tomato sauce, or their natural juices.

Soused fish

Sousing is a method of poaching oily fish in vinegar and water with various flavourings. After sousing, the fish is served cold in the cooking liquor.

Processed fish

QUENELLES

These are prepared from a mixture of finely minced raw fish pounded with cream, egg-white, and salt. They are shaped with the aid of two spoons, poached in fish stock, and usually served hot with a suitable sauce and garnish.

OCEAN STICKS/FISH STICKS

These are frozen reconstituted sticks of white fish flavoured with crab or crab flavouring. They are served grilled or deep- or shallow-fried, used for fish stews and soup, or eaten cold.

FISH PASTE

A ready-to-use filling for sandwiches and rolls, fish paste is prepared from fish, shellfish, cereals, flavouring, etc.

FISH MOUSSE

This is prepared from finely minced smoked, cooked, white or oily fish, blended with seasoning and flavouring, usually enriched with cream and set with gelatine.

FISH PÂTÉ

This is very similar to fish mousse, but set with butter.

FISH FINGERS

These are frozen fingers of reshaped raw white fish, without skin or bone, which are egg-and-crumbed ready for cooking. They are served grilled or shallow- or deep-fried. The best quality are processed from cod.

10.7 Caviar

Caviar (*caviar* (m)) – the uncooked roe of the female sturgeon – is one of the western world's most expensive and prized foods. It is served chilled on a bed of ice for an hors-d'oeuvre, or as a garnish on toasted canapés and egg and fish dishes. It is purchased in sealed glass jars or cans.

The best-quality caviar is silver-grey in colour with large, uniformly shaped, well-rounded eggs which have a mild taste. The roe is removed from the fish, cleaned of membrane, and gently pressed through a hemp sieve before salting. The best caviar will contain only 3–4% of salt.

An alternative method of preservation is to dip the roe briefly in hot water, followed by pressing between cloths. The result is sold as pressed caviar but is inferior in quality.

Caviar eaten as an hors-d'oeuvre can be accompanied by hot buttered toast, Melba toast, blinis, finely chopped onion and parsley, sieved hard-boiled egg, and lemon wedges.

Botarga (red caviar) is processed from the roe of salmon, pike, carp, tuna, and grey mullet. It is coarse and red and is mainly used for garnishing and decorating.

A mock caviar can be obtained from lumpfish and its use is similar to that of botarga.

Sturgeon is classified as a freshwater fish as it spawns in fresh water. The flesh is firm, meaty, and well-flavoured. It is sold fresh, dried, and smoked and is popular in east-European countries.

10.8 Classification of shellfish

Shellfish (*coquillage* (m)) are harvested or collected mostly from a salt-water environment (tidal mud flats, open seas, estuaries, etc.). The term 'shellfish' is used to cover a wide variety of marine or freshwater creatures without a backbone. For culinary purposes the term can also be used to include a number of shell-less marine creatures – cuttlefish, squid, and octopus – and also snails, land-based molluscs. Table 10.6 describes the two main categories of shellfish: crustaceans and molluscs.

Shellfish may be used for

- snack items – cockles, whelks, winkles seasoned with vinegar;
- sandwich fillings, topping for canapés;
- soup;
- hors-d'oeuvre or seafood cocktails;
- hot starters for luncheon or dinner menus;
- part of a salad for a light luncheon;
- the fish course on a dinner or function menu;
- the main course on a luncheon or dinner menu;
- a garnish for rice, fish, egg, poultry, veal, and lamb dishes.

Table 10.6 Classification and points to aid identification of shellfish

Crustaceans	Molluscs
Covered in a hard, horny carapace (shell).	Hinged shells (bivalves) or a single shell (univalves).
Extremities usually jointed – legs, tail, claws, etc.	No limbs.
Considerable mobility.	Limited mobility.
Shell often changes colour when cooked – the blue-black lobster turns bright red, for example.	Bivalves (scallops, oysters, mussels) are generally held in higher esteem than univalves (winkles, whelks). Some examples, such as oysters, can be eaten raw.

10.9 Purchasing and storing shellfish

Quality purchasing points for shellfish

- Shellfish must be alive when purchased, if not already cooked.
- Live bivalves – mussels, oysters, and scallops – must be tightly closed.
- Live snails, whelks, and other univalves will shrink back into their shells when touched.
- The legs of dead crustaceans will hang limp and lifeless.
- The tail of a fresh lobster will be tightly curled beneath it.
- Shrimps and prawns are rarely sold alive, having usually been cooked in boiling salted water immediately after being caught.
- Crabs, lobsters, and crawfish should feel heavy for their size – avoid those with a soft new shell.
- Ensure that all shellfish are purchased from a reputable dealer who can guarantee that they were gathered from an area of clean water.
- Shellfish are also available tinned, cooked, and pickled in either vinegar or brine.
- Prawns, lobster, crayfish, mussels, cockles, and crabmeat are available frozen after cleaning, cooking, and shelling.
- Raw scallops and scampi are sold frozen, covered in a protective coating of ice.

Storage of shellfish

LOBSTERS, CRABS, AND CRAYFISH

When purchased alive, these shellfish should be cooked as soon as possible after delivery. Never leave live shellfish in a hot kitchen to dehydrate – always place them in a cool position away from direct sunlight or in the bottom of the refrigerator. If covered with damp seaweed or a damp sack, lobsters, crabs, and crayfish will stay alive and in good condition for several hours.

MUSSELS, SCALLOPS, AND OYSTERS

Stone in a cool position away from direct sunlight or in the bottom of the refrigerator. If suitable, leave in the box or container in which the shellfish were delivered. Covered with damp seaweed or a damp sack in the refrigerator, oysters and mussels will stay alive for two to three days, provided they were fresh when purchased. It is advisable to cook scallops within a few hours of delivery.

Cooked shellfish are stored under refrigeration or deep-frozen for later use.

10.10 Uses of shellfish

Tables 10.7 and 10.8 describe the principal crustaceans and molluscs and their catering uses.

Cephalopod molluscs (Table 10.9) can easily be ignored as being unpalatable – looking like inflated bags with heads and tentacles – but when carefully prepared they can be used to create a varied and interesting group of dishes.

Table 10.7 Crustaceans

Type	Description	Availability	Catering uses
Crab Edible or common crab (*crabe* (m))	A large powerful crab measuring over 20 cm (8 inches) across the shell. The large claws when cracked open provide white meat, the brown meat being found in the shell. Crabs are medium-dark rosy-brown in colour. Edible crabs are cooked in boiling salted water. Only the guts and gills are discarded.	Fresh (cooked or raw), tinned, and frozen. Available all year round – fresh best in summer.	Dressed crab – both the brown and the white meat are arranged in the cleaned shell and decorated with sieved hard-boiled egg, chopped parsley, paprika, anchovy fillets, capers, etc. Soup – bisque, bouillabaisse. Pâté/mousse. Soufflé – hot.
Spider crab (*araignée* (f))	The long thin legs of this crab suggest those of a spider. The yellowish-red to chestnut shell is covered with small spikes.	Fresh (cooked or raw), tinned, and frozen.	Stuffing for chicken, veal, etc. Filling for quiches or flans. Cocktails or filling for avocado pears. Garnish for rice dishes.

Blue crab, shore crab, and eriphie crab are popular in mainland Europe – mainly for the making of soups – but are rarely eaten in the UK.

Type	Description	Availability	Catering uses
Crawfish/spiny lobster/red lobster (*langouste* (f))	Crawfish are reddish-brown in colour, with tiny spines dotted over the shell. They grow to 4.5–5.5 kg (10–12 lb). Most of the flesh is contained in the tail. Crawfish do not change colour when cooked.	Fresh (cooked or raw) and frozen. Fresh best in summer.	As for lobster.
Crayfish (*écrevisse* (f))	This is a freshwater crustacean that lives in the muddy banks of rivers, streams and lakes. In appearance it is like a miniature lobster. Crayfish are pale pink in colour and once cooked the shell changes to a dark reddish-brown. Only the tails are eaten.	Whole fresh (cooked or raw) and frozen.	Soup – bisque d'écrevisses. Boiled. Stewed. Mousse – hot/cold. Sauce – Nantua sauce. Garnish – hot and cold fish and chicken.
Lobster (*homard* (m))	Lobsters are a dark bluish-black colour which changes to red when cooked. They may grow up to 60 cm (2 ft) in length with two large powerful claws (crusher and ripper claws). The claws contain well-flavoured white meat, as does the tail/abdomen. Hen (female) lobsters can contain eggs in the form of red roe or coral.	Alive or cooked in the shell, fresh or frozen. All year round. Fresh best in summer.	Soup – bisque de homard. Sauce – sauce américaine. Grilled – split lengthways before cooking. Boiled – in court-bouillon and served cold for salads or decorated for presentation on a cold buffet. Mousse – hot/cold. Soufflé – hot.
Prawns Dublin Bay prawn Norway lobster/scampi (*langoustine* (f))	Rose-grey to pink in colour, resembling a miniature lobster growing to 18 cm (7 inches) in length. Only the tail is used.	Usually only available shelled and frozen raw, encased in an ice glace, or egg-and-crumbed for deep frying.	Deep frying – egg-and-crumbed. Shallow frying meunière style. Stewing – provençale. Garnish for fish, chicken, and veal dishes. As part of a 'fruits de mer' mixture. Scampi can also be substituted for lobster in a number of dishes.
Common prawn (*crevette rose* (f))	A pale, semi-transparent pink colour when raw, turning an opaque pinkish-red when cooked. Caught from shallow inshore waters, 9–10 cm (4 inches) in length.	Usually only available cooked (whole or the tail) shelled, frozen, or tinned.	Cocktails – usually accompanied by a mayonnaise-based sauce. Salads. Garnish for fish, egg, chicken, veal, avocado, and rice dishes. Soup – bisque de crevettes roses. As part of a 'fruits de mer' mixture.
Jumbo prawn/Mediterranean prawn (*crevette rouge* (f))	These large prawns grow up to 20 cm (8 inches) long and are light-pinkish to yellowish-grey in colour, turning pink-red when cooked.	Usually available cooked whole, fresh or frozen. The raw tails are also available frozen.	Hors-d'oeuvre whole, unpeeled on a bed of crushed ice. Salads. Grilled or shallow-fried (raw tails only).

Table 10.7 Crustaceans (*continued*)

Type	Description	Availability	Catering uses
Shrimp (*crevette grise* (f))	Shrimps are smaller than prawns, semi-transparent grey in colour with dark spots, changing to reddish-brown when cooked.	Usually only available cooked – may be shelled, smoked, frozen, tinned, or dried.	Soup – bisque de crevettes. Potted in butter. Snack item.

Table 10.8 Molluscs

Type	Description	Availability	Catering uses
Cockle (*coque* (f))	Cockles are gathered from the muddy shoreline. Their shells are creamy white in colour and the 'ribs' radiate out from the hinged end of the rounded shell.	Rarely available fresh but are usually sold shelled, frozen or pickled.	Soup – popular ingredient in Italy. Garnish for pasta dishes. Ingredient in a 'fruits de mer' mixture. Snack item – seasoned with vinegar.
Mussel (*moule* (f))	Mussels are popular bivalves with a bluish-black shell, which has a pointed hinged end.	Available fresh autumn and winter, also frozen and pickled.	Soup – as the main ingredient or a garnish item. Ingredient for a 'fruits de mer' mixture. Garnish for rice, pasta, and fish dishes. Snack item – seasoned with vinegar. Popular mussel dishes include stuffed, curried, grilled, poulette, and marinière.
Oyster (*huître* (f))	Oysters are the most highly valued of all the molluscs. They are greyish in colour with a rough ridged shell. A number of varieties are cultivated, including the native, Portuguese, and Marenne. They are mainly eaten raw, when there is an R in the month. Oysters are opened at the hinged end, turned, bearded, and placed into the convex upper shell.	Purchased fresh by the dozen in wooden barrels or baskets packed in ice and seaweed, September–April	Raw – with lemon juice. Garnish for steak-and-kidney pudding, carpetbagger steak, and fish dishes. Alternatively, oysters can be steamed, poached, grilled, and baked.

Table 10.8 Molluscs (*continued*)

Type	Description	Availability	Catering uses
Scallop (or scollop)/Pilgrim shell (*coquille Saint-Jacques* (f))	Scallops have a fan-shaped ribbed, pinkish-red convex upper shell, the under shell being white and flat. The edible parts of a scallop consist of the large round white muscle and the orange-red tongue or coral. The frill, although edible, is rarely eaten.	Available fresh (November–March), opened and cleaned, or frozen (raw).	Ingredient for 'fruits de mer' mixture. Mousse – hot or cold. Stuffing for fish, suprêmes of chicken, escalopes of turkey. Poached, deep-poached in court-bouillon, deep-fried, etc. and served with a suitable sauce or garnish.
Whelk	This has a greyish-brown spiral shell, considerably larger than the winkle's. The white foot is tough and somewhat indigestible. Cooked as for winkles.	Fresh all year	Snack item seasoned with vinegar
Winkle (*bigorneau* (m))	Winkles have small black spiral shells and are found attached to rocks, harbour walls, etc. They are cooked in boiling salted water.	Fresh all year	Snack item seasoned with vinegar.

Other edible molluscs include the top-shell conch, clam (chowder, cherrystone, littleneck), horn-shell, Noah's Ark, dog-cockle, date-shell, fan mussel, warty-Venus, Razor-shell, ormer, and limpet.

Table 10.9 Cephalopod molluscs

Type	Description	Availability	Catering uses
Cuttlefish (*seiche* (f))	Cuttlefish are oval, growing up to 25 cm (10 inches) long, and common off the south coast of England.	Available fresh or frozen.	Stewing – often with a base mixture of onion, garlic, olive oil, and tomatoes. Stuffed – with veal, pork, forcement, breadcrumbs, etc. Garnish for soup, risotto, pasta, and polenta dishes.
Octopus (*pieuvre* (f)/ (*poulpe* (f))	An octopus may grow up to 3 m (10 ft) long. It has eight tentacles, each lined with a twin row of suckers. The flesh is tough and has to be beaten with a heavy stick or mallet to tenderise it before cooking.	Available fresh, frozen, and dried.	Stewing – as for cuttlefish. Garnish for risotto and pasta dishes.

80   Commodities

Table 10.9   Cephalopod molluscs (*continued*)

Type	Description	Availability	Catering uses
Squid/calamary (*encomet* (m)/ *calmar* (m))	When purchased, squid are semi-transparent and pearly-grey in colour. They have a diamond-shaped swimming fin at the rear of the body.	Available fresh or frozen.	Stuffing – using a variety of different mixtures. Soup – the ink can be used to colour the soup. Deep frying or shallow frying. Stewing – as for cuttlefish. Garnish for rice, pasta, and polenta dishes.

10.11 Other commodities classed as seafood

Table 10.10 describes the catering uses of snails. Although snails are actually land-based molluscs, they are often classed as shellfish for cullinary purposes.

Sea-urchins and sea-anemones are sometimes eaten but are unlikely to be included on the menu in the UK.

Table 10.10   Snails

Type	Description	Availability	Catering uses
Snail (*escargot* (m))	Snails are land-based univalve molluscs with a light pearly-brown spiral shell. The flesh is rather tough to eat.	Available tinned or prepared in the shells with garlic butter and frozen. If tinned, the shells are sold separately.	Popularly served in the cleaned shell with garlic butter on a special dish with round hollows. A portion usually consists of six snails.

11 Eggs

11.1 Composition and structure

Although eggs (*oeufs* (m)) from a number of sources are suitable for catering purposes, it is the hen's egg that is by far the most important for the caterer. Eggs from other birds, such as the duck, the goose, the gull, and the quail, are occasionally used, but this section is concerned with the hen's egg.

There is little difference in the nutritional value of an egg, whether it has been laid by a battery hen or by a free-range bird. The two most noticeable differences are likely to be in the colour of the shell, which is due to the breed of hen, and the colour of the yolk, which depends on the amount and types of carotenes that the bird eats (see page 145).

Eggs are an extremely versatile food commodity, suitable for inclusion in a wide range of products and dishes, and it is difficult to imagine a standard menu that has not used some or all of the components of egg. Eggs may be used as a complete dish, to enrich other dishes, to provide aeration, for binding, or to encourage emulsification of fats and oils, and may occur in many of the courses in a menu from hors-d'oeuvres to sweets.

The porous shell is composed largely of calcium carbonate. There are two shell membranes lying close together immediately inside the shell except at the large end where they separate to form an air space (fig. 11.1). The white of an egg contains a mixture of proteins, sometimes referred to as *albumen*. An important constituent of the yolk is *lecithin*, which is an emulsifier.

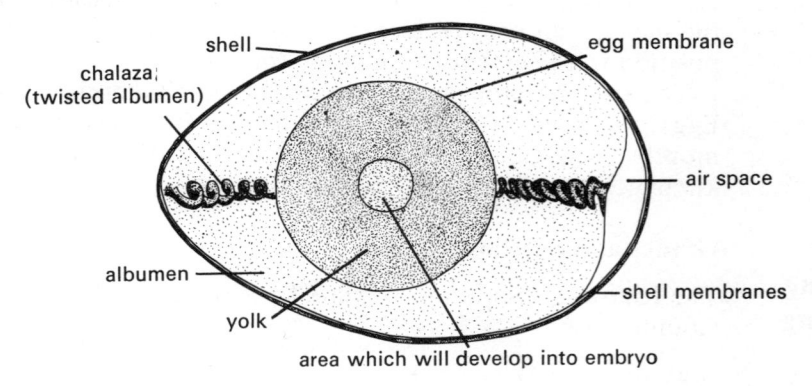

Fig. 11.1 View of a hen's egg with the top half of the shell removed

11.2 Quality points for fresh eggs

- *Shell* Clean, undamaged and slightly rough.
- *White* A large proportion of thick white to thin white.
- *Yolk* Firm, round/domed shaped, good yellow colour.
- *Smell* Pleasant – bad eggs smell of hydrogen sulphide.

As eggs become older they deteriorate and the thickness (viscosity) of the white decreases, giving a lower proportion of thick white. This is due to changes which take place within the egg on storage and the passage of gases which occurs through the air space and the porous shell.

The age of an egg can affect the quality and appearance, as shown in figs. 11.2 to 11.4.

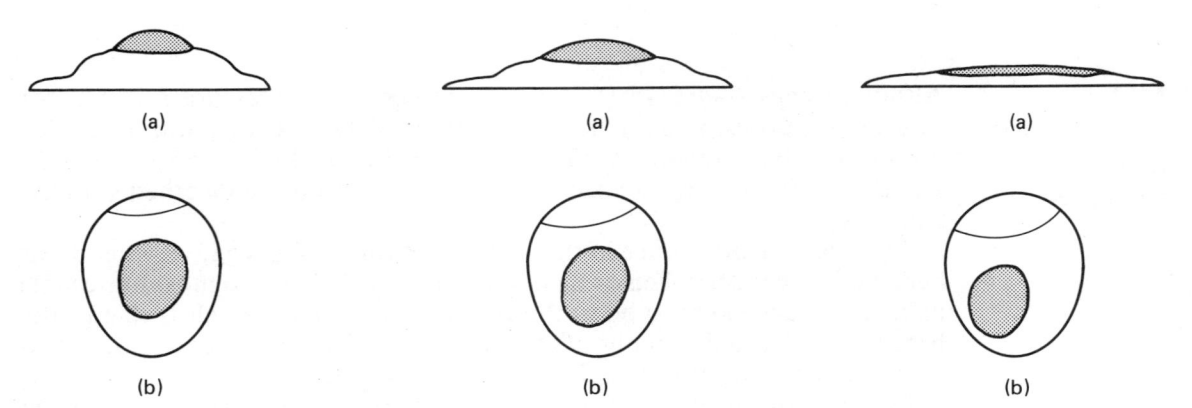

Fig. 11.2 A fresh egg   **Fig. 11.3** An egg that is beginning to deteriorate   **Fig. 11.4** A stale egg

Figure 11.2(a) represents a fresh egg taken from its shell and placed on a flat surface. Note the large amount of thick white and the well-formed yolk. Figure 11.2(b) shows the egg in its shell, with a small air space and a centrally placed yolk.

Figures 11.3(a) and (b) show some deterioration, with the white and yolk beginning to lose their shape when the egg is broken. The whole egg shows an enlarged air space, and the yolk loses its central position.

Figures 11.4(a) and (b) show the characteristic appearances of a stale egg. The yolk and the white lose their shape when the egg is broken, and in the shell the air space is larger still and the yolk has moved from its normal position to the extent of touching the shell.

The storage temperature affects the time taken for eggs to deteriorate. Eggs stored at 3 °C (37 °F) will remain in first-class condition for about 3 months, whereas deterioration will occur after only a few days in a hot kitchen.

11.3 Purchasing and storing eggs

Grades and purchasing units

The following minimum weights for eggs are laid down by the European Community:

grade 1 70 g
2 65 g
3 60 g
4 55 g
5 50 g
6 45 g
7 under 45 g

The most popular grades are 2–4 (from 2½ to 1½ oz).

Traditionally, eggs are packed in dozens or multiples of a dozen, but some eggs are now being packed for retail sale in cartons of 10.

All eggs leaving the packing stations are graded and the egg-boxes are date-stamped.

Storage

Eggs must be stored in a cool but not a dry situation. A refrigerator at 0–5 °C (32–41 °F) is ideal.

No strong-smelling foods such as cheese, onions, or fish should be stored near the eggs, because the porous nature of the shells enables the eggs to absorb the strong smells and become flavoured.

Commercially, eggs are stored at just above freezing point in an atmosphere where the humidity and the carbon-dioxide content of the air are controlled. They will keep for up to nine months under these conditions.

Preservation of eggs

Frozen eggs and dried eggs are prepared commercially. In both cases the egg is either frozen or spray-dried at a temperature which does not affect the protein. These are used by bakers and confectioners.

11.4 Spoilage of eggs

Eggs and egg products are excellent food material for many bacteria. Fresh eggs may be contaminated with salmonellae (see page 179). As the eggs are laid, salmonellae from the hen's intestinal tract may enter the egg through the small pores in the shell. Cooking can destroy these bacteria, but if the egg is not cooked at all (as in mayonnaise) or only slightly cooked and is then allowed to stand in food for some hours at room temperature, food poisoning can result if the food is eaten.

In 1988 the use of raw or partly cooked eggs and egg product was banned in UK hospitals because a type of salmonella (*Salmonella enteriditis*) had been found in some eggs and poultry. The food poisoning caused by this bacterium was particularly harmful to the old, the sick, and pregnant women. For general use the yolk and the white were recommended to be cooked until solid. In the USA, recommendations were made to boil eggs for 7 minutes or to fry them for 3 minutes on each side.

As an egg ages it becomes more alkaline and produces *hydrogen sulphide*, a gas with a characteristic objectionable smell. Long cooking times at high temperatures encourage the development of this odour, even in freshly laid eggs. Some of the sulphur in the egg combines with the iron in the egg to form a greyish-green strong-tasting compound that can be seen as a layer around the yolk of hard-boiled eggs that have been overcooked or not cooled sufficiently quickly in cold running water.

11.5 Uses and properties of eggs

The protein in eggs coagulates on heating and on beating (see page 158), and this property allows eggs to be used for a variety of purposes, as follows.

Enriching

Egg improves the quality and texture of sugar paste.

Egg is also added in the form of a liaison (egg-yolk and cream) to velouté sauces and soups by incorporating into liquids at not more than 70 °C (158 °F).

Thickening

Sauce anglaise, ice-cream, milk puddings, and bavarois are thickened by the coagulation of the egg protein.

Colouring

The Maillard reaction when egg is heated (see page 159) is made use of to colour foods by brushing egg-wash on goods to be baked, by glazing of poached fish dishes by including a sabayon (whisked to form a foam), and in frying batters.

Emulsifying

An emulsion consists of fine droplets of a liquid (such as oil) dispersed in another liquid (such as water) or in a solid (such as fat).

The lecithin in egg-yolk is able to emulsify a greater quantity of fat or oil than is present in the egg-yolk itself. This property is utilised in the preparation of mayonnaise and hollandaise sauce, which contain high proportions of fat or oil dispersed in water.

Binding

Egg-yolks included in croquette potatoes, rissoles, and stuffings coagulate on heating, ensuring that the ingredients are held together during and after cooking.

Clarifying

Egg-white, when added to a liquid and heated, slowly coagulates and rises to the surface, taking impurities with it. This is made use of in clarifying consommé, aspic, and fruit jellies.

Aerating

Egg protein partially coagulates as it is beaten and at the same time entraps tiny bubbles of air into the structure. This property of eggs can be used to produce a variety of dishes, such as meringues, soufflés, and Genoese sponges.

Garnishing

Eggs add colour and variety to hors-d'oeuvres and appetizers.

Main meals

Omelettes, eggs sur le plat, etc.

11.6 Methods of cooking eggs

- Poached (*oeufs pochés*)
- Hard-boiled (*oeufs durs*)
- Boiled (*oeufs à la coque*)
- Soft-boiled (*oeufs mollets*)
- In cocotte (*oeufs en cocotte*)
- Scrambled (*oeufs brouillés*)
- Baked (*oeufs sur le plat*)
- Fried (*oeufs frits*)
- French-fried – deep-fried (*oeufs frits à la française*)
- Omelette (*omelette*)

12 Milk and milk products

12.1 Milk

In the United Kingdom, 'milk' generally refers to milk from cows, though goats milk supplies a small specialist market. In certain parts of the world the milk of camels, sheep, buffalo, or mares also plays an important part in providing a locally produced food item.

Milk (*lait* (m)) is a nutritious food, particularly for young children. It is very commonly used in many dishes such as soups, sauces, puddings, desserts, and cakes and for hot and cold drinks. The trend in the UK and the rest of Europe is towards consuming more skimmed or semi-skimmed milk. This reflects the present concern over the quantity of animal fat consumed in the western diet (see page 142).

Types of milk

- *Pasteurised milk*   The milk is heated for sufficient time to kill any pathogenic bacteria (see page 171) and is then rapidly cooled. The treatment does not destroy all the micro-organisms or spores present.
- *Homogenised milk*   This is milk that has been processed so that the cream does not separate and form a layer on top of the milk. It is usually pasteurised.
- *Sterilised / ultra-heat-treated (UHT) / longlife milk*   This is homogenised milk heated to a high temperature for a very short period of time to produce a sterile product that will keep for up to 6 months without refrigeration. Heating changes the taste, which is easily recognised when compared with fresh milk.
- *Skimmed milk*   This is milk that contains only a very small percentage of the milk fat but all the minerals and protein of whole milk. Fortified skimmed milk has the fat-soluble vitamins added that were lost during processing.

  Skimmed milk has a different taste from whole milk but this difference is less noticeable in semi-skimmed milk, where only part of the milk fat has been removed.
- *Buttermilk* is a by-product of butter-making and contains much of the mineral and protein content of whole milk.
- *Condensed milk* is milk from which a large proportion of the water has been removed. Sugar may be added. It is often used for confectionery and sweet dishes.
- *Evaporated milk* is similar to condensed milk but without added sugar and with more water.
- *Dried or powdered milk* is prepared from skimmed milk, from which most of the water content has been removed. When reconstituted, it can be used in a similar manner to fresh milk. Dried milk powder is often used in the manufacture of bread and yeast products.

Milk and milk products 87

Storage

When stored in a refrigerator in the container in which it was purchased, or alternatively in a covered container away from strong-smelling foods, fresh milk will keep fresh for a period of up to 4 days.

12.2 Cream

Cream (*crème* (f)) is obtained by skimming off the top of whole milk. The type of cream depends on its fat content (Table 12.1).

Table 12.1 Types of cream

Type	Butterfat content	Description	Keeping qualities	Uses
Single cream	18%	Not suitable for whipping.	3–4 days in a refrigerator. Use within 48 hours of opening the container.	Served with coffee. Added to sauces and soups. Poured over fruit salad and sweet dishes.
Whipping cream	38–40%	Will only maintain its volume for a limited period once it has been whipped.	3–4 days in a refrigerator. Use within 48 hours of opening the container.	Served with or used to decorate sweet dishes. Added to sauces, soups, and other savoury preparations.
Double cream	48–50%	When whipped it will double in volume and hold its shape without collapsing for longer periods of time than whipping cream.	3–4 days in a refrigerator. Use within 48 hours of opening the container.	Served with or used to decorate sweet dishes. Added to soup, sauces, and other savoury preparations. Used as a thickening agent for savoury sauces.
Sour cream	18%	Single cream, soured and thickened by adding an edible acid. It is usually sold in plastic tubs. It can be prepared in the kitchen by adding lemon juice to fresh cream.	3–4 days in a refrigerator. Use within 48 hours of opening the container.	Added to sauces at the end of cooking to provide a sharp tangy flavour. Salad dressing.
Clotted cream	48–55%	Prepared by heating and concentrating the cream to produce a high fat content. When cooled it has a distinctive taste.	3–4 days in a refrigerator. Use within 48 hours of opening the container.	Traditionally served with afternoon teas in the West Country.
Sterilised	23%	Sold in small cans or bottles, this type of cream has a 'cooked' taste and is more suited to the domestic market.	If not opened should keep indefinitely. Use within 48 hours of opening the container.	Poured or spooned over fruit salad and other sweet dishes.

Table 12.1 Types of cream (*continued*)

Type	Butterfat content	Description	Keeping qualities	Uses
UHT	Varies with the type of cream.	Sold in foil-lined containers or individual pots for serving with coffee.	2–3 months if unopened. Does not need refrigerated storage. Use within 48 hours of opening the container.	As for fresh cream.

12.3 Yoghurt and fermented milk

Yoghurt (*yaourt* (m)) is a semi-solid milk product produced by inoculating warm milk with a bacterial culture. It is available plain or flavoured with fruit purée. Plain yoghurt is used in the preparation of curry dishes, salads, salad dressing, and marinades.

Yoghurt can be made from either cows', sheep's, or goat's milk. Live yoghurt has not been heated to destroy the bacteria.

Fermented milk drinks are popular in various parts of the world. These can be prepared from a variety of milks.

12.4 Cheese

Cheese (*fromage* (m)) is made from the milk of cows, goats, sheep, buffalo, asses, camels, and mares. In the UK and the rest of Europe, most cheeses are manufactured from either cow's, goat's or sheep's milk, which can be full-cream or partly or fully skimmed milk, milk with added cream, or cream on its own.

Although once an important cottage industry, most cheese-making in the UK now takes place under factory conditions. A small but increasing number of farmers produce their own cheeses, however, and a considerable number of new varieties have recently become available.

Even though there are many different types of cheese produced – varying in colour, size, texture, and flavour – the same basic cheese-making process is common to all. The flavour of the cheese will be affected by the quality and type of milk used, the moisture content of the cheese, the percentage of salt added, and the differences in the manufacturing and ripening processes.

Cheese-making involves the following important stages: clotting milk with either rennet or a bacterial starter (see page 176), cutting the curd, heating, stirring, and settling to dispel the watery whey. This may be followed by milling, salting, moulding, and ripening. The actual sequence and duration of each stage will determine the texture and acidity of the finished cheese.

Cheeses are often named after the region or town in which they were first produced, but many of the more popular types are now manufactured outside the original area of production. For example, cheddar cheese is produced and eaten world-wide. Other cheeses are sold under a trade name, such as 'Lymesworld' and 'Bel-paese.'

Classification of cheeses

Cheeses can be classified in the following way, with each group having similar characteristics:

- *Hard cheeses* These are pressed to squeeze out as much of the whey as possible. A long period of ripening is required to develop the full flavour. These are difficult to cut, but ideal for grating.
- *Semi-hard cheeses* These are pressed sufficiently to produce a firm, smooth texture that is easy to cut. The ripening period varies with the type of cheese.
- *Soft cheeses* These are lightly pressed and have a soft spreadable texture that makes them stick to the knife when cut. They have a short ripening period.
- *Blue-veined cheeses* The open texture of these cheeses allows the mould spores which are introduced to grow into mould and spread throughout the cheese.
- *External-mould cheeses* Cheeses with a dry rind may be encouraged to grow certain types of mould on their surface. If the rind is kept moist, some bacteria may be grown on the rind.

The growth of bacteria or moulds on or in the cheeses will give them characteristic flavours.

The more the cheese is pressed, the lower the water content and the harder the cheese.

Purchasing and storing cheeses

The following general points should be considered when purchasing cheeses, to ensure a prime-quality product:

- All cheese should have a pleasant smell without traces of ammonia, which is associated with an over-ripe cheese.
- The cut surfaces should not appear dry and shrunken.
- The crust of external-mould cheeses should not be dark and sunken or the middle over-runny.
- The skin or rind of the cheeses should not show signs of mildew spots, which are an indication of damp storage.

In many establishments, individual portions of cheese are purchased in preference to whole cheeses. However, although less wasteful, individual portions often lack the flavour, quality, aroma, and taste of whole cheese.

Cheeses are best stored in a dark, cool position away from direct sunlight, in the original boxes or wrappings, or wrapped in foil to prevent the cheese from drying out. External-mould cheeses need extra care in hot weather to prevent the crust from ripening more quickly than the centre. To ensure the maximum flavour and aroma, cheese should be left at room temperature for a short period before service.

With the increased use of refrigeration it has become the accepted practice to store cheeses in the refrigerator. This is perfectly acceptable in helping to maintain the product in good condition, but it does adversely affect the texture, causing the cheese to have a stodgy eating quality.

Uses of cheese

Cheeses are used for sandwich fillings; salads; bar meals (such as ploughman's lunch); flavouring pastry, soufflés, mousses, and sauces; and as a topping for pizza and Welsh rabbit, a filling for stuffed mushrooms, or a garnish for soups. Cheese can be eaten as a cheese course or with apples. Cheese is also used in a fondue or cut into cubes and deep-fried.

Tables 12.2. to 12.8 list the commoner cheeses and their countries of origin.

Table 12.2 British cheeses

Type	Classification	Description
Caerphilly	Semi-hard	A close, crumbly-textured cheese with a mild, pleasant, distinctive, slightly salty flavour. Caerphilly is pale creamy-white in colour.
Cheddar	Hard	A close, smooth-textured cheese, creamy-golden in colour with a mellow, nutty flavour. Probably the best-known of all British cheeses.
Cheshire	Hard	A loose, open-textured, crumbly cheese, with a mild, mellow, slightly salty flavour. Available in red, white, or blue varieties.
Derby and Sage Derby	Hard	A smooth, close-textured cheese with a clean, tangy flavour. Derby is pale honey in colour, or coloured/flavoured with the juice of sage leaves which gives the cheese a layered green appearance.
Double Gloucester	Hard	A close buttery-textured cheese, orange-red in colour with a distinctive nutty flavour, similar to Cheddar.
Lancashire	Semi-hard	A soft, loose, crumbly-textured cheese, creamy-white in colour with a mild pleasant flavour. A popular cheese for use in cooking, the flavour becomes stronger as it matures.
Leicester	Hard	A loose, crumbly-textured cheese with a rich, strong red colour and a mild, mellow taste.
Stilton	Blue-veined	A very popular cheese with a fairly soft, close, crumbly texture and a tangy, creamy taste. The outer rind is brownish-grey in colour with a wrinkled appearance.
Wensleydale	Semi-hard	A flaky, fairly close-textured cheese with a honeyed, slightly salty taste. It is pale creamy-white in colour.

Other types of British cheese include Dunlop, White Stilton, Lymeswold, Blue Wensleydale, Blue Dorset, Red Windsor, Bonchester, Colwick, Blue Cheshire, and Blue Shropshire.

Table 12.3 French cheeses

Type	Classification	Description
Brie	External-mould	Manufactured from cows' milk, with a number of different varieties on the market. A soft, round, flat cheese, with a velvety external mould, Brie has a characteristic sharp taste, which develops with maturity. The centre of the cheese softens when ripe. When over-ripe, the crust darkens and the cheese develops a strong smell of ammonia. It is available in whole rounds or cut into wedges.
Camembert	External-mould	A small, round, flat cheese, similar to Brie. The centre of the cheese, like Brie, softens when ripe. The thin velvety rind is white in colour, and the centre is pale yellow. It is available whole or in individual portions.
Carré de l'Est	External-mould	Similar to Camembert but square in shape and somewhat darker in colour.
Coulommiers	External-mould	Smaller in size than Brie, this cheese has a distinctive almond taste. The rind is velvety white when ripe.
Gervais or Petit Suisse	Soft/cream	Manufactured from a mixture of milk and cream, Gervais has a soft creamy texture. It is sometimes sprinkled with sugar before eating.
Roquefort	Blue-veined	This expensive cheese is produced from unpasteurised ewes' milk in the Roquefort region of France. It has a soft, creamy, crumbly texture with a distinctive sharp flavour. It is wrapped in tin foil. Each cheese weighs about 2 kg (4½ lb).
St Paulin/Port Salut	Semi-hard	A round, flat cheese with a strong, leathery rind. The cheese is pale in colour with a soft rubbery texture and a mild, slightly bland taste.

Other types of French cheese include Boursin, Tommes au raisin, Bresse-bleu, Cantal, Pipo Crem, and Fourme d'Ambert.

Table 12.4 Dutch cheeses

Type	Classification	Description
Edam	Semi-hard	Distinctive, easily recognised ball shape with a red rind. It is produced from semi-skimmed cows' milk. Edam cheese is yellow in colour with a firm, dry, rubbery texture and a pleasant mild flavour.

Table 12.4 Dutch cheeses (*continued*)

Type	Classification	Description
Gouda	Semi-hard	Similar to Edam, but round and flat in shape like a millstone. It has a dull mustard-yellow-coloured rind. The cheese is paler in colour than Edam, with a softer texture.

Table 12.5 Swiss cheeses

Type	Classification	Description
Gruyère	Hard	Large millstone-shaped cheeses, pale yellow in colour, with a soft waxy texture. Gruyère is easily recognised by the large shiny holes dispersed throughout the cheese. The flavour is nutty and sweet. It is an excellent cheese for cooking, and is traditionally used for French onion soup.
Emmental	Hard	Similar to Gruyère, but with much smaller holes.

Table 12.6 Danish cheeses

Type	Classification	Description
Danish Blue/Danablu	Blue-veined	The best known of the Danish cheeses, having a soft creamy texture. The taste is distinctive and sharp.
Mycella	Blue-veined	Similar to Danish Blue but with a milder taste.

Table 12.7 Italian cheeses

Type	Classification	Description
Bel-Paese	Cream/soft	Shaped like a small millstone. The taste is mild and creamy, the texture close and slightly rubbery.
Dolcelatte	Blue-veined	Similar to Gorgonzola, Dolcelatte has a soft creamy texture and a pleasant sharp taste.
Gorgonzola	Blue-veined	Prepared from cows' milk. It has a soft, slightly crumbly texture and a sharp distinctive flavour.
Mozzarella	Semi-hard	This cheese was formerly made from buffaloes' milk, but today is produced entirely from cows' milk. It is available in a variety of shapes and sizes, also shredded. It is used extensively for pizzas and is mild, almost bland, in flavour with a soft rubbery texture.

Milk and milk products

Table 12.7 Italian cheeses (*continued*)

Type	Classification	Description
Parmesan	Hard	Parmesan is famous as a cooking cheese. The cheeses are matured for many months. They are golden yellow in colour, with a strong distinctive taste and a very hard thick rind. Available whole or grated.

Table 12.8 Other cheeses

Type	Description
Cottage cheese	This is an unripened, skimmed-milk cheese which is low in fat with a soft, granular, lumpy curd. It is used in salads and sandwiches and for stuffing fruit, fish, pasta, etc.
Curd cheese	Curd cheeses are unripened cheeses made from the separated curds of cows' milk, with a pleasant sharp taste. Curd cheese is popular for making cheesecakes.
Cream cheese	These unripened cheeses are prepared from full-cream milk and are usually sold wrapped in foil.
Fromage blanc/fromage frais	This is made from skimmed milk. The cheese is light, contains very little fat, and is low in calories. It is often used to replace cream in recipes and can be used in the preparation of both savoury and sweet dishes. It is available plain or flavoured with fruit purée.

12.5 Butter

Butter (*beurre* (m)) is obtained by churning cream (see page 87). The flavour can be altered by allowing the cream to 'sour' slightly before it is made into butter. It may also contain added salt and colour. Butter contains more than 80% fat.

Because of its flavour and texture, butter is used in a wide range of cooking processes. It can be used for sauces, soups, finishing vegetables, decorating cold dishes, and making cakes and pastries.

Clarified butter is produced by heating the butter and allowing the fat portion to rise to the surface. The water and solids sink to the bottom. Clarified butter is therefore mainly fat and can be used for shallow frying and hot butter sauces.

13 Fats and oils

13.1 Uses of fats and oils

Fats are solid or semi-solid at room temperature. Oils are liquid at room temperature. Fats and oils can have similar uses in cooking, no matter whether they are of plant or animal origin. They can be used for shallow or deep frying, as 'shortening' for inclusion in flour products, or for making emulsions (see page 84). Butter has special uses because of its characteristic flavour.

Fat or oil used for frying should be able to be heated to a high enough temperature to sear the food quickly before the smoke-point is reached (see page 158). Vegetable oils have a higher smoke-point than animal fats. If the food is not seared quickly, fat or oil may penetrate and make the food soggy and greasy. The fat or oil used for deep-frying will gradually deteriorate with use and the smoke-point will eventually fall to a temperature below that which is needed to sear the food quickly. At this stage you should not use the fat or oil, since a satisfactory cooked product will not be achieved. Since the fat or oil is now rancid, it may also contain some compounds that are toxic.

The rate at which the frying fat or oil deteriorates can be slowed down by using it correctly. If the fat or oil is heated for no longer than is necessary, if the food is dried before being immersed in the hot fat or oil, and if the fat or oil is strained free from food particles after use, the useful life of the fat or oil will be extended. If possible, the cold fat or oil should be stored so that it is not exposed to air or sunlight. In practice, this means that you can save money by looking after the fat or oil you use for deep frying.

Some solid fats used for frying contain an 'antispattering' agent which reduces the amount of spitting that occurs when the fat is heated.

When fat is used as a shortening agent, as in pastry, the fat coats the protein particles in the flour and prevents them from forming into larger particles when water or milk is added. The more fat that is added, the 'shorter' or more crumbly the pastry will be. Some fats are chemically altered to encourage creaming, whereby air is incorporated into the fat when it is beaten. This air expands when the food is cooked and improves aeration.

Oils are used to make emulsions such as mayonnaise. An emulsifying agent, usually egg-yolk, is needed to prevent the oil separating from the aqueous liquid.

13.2 Types of fat and oil

Lard

Lard is a solid fat melted out of firm pork fat by heating. It can be used for shallow and occasionally deep frying and for making short-crust and hot-water paste.

Suet

Suet is the solid fat deposits from around the kidneys of various animals. In the case of suet, unlike lard, the fat has not been extracted from the fatty tissue by rendering. Beef suet is generally used for suet puddings and mincemeat.

Dripping

Dripping is obtained from beef. The 'drippings' from the roast meat are 'clarified' when the fat floats to the top and solidifies. It can be used for shallow frying.

Olive oil

Olive oil is the oil extracted from olives grown in the Mediterranean countries. The best quality is usually extracted by cold pressing. The characteristic flavour of good-quality olive oil makes it especially suitable for making mayonnaise and vinaigrette. It is sometimes used for shallow frying, but its low smoke-point makes it unsuitable for deep frying.

Other oils

Many other oils are used nowadays for both deep and shallow frying and for inclusion in food items. Groundnut oil, sunflower oil, soya-bean oil, corn oil, and palm oil are some of those used.

Margarine

Margarine is a synthetic emulsion containing more than 80% fats or oils. The oils may be from plants, animals, or marine creatures and are selected and chemically treated to make a product with a particular consistency. For spreading, the margarine needs to be 'plastic', whereas margarine used in making cakes and pastries may need to have a harder consistency so that it does not melt and soak into the flour while the mixture is being prepared at room temperature. Hard margarine, with a high melting point, is especially used for making puff pastry. Margarines may also be flavoured with some butter or milk products, and those for retail sale must by law have vitamins A and D added.

Many of the uses of margarine are similar to those of butter (see section 12.5), except that margarine may give an inferior product where the flavour of butter is important.

The types of oil used in making margarines have become of interest due to the effect of polyunsaturated fats on health (see page 142). You should not be misled, however: some margarines are made from vegetable oils that are high in polyunsaturates, but, in order to make the margarine solid, these are turned into saturated fats. 'Vegetable' margarines are not *necessarily* high in polyunsaturated fats.

Compound fats

These baking compounds are usually based on vegetable oils and are prepared for specialist use. They are not generally available in small purchasing units and are mainly used by bakers and bakery firms. (Where cost is not a prime consideration, butter might be the first choice of the hotel patissier.)

Low-fat spreads

Low-fat spreads contain a larger proportion of water and consequently less fat or oil than margarine. They are not legally allowed to be sold as 'margarine'.

Butter

The properties and uses of butter are described in section 12.5.

14 Vegetables, salads, and pulses

Vegetables have been cultivated for over 6000 years and provide a valuable source of nutrients. Today, vegetables have taken on an even more important role as a growing number of people question the morality of rearing and killing animals for human consumption.

The term 'vegetable' in common usage has come to include any edible part of any plant – vegetables may be roots, rhizomes, tubers, stems, leaves, flowers, seeds, etc. This section also includes salads and pulses.

Vegetables have many uses, including:

- as an accompaniment to the main dish of meat, fish, poultry, or game;
- in their own right as a vegetable course – asparagus and globe artichokes, for example;
- as a base for many different types of soup;
- as a flavouring in soups, sauces, braises, stews, etc.;
- raw and cooked as a salad ingredient;
- as an attractive and decorative garnish item;
- as a valuable source of nutrients for vegetarians.

14.1 Classification of vegetables

Vegetables are not easy to classify by rule of thumb, and a number of different approaches can be adopted. For a simple general classification – often useful when selecting a suitable method of cooking – vegetables can be divided into three broad groups:

- green vegetables (including cauliflower) – plants with the edible portion(s) harvested above the ground;
- root vegetables (including tuber) – plants with the edible portion(s) harvested beneath the ground;
- salad items – usually eaten raw.

The more comprehensive classification shown in Table 14.1 is based on grouping together vegetables that provide a similar edible portion. This type of grouping is the one most often used.

Table 14.1 Classification of vegetables

Classification	Examples
Green and leafy	Cabbages of all kinds; leaf beet; sorrel; curly endive; lettuces of all kinds; watercress; mustard cress; corn-salad; spinach; kale.

Table 14.1 Classification of vegetables (*continued*)

Classification	Examples
Flower heads	Calabrese; white and purple sprouting broccoli; cauliflower; asparagus; globe artichoke.
Seeds of leguminous green vegetables	Broad beans; runner beans; French beans; mange-tout; peas.
Fruit	Aubergines; cucumbers; courgettes; marrows; pumpkins; squashes; tomatoes; green, red, and yellow peppers.
Blanched stems	Leeks; celery; endive.
Roots	Beetroot; carrots; parsnips; swedes; turnips; kohlrabi; salsify; scorzonera; celeriac; radishes.
Tubers	Potatoes; sweet potatoes; Jerusalem artichokes.
Bulbs	Onions; shallots; garlic; salad onions.
Cereals	Sweetcorn (maize); rice – see sections 3.3 and 3.5.
Pulses	Butter beans; kidney beans; flageolets; haricot beans; lentils; split peas.
Fungi	Chanterelles; common or field mushrooms; truffles; ceps; morels.

14.2 Purchasing and storing vegetables

Availability of fresh vegetables

Some vegetables have a definite season, but others are available all the year, the home-grown supply being supplemented by those imported from other countries. Often, as the supply from one country nears its end, that from another becomes available. Root vegetables, bulbs, and tubers keep well in store and so their period of availability is extended over many months. A number of perishable salad items are grown in hot-houses in the colder months of the year, outside the normal growing season. Poor weather conditions during the sowing, growing, and harvesting periods will often reduce the supply normally available and cause an increase in the selling price.

Frozen, tinned, and dried vegetables provide alternatives to the use of fresh. These require virtually no preparation and only the minimum of cooking, making them an attractive proposition to the caterer (see pages 132–3).

Quality, purchasing, and storage of fresh vegetables

A vegetable store should be located on the north-facing wall of the building, with limited natural light. It should be cool, well-ventilated, and easy to clean. Good stock rotation is necessary at all times.

Root vegetables should be

- clean and free from soil and stones;
- well-shaped, firm and not damaged by harvesting equipment;
- free from signs of damage from frost, pests, and disease;
- stored in a cool, dry, well-ventilated, darkened position in mobile bins (potatoes), or on slatted racks or in open-mesh bins;

- purchased at regular intervals (deterioration in quality will occur during prolonged storage);
- medium in size, representing the best value – large examples are often over-mature and coarse.

Green vegetables should be

- crisp, firm, compact, and well-shaped;
- of an appropriate colour, showing no signs of discolouration – cabbages and other green leaf vegetables should be free of yellow leaves;
- medium in size (in relation to their maximum size);
- free from damage caused by frost, pests, and disease;
- stored in a cool, dry, well-ventilated, darkened position on shallow, slatted racks;
- purchased at very regular intervals (daily is best).

Cauliflowers should feel heavy in relation to their size. Green vegetables that are tired or wilted in appearance or offered for sale with too much unwanted stalk or outer leaves should be avoided.

Most of the points that apply to green vegetables can be followed when selecting and purchasing salad items. These are best stored in the refrigerator, care being taken only to order sufficient for any one day. When stored for longer periods, salad items quickly deteriorate.

Grading and quality-control standards

Quality grading has gradually been introduced by the European Community and regulations now cover many of the commonly available fruit and vegetables. The following four grades have been recognised, but are not necessarily applicable to all types of fruit and vegetable:

- Extra class – top quality
- Class 1 – good quality
- Class 2 – fair, reasonable quality
- Class 3 – poor, low quality

The Ministry of Agriculture, Fisheries and Food has prepared advisory leaflets explaining the standards required.

Frozen vegetables

Many types of vegetables are available frozen. These are often grown with the field officer of the processing company advising the farmers. These vegetables are harvested in prime condition, transported, processed, and frozen within a few hours.

Frozen vegetables are stored at $-18\ °C$ ($0\ °F$) and can be kept for up to 3 months. They can be cooked straight from the freezer. This type of product requires only a few minutes' cooking (see page 196).

14.3 Vegetables and their uses

Table 14.2 describes the principal vegetables and salad items and their catering uses.

Vegetables and salad items are cheapest when the market is supplied by home-grown produce. Salad items are usually only available fresh, whereas most vegetables are available fresh or preserved (tinned, frozen, and dried).

Edible fungi and their uses are described in Table 14.3.

Table 14.2 Vegetables and their uses

Name	Classification	Description	Availability	Catering uses
Artichoke – globe (*artichaut* (m))	Flower head	The true artichoke, thistle-like in appearance. Only the unopened, bluish-green flower bud is eaten.	Fresh from June to September. The fleshy, disc-shaped bases of the buds are sold tinned as artichoke bottoms (*fonds d'artichaut* (m)).	Hot or cold vegetable (whole). Salad ingredient. Garnish for fish, chicken, and meat dishes (bottoms only).
Artichoke – Jerusalem (*topinambour* (m))	Tuber	Not a true artichoke, but the tubers of a sunflower; light brownish-white in colour and sometimes extremely knobbly. The flesh is white and rather watery.	Fresh from November to March.	Hot vegetable. Soup.
Asparagus (*asperge* (f))	Flower head	Only the young, immature shoots of the plant are eaten, which should be straight, with tightly closed heads. Dry, withered, and discoloured stems are signs of overmaturity and long storage.	Fresh all year, cheapest May–June. Also available tinned and frozen.	Hot or cold vegetable. Soup, hors-d'oeuvre. Salad ingredient. Garnish for egg, fish, chicken, and meat dishes.
Aubergine (egg plant) (*aubergine* (f))	Fruit	Long, purple-skinned, pear-shaped vegetables with dull white flesh. Those with dull, wrinkled, or blotched skins are deteriorating in quality. White-skinned varieties are also available.	All year, but cheapest June–September.	Hot vegetable. Hors-d'oeuvre (hot). Garnish for chicken and meat dishes.
Beans Broad (*fève* (f))	Seeds	Large, pale greenish-grey beans produced in large flat pods. The skin has a tendency to be tough and the beans benefit from being skinned.	Fresh all year, cheapest June–July. Also available frozen.	Hot vegetable.
French (fine beans) (*haricot vert* (m))	Seeds	The young, green, immature pods are eaten whole while the seeds are still small. Mature pods are large and stringy. French beans are also cultivated for their seeds, which are eaten green as flageolets or dried as haricots.	Fresh all year, cheapest July–September. Also available tinned and frozen.	Hot vegetable. Soup. Salad ingredient. Garnish for soup and chicken and meat dishes.

Table 14.2 Vegetables and their uses (*continued*)

Name	Classification	Description	Availability	Catering uses
Runner (*haricot d'Espagne* (m))	Seeds	Large, long green pods with purple seeds, usually sliced thinly before cooking. Pods that are stringy, limp, or yellowed are old and of inferior quality.	July–September. Also available frozen.	Hot vegetable.
Beetroot (*betterave* (f))	Root	These are usually dark crimson-red in colour, round or elongated in shape. The best examples are medium in size, with even-coloured flesh free from any stringiness. Beetroot are never peeled or cut before cooking.	All year, and can be purchased cooked or raw. Also available pickled in vinegar – sliced, cubed, or whole.	Hot vegetable. Hors-d'oeuvre. Salad ingredient. Garnish for soups and meat dishes.
Broccoli (*brocoli* (m))				
Calabrese	Flower head	Large green compact flower heads (curd) similar to a small cauliflower. Heads that are open and yellowing with limp green leaves at the base of the stem are deteriorating in quality.	Fresh all year, cheapest August–October. Also available frozen.	Hot vegetable. Salad item.
Sprouting	Flower head	Purple and white varieties are available and are small flower heads on tender stalks, surrounded by small green leaves.	February–April as an alternative to spring cabbage	Hot vegetable.
Brussel sprout (*chou de Bruxelles* (m))	Green and leafy	Small hard, green buds resembling miniature cabbages growing from the base of the leaves. Sprouts should be firm, compact, and of a good shape – those that are loose and yellowing are of poor quality.	October–March. Also available frozen.	Hot vegetable. Soup (very occasionally).
Cabbage (*chou vert* (m))	Green and leafy	Numerous different varieties are available, providing a steady supply throughout the year. All have one common feature, in that the bud is surrounded by leaves that turn inwards and clasp it tightly to form the head. The solid inner portion is termed the 'heart'.	All year.	Hot vegetable.
		Spring varieties provide tender greens in early spring or mature heads later in early summer. They are generally conical in shape and smaller than those sold in summer and winter: popular examples include Early Market, Harbinger, and Wheeler's Imperial.	Spring.	Hot vegetable.

Table 14.2 Vegetables and their uses (*continued*)

Name	Classification	Description	Availability	Catering uses
Red cabbage (*chou rouge* (m))	Leafy	Red cabbages, popular for pickling, can also be prepared as a hot vegetable	Fresh all year at a stable price. Also available pickled.	Hot vegetable. Pickling.
White cabbage/ Dutch cabbage (*chou pommé* (m))	Green and leafy	Large ball-shaped cabbages, extremely firm and crisp and heavy in relation to size. The heart is pale yellow-green, shading to white at the centre.	All year.	Hot vegetable. Hors-d'oeuvre. Coleslaw.
Carrot Main crop (*carotte* (f))	Root	Both stump and long-rooted varieties are available. Carrots should be even in size and free from damage by harvesting machinery, pests, and disease. Roots that are split or forked are best rejected.	All year. Also available tinned and frozen, whole, sliced, and diced.	Hot vegetable. Soup. Salad ingredient. Garnish for soups and fish, poultry, and meat dishes. Flavouring for soups, stews, braises, etc.
Bunched		These are small, immature thinnings of the main crop, sold in bunches with the foliage (tops) left on.	April–June.	Hot vegetable. Salad ingredient.
Cauliflower (*chou-fleur* (m))	Flower head	Members of the cabbage family, cauliflowers have crisp, firm, white heads (curds). Curds that are loose and open or spotted and discoloured should be rejected.	Fresh all year, cheapest July–October. Also available frozen.	Hot vegetable. Soup. Hors-d'oeuvre. Salad ingredient. Garnish for poultry and meat dishes.
Celeriac (turnip-rooted celery) (*céleri-rave* (m))	Root	Similar in taste to celery, the off-white coloured, turnip-shaped root should feel heavy in relation to its size, and be free from blemishes and soft spots. Celeriac discolours quickly when cut.	Fresh all year, cheapest November–February. (Usually only available fresh.)	Hot vegetable. Soup. Salad ingredient. Garnish for poultry and meat dishes.
Celery (*céleri* (m))	Blanched stem	Unlike celeriac, celery does not produce a basal knob but long leaf stalks.	All year. Also available tinned.	Hot vegetable. Soup. Hors-d'oeuvre. Salad ingredient. Garnish for meat, game, and cheese. Flavouring for soups, stews, braises, etc.
Chicory (*endive* (f))	Blanched stem	Long pointed leaves, growing closely packed together into narrow spears. Unless carefully blanched, chicory is extremely bitter. The leaves, creamy white in colour, shading to light yellow-green at the tips, should not show any signs of browning or discolouration.	Fresh all year, cheapest November–March. (Usually only available fresh.)	Hot vegetable. Salad ingredient.
Chinese cabbage/leaves	Green and leafy	These form an oval or elongated head of shiny leaves resembling a cos lettuce, with wide, flat stalks.	All year, but not all varieties.	Hot vegetable. Salad ingredient. Decoration for cold egg, poultry, meat, and fish dishes.

Table 14.2 Vegetables and their uses (*continued*)

Name	Classification	Description	Availability	Catering uses
Courgette (*courgette* (f))	Fruit	A variety of marrow producing an abundant supply of fruit that are picked while young and tender.	All year, cheapest July–September. Also available frozen, sliced and whole.	Hot vegetable. Hors-d'oeuvre. Garnish for fish, poultry, and meat dishes.
Cress (*cresson* (m)) (mustard and cress/hot and cold)	Green and leafy	Delicate, small, green leaves on long, thin, white stems. Grown in disposable punnets.	All year.	Salad ingredient. Garnish for sandwiches, plated cold meat, etc.
Watercress (*cresson de fontaine* (m))	Green and leafy	A water plant with dark-green glossy leaves, with a distinctive peppery taste. Sprigs with short stalks free from roots and yellow leaves are best.	All year, but expensive and scarce in periods of prolonged cold weather.	Soup. Salad ingredient. Garnish for grilled and roast meats.
Cucumber (*concombre* (m))	Fruit	Cucumbers should be dark-green in colour, crisp, firm, and fairly straight, without any signs of flabbiness. A small type of ridge cucumber is known as a 'gherkin' and is mainly used for pickling.	All year.	Hot vegetable. Soup. Salad ingredient. Garnish for cold egg, fish, poultry, and meat dishes; also hot fish and chicken dishes.
Endive (*endive frisée* (f))	Green and leafy	Resembles a loose, curly-leafed lettuce in appearance. The leaves are crisp, with a slightly sharp, bitter flavour, white at the base, shading to yellow-green at the top.	Fresh all year, cheapest April–June.	Hot vegetable. Salad ingredient.
Fennel (Florence) (*fénouil* (m))	Modified leaf structure	The swollen bases of the stalks are closely packed together to form a bulb that has a distinctive, sweet, aniseed taste. Bulbs should be firm and creamy white with a tinge of green.	All year.	Hot vegetable. Salad ingredient.
Garlic (*ail* (m))	Bulb	A member of the onion family, with a pronounced, distinctive flavour. The round, whitish-coloured bulb (head) is divided into many segments called 'cloves'.	Fresh all year or dried for flakes and garlic salt. Also available as garlic purée.	Garnish for poultry and meat dishes. Flavouring for soups, sauces, salads, poultry and meat dishes, etc.
Lamb's-lettuce/corn-salad (*mâche* (f))	Green and leafy	Small delicate green leaves with rounded ends, joined at the base of the stems to form small clumps.	All year, but not all varieties.	Salad ingredient.
Leek (*poireau* (m))	Blanched stem	Leeks are members of the onion family. Those with a long, white stem are best. Stems which are split or discoloured, with a hard woody centre, or an excessive amount of dark-green leaves are of an inferior quality.	Fresh all year at a stable price, but of poor quality May–July.	Hot vegetable. Soup. Hors-d'oeuvre. Garnish for eggs, fish, poultry, and meat dishes. Flavouring for soups, sauces, stews, and braises.

Commodities

Table 14.2 Vegetables and their uses (*continued*)

Name	Classification	Description	Availability	Catering uses
Lettuce (*laitue* (f))	Green and leafy	Lettuce is popular as a salad ingredient. A number of different varieties are available, providing a steady supply throughout the year. All lettuces when purchased should be fresh and well-coloured without wilting, yellowing, or browning of the heart. Varieties of lettuce include butterhead/cabbage, cos, and crispheads (Iceberg and Webbs Wonderful).	All year, but not all varieties.	Hot vegetable. Soup. Salad ingredient. Garnish for hot poultry and meat dishes. Decoration for cold egg, fish, poultry, and meat dishes etc.
Oak-leaf lettuce (*feuille de chêne* (f))	Green and leafy	The leaves are shaped like those of the oak tree, with a brown fringe, and have a delicate taste.	All year, but not all varieties.	Salad ingredient.
Marrow (vegetable marrow) (*courge* (f))	Fruit	When young and tender the marrow skin is dark green in colour and the marrow easy to peel. The large, flat, oval-shaped pips are removed before cooking.	June–September. Also available frozen.	Hot vegetable.
Onion (*oignon* (m))	Bulb	The onion is an extremely versatile vegetable and is extensively used for flavouring savoury dishes/preparations. The bulbs should be well-shaped, firm, dry, and without signs of softness or decay.	All year. Also available frozen (slices, button onions), dried, and pickled.	Hot vegetable. Soup. Flavouring for soups, stews, braises, etc.
Button onion (pickling onion)	Bulb	Small, even-sized bulbs. When stored too long, they will show signs of shooting.	September–December	Garnish for poultry and meat dishes.
Salad onion (spring onion)	Bulb	These are small, immature onions harvested before the bulb develops. The tops should be dark green, without signs of wilting or yellowing.	All year.	Salad ingredient. Also used extensively in oriental cookery.
Parsnip (*panais* (m))	Root	Parsnips are long, tapered roots of yellow-buff colour with a distinctive sweet taste. The roots should be of even size, firm, and without signs of softness or disease, especially around the top.	September–March	Hot vegetable. Soup.
Peas Garden pea (*petit pois* (m))	Seed	Peas should be harvested while young, when they are tender and of a good medium-green colour.	Fresh English peas July–August. Gradually becoming available at other times of the year. Also available tinned, frozen, and dried.	Hot vegetable. Soup – hot or cold. Salad ingredient. Garnish for poultry and meat dishes.

Table 14.2 Vegetables and their uses (*continued*)

Name	Classification	Description	Availability	Catering uses
Mange-tout (m) (sugar peas/ eat-all)	Seeds	These peas do not have the normal tough lining to the pod. They are harvested when the peas are small and underdeveloped. The pods should be of a good colour and crisp without signs of yellowing. They are eaten whole.	All year, cheapest July–August.	Hot vegetable. Salad ingredient.
Petit pois	Seed	This is a variety of pea that is harvested when the seeds are small, sweet and tender.	Fresh – July–August. Canned or frozen – all year.	Hot vegetable. Salad ingredient.
Okra (lady's fingers/ gumbo)	Fruit	Pointed, flat-sided, round pods, green in colour, produced by an annual plant belonging to the cotton family.	Fresh all year. Can also be purchased tinned or dried.	Hot vegetable. Salad ingredient.
Peppers (capsicums/ pimentos) (*piment* (m))	Fruit	Hollow green, red, or yellow pods with shiny skins. The stalk and seeds must be removed before use. Pods that are limp, dull, and wrinkled are deteriorating in quality.	Fresh all year, cheapest July–August. Also available tinned and frozen.	Hot vegetable. Hors-d'oeuvre. Salad ingredient. Garnish for pasta, rice, fish, poultry, and meat dishes.
Potato (*pomme de terre* (f) (old); *pomme nouvelle* (f) (new))	Tuber	Approximately 50 varieties of potatoes are grown commercially in the UK, often for a number of specific uses – for example, for early eating, for baking, for chipping, for roasting etc. It is compulsory to show the name of the variety on all 25 kg (½ cwt) bags. Potatoes should be clean, firm, and disease-free, showing no signs of greening.	All the year, but not all varieties. New potatoes are available fresh all year, but are of poor quality September–February. Tinned new potatoes and potato powder and granules are available all year.	Only used cooked. Hot vegetable. Soup. Hors-d'oeuvre. Salad ingredient. Garnish for fish, poultry, and meat dishes.
Radish (*radis* (m))	Root	The small red varieties of radish are the type most often grown, but black and white radishes are also available.	Fresh all year at a stable price.	Salad ingredient.
Redicchio/red chicory	Leafy	The leaves, red to scarlet in colour with white ribbing, are crisp with a sharp, tart flavour.	All year, but not all varieties.	Salad ingredient.
Salsify (oyster plant) (*salsifis* (m))	Root	The long slender roots are covered with a brown skin and have white flesh. Roots should be firm and well-shaped, without soft spots and blemishes.	November–March, best in February.	Hot vegetable.

Table 14.2 Vegetables and their uses (*continued*)

Name	Classification	Description	Availability	Catering uses
Shallot (*échalote* (f))	Bulb	Shallots are members of the onion family, but with a more delicate flavour. Bulbs range in colour from light yellow to pale pink, violet, and golden brown. Bulbs should be firm and dry, showing no signs of sprouting or softness.	All year, cheapest in July–August.	Garnish for poultry and meat dishes. Flavouring for many kinds of savoury preparations/dishes. Pickling.
Sweetcorn (*maïs* (m))	Seeds (cereal)	Botanically sweetcorn is a member of the grass family. The seeds (kernels) are tightly packed into rows on cobs. These should be well-filled with soft pale-yellow kernels. Avoid those which are dark-yellow and hard.	Fresh all year, cheapest August–September. Also available frozen (whole kernels) and tinned (whole kernels and 'creamed' (broken kernels)).	Hot vegetable. Salad ingredient. Soup. Garnish for soups and rice and poultry dishes.
Turnip (*navet* (m))	Root	Turnips may be round or elongated in shape, the flesh and skin being white in colour. Roots should be firm, without damage from harvesting or disease, and completely free from woodiness.	Fresh all year. The small early-season roots make an excellent hot vegetable.	Hot vegetable. Soup. Garnish for poultry and meat dishes.
Spinach (*épinard* (m))	Green and leafy	Spinach has pointed leaves, which should be fresh in appearance, crisp, and with a minimum of excess stalk or damage by pests.	Fresh all year, cheapest May–September. Also available frozen and tinned.	Hot vegetable. Garnish for eggs, fish, poultry, and meat dishes. Salad ingredient – young leaves only. Soup.
Swede (*rutabaga* (m))	Root	Similar to turnips but larger, with yellow flesh that is milder and sweeter in taste. Roots should feel heavy for their size. Large mature roots are often coarse and fibrous.	September–April.	Hot vegetable. Soup. Garnish for poultry and meat dishes.
Tomato (*tomate* (f))	Fruit	An extremely versatile 'vegetable' that can be used in numerous different ways. A number of varieties are grown commercially, ranging in size from the small cherry tomatoes to the large beefsteak. Fruits should be firm and ripe, with smooth shiny skins and without signs of damage by pests or disease.	Fresh all year, cheapest July–September. Also available tinned, sieved, and concentrated.	Hot vegetable. Soup. Sauce. Hors-d'oeuvre. Salad ingredient. Garnish for soup, pasta, rice, eggs, fish, poultry, and meat dishes. Flavouring for many stews and braises etc. Chutney, ketchup.

Table 14.3 Edible fungi

Name	Classification	Description	Availability	Catering use
Cep (*cèpe* (m))	Fungus	Ceps are fleshy, flat brown caps with stout stalks and delicate white veins.	Fresh – September–December. Tinned, dried – all year.	Hot vegetable. Garnish for meat dishes.
Chanterelle (f)	Fungus	Yellow-coloured, with irregular, funnel-shaped caps, delicately ribbed stalks, and a pleasant smell of apricots.	Fresh – July–December. Tinned, dried – all year.	Hot vegetable. Garnish for meat dishes.
Morel (*morille* (f))	Fungus	The colour varies from pale yellow-brown to brown or black-grey and the cap is conical and covered with prominent ridges. The stalk is stout, whitish, hollow, and brittle.	Fresh – March–June. Tinned, dried – all year.	Garnish for meat dishes. Flavouring for soup and stews etc.
Mushroom Common or field mushroom (*champignon* (m))	Fungus	Mushrooms vary considerably in appearance. Field mushrooms usually have a white, rather silky cap. The stalk is also white.	June–October.	Hot vegetable. Soup. Garnish for poultry and meat dishes.
Cultivated mushroom (*champignon de couche* (m))	Fungus	Cultivated mushrooms have now replaced the field variety for most catering uses and are available in three sizes: • Button – white with pale pink gills, unopened. • Cup/caps – white, with cap (pileus) partially opened. • Flat – darker colour, fully opened with dark-brown gills. Mushrooms should be purchased daily and used within 24 hours.	All year – in three sizes. Also available tinned and frozen.	Hot vegetable. Soup. Hors-d'oeuvre. Salad ingredient. Garnish for eggs, pasta, rice, sauces, fish, poultry, and meat dishes. Flavouring for many savoury dishes.
Truffle (*truffe* (f))	Fungus	Truffles are an extremely expensive, highly prized luxury item. Whole truffles have a knobbly, warty appearance, with firm, veined flesh that can be cut into slices. The flavour is strong and aromatic. They are usually black in colour. A white variety is occasionally available.	Rarely available fresh outside of the immediate area of growth. Usually purchased tinned.	Garnish/decoration for sauces, hot egg, fish, poultry and meat dishes. Also used to decorate cold buffet items.

14.4 Dried pulses

This group of commodities consists of the dried edible seeds of plants of the legume family and includes beans, peas, and lentils, which have become popular outside their main growing regions. Pulses have always been used in the cooking of the Middle East, Asia, Mexico, and the Caribbean. In the

UK and the rest of Europe, pulses have increased in popularity with the escalating cost of animal protein and the growth of interest in vegetarian cooking.

As well as being available in their dried state, pulses are also sold cooked and tinned, processed into flour, fermented into soy sauce, etc. Certain types of dried beans – for example mung beans – can be sprouted and the shoots eaten as a fresh vegetable or salad item.

Today most pulses are dried and graded by machinery, ready for use in the preparation of soups, casseroles, croquettes, salads, and vegetable dishes. Beans and peas which become tender and floury when cooked are best used in casseroles, where they absorb the flavour of the spices and herbs, while those with a firmer texture make excellent salads. Pulses have a long shelf-life if stored in a dry, cool position, but are best when used within 5 to 6 months of purchase. Most pulses require soaking in cold water before cooking.

CHICK PEAS

These are popular in Oriental and Middle Eastern cookery. These large, hazlenut-shaped peas are golden beige in colour with a distinctive crunchy, nutty flavour. They can also be milled into flour and used to make hummus.

BLACK-EYED PEAS

These are very popular in the southern states of America, where they are cooked with salt pork. They are small, whitish-coloured beans with a distinctive black or yellow eye.

FLAGEOLETS

Flageolets are the pale green seeds of the French bean. They have an elongated kidney shape with a delicate taste, and are usually eaten as a vegetable, particularly in France with roast lamb.

HARICOT BEANS

Haricot beans are white, plump, kidney-shaped dried seeds of the French bean, commonly eaten canned in tomato sauce. They are used in the classical French dish of cassoulet, where they are cooked with sausages, pickled pork, and duck.

LENTILS

There are a number of different varieties of lentil, including the common red and green. Lentils have a flattish, round shape and can be purchased split or whole. They are often used in the preparation of soup and can, on occasions, be cooked without first soaking.

PEAS

The two common types of dried peas are the whole, marrowfat peas and the yellow or green split peas. Marrowfat peas lost much of their popularity with the introduction of frozen peas, but split peas continue to be used for the making of soup and pease pudding.

MUNG BEANS

These are tiny olive-green beans and are widely used to provide bean-shoots for eating raw in salads or in the preparation of many oriental dishes.

RED KIDNEY BEANS

These beans are dark maroon-red in colour and have a floury texture and a fairly sweet flavour. They are best-known as a basic ingredient in chilli con carne. They must be boiled rapidly for at least 10 minutes before being used (see page 155).

SOYA BEANS

These small oval beans have been featured in oriental cuisine for many years and are important in the preparation of meat substitutes. Soya beans are also used to produce oil, bean curd (called tofu), flavouring pastes, condiments, and flour.

15 Fruit and nuts

15.1 Classification of fruit

Caterers usually use the word 'fruit' to describe the edible seed-bearing portion of some cultivated or wild shrubs, trees, and plants. Fruit (*fruit* (m)) can be eaten raw; served at the beginning or end of a meal; made into ice-cream or sorbets; eaten as a snack item; used to decorate and garnish numerous fish, poultry, meat, and game dishes; or used to produce a wide range of cakes, pastries, and desserts.

The classifications of fruit are shown in Table 15.1.

Table 15.1 Classification of fruit

Classification	Examples
Soft fruit	Raspberries, strawberries, blackberries, currants, gooseberries.
Citrus fruit	Lemons, oranges, limes, grapefruit, pomegranates
Hard fruit	Apples, pears
Tropical fruit	Mangoes, bananas, pineapples, figs, dates, grapes, melons, kiwi fruit, papaw
Stone fruit	Plums, apricots, peaches, cherries, greengages

15.2 Purchasing and storing fruit

Quality purchasing points for fresh fruit

- Soft fruit quickly deteriorates. This process is speeded up in fruit that has been bruised or damaged or is over-ripe or already diseased.
- Fruit should appear fresh and firm to the touch. It should be clean, free from disease or pest damage, and unbruised.
- Hard fruit discolours quickly when bruised or damaged, and the presence of moulds, shrivelling, or wilting shows that the fruit should not be purchased.
- The degree of ripeness in fruit can often be judged by the colour. Over-ripe citrus fruits shrivel and shrink in size; stone fruit and soft fruit become soft and watery.

Quality grades for European fruit are the same as those for vegetables (see page 99). For tropical produce, standards are set by the Organisation for Economic Co-operation and Development (OECD) and the United Nations Economic Commission for Europe.

Storage

- Wherever possible, fruit should be purchased daily in small quantities, particularly those types that deteriorate quickly.

- Examine all fruit immediately after delivery, putting to one side any that are damaged or mouldy.
- A cold, airy store will retard ripening. Fruit should not be stored in a very dry atmosphere.
- Hard fruit, citrus fruit, and peaches and other types of stone fruit are best stored in the boxes in which they were delivered.
- Soft fruit should be handled as little as possible and be stored in a refrigerator.
- Bananas when stored at too low a temperature quickly turn black.

Preserved fruit

Fruit can be preserved by drying, freezing, tinning, bottling, or crystallising. Frozen fruit has lost some of its impact on the market with the rapid expansion of the fresh-fruit market over the last 10 years – fresh strawberries, raspberries, mangoes, kiwi fruit, and other exotic fruit are now commonly available all year.

15.3 Fruit and their uses

Table 15.2 describes the principal types of fruit and their catering uses.

Fresh fruit is at its cheapest when the market is supplied by its traditional source – for the UK, for example, strawberries and raspberries from UK growers, peaches from Spain and Italy. Importing fruit from distant countries increases the purchase price, as does the use of artificial heating to grow and ripen fruit.

Table 15.2 Fruit and their uses

Type	Description	Availability	Catering uses
Apple (*pomme* (f)) Dessert apples	Dessert apples vary considerably in taste, texture, and aroma. Popular varieties include Cox's Orange Pippin, Golden Delicious, and Granny Smiths.	Fresh all year, but not all varieties. Dried apple rings available all year.	Eaten raw, sometimes with cheese, or as an ingredient in fresh fruit salad.
Cooking apples	Valued for its tart, acidic flavour, Bramley Seedling is the most popular variety. Other varieties include Howgate Wonder, Lord Derby, and Grenadier.	Fresh all year, cheapest September–December. Also available tinned (apple pack) and frozen.	Baked filling for pies, puddings, strudels, pastries, crumbles, and charlottes. Garnish for pork and poultry dishes. Apple sauce. Mincemeat, jam, and chutneys. Cider and cider vinegar. Apple fritters. Pies and puddings.
Apricot (*abricot* (m))	Slightly flattened, smallish in size with smooth, yellowish-orange skin.	Fresh all year, cheapest June–July. Also available tinned, frozen, dried, crystallised, and bottled in brandy.	Eaten raw, stewing, compotes, salads, garnish for pork dishes, filling for pies, pastries, flans and puddings. Garnish for rice condé. Jam, wine, and liqueur.

Table 15.2 Fruit and their uses (*continued*)

Type	Description	Availability	Catering uses
Avocado (*avocat* (m))	A large pear-shaped fruit with a thick green skin. When ripe, the pale green flesh is soft and creamy. Avocados are sliced in half lengthways and the stone is removed before use. Small finger-sized stoneless avocados can also be purchased.	Fresh all year.	Eaten raw as an hors-d'oeuvre stuffed with prawns or crabmeat or filled with a vinaigrette dressing. Mousse. Served hot with a suitable sauce or garnish. Garnish for chicken and fish dishes.
Banana (*banane* (f))	Grown in hot tropical countries, bananas are picked and transported green and then ripened. Bananas are best eaten raw when the skin is golden-yellow in colour.	Fresh all year. Also available dried (whole, slices) all year.	Eaten raw. Garnish for fish and chicken dishes. Banana fritters; filling for flans, pies, and puddings.
Blackberry (*mûre* (f))	The cultivated varieties are much larger than the wild counterparts. When purchased, blackberries should be a deep rich colour, free from mould.	Fresh August–October. Also available tinned and frozen all year.	Eaten raw. Stewed, compote. Filling for tarts, pies, and puddings. Jam, wine.
Cherry (*cerise* (f))	A small stone fruit of which there are many varieties. They should be stored for only 1–2 days after purchase. Morello cherries are popular for cooking.	Fresh all year, cheapest June–July. Also available tinned, frozen, and bottled in brandy.	Eaten raw. Filling for flans, tarts, pastries, and pies. Garnish for duck and chicken dishes. Jams, wine, and liqueur. Glacé cherries – cakes.
Currant (*groseille* (f))	There are three varieties: black, red, and white. The black variety produces the heaviest crop.	Fresh June–August. Also available tinned, frozen, and bottled in brandy.	Eaten raw. Filling for tarts, flans, and pastries. Compotes, sorbets, and ice-cream. Garnish for meat and game dishes. Jams, liqueur, syrup.
Date (*datte* (f))	The fruit of the date palm, the most popular variety being the Deglet Noir.	Fresh at a stable price all year. Also available semi-dried and dried all year.	Eaten raw. Flavouring for cakes, pastries, and pudding.
Fig (*figue* (f))	Green, white, purple, and black varieties of fig are available. Only the stalk is not edible – the skin, flesh, and pips are all eaten.	Fresh all year, cheapest August–October. Also available tinned and dried, all year.	Eaten raw, on their own or as part of a fruit salad. Compote or baked. Garnish for roast duck.
Gooseberry (*groseille verte* (f))	Grown for both desset and culinary use, gooseberries can be green, yellow, or red, depending on the variety.	Fresh May–July. Also available tinned, frozen, and bottled all year.	Eaten raw. Filling for pies, puddings, and tarts. Stewing, compote.
Grapes (*raisin* (m))	Grown on vines. Grape growing is the world's largest fruit industry. Grapes are classified as dessert grapes, raisin grapes, wine grapes, canning grapes, and juice grapes.	Fresh all year. Also available tinned and dried all year.	Eaten raw. Garnish for pastries, flans, fruit salad, petits fours. Served with fish and poultry dishes. Wine, unfermented juice. Sorbet.
Grapefruit (*pamplemousse* (m))	A large citrus fruit with a pale yellow skin. The flesh is firm and tart. There are a number of varieties available, with either white or pink flesh.	Fresh all year. Tinned (segments) all year.	Eaten raw at breakfast or for an hors-d'oeuvre. Garnish for chicken and fish dishes. Grilled and served hot. Marmalade, juice.

Table 15.2 Fruit and their uses (*continued*)

Type	Description	Availability	Catering uses
Greengage (*reine-claude* (f))	A stone fruit similar to a sweet plum, yellowish-green in colour.	Fresh July–August. Tinned and bottled all year.	Eaten raw. Filling for pies, tarts, and flans. Jam.
Kiwi fruit	Kiwi fruit are the size of a small lemon and have a thin, brown, furry skin. When cut, the flesh is a pale green shading to white in the centre. The small edible seeds are black in colour.	Usually only available fresh, at a stable price all year.	Eaten raw. Garnish for fruit salad, pastries, and flans. Served with veal and chicken dishes.
Lemon (*citron* (m))	Lemons are grown in the warm Mediterranean countries, California, and Florida and are picked green and ripened after harvest until the skin turns yellow. They are widely used for both garnishing and flavouring a large variety of dishes.	Fresh all year. Crystallised all year.	Garnish – for hot deep- and shallow-fried, grilled, baked, and deep-poached fish dishes. Grilled and shallow-fried veal dishes. Cold fish, smoked fish, oysters, shellfish dishes. Flavouring (both the juice and grated zest can be used) hot or cold, savoury or sweet sauces. Cordials, stuffings, fillings, syrups, sorbets. salad dressings, vinegars, etc.
Mango (*mangue* (f))	Oval or kidney-shaped, the skin changes from green to bright orange/yellow when ripe. The juicy yellow/orange flesh conceals a large flat stone.	Fresh all year at a stable price. Tinned all year.	Eaten raw. Mousse, ice-cream, sorbet.
Melon (*melon* (m))	There are several different varieties, varying in size, colour, flavour, aroma, and availability. The main types of commercially grown melon are Honeydew, Cantaloupe, Ogen, Charentaise, Galia, and watermelon.	Fresh (whole or portions) all year - but not the same variety. Honeydew cheapest in summer. Frozen (balls or cubes) all year.	Eaten raw in salads, cocktails, fruit salad, wedges, sorbet.
Orange (*orange* (f))	Several varieties are grown throughout the world. Seville or Bigarrade oranges are used for the manufacture of marmalade.	Fresh all year. Tinned (segments) and bottled in brandy all year.	Eaten raw. Ingredient for fruit cocktails, salads, fruit salads. Garnish for meat and poultry dishes. Juice, syrup, sorbets, mousse, soufflé, liqueurs, marmalade.
Papaw/pawpaw/papaya (*papaye* (f))	Papaws have a very rich perfume when fully ripe. They are elongated in shape and the black seeds must be removed before the pinkish-orange flesh is eaten.	Fresh all year at a stable price. Tinned all year.	Eaten raw. Ingredient for fruit salad.
Peach (*pêche* (f))	There are two main types of peach: free-stone and cling-stone. Free-stones are mainly used for freezing and eating raw; cling-stones for canning.	Fresh all year, July–September. Tinned (halves and slices), frozen, and bottled all year.	Eaten raw. Ingredient for fruit salad. Filling for pastries, flans, and tarts. Garnish for gammon, pork, and chicken dishes. Liqueur, brandy.
Pear (*poire* (f))	A popular fruit, but difficult to ripen. Pears remain at their best for only a few days.	Fresh all year, but not the same variety. Tinned (halves) and dried all year.	Eaten raw. Ingredient for fruit salad, salads, rice condé, flans, and tarts. Stewed, compote.

Table 15.2 Fruit and their uses (*continued*)

Type	Description	Availability	Catering uses
Pineapple (*ananas* (m))	Principally grown in the West Indies and Central America. Pineapples are yellowish-red in colour when ripe, resembling a large pine-cone. The hard core is usually removed before use.	Fresh all year. Tinned (rings, cubes, and pieces), dried, and crystallised all year.	Eaten raw. Ingredient for fruit salad, salads, rice condé, flans, pastries, and tarts. Fritters, juice, garnish for gammon dishes.
Plum (*prune* (f))	A stone fruit extensively grown in the UK and Europe. There are numerous varieties, producing early and late crops, some of which are used for cooking, others for dessert purposes.	Fresh all year, cheapest July–October. Tinned, bottled, and dried (prunes) all year.	Eaten raw. Ingredient for fruit salad. Filling for tarts and pies. Stewing, compote, jam, liqueur.
Pomegranate (*grenade* (f))	Round in shape, the size of a tennis ball, with a hard leathery brownish-red skin. Only the crisp juicy seeds are eaten.	Usually only available fresh, September–December.	Eaten raw. Sorbet, juice, syrup.
Raspberry (*framboise* (f))	Raspberries have a wonderful flavour, but are very perishable, keeping only 1–2 days.	Fresh all year, cheapest June–August. Tinned, frozen, and bottled all year.	Eaten raw. Filling for pastries, tarts, pies, and flans. Soufflé, mousse, sorbet, ice-cream, and sauce. Jam, liqueur, vinegar.
Rhubarb (*rhubarbe* (f))	Rhubarb is valued early in the year when many other types of fresh fruit are unavailable. Rhubarb can be 'forced' under cover to provide an early crop of tender young stems in February/March. Only the fleshy stems are eaten.	Fresh February–August. Tinned all year.	Compote. Filling for crumble, pies, tarts, and flans. Wine and jam.
Strawberry (*fraise* (f))	A pulpy red fruit with the surface studded with yellow seeds.	Fresh all year, cheapest May–September. Home-grown available mid-May–October. Tinned and frozen all year.	Eaten raw. Filling for flans and pastries. Soufflé, mousse, sorbet, sauces, jam, liqueur.

Clementines, tangerines, satsumas, and mandarins – sometimes collectively called 'easy peelers' – were once only available at Christmas time. These can now be purchased from September to June.

Other types of exotic fruit increasingly available fresh are passion fruit, lychees, guava, kumquats, nectarines, prickly pear, quince, cape gooseberries, starfruit, ugli fruit, and persimmons or sharon fruit.

15.4 Nuts

Nuts (*noix* (f)) are usually seeds contained in a hard shell – think of walnuts and almonds. Sometimes the shell is more like a thick skin, as in chestnuts. The seed inside the shell is called the kernel.

Nuts are used in many different preparations, both savoury and sweet. Many nuts are at their best in late autumn and early winter, when first picked. Those with clean, unblemished shells that feel heavy for their size are likely to provide the best quality. Shelled nuts when stored for too long become stale and rancid and develop an unpleasant taste, caused by the oil in the nuts going rancid.

Table 15.3 describes the principal types of nut and their catering uses.

Fruit and nuts

Table 15.3 Nuts and their uses

Type	Description	Availability	Catering uses
Almond (*amande* (f))	There are two main types of almond; sweet almonds and bitter almonds. Bitter almonds owe their flavour to small quantities of prussic acid.	*Sweet*: Whole unshelled, October–January; shelled whole, split, flaked, nibbed, ground and salted all year. *Bitter*: Shelled whole all year.	Eaten raw. Decoration/flavouring for cakes. Ingredient in potato dishes, stuffings, salads. Garnish for fish dishes. Oil. Nougat, praline, salted. Essence – flavouring for sauces, pastries, and cakes. Eaten raw. Decorating cakes. Coated with chocolate.
Brazil (*noix du Brésil* (f))	The fruit of a large tree grown extensively in Paraguay and Brazil. The brown, curved shell has three distinct edges.	Whole unshelled October–January. Whole shelled all year.	Eaten raw. Decorating cakes. Coated with chocolate.
Chestnut (*marron* (m))	A large nut with a floury texture when cooked. Chestnuts grow two or three together in a prickly case.	Whole unshelled October–January. Shelled, tinned, dried, and flour all year.	Braised roasted and eaten hot. Ingredient for stuffings. Garnish for vegetable dishes and game dishes. Marron glacé. Flour for cakes and biscuits, soup, purée, soufflé.
Coconut (*noix de coco* (f))	The thick, hard shell of this fruit of a tropical palm tree is covered with a fibrous outer husk. The flesh is white in colour and sticks to the shell. The hollow centre is filled with a milky white liquid. Coconut milk is available in semi-hard blocks and as a dried powder.	Whole unshelled, all year. Shelled, shredded, and desiccated all year.	Eaten raw. Ingredient in puddings, pastries, cakes, curries, oil. Coconut milk is used in Indian and oriental savoury and sweet dishes.
Hazelnut/cobnut/filberts (*noisette* (f))	The fruit of a small tree, grown throughout Europe. The nuts are small in size with a thick brown shell.	Whole unshelled September–December. Shelled whole all year.	Eaten raw. Ingredient in cakes and stuffings. Oil.
Ground-nuts/peanuts (*cacahouette* (f))	Harvested from beneath the ground, the small nuts, which have a dull reddish skin, are produced two or three to a shell.	Whole unshelled all year. Shelled whole, ground, salted, and dry-roasted all year.	Eaten raw. Substitute for ground almonds. Oil, salted, roasted.
Pistachio (*pistache* (f))	Form the reddish-brown fruit of the pistachio tree. The nuts, when shelled and blanched to remove the skin, are a light, delicate green colour.	Whole unshelled all year. Shelled whole and salted all year.	Used to decorate cakes and desserts. Ingredient for stuffing galantines and sausages. Salted. Ice-cream.
Walnut (*noix* (f))	A large brown nut, walnuts are probably the most widely used nut in British cooking.	Whole unshelled October–January. Shelled halves and pieces all year.	Used to decorate cakes and desserts. Ingredient for stuffings and pâté. Garnish for salad and poultry dishes. Walnut oil, salad dressing.

Other types of nut include cashews, pecans, and pine-nuts.

16 Sugars and syrups

16.1 Sugars

Sugars (*sucres* (m)) are extracted from sugar cane and sugar beet. White sugar consists of pure sucrose (see pages 140–1). Brown sugars contain traces of other substances which have been derived from the cane or the beet in the process of extracting the sugar.

The extraction of sugar is a complex process but basically involves crushing the raw material and washing out the sugar juice with water. This syrupy liquid is then concentrated by boiling and the sugar crystals are allowed to form. The liquid left behind is molasses or black treacle.

The pure white sugars – granulated, castor, and nib – differ from each only in their crystal size. They have different uses in catering:

- *Granulated sugar* Large crystals which are best used when the sugar is to be dissolved in a liquid – for example in syrups, sweet sauces, and sugar-boiling. Cubes of granulated sugar are used mainly to serve with hot beverages.
- *Castor sugar* Small even-sized crystals, used mainly for the preparation of cakes, pastries, and biscuits.
- *Nib sugar* Clusters of large sugar crystals used mainly to decorate Bath buns, rock cakes, and fancy tea-breads.
- *Icing sugar* Sugar crystals crushed to a powder. Used for royal icing and water icing and for dusting cooked pastries.

Various brown sugars are produced by crystallising the sugar at different stages of the purification process and will contain small amounts of substances other than sucrose. The darker the colour, the more pronounced is the flavour. In a similar manner to white sugar, brown sugars can be made in a variety of crystal sizes. They are used in the preparation of Christmas, wedding, birthday, and Dundee cakes and in hot beverages.

Other uses for sugar include:

- to provide extra colour on baked goods (see pages 157 and 159);
- as a preservative in jams, marmalade, canned fruit, and glacé fruit (see page 178);
- to help yeast grow faster when added to batters and baked yeast goods (see page 176);
- to improve the keeping qualities of cakes and pastries, by keeping them moist.

Purchasing

Sugars are available in a range of pack sizes to suit the needs of the caterer. Individual portions of sugar are popular for serving with hot beverages.

Storage

Sugar absorbs moisture from the atmosphere and is best stored in airtight containers in a dry well-ventilated store. Brown sugar forms a solid lump if kept for too long.

16.2 Syrups (*sirops* (m))

- *Golden syrup* (mélasse raffinée (*f*)) A by-product of sugar refining, the syrup is filtered, concentrated, and used in the preparation of gingerbread, brandy snaps, and biscuits.
- *Treacle* (mélasse (*f*)) Darker than golden syrup, and with a more pronounced flavour, this is often used to provide colour in rich fruit-cakes.
- *Honey* (miel (*m*)) A natural syrup produced by bees from the nectar of flowers, this is available as a clear golden-coloured syrup or a thick opaque crystallised mass and contains glucose and fructose as well as sucrose (see pages 140–1).
- *Corn syrup* contains a mixture of sugars and polysaccharides (see page 141) and is made from corn starch. It is used mainly in confectionery work.
- *Maple syrup* is made by concentrating the sap of the sugar maple tree and is very largely sucrose. It may contain some of the volatile flavourings present in the maple tree. It is used for baking and confectionery work.

17 Non-alcoholic beverages

Tea and coffee are classified as hot non-alcoholic beverages. They can be served after a meal, with a snack or light meal, or on their own as a refreshing drink. Although these items have little food value, other than that of any milk or sugar that may be added, they can leave a lasting impression on the customer. Many a good meal has been spoiled by the service of poor-quality tea or coffee.

Tea has always been served with an English breakfast or afternoon tea, whereas coffee has usually been favoured at lunch and dinner. Nowadays, however, both tea and coffee are available with most meals.

Tea and coffee can be dispensed from the stillroom or the service counter, or be prepared in front of the customer in specially designed equipment. Other types of non-alcoholic drink which are offered for sale include cocoa, hot chocolate, and various proprietary beverages.

17.1 Tea

Tea (*thé* (m)) is considered to be the national drink of the United Kingdom and is probably more widely drunk throughout the world than coffee.

The best-quality teas are from bushes grown at high altitudes in India, Sri Lanka ('Ceylon'), and China, one of the most famous being Darjeeling, which is cultivated in the foothills of the Himalayas. The quality of the tea also depends on the size of the leaf that is picked and the time of the year. The tip leaf and the two leaves immediately below form the 'standard pluck': if more leaves are picked the tea will have a coarser flavour.

After picking, the leaves are allowed to wither slightly before being rolled to release the leaf juices. Fermentation, which follows the rolling, will determine the type of tea produced. Black tea is fermented for 19–20 hours, oolong for 3–4 hours, whereas green tea is not fermented. Tea is graded for quality by the taste and by the size of the leaf.

Tea is best stored in dry, clean, airtight containers in a dry, well-ventilated position away from strong-smelling foods.

When making tea, allow 45–60 g (1½–2 oz) of dry tea to 4.5 litres (1 gallon) of water. 500 ml (1 pint) of milk will be sufficient for 20–30 cups.

Tea can be drunk hot on its own or with the addition of milk and/or sugar.

Lemon tea is drunk in a 250 ml (½ pint) glass in an ornate metal stand, without milk but with a slice of lemon.

Iced tea should be served well chilled in a glass tumbler garnished with a slice of lemon.

17.2 Herb teas

Herb teas are not really teas and are better referred to as 'tisanes'. There is a range of single and blended flavours available.

- Single flavours include camomile, rosehip, fennel, peppermint, and comfrey.
- Blended flavours include mixed fruit (apple, mallow, rosehip, and orange and lemon peel), honeybush (African honeybush, redbush, and hibiscus), and mint royal (peppermint, mallow, pennyroyal, and larkspur flowers).

17.3 Coffee

Although originally grown in North Africa and the Middle East, coffee (*café* (m)) is now enjoyed world-wide. It is grown in plantations, and the coffee trees are pruned to arrest growth at between 2 and 2.75 m. The coffee beans are contained in pairs in a small cherry-like fruit which is dark-red to bluish-black in colour. Only the beans are processed into coffee – the fruity pulp, shell, and silvery skin are discarded during processing.

Major coffee producers

- *Central and South America* are the world's largest coffee producers. Much of the coffee grown is of an inferior quality and used mainly for the production of instant coffee.
- *The West Indies* is considered by many to produce the world's best-quality coffee, but it is of course very expensive to buy.
- *Central Africa*   Kenya and Tanzania export coffee that is rich and full-bodied in character.
- *Yemen* is the original producer of Mocha coffee, which is often blended with the lighter coffees of India.
- *India*   Mysore, India's best-known coffee, is used extensively for blending with other coffees to provide a smooth subtle flavour.

Roasting and grinding

The beans are roasted to develop the characteristic flavour, the degree of roasting depending on the final blend and the preference of the consumer. A Continental blend is prepared from a selection of dark-roasted beans. Other degrees of roasting include light and medium.

Once roasted, the beans need to be stored in airtight containers to prevent the beans from absorbing moisture. Whole beans lose their flavour less quickly than ground coffee.

The grind of coffee you choose will depend on the method of making coffee. A better-quality cup of coffee will result if the correct grind is purchased – for example:

- espresso method – very fine grind;
- filter method – fine grind;
- jug method – medium grind;
- still set – medium grind.

The hardness of the water supply will affect the flavour of the infused coffee, as will the fineness of the grind, so it is best to try a number of different blends before making the final choice.

Loose ground coffee is best stored

- in airtight containers;
- in a dry, cool, well-ventilated position;
- away from strong-smelling foods which may affect the flavour of the coffee.

Preparing fresh coffee

Ground coffee for catering use is best purchased in foil vacuum-packs in set quantities, each producing a given quantity of coffee when infused with hot water. When using loose ground coffee, allow 275–340 g (10–12 oz) to 4.5 litres (1 gallon) of water.

Fresh coffee can be produced by a number of different methods, including:

- *Jug method* A measured quantity of ground coffee is placed into a pre-warmed jug and covered with boiling water. The coffee is allowed to infuse for a few minutes, after which the coffee is strained from the grounds. This method of making coffee is more suitable for domestic use.
- *Filter method* A variation of the jug method, where a cone-shaped filter and a disposable filter bag are placed on top of the jug. Boiling water is poured on to the ground coffee which infuses and drains into the jug.
- *Electric filter coffee machine* This machine uses the same principle as the filter method. Water above the filter is electrically heated to the required temperature and allowed to drain throught the fine-ground coffee into a flask which stands on a heated plate. The water reservoir must be topped up with cold water.
- *Percolator method* This method uses an electrically heated coffee percolator which is filled with cold water and brought to the boil. The water rises up a hollow centre tube, infuses with the ground coffee, and drains back to repeat the process for as long as it is heated.
- *Cona method* Similar to the percolator method, the bottom glass bowl is filled with cold water and brought to the boil so that the water rises and infuses with the ground coffee in the upper bowl (fig. 17.1). The coffee drains back when the heat is reduced.
- *Espresso method* Using this method, each cup of coffee is freshly made to order. Steam and water are forced under pressure through finely ground, high-roast coffee. This type of coffee machine (fig. 17.2) will also be fitted with a steam injector to heat the milk used to make frothy cappuccino.
- *Still set* The most popular method of making coffee in large quantities. A still set consists of a small central infuser with an urn on each side (fig. 17.3). A disposable filter is placed into the infuser, and the ground coffee is placed on top. Boiling water is added and the resulting coffee is drained into one of the storage urns. The milk is heated in a separate steam-jacketed container ready for service.
- *Using a disposable, individual filter* – for example Rombout coffee.

Non-alcoholic beverages 121

Fig. 17.1 A Cona coffee-maker

Fig. 17.3 A coffee machine and milk urn

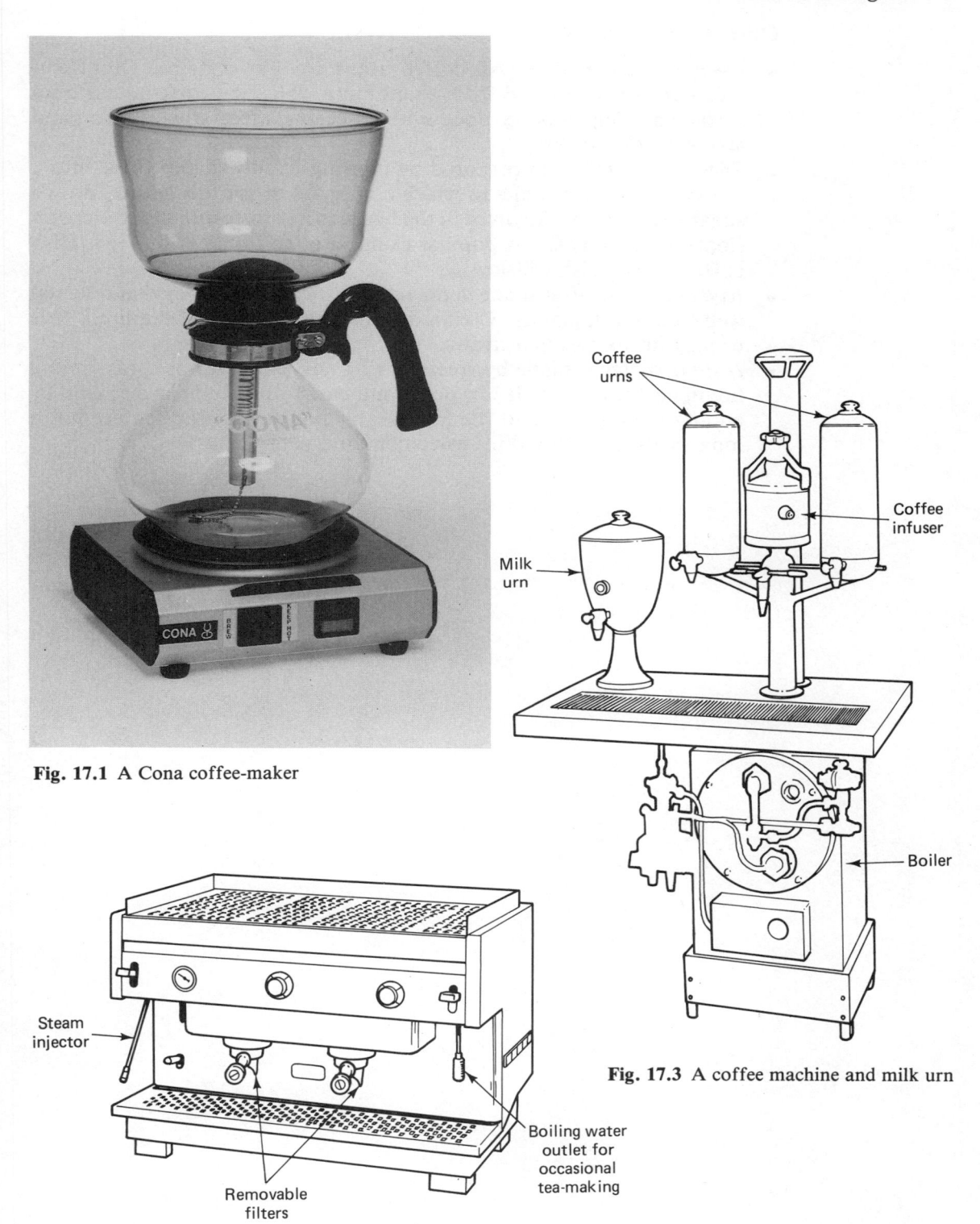

Fig. 17.2 An espresso coffee-machine

Other types of coffee

- *Decaffeinated coffee* All coffee beans contain caffeine. Decaffeinated coffee is processed from beans from which the caffeine has been extracted. This process does not noticeably affect the flavour and aroma of the coffee.
- *Speciality coffees* are prepared by pouring freshly made coffee into a pre-warmed Paris goblet to which a measure of spirit is added. Brown sugar must also be dissolved in the black coffee to ensure that the cream floats on the surface. A popular example of this type of coffee is Irish coffee, using Irish whiskey.
- *Iced coffee* Coffee made in the normal way may be cooled and served well-iced in tall glasses. Cream or milk can be added if required. It is usually drunk through straws.
- *Instant coffee* is made by freeze-drying (see page 178) or spray-drying liquid coffee extract. It is quickly and easily prepared for drinking by adding boiling water to the granules or powder. Instant coffee has a long shelf-life if stored in sealed containers.

18 Herbs and spices

Herbs (*herbes* (f)) and spices (*épices* (f)) have been used for centuries to enhance the flavour of food. At one time they were very important in masking the unpleasant flavour of stale food. Nowadays this is not necessary and you use herbs and spices more sparingly to give particular flavours and aromas.

It is not easy to distinguish between herbs and spices – nor is it particularly important! Many herbs, but not all, are the leaves, stems, or flowers of plants and are often available fresh or dried. Spices are obtained from flowers, seeds, leaves, bark, or roots and in the UK are usually used dried. Herbs and spices owe their flavour and aroma to the volatile oils which they contain.

18.1 Herbs

In every region of the world, dishes have been developed that use herbs that grow locally: fish flavoured with dill in Scandanavia; roast meats served with mint, sage, and horseradish in the UK; and a variety of dishes using basil, oregano, and garlic in Italy, for example. As with many commodities, the amount of herbs used will depend on the consumer's preference and the type of dish being prepared.

Herbs can be used individually or as mixtures of herbs:

- *Bouquet garni* is a popular combination of herbs used for flavouring soups, sauces, stocks, stews, and braises. It contains parsley stalks, thyme, and bay leaves.
- *Fines herbes* is a mixture of finely chopped fresh tarragon, chervil, and parsley and is used in many classical recipes.
- *Mixed herbs* are, not surprisingly, mixtures of dried herbs, usually including bay leaves, parsley, and thyme as well as some other herbs.

Most herbs are available either fresh or dried, but many chefs prefer to use fresh. Parsley, mint, and chives are nearly always used fresh. The range of dried herbs is nowadays very wide.

The volatile oils that give herbs their flavour are more concentrated in dried herbs than in fresh ones. This means that when you use dried herbs you will not need to use as much as you would do if you used fresh herbs. Fresh herbs are often chopped or bruised before use, to release the volatile oil from the plant cells. Some herbs, especially mint, should be added towards the end of the cooking period, otherwise the volatile oil will evaporate before the food is served.

Fresh herbs should be purchased as frequently as possible. Dried herbs should be bought in small quantities that can be used up in a few weeks and stored in airtight containers.

18.2 Spices

Spices can come from any part of a plant and are dried before use. They are often ground and used in powder form. Many of them come from the hot, tropical regions of the world.

Once ground, spices quickly lose their pungent flavour and aroma. They should be purchased in smallish quantities from reputable suppliers who will not have adulterated the spice by adding anything to it, and they should be stored in well-closed containers. As with herbs, spices can be used singly or in mixtures:

- *Mixed spice* This is a mixture of ground spices, mainly used in preparing cakes, pastries, and biscuits. A typical commercial mixture

Table 18.1 Uses for herbs and spices

	Angelica	Basil	Bay-leaves	Chervil	Chives	Coriander leaves	Dill	Fennel	Garlic	Horseradish	Marjoram	Mint	Oregano	Parsley	Rosemary	Sage	Sorrel	Tarragon	Thyme
Soups		•	•	•	•			•	•			•		•			•	•	•
Egg dishes			•	•		•			•				•				•	•	
Fish/shellfish dishes			•	•	•	•	•	•	•	•				•				•	•
Poultry dishes			•	•				•	•		•		•	•	•	•		•	•
Butchers' meats			•			•			•	•		•	•	•	•	•		•	•
Game			•						•				•	•					•
Vegetable dishes	•		•				•	•	•		•	•	•			•			
Potato dishes				•			•	•				•		•					•
Salads and cold preparations	•		•	•		•		•	•			•	•				•		•
Sweet dishes	•											•							
Cakes and pastries																			
Sauces/stocks		•	•					•		•			•					•	•
Pasta and farinaceous products		•	•		•			•		•			•	•					
Savoury flans, pies, puddings, pizza dishes, etc.		•	•					•		•		•	•						•

will contain cinnamon, caraway, ginger, mace, nutmeg, and a bulking agent such as rice flour.
- *Five-spice powder* This is a blend of five different ground spices – anise pepper, star anise, cassia, cloves, and fennel seeds. It is used mainly in Chinese cooking for flavouring savoury dishes.
- *Garam marsala* This mixture of ground spices is used in Indian cookery during the latter stages of cooking or as a condiment. It contains black pepper, cumin, cinnamon, clove, mace, cardamom, coriander, and bay-leaf.
- *Quatre épices* A blend of ground white pepper, cloves, ginger, and nutmeg.

Spices

Allspice	Caraway	Cardamom	Cayenne	Cinnamon	Cloves	Coriander	Ginger	Juniper	Mace	Nutmeg	Paprika	Pepper	Poppy seeds	Saffron	Sesame seeds	
			•		•				•	•	•	•		•		Soups
										•	•	•				Egg dishes
			•				•		•	•	•	•		•		Fish/shellfish dishes
			•	•			•		•	•	•	•		•		Poultry dishes
			•		•		•			•	•					Butchers' meats
•	•			•	•		•			•						Game
	•				•				•	•	•					Vegetable dishes
	•								•	•	•					Potato dishes
				•	•					•	•					Salads and cold preparations
	•			•	•		•		•	•						Sweet dishes
									•				•	•	•	Cakes and pastries
	•		•	•		•			•	•	•		•			Sauces/stocks
			•		•	•					•		•			Pasta and farinaceous products
•			•	•	•	•	•	•			•	•				Savoury flans, pies, puddings, pizza dishes, etc.

- *Épices fines* A blend of ground white pepper, paprika, mace, nutmeg, cloves, cinnamon, bay-leaves, sage, marjoram, and rosemary.
- *Curry powder* This is a blend of powdered spices which varies for each type of curry, to give the required taste and hotness. A typical list of ingredients will include ginger, chillies, mustard seed, cumin, turmeric, black pepper, cinnamon, nutmeg, cloves, coriander, and fenugreek.

18.3 Uses of herbs and spices

Table 18.1 shows the types of dish in which the most popular herbs and spices may be used.

Other types of herb occasionally used in the kitchen include borage, burnet, fenugreek, hyssop, lavender, lemon balm, lemon grass, lovage, winter savory, and yarrow.

Other types of spice occasionally used in the kitchen include anise, annatto, cassia, cumin, fenugreek, tamarind, and turmeric.

19 Condiments

Condiments (*condiments* (m)) are substances that are added to food during cooking or at the table to improve or contribute to the flavour.

19.1 Salt

Salt (*sel* (m)) – the chemical sodium chloride – is used in numerous different ways, including preserving foods, enhancing the flavour of foods, and for making into a salt crust to wrap around small pieces of meat before baking. Salt is used before, during, or after cooking, or on the table. The quantity used will often depend on the preference of the consumer.

In response to the concern expressed over the high levels of sodium in the western diet, some chefs have developed a style of cooking that has eliminated salt altogether. However, many people find that food prepared and cooked without some salt is tasteless and unappetising. Alternatively, low-sodium salt substitutes are available that taste very similar to salt.

Salt is hygroscopic – it absorbs moisture from the atmosphere – so it sometimes has an anti-caking agent added to prevent the crystals sticking together in moist conditions.

Salt is obtained from mines, underground lakes, and sea-water.

- Rock-salt is available in three grades – superfine, fine, and medium crystal.
- Sea-salt is produced by the natural evaporation of sea-water in shallow lagoons. It is considered by some to have a better flavour than rock-salt and is available as either large or fine crystals.

Garlic salt, onion salt, and celery salt are seasoned salts used in place of the fresh ingredient or when only small quantities are required.

19.2 Pepper

Pepper (*poivre* (m)) is harvested from the *Piper nigrum* plant, native to India and grown throughout south-east Asia. The fruit, called peppercorns, grow on long hanging spikes, turning a reddish colour when ripe.

- Black peppercorns are the green, unripe fruits which are sun-dried until the skin wrinkles and blackens. They are available whole or coarsely or finely ground and are commonly used to flavour most types of savoury dishes or preparations. Black pepper has a stronger, more aromatic flavour than white.
- White peppercorns are not harvested until the fruit is ripe. They are soaked, skinned, and sun-dried. They are available whole or finely ground (for use as a table condiment) and used in white soups, sauces, and stews when the visual presentation would be spoiled by black pepper. White pepper is hotter in flavour than black pepper, but with a much less aromatic flavour.

- Green peppercorns are available in jars or tins. The unripe berries are used whole to give a hot piquant flavour to sauces to accompany meat dishes, such as pork, and also for flavouring selected vegetable dishes, such as swede.

Pepper could also be classed under 'Spices'.

19.3 Monosodium glutamate (MSG)

This is obtained from the protein of plants or micro-organisms. It is usually available as small white crystals and is used to enhance the flavour of other foods. It is used extensively by food manufacturers, and is also popular in Chinese cooking.

19.4 Vinegar

Vinegar (*vinaigre* (m)) contains acetic acid. It is used in cooking to add a piquant flavour to numerous sauces and salad dressings. It is also used as part of the marinade for red meats and game and for pickling herrings and certain types of vegetable, for example onions and red cabbage.

Fermented vinegar is produced by the action of micro-organisms on dilute alcohol, turning it into acetic acid. Vinegar can be produced from any kind of alcoholic liquid, and the type of vinegar used often reflects the national drink of the country: wine vinegar in France, malt vinegar in England, and distilled vinegar in Scotland. Cider vinegar is popular in North America.

Non-fermented (or non-brewed) vinegar is sharp and harsh-tasting. This type of vinegar is produced by a number of methods, including diluting chemically produced acetic acid with water and colouring it with caramel.

Herb vinegars are good-quality vinegars flavoured with the named herb to give the required taste, for example tarragon, thyme, dill, garlic, chilli, etc.

Fruit vinegar is produced by steeping ripe fruit in good-quality vinegar. Raspberry vinegar is probably the most popular, but other types include blackberry, red or black currant, and strawberry.

Lemon vinegar is a blend of white-wine vinegar and lemon juice used for salad dressings and fish dishes.

Occasionally sherry vinegar and rice vinegar are also used in the kitchen in the UK.

19.5 Mustard

Mustard (*moutarde* (f)) is prepared by grinding the seeds of various plants, the two most commonly used being the white and black mustard plants.

English mustard – a mixture of ground black and white mustard seed, coloured with turmeric – is the hottest in taste. It is available as a yellow powder or a smooth ready-mixed paste. English mustard is served with roast and boiled beef, cold ham or ham sandwiches, and grilled steaks. It is also used to flavour sauces including mayonnaise, Robert sauce, charcutière sauce, and cheese sauce.

French mustard is available only as a ready-mixed paste. It is darker in colour than English mustard but with a sweeter, milder taste and is served with grilled steaks or for flavouring vinaigrette dressing.

Other types of mustard include German mustard, Dijon mustard, Bordeaux mustard, and whole-grain mustard.

19.6 Bottled sauces

SOY SAUCE

This is prepared from soya beans, wheat flour, and molasses and is light or dark in colour with a distinctive salty taste. It is popular in the Far East for flavouring and seasoning all types of savoury dishes.

TABASCO SAUCE

This is a thin, fiery hot-tasting sauce that is light-red in colour. It is prepared from vinegar and the pulp of the red peppers grown in the Tabasco region of Mexico.

TOMATO KETCHUP

A very popular sauce used mainly as a table condiment, this is prepared from tomatoes, vinegar, sugar, salt, and various spices.

WORCESTERSHIRE SAUCE

A fairly thin, dark-brown sauce with a sweetish, fairly pungent flavour, this is used in many recipes including soups, gravies, sauces, and tomato juice.

Other bottled sauces include hoisin sauce, oyster sauce, tartare sauce, and bottled salad dressings – mayonnaise, cocktail sauce, thousand island dressing, etc.

20 Pickles and chutneys

Pickles and chutneys are used to garnish or accompany a wide range of savoury dishes, providing a contrast to the main ingredient.

20.1 Pickles

In this context, the word 'pickle' covers those vegetable and fruit products that have been preserved in vinegar or brine.

CAPERS

These are the preserved unopened buds of a shrub native to the Mediterranean countries, used for garnishing steak tartare, sauces, veal, and egg and fish dishes.

GHERKINS

A variety of small cucumber grown exclusively for pickling. They are used to accompany cold meats, pies, and sausages. They are also an ingredient for sauce tartare.

OLIVES

These are harvested from a tree native to the Mediterranean, either when green or, for black olives, when fully ripened. They are sometimes pitted and stuffed before pickling. They are used to garnish sauces, veal, and fish and chicken dishes, or as part of an hors-d'oeuvre or bar snack.

ONIONS

Pickled onions are available in a variety of sizes. They are used to garnish cold sliced meat, sausages, meat pies, pâté, cheese, and sandwiches.

Other types of pickle include piccalilli; mixed vegetable pickles; lime pickles; and pickled red cabbage, eggs, and walnuts.

20.2 Chutneys

Chutneys are thick mixtures of cooked vegetables and/or fruits which are sweet and spicy in flavour. They are usually fairly dark in colour. Cooked chutney includes vinegar to act as a preservative and to influence the flavour.

Mango chutney is often used as an accompaniment to curried dishes. Tomato chutney is popular served with cold sliced meats and British cheeses.

21 Essences, flavourings, and colourings

Essences, flavourings, and colourings are concentrated, and their addition to food must be done with care.

- Essences are usually alcoholic solutions of the volatile components extracted from natural materials. Common examples are almond, lemon, orange, peppermint, and vanilla essence. Some natural essences are also available from soft fruits.
- Artificial flavouring are made from chemicals that are synthesised to be similar to the natural compounds and blended to produce an acceptable imitation. Examples are brandy, rum, coconut, and banana flavourings.

Because of their volatile nature, flavourings and essences should be stored in well-closed containers in a cool place.

- Colourings may be natural or artificial and their use is subject to various complicated regulations.

    Natural colours are usually obtained from plants, and a number of commodities are used to impart colour – for example, turmeric, egg-yolk, brown sugar, caramel, chocolate, and cocoa.

    There is an extensive range of artificial colourings, which may be alcohol- or water-based. There are legal restrictions on the chemicals that may be used, the concentration, and the type of food in which they may be used.

Artificial flavourings and colourings may be classed as food additives – see chapter 23.

22 Convenience foods

22.1 When convenience foods might be used

It is difficult to define convenience foods accurately, so we will use a definition from Arnold Bender's *Dictionary of Nutrition and Food Technology*: convenience foods are 'processed foods in which a considerable amount of the preparation has already been carried out by the manufacturer'.

Although some people would include items such as manufactured cakes, biscuits, breakfast cereals, sliced bread, and bottled sauces under the heading 'convenience foods', most caterers use the term to mean those types of food that have been processed to an advanced stage, or modified in some way, so that the need for labour, craft skills, preparation, and cooking time is greatly reduced.

Convenience foods have been used for many years and have developed out of the need to preserve food. If food and food products are preserved in a readily available form, time, labour, and storage space are saved. We look at some examples of these elsewhere in the book:

- dehydrated stock cubes and soups;
- tinned vegetables and fruit;
- bottled sauces, chutneys, and pickles;
- frozen steaks, fish, and vegetables.

Convenience products are used in a wide range of catering establishments. These vary from those operations that are totally dependent on convenience foods, such as some fast-food and take-away outlets, to those that only use sufficient to ease the work-load of the kitchen personnel and to speed up preparation, production, and service. Very few caterers can claim not to use any type of convenience product.

You could well find that you can use convenience foods to advantage in the following situations:

- where you have staff shortages or staff recruitment problems;
- where you haven't enough storage space for bulky fresh products;
- where you have a problem in obtaining a regular supply of fresh commodities (because of seasonal shortages, too high a purchase price, or the geographical location of the establishment);
- where you have only a limited space for food preparation;
- where you have not the specialised preparation equipment available;
- where your kitchen personnel do not possess sufficient craft skills.

Convenience foods can be classified either by the method of preservation used – such as freezing or drying – or by the extent to which the food has been processed – for example:

- partially processed items – peeled potatoes, shredded vegetables, and minced beef, for example;

- items ready to cook or reheat – chips, burgers, and frozen vegetables, for example;
- items ready to serve – pâtés, quiches, and gâteaux, for example;
- items that are incorporated into other dishes – tomato purée, dried herbs, and spice mixtures, for example.

22.2 Labour and food costs

The use of convenience foods in the catering industry has increased considerably in recent years. Much of this growth should be seen in the context of the need to reduce labour costs. Not only are fewer staff needed to produce a similar number of meals if convenience foods are used; the remaining staff do not need to be so highly skilled.

The cost of many convenience foods is higher than that of the fresh foods in season, but manufacturers argue that the cost of labour, fuel, wastage, and equipment depreciation must also be considered. Convenience foods do offer an alternative to fresh commodities at periods of the year when the cost of fresh items would be very high. If the caterer has the choice of substituting a convenience item or taking a dish off the menu, it may be that a convenience item can offer a high-quality, reasonably priced alternative.

22.3 Special points concerning convenience foods

- The large range of convenience foods available allows the caterer to offer a wider range of menu dishes.
- Convenience foods are consistent in standard, with a stable pricing structure.
- Wastage can be reduced considerably, particularly in situations where menu items are cooked or reheated straight from the freezer.
- Cleaning, fuel, and maintenance costs are reduced when the kitchen is opened for shorter periods.
- Many catering operations are not geared to using up left-over cooked and raw items. When cooking to order, excess is not produced if convenience foods are used.
- Portion control is made easier by using a specified portion size. Many items are available in single-portion packs or individually frozen.
- An unexpectedly high demand can be accommodated more easily using convenience foods.
- Convenience foods require less storage space, and stock control is easier.
- Always follow the manufacturers' recommendations.

23 Food additives

One of the problems of writing about food additives is that we have to decide what we mean by 'additives'. If we add parsley to butter to make maître d'hôtel butter, is the parsley an additive? If we add gelatin to a lemon mousse, is the gelatin an additive? The parsley affects the flavour and the colour, and the gelatin alters the texture. Many additives affect the flavour, the colour, and the texture of food, as well as having other properties.

Another approach would be to talk about additives as 'chemicals'. However, we have been adding chemicals to food for thousands of years – salt (sodium chloride), for example, has long been used as a preservative and to enhance the flavour. In any case, some of today's 'additives' are found naturally in some foods – for example, lecithin is found in egg-yolk and ascorbic acid (vitamin C) is found in many fruits and vegetables (see pages 152–3).

As a professional caterer you will not worry about additives because you will never use them . . . *or will you*? What about acetic acid (E260) in vinegar? lactic acid (E270) in sour milk or sour cream? curcumin (E100) in turmeric and curry powder? citric acid (E330) in lemon juice?

Additives are substances added to food by food manufacturers to perform certain functions. The commonest of these are:

- to preserve food,
- to colour food,
- to flavour food,
- to improve the texture and appearance of food,
- to make the food easier to process,
- to increase the nutritional content.

Additives are controlled by law in order to prevent any harmful effects on the consumer. The legislation is very complex but relates to the purity of the additives, the foods that they can be used in, and the maximum amount that can be used. Some additives have 'E' numbers. These are substances that have been generally recognised as being safe by the European Community. However, not all additives have E numbers as yet.

The use of E numbers is helpful for two reasons:

- When used in food labelling, the E number is usually shorter than the chemical name that is represents.
- People who know that they should avoid certain food additives because they are sensitive to them can readily memorise the E numbers and identify them on food labels.

Further information on E numbers and the additives that they represent can be found in *New E for Additives* by Maurice Hanssen (Thorsons, 1987).

PART THREE
Catering and food science

Don't let the word 'science' stop you from reading this part of the book. We are going to try to explain, in simple terms, the use that our body makes of foods and why certain things happen during the storage, preparation, cooking, eating, and digestion of foods. If we can understand why things behave in the way in which they do, we will then, to some extent, be able to control them – which is, of course, what all good caterers should be able to do.

You may not have previously had the opportunity to learn any science. Don't let that put you off! On the other hand you may have studied 'integrated science' at school or college; or you may have studied physics, chemistry, and biology as separate subjects. This part of the book follows none of these approaches – its starting point is *food*. We shall consider how the body breaks food down into its basic components and what use the body makes of these components, why and how food is cooked, and what happens to food as a result of being cooked. We shall also consider the role of micro-organisms – bacteria and fungi – in making food and in making people ill as a result of eating some food. The chapters in this part of the book consider these more or less in that order:

Chapter 24 Nutrition

- How food is broken down in the body – that is, digestion.
- What use the body makes of the components of food.
- Which of these components are needed by the body, and in what quantities.
- What are the effects of having too little or too much of some of these components.
- Which foods provide those food components which the body needs (nutrients).
- What is the effect of cooking processes on these nutrients.

Chapter 25 Food science

- How food is cooked.
- What substances food contains which are affected by cooking.
- What happens to these substances as a result of being cooked.

Chapter 26 Microbiology and hygiene

- Why some sorts of micro-organisms are of interest to caterers.
- What conditions they need.

- Where they are found.
- How they are spread.
- How they can be prevented from spreading.
- How they can be killed.
- What sort of illnesses can be caused by eating food contaminated by microbes.
- What micro-organisms are sometimes used in food production.
- How the risk of food poisoning can be reduced by attention to personal hygiene, kitchen hygiene and work practices, food storage, and elimination of pests.
- The factors that cause food spoilage.
- Food preservation.

24 Nutrition

Many people in the catering industry are concerned with food at some stage, whether with its preparation, its cooking, or its service. Eating also gives many people pleasure and provides many people with the means of making a living. You will probably fall into both categories. What we must also bear in mind, however, is that we all *need* food to remain alive, no matter whether this food is at the basic level of some third-world countries or at the more luxurious standards of some western societies. This, of course, is because food contains materials that the body needs so that it can continue to function (remain alive). The science of nutrition considers what these necessary materials are, how the body gets them from food (digestion), what the body does with them, and how much of them the body needs.

24.1 Components of food

Food comes from items which were once living. Some foods can be made artificially in the laboratory, but this is a very expensive process so almost all of our commodities come from plants or animals. Since plants and animals are made up of small living units called cells, many of our foods are composed of cells or are extracted from cells in processing – for example oil, sugar, and flavourings. A few commodities are not made up of cells – foods such as milk and milk products and eggs, although produced by animals made up of cells, do not themselves contain cells. So what is the connection with nutrition? You will have already guessed – *we* are made up of cells. The caterer's role is to get the material in the plant or animal cell into such a form that customers can make use of that material and convert it into material for their cells.

The components of cells which we need are called *nutrients*. In addition we need water and roughage from the cell walls, but these are not normally considered as nutrients.

Nutrients are classified into five groups, which the body deals with differently and which have different functions in the body:

- carbohydrates (page 140),
- proteins (page 141),
- fats and oils – also known as lipids (page 142),
- minerals (page 143),
- vitamins (page 144).

(Remember that we also need water and fibre (roughage).)

These nutrients occur in food in rather complex forms, and the body needs to break them down (digest them) before they can be absorbed into the blood and used by the body.

24.2 Digestion

Digestion consists of two main processes: physical breakdown of food and chemical breakdown.

Physical breakdown (mechanical breakdown)

Quite a lot of physical breakdown occurs during cooking (see page 156 about digestibility). After eating, mechanical breakdown of food takes place

- in the mouth by chewing – *mastication*;
- in the stomach by churning – *stomach movement*;
- in the small intestine by wave-like muscular contractions which, helped by the presence of indigestible fibre (see pages 140 and 149), force the contents onwards along the gut – *peristalsis*;
- in the small intestine by the effect of bile which breaks the fat droplets into much smaller globules – *emulsification*.

Chemical breakdown

The chemical breakdown of food in the digestive tract is brought about by substances called *enzymes*, which make chemical reactions take place much faster than they would normally.

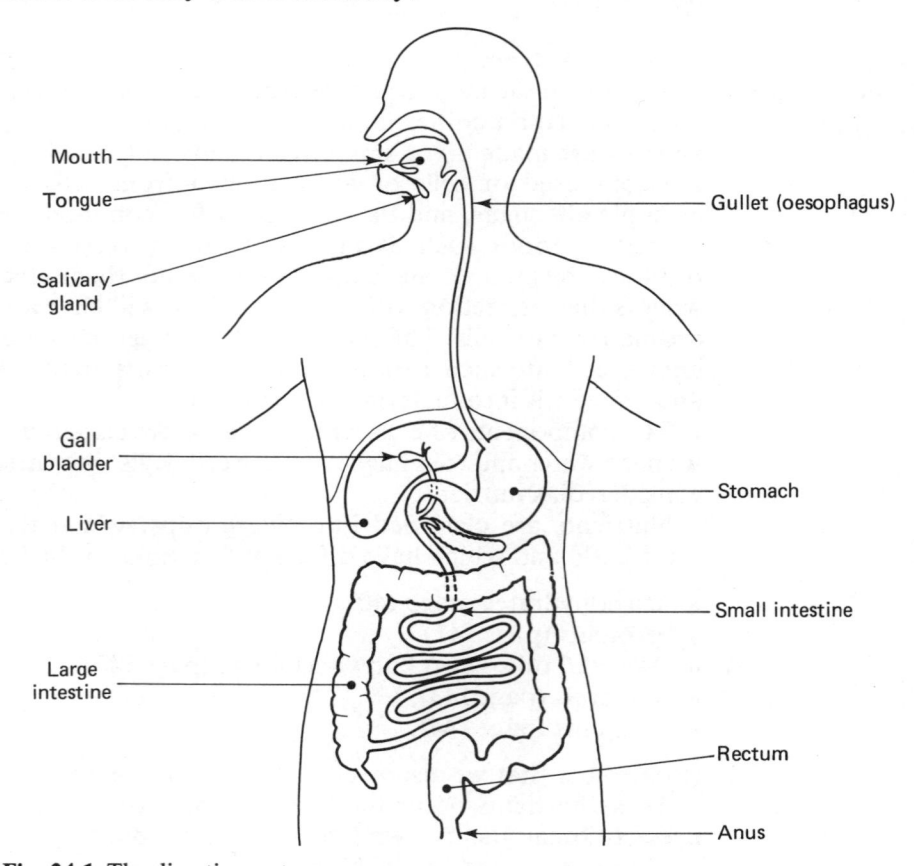

Fig. 24.1 The digestive system

The three most important groups of digestive enzymes are

- amylases – these speed up the breakdown of starch to sugars;
- proteases – these speed up the breakdown of proteins to amino acids;
- lipases – these speed up the breakdown of lipids to fatty acids and glycerol.

(We'll have a look at what the body does with the breakdown products a little later.)

These enzymes are contained in digestive juices which are secreted into the digestive tract (alimentary canal) at various points along the way (fig. 24.1) – for example:

- saliva in the mouth – produced by salivary glands;
- gastric juice in the stomach – made by the stomach lining;
- pancreatic juice in the small intestine – made by the pancreas;
- intestinal juice in the small intestine – made in the intestinal wall;
- bile in the small intestine – made in the liver and stored in the gall bladder. (Bile does not contain enzymes but it does help break up the fat droplets, as we said a little earlier.)

In the next chapter we shall talk about the role of cooking in making food palatable and digestible. Often the processes of digestion can be upset by unpalatable food served under the wrong conditions. This is where you can help by providing food and surroundings which encourage digestion to take place.

24.3 Absorption

As a result of digestion, small particles are formed which can enter the bloodstream through the walls of the digestive tract and be carried around the body to any cell that needs them. So you see we have completed the cycle of getting material out of animal and plant cells into our own.

- Carbohydrates are absorbed as glucose or other monosaccharides (see page 141).
- Proteins are absorbed as amino acids (see page 141).
- Fats (lipids) are absorbed as fatty acids and glycerol (see page 142).

Most of the absorption takes place in the small intestine, although simple substances such as glucose can be absorbed from the mouth or the stomach. Most of the water in food is absorbed from the large intestine. The remaining material which is not absorbed or digested is passed through the alimentary canal to the rectum, from which it is eliminated, via the anus, as faeces.

24.4 Functions of nutrients

The nutrients that are needed by the body and are obtained from food can be considered under three headings, according to their function:

- *Those that provide energy.* Energy is necessary for all bodily processes and activities – for example, breathing, heart-beat, working, and running. It can be provided from carbohydrates, proteins, fats (lipids), and alcohol, and these are referred to as *calorific nutrients* (see page 147).
- *Those that provide material for growth and repair.* New tissues are

constantly needed – for example, muscle, bone, and blood. Growing children and other groups of people, such as pregnant women, need more of these than others (see page 145). Proteins and minerals are the body's main building materials.
- *Those that regulate body processes.* The many complicated processes that go on in the body to keep us alive and healthy need to be controlled. This is the function of many vitamins and some minerals (see page 144).

Functions of carbohydrates

The main groups of carbohydrates that are eventually digested and absorbed into the body are sugars and starches. Their function is to provide the body with energy. Any carbohydrate not used for this will be converted into fat and stored in the body. Although fibre (or roughage) is made up of carbohydrate material (cellulose), it is not digested but remains in the intestine to add bulk to the intestinal contents. Alcohol (ethanol), although not strictly a carbohydrate, can also provide some parts of the body with energy – but not the muscles!

SUGARS

There are a number of sugars important in nutrition:

- Sucrose comes from cane and beet sugar.
- Lactose occurs in milk.
- Fructose is found in honey and fruit.
- Maltose and glucose do not occur commonly in food (unless you count

Table 24.1 Average sugar content of selected foods (g per 100 g) (calculated as monosaccharides)

Food	Sugars
Honey	76.4
Jam	69.2
Milk chocolate	56.5
Chocolate biscuits	43.4
Muesli	26.2
Tomato ketchup	22.9
Peaches in syrup	22.9
Ice-cream	19.7
Bananas	16.2
Oranges	8.5
Cornflakes	7.4
Baked beans	5.8
Milk (as lactose)	4.6
White bread	2.8
Canned tomato soup	2.6
Beer (bitter)	2.3

Mars Bars!) but are produced by digesting the starches found in cereals and some root vegetables.

These sugars are easily digested and absorbed. They are sometimes divided into two groups of 'simple' and 'double' sugars:

- simple sugars (monosaccharides) – glucose and fructose;
- double sugars (disaccharides) – lactose, maltose, and sucrose.

The disaccharides are split into monosaccharides during digestion, and indeed in some cookery processes:

- Lactose produces glucose and galactose (another single sugar).
- Maltose produces glucose.
- Sucrose produces glucose and fructose.

Table 24.1 shows the sugar content of various foods – the main sources of sugars in the diet are sugar, sweets and chocolates, milk (containing lactose), fruit and fruit products, and biscuits and cakes.

NACNE (the National Advisory Commission on Nutrition Education) has advised restricting the intake of sugar and sugar products because too much may lead to obesity and damage to teeth (dental caries). Alternative artificial sweeteners such as saccharin, aspartame, and acesulfame K provide very little energy.

STARCHES (see also page 157)

Starch occurs in plant cells in the form of starch granules and is made up entirely of glucose units joined together.

The digestion of starch to maltose and finally to glucose is more complicated than the digestion of sugars. In order to make starch more easily digested, it needs to be cooked. Dry heat on starch produces dextrins; moist heat gelatinises the starch, as we shall see in the next chapter (pages 157–8).

ALCOHOL

All alcoholic beverages contain ethanol. Although it has other effects on the body, it can provide energy. It is easily absorbed.

Functions of proteins

Although, under certain circumstances, proteins can be used by the body as a source of energy, their most important use in the body is to provide material for new tissue for growth, replacement, or repair.

Proteins are made up of amino acids which the body uses as building blocks to make up the sort of tissue that is required. Amino acids contain nitrogen in a form that the body can use and are the only source of this material in a normal diet. This is why proteins are so important in our diet.

If the protein that we eat contains the exact selection of amino acids that our body needs in approximately the correct proportions, it is referred to as 'complete' or *high-biological-value protein*. With the exception of gelatin, animal sources provide protein with a high biological value – examples are meat, fish, eggs, and milk.

Essential amino acids must be provided in the diet because they cannot be made in the body, as can some amino acids. If a food does not contain all the essential amino acids in the required proportions, it is referred to as an 'incomplete' or *low-biological-value protein*. This type of protein occurs in plant foods such as cereals, fruit, vegetables, and nuts. One important exception is the protein from soya, which has a high biological value.

A mixture of proteins from different plant sources can together provide high-biological-value protein. This is called the *complementary value* of proteins, and is why strict vegetarians do not suffer from protein deficiency if they eat a diet containing a good mixture of plant foods.

Functions of fats (lipids)

In nutrition, the term fat (lipid) is used to include both solid fats and liquid oils. Chemically they are both made up of glycerol and fatty acids. Whether they are solid or liquid at room temperature depends on the type of fatty acids that the fats or oils are made up of.

Solid fats contain more saturated fatty acids than oils. Oils contain more unsaturated and polyunsaturated fatty acids than fats. Don't worry about the chemistry of fatty acids – 'saturated' means that the fatty acid contains all the hydrogen that it can; 'mono-unsaturated' and 'polyunsaturated' mean that it doesn't. What really matters is that the type of fatty acid will affect the fat. So saturated fats contain a fair proportion of saturated fatty acids – these tend to be found in foods of animal origin such as lard, milk, and eggs – whereas mono-unsaturated or polyunsaturated fats contain a higher proportion of mono-unsaturated or polyunsaturated fatty acids and are to be found in foods of plant origin like soya oil, sunflower oil, corn oil, etc. Fish oils are also rich in mono-unsaturated and polyunsaturated fats.

There is also a nutritional difference between fats and oils which we will discuss a little later on.

Whatever the composition of the fat, it is used by the body to produce energy. In fact, weight for weight, it produces more than twice as much energy as carbohydrate (see page 147). Any fat not needed by the body for energy is stored in the body and can form a protective layer around the kidney – like suet, if you get it from a butcher! – or under the skin to form a layer that reduces heat loss from the body. It is sometimes stored within the muscles, which gives the marbling effect you have seen in meat. (Any carbohydrate, protein, or alcohol not used for energy is also converted to fat and stored in the body.)

Fats and oils are needed in the diet in addition to carbohydrates and proteins because they are necessary for the fat-soluble vitamins (see page 145) to be absorbed.

The importance of whether or not a diet should contain more mono-unsaturated and polyunsaturated fats and less saturated fats is tied up with the level and type of cholesterol in the blood. Cholesterol, as you probably know, is one of the substances often mentioned as contributing to heart disease, but the situation is not straightforward. What we as caterers should know is that a higher proportion of polyunsaturated and mono-unsaturated fats in people's diets will ensure that the cholesterol in the blood will be in a form that is much less likely to contribute to heart disease and may even play a part in reducing the risk. More lean meat and plant oils and less eggs and cream!

Table 24.2 shows the fat content of various foods.

Table 24.2 Typical fatty acid composition of some foods as bought

Food	Total fat (g per 100 g edible portion) (includes mono-unsaturated fats)	Approx. ratio of polyunsaturated to saturated fatty acids
Corn (maize) oil	99.9	4:1
Butter	81.0	1:17
Margarine		
hard	81.0	1:4
polyunsaturated	81.0	3:1
Salted peanuts (roasted)	49	2:1
Potato crisps	35.9	1:1.5
Cheddar cheese	33.5	1:15
Milk chocolate	30.3	1:15
Pork (average)	25.5	1:2
Mackerel	22.9	1:1
Chicken	12.8	1.5:1

NACNE and COMA recommend that the ratio of polyunsaturated fatty acids to saturated fatty acids should be as high as possible. This ratio is called the P:S ratio.

Functions of minerals

The body contains a very large number of minerals, and so does the food we eat, so there are only a few that need to be specially considered from the point of view of nutritional requirements. Anyone who eats a reasonably mixed selection of food will get most minerals, but there are some exceptions that need to be considered:

CALCIUM

The major function of calcium in the body is to provide the physical structure of bones and teeth, in combination with another mineral called phosphorus. It also plays a part in the contraction of muscles and in blood clotting. Vitamin D (cholecalciferol – page 145) is necessary for the body to absorb and use calcium.

IRON

The red colour of the blood is due to the *haemoglobin* in the red blood cells. The haemoglobin contains iron and is the compound that carries oxygen in the blood to the cells where it is used in the release of energy from calorific nutrients (see page 139). Iron also occurs in another reddish pigment which is found in muscle cells – *myoglobin*. This is what gives raw meat its colour.

Iron is absorbed by the body much more easily if vitamin C (ascorbic acid) is present in the food (see page 144).

SODIUM

Sodium occurs in the fluids in the body mainly in the form of sodium chloride (common salt). People working in hot conditions who lose a lot of sweat also lose a lot of sodium. This may need to be replaced in the diet. Because many people are now concerned with reducing the amount of salt that they eat, because of possible links with high blood-pressure in certain susceptible people, caterers may need to reduce the amount that they add to their dishes.

IODINE

This is needed in order for the thyroid gland to produce the hormones that control the body's basal metabolism (see page 146). It is found in sea food and is often added to table salt.

Functions of vitamins

Vitamins are needed by the body in only very small amounts. They all play a part in regulating body processes, and hence all of them contribute to healthy growth and development.

Vitamins are usually classified into two groups: water-soluble and fat-soluble. This distinction is important when we consider that they are supplied by food:

- Water-soluble vitamins are easily lost when we cook or prepare food in water (see pages 154 and 194). Also, they are not stored in the body to any extent, and so we ought to have a daily supply.
- Fat-soluble vitamins are not lost in cooking to any extent and *are* stored in the body, so a daily supply is not usually essential. This also means that we can have too much of some of them, since they can accumulate in the body and have harmful effects – for example, excessive amounts of vitamin D are poisonous.

Water-soluble vitamins

VITAMIN-B GROUP

There are quite a lot of vitamins in this group, but we are going to mention only three as being most important from the caterer's point of view:

- thiamin (vitamin B1),
- riboflavin (vitamin B2),
- nicotinic acid or niacin.

These are all concerned with releasing energy from the calorific nutrients (see page 139). (Nicotinic acid has nothing to do with nicotine.)

VITAMIN C (ASCORBIC ACID)

The three main functions of vitamin C in the body are

- the formation of connective tissue,
- the release of energy,
- the absorption of iron from food.

Fat-soluble vitamins

VITAMIN A (RETINOL)

This may be eaten as *retinol* in foods of animal origin or as *carotenes* (orange/yellow pigments) in foods derived from plants.

Vitamin A has many functions in the body. It keeps the mucous membranes in a healthy condition and helps to prevent the entry of disease into the body. (Mucous membranes line the respiratory system – the windpipe and the lungs – and the digestive tract.) It also allows us to see better in very dim light – although even that won't help us to see in the dark!

A massive overdosage of vitamin A can, however, cause dry hair, rough itchy skin, headache, and vomiting.

VITAMIN D (CHOLECALCIFEROL)

This vitamin is concerned with the absorption and utilisation of calcium in the body (see page 143) and so is very important in developing firm bones and teeth. It can be produced in the body by the action of ultra-violet light, found in sunlight, on a fatty substance under our skin. An excessive intake of vitamin D can, however, lead to loss of appetite, vomiting, loss of weight, and intense thirst.

24.5 The body's need for nutrients

For most of us, food is the only way in which we get our nutrients (unless we take vitamin or mineral tablets). As caterers we must always remember that, although our customers should enjoy the food that we provide them with, we are also providing them with nutrients.

In the same way that not everyone needs the same amount of food, so not everyone needs the same amount of nutrients. Tables which give the recommended daily amounts of some nutrients are published in the Ministry of Agriculture, Fisheries and Food's *Manual of Nutrition* (HMSO). You are not expected to memorise these amounts, but they are useful for pointing out some differences. As you will see, pregnant women need more calcium, iron, and vitamin D than other women; and men, on average, need more energy than women.

These tables are produced by the Department of Health, but other organisations also make suggestions from time to time. Two of the most important are COMA (the Committee on Medical Aspects of Food Policy) and NACNE (the National Advisory Committee on Nutrition Education). Both of these have published reports concerned with making our diet more healthy by reducing the amount of saturated fats, sugar, and salt that we eat and increasing the amount of fibre, as well as reducing our alcohol consumption. These reports have led to the increasing demand from customers for foods that follow these guidelines:

- less butter, cream, and eggs;
- less animal fat;
- less salt;
- less sugar;
- increased amounts of unrefined cereals.

The body's need for nutrients, then, is supplied by food. This food can be referred to as our *diet*. We tend to think of a diet as being something that restricts our intake of food, but a diet really is any selected intake of food and drink.

The usual basis of any diet is the amount of energy it provides. If our diet provides the correct amount of energy, it is likely that most of the other nutritional requirements will be met if we eat a good mixture of foods.

Energy needs

The units of energy used in nutrition are kilocalories or kilojoules. Since both of these units are in use, you ought to know that one kilocalorie is equivalent to 4.2 kilojoules. We are going to use kcal as the abbreviation for kilocalories and kJ as the abbreviation for kilojoules.

The amount of energy a person needs depends on a number of factors, but these can be considered under two headings:

- *Basal metabolism* – the energy needed to keep the body alive without any physical activity. This will depend on age, size, and sex. Other things being equal, men have a higher basal metabolism than women, and big people have a higher basal metabolism than small people.
- *Physical activity* – the additional energy needed to do things. Occupation and leisure activities will affect these energy requirements. Any form of work or play that involves a lot of activity will use up more energy than a form that involves less activity.

Table 24.3 shows some examples of the total daily energy needs of various groups of people.

Table 24.3 Daily energy needs of certain groups of people

Group	Energy needs MJ	kcal
Boys 15–17	12.0	2880
Men 18–34 sedentary	10.5	2510
moderately active	12.0	2880
very active	14.0	3350
35–64 sedentary	10.0	2400
moderately active	11.5	2750
very active	14.0	3350
65–74	10.0	2400
Girls 15–17	9.0	2150
Women 18–54 most occupations	9.0	2150
very active	10.5	2500
55–74	8.0	1900
pregnant	10.0	2400
lactating	11.5	2750

For further figures you should consult the tables published by the Ministry of Agriculture, Fisheries and Food in *Manual of Nutrition* (HMSO).

If the food we eat contains more energy than we use, we may put on weight. If we eat less than we need, we should lose weight. Unfortunately, there are many factors that affect body weight, so that in practice this last idea doesn't always work!

Foods supplying energy

Our energy needs can be met by the calorific components of food: carbohydrate, protein, and fat. Most of us eat a mixture of these. They do not all produce energy at the same rate. The following approximate figures give a comparison, although you must realise that these figures are for *pure* nutrients and very few of our foods are made up of nothing but nutrients. Sugar is nearly 100% carbohydrate, and lard and cooking oil are 100% fat, but apart from these and similar examples foods contain other material such as water and fibre, from which we cannot produce energy.

- Carbohydrates produce 16 kJ (3.75 kcal) per gram.
- Proteins produce 17 kJ (4.0 kcal) per gram.
- Fats produce 38 kJ (9.0 kcal) per gram.

(Alcohol produces 29 kJ (7.0 kcal) per gram.)

Milk, for example, is a food that contains a lot of water and a mixture of energy-giving nutrients.

We can calculate the energy provided by 100 grams of milk. (You can also look it up in a table, as we explain later.) Each 100 grams of milk contains 4.7 g carbohydrate, 3.3 g protein, and 3.8 g fat (and a lot of water which doesn't produce any energy), so its energy content is

$$(4.7 \text{ g} \times 16 \text{ kJ/g}) + (3.3 \text{ g} \times 17 \text{ kJ/g}) + (3.8 \text{ g} \times 38 \text{ kJ/g})$$
$$= 75.2 \text{ kJ} + 56.1 \text{ kJ} + 144.4 \text{ kJ}$$
$$= 275.7 \text{ kJ} \quad (\text{or } 275.7 \div 4.2 = 65.6 \text{ kcal})$$

The actual figure for liquid milk shown in food composition tables is 272 kJ (65 kcal) per 100 grams. The difference is because the energy figures we have used here are approximate. Since the portion sizes we use in catering are not usually very accurate, the approximate figures we have given are perfectly acceptable.

Almost all foods contain water and fibre, from which we cannot get energy. Foods with a high proportion of either or both will provide less energy than those with less water or fibre. Weight for weight, vegetables and fruit provide less energy than bread for example. Similarly, because fat provides more than twice as much energy as sugar from the same weight, foods that contain a lot of fat will provide more energy than those that contain very small amounts. Thus 100 g of cheese provide more energy than 100 g of chicken.

In an average household diet in the United Kingdom, energy is obtained from foods in the proportions shown in fig. 24.2. (This pie chart does not include energy from alcoholic beverages.)

Food composition tables list the energy that the body can obtain from many common foods. The figures for made-up foods not in the tables can be estimated from the figures for the components given in recipes. For example, 150 g of uncooked short pastry contains

148 *Catering and food science*

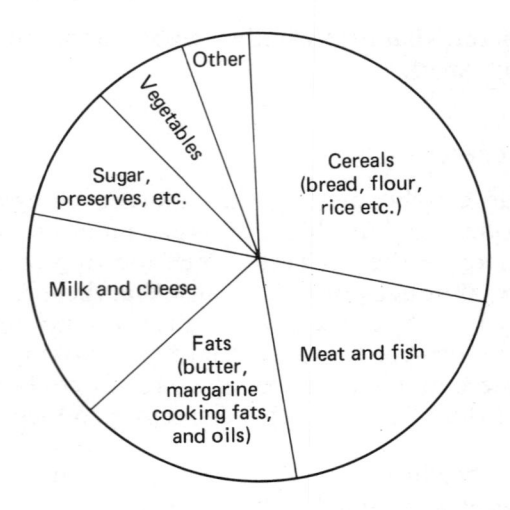

Fig. 24.2 Where energy is obtained from in the average UK diet

100 g flour providing 1493 kJ per 100 g,
25 g margarine providing 3000 kJ per 100 g,
25 g lard providing 3667 kJ per 100 g,
pinch of salt ⎫
water   ⎬ no kJ

Its energy content is therefore

$$\left(100\,g \times \frac{1493\,kJ}{100\,g}\right) + \left(25\,g \times \frac{3000\,kJ}{100\,g}\right) + \left(25\,g \times \frac{3667\,kJ}{100\,g}\right)$$

$$= 1493\,kJ + 750\,kJ + 917\,kJ$$

$$= 3160\,kJ \quad (\text{or } 3160 \div 4.2 = 752\,kcal)$$

Assuming that 150 g makes three portions, the energy provided by each portion will be 3160 kJ ÷ 3 = 1053 kJ (251 kcal).

24.6 A balanced diet

You will remember that we said that a diet was any selection of food. If we choose our food wisely within the framework of the energy that we need and that the food supplies, we can obtain a balanced diet – that is, a diet that supplies all our nutritional needs in the correct amounts. In practice this is not difficult to achieve in the western world – any reasonable selection of food will provide the protein, minerals, and vitamins needed. It is only when people do not have enough to eat or when they eat too much or when they omit whole groups of food from their diet that the diet may become unbalanced.

Probably the commonest effect of an unbalanced diet in the United Kingdom is overweight caused by eating too many calorific foods. It is possible under some circumstances also to have too much vitamin A and too much vitamin D.

A few people in the western world may suffer from a diet which is deficient in some aspects. (Sadly, this situation is all too common among the two-thirds of the world's population who don't get enough to eat.)

- A deficiency of energy will lead to loss of weight.
- A deficiency of thiamin (vitamin B1) may cause tiredness and lethargy or, in severe cases, beri-beri.
- Too little vitamin C may lead to difficulty in wound-healing and bleeding gums. Severe deficiency causes scurvy.
- A deficiency of either calcium or vitamin D can lead to poor bone and teeth formation. This causes rickets (bendy bones) in children and osteomalacia (softened bones) in adults.
- A shortage of iron in the diet may lead to one form of anaemia – this causes the individual to look pale and feel tired.
- A deficiency of iodine causes goitre – a swelling of the neck.
- A lack of fibre in the diet is increasingly being blamed for some of our modern illnesses. Certainly a fibre deficiency will encourage constipation and conditions associated with with constipation, such as haemorrhoids (piles). Table 24.4 shows the dietary fibre content of various foods. (Remember, only foods of plant origin contain dietary fibre.)

Table 24.4 Dietary fibre content of some foods, g per 100 g edible portion

Food	Dietary fibre content
All Bran	26.0
Shredded Wheat	11.2
Weetabix	9.3
Wholemeal bread	8.5
Peanuts	8.1
Baked beans	7.3
Brown bread	6.4
Spaghetti	5.6
Digestive biscuits	5.1
Brown rice	4.2
White bread	4.1
Cabbage	3.4
Banana	3.4
White rice	3.0
Carrots	2.9
Apples	2.0
Potatoes	1.8

Remember that only foods of plant origin contain dietary fibre.

24.7 Contribution of foods to a diet

We are now going to consider what some of the more common foods provide in the way of nutrients, and fig. 24.3 shows the sources of nutrients in the diet of a typical family in the UK.

150 *Catering and food science*

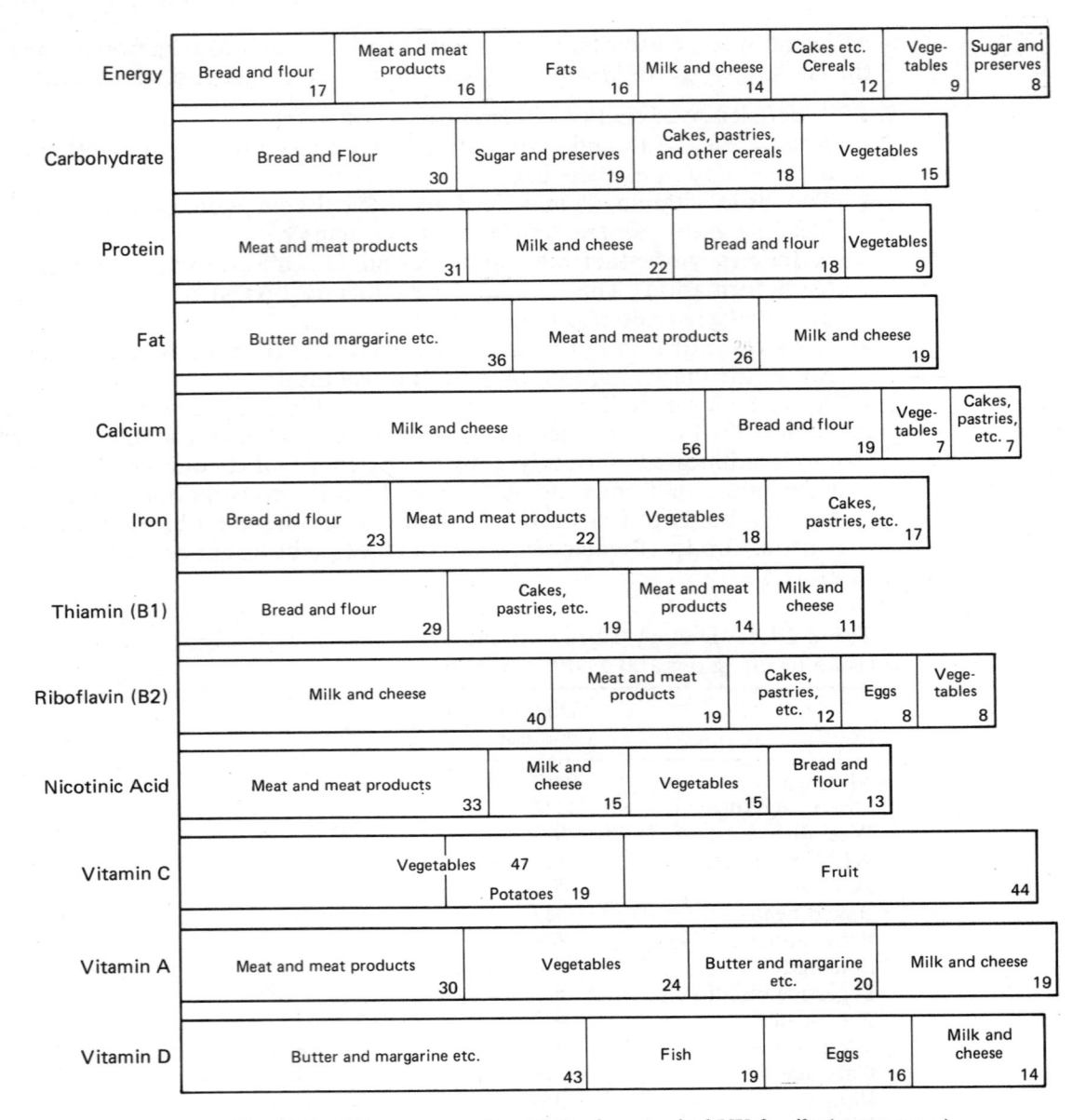

Nutrient	Sources (percentages)
Energy	Bread and flour 17 | Meat and meat products 16 | Fats 16 | Milk and cheese 14 | Cakes etc. Cereals 12 | Vegetables 9 | Sugar and preserves 8
Carbohydrate	Bread and Flour 30 | Sugar and preserves 19 | Cakes, pastries, and other cereals 18 | Vegetables 15
Protein	Meat and meat products 31 | Milk and cheese 22 | Bread and flour 18 | Vegetables 9
Fat	Butter and margarine etc. 36 | Meat and meat products 26 | Milk and cheese 19
Calcium	Milk and cheese 56 | Bread and flour 19 | Vegetables 7 | Cakes, pastries, etc. 7
Iron	Bread and flour 23 | Meat and meat products 22 | Vegetables 18 | Cakes, pastries, etc. 17
Thiamin (B1)	Bread and flour 29 | Cakes, pastries, etc. 19 | Meat and meat products 14 | Milk and cheese 11
Riboflavin (B2)	Milk and cheese 40 | Meat and meat products 19 | Cakes, pastries, etc. 12 | Eggs 8 | Vegetables 8
Nicotinic Acid	Meat and meat products 33 | Milk and cheese 15 | Vegetables 15 | Bread and flour 13
Vitamin C	Vegetables 47 | Potatoes 19 | Fruit 44
Vitamin A	Meat and meat products 30 | Vegetables 24 | Butter and margarine etc. 20 | Milk and cheese 19
Vitamin D	Butter and margarine etc. 43 | Fish 19 | Eggs 16 | Milk and cheese 14

Fig. 24.3 Major sources of nutrients for a typical UK family (percentages)

Milk and milk products

MILK

Although cow's milk is a complete food for calves, it does not contain enough iron or vitamin C for human babies. It is a valuable source of protein, calcium, and riboflavin (vitamin B2) in most people's diet. The protein is of a high biological value (see page 141). The fat that whole milk contains is largely saturated (see page 142), and many people are turning to skimmed milk to reduce their intake of saturated fat.

CREAM

Since this has a higher fat content than milk, it will provide more energy and more fat-soluble vitamins – vitamin A and vitamin D. Cream contains less protein and calcium than milk.

CHEESE

The nutrient content will depend on whether the cheese is made from whole milk, skimmed milk, or cream. For example, cheddar cheese made from whole milk will contain the nutrients present in milk, except carbohydrate and vitamin C, in a more concentrated form.

BUTTER

See page 152.

Meat

CARCASS MEAT

Lean meat is animal muscle. The muscle fibres are held together by connective tissue. The amount of connective tissue will depend on the age of the animal and the part of the animal from which the meat is taken. Meat with the least connective tissue has the best eating qualities (see page 26). All meats have a similar nutritional content and provide high-biological-value protein, iron, and B-group vitamins. The fat is largely saturated fat and can occur within the muscle or around it. The fat content will have a big effect on the energy content.

OFFAL

Liver and kidney provide the same nutrients as carcass meat. In addition they contain more iron and vitamin A. Liver is a particularly rich source of vitamin A.

Fish

The flesh of fish is similar in nutritional content to lean meat, but because it contains very little connective tissue it is not tough and cooks quickly. The protein it contains is of a high biological value.

Fish which contain reasonable amounts of oil in their flesh (oily fish) provide more energy than white fish and are a valuable source of vitamin D.

All fish livers contain large amounts of vitamin A and vitamin D.

Eggs

Both the white and the yolk of eggs contain protein of a high biological value. In addition, the yolk contains some saturated fat and some vitamins, notably vitamin D.

Fats

BUTTER

This is made from cream and will therefore contain the saturated fat and fat-soluble vitamins associated with cream. Although it is sometimes referred to as a dairy product, it does not provide protein or calcium.

MARGARINE

The nutritional composition of margarine is very similar to that of butter. Some margarines are made from unsaturated or polyunsaturated fat. Margarines made from vegetables oils may have some of their fats changed to saturated fats during the manufacturing process. The fat content and vitamin A and vitamin D content for all margarines have to reach a legal minimum.

LOW-FAT SPREADS

Because of their much lower fat content, these are not allowed to be labelled as margarines. Weight for weight they will provide less energy than margarine, because some of the fat has been replaced by water.

LARD AND COOKING OILS

These are virtually 100% fat or oil. They supply energy in the diet.

Sugar and preserves

Sugar is more than 99% carbohydrates and provides nothing but energy. Preserves may contribute very small amounts of vitamin C as well.

Fruit and vegetables

All fruit and vegetables contribute fibre to the diet.

POTATOES

Because of the amount normally eaten, potatoes are an important source of vitamin C in most people's diet. They also contribute useful quantities of protein (low biological value), iron, and B-group vitamins.

ROOT VEGETABLES

These provide little but fibre. Carrots are a very rich source of carotenes from which the body can make vitamin A. Some root vegetables contain small amounts of carbohydrates.

GREEN LEAFY VEGETABLES

These are an important source of vitamin C and may provide some vitamin A (carotenes) and iron.

PEAS, BEANS, AND NUTS

These are important sources of protein – especially for vegetarians, who need a mixture of low-biological-value proteins (see page 142). They also provide iron, and nuts will contain fat.

FRUIT

Fresh fruit is normally a valuable source of vitamin C, but apples, pears, plums, and cherries contain much less than other fruits such as oranges and black currants.

Cereals

BREAD AND FLOUR

In nearly everyone's diet, these are important contributors of all the nutrients except for the fat-soluble vitamins and vitamin C. The protein is of a low biological value, and iron and calcium as well as some of the B-group vitamins are added to white flour to replace those vitamins and minerals lost in the milling process. White flour contains less fibre than wholemeal flour.

CAKES, PASTRIES, BISCUITS, AND BREAKFAST CEREALS

These products often contain added sugar, fat, and eggs and so in addition to the cereal they provide a wide range of nutrients. They are unlikely to provide much vitamin C or vitamin A. Breakfast cereals often have minerals and vitamins added.

WHOLE CEREALS

Whole cereals such as brown rice are valuable contributors of fibre to the diet.

Textured vegetable protein (TVP)

This is made from plant proteins and may have egg added to it. The mixture of proteins gives it a high biological value. If it is also enriched with some of the B-group vitamins, it will be nutritionally similar to meat.

24.8 The effect of cooking processes on nutrients

In this section we shall outline the effects of cooking on the nutritional value of foodstuffs. In the next chapter (section 25.2) we shall look at the effects of cooking on other aspects of food.

Carbohydrates

Soluble carbohydrates such as sugars will be lost in the cooking water. If sugar is added to fruit during cooking, this will increase the carbohydrate and energy content.

When sugar caramelises (see page 157) it loses some of its energy content.

Starch granules gelatinise in moist heat (see page 157) and become more digestible. In dry heat they dextrinise (see page 158) and are easier to digest. In both cases the nutritional value is virtually unchanged.

Proteins

Normal cooking processes allow proteins to become more readily available for digestion. In moist heat the connective tissue collagen is converted to a soluble protein called gelatin, which is readily digested. The nutritional value of proteins is affected only by drastic overcooking.

Fats

Unless fats are heated to the 'blue smoke' stage (see page 158), no change in the nutritional value of the fat occurs. If heated further, decomposition occurs.

Minerals and vitamins

Vitamin C, thiamin (vitamin B1), and some minerals are lost when vegetables are cooked by boiling. However, in hard-water areas the food may absorb calcium from the cooking water. Salt added to cooking water will increase the sodium content of food cooked in it. Finely chopped particles of food will lose more of their water-soluble components than if the food is cooked in large pieces.

Dry heat may increase the loss of vitamin C and thiamin. Foods kept hot for some time before service will lose significant amounts of vitamin C.

Little loss of fat-soluble vitamins occurs in normal cooking processes.

24.9 The effect of storage and preparation on nutrients in food

Storage

Provided that the appropriate storage conditions are followed, the only significant loss is likely to be of vitamin C. This loss occurs due to the natural processes that continue when fruit and vegetables are stored.

If butter and margarine are allowed to go rancid, the fat-soluble vitamins may be destroyed.

Riboflavin (vitamin B2) is affected by the ultra-violet light in sunlight. Milk exposed to sunlight loses some of its riboflavin and vitamin C.

Preparation

A loss of vitamin C may occur if fruit and vegetables are damaged unnecessarily in their preparation. Damage to plant cells releases an enzyme that destroys the vitamin. This is why tearing leafy vegetables is preferable to chopping them, as fewer cells are damaged. Washing chopped fruit or vegetables in large volumes of water or in running water will remove more of this important vitamin.

Food service

The length of time for which food is kept hot between cooking and service will influence the loss of vitamin C. If the food is mashed or puréed, the loss will be even greater because of the reaction with the oxygen in the air.

24.10 Nutritional value of convenience foods

No general statement can be made regarding the nutritional content of convenience foods – any loss of nutrients will depend on how the food has been treated during its processing, storage, and cooking. For example, frozen peas stored at the correct temperature and cooked and served quickly are likely to contain more vitamin C than fresh peas that have spent some time in the market and that have been stored and cooked badly.

The vitamin content of tinned foods may be less that that of their fresh counterparts because of the heating process that occurs during canning and because some of them contain preservatives that destroy some vitamins. Some contain added vitamins, however.

Dried foods will contain none of the original vitamin C, although vitamin C may be added to the product after drying – as with instant mashed potato, for example.

As a general observation, you can reckon that frozen foods are likely to be of similar nutritional quality to fresh foods if they are frozen at their best and are stored and cooked in the correct manner. Tinned and dried foods are often nutritionally inferior with respect to their content of water-soluble vitamins, unless these are added afterwards to replace those lost in processing.

24.11 Anti-nutritional food components

We have discussed the body's needs for nutrients and how various foods meet these needs. However, there are many foods that contain substances which interfere with the digestion and absorption of nutrients:

- Oxalic acid in rhubarb and spinach and phytic acid in some cereals will prevent some minerals from being absorbed, notably calcium.
- Red kidney beans and a few other foods contain relatively large amounts of substances called lectins, which can cause vomiting and diarrhoea. These will affect food being digested and absorbed. These substances used to be known as haemagglutinins. They are destroyed by rapid boiling (see page 109).
- Cabbage, cauliflower, and turnips are among common foods which contain goitrogens. These goitrogens can also be found in milk from cows fed on kale and turnips. If these are consumed in large quantities they appear to increase people's tendency to develop goitre (an enlargement of the thyroid gland, which appears as swelling of the neck.) These substances interfere with the uptake of iodine from the diet or the production of the hormone thyroxine by the thyroid gland.
- Trypsin inhibitors are found in many plant foods, especially soya beans. These interfere with the digestion and absorption of some proteins. Soya flour is sometimes pretreated to inactivate this inhibitor.
- Antivitamins are quite common in food. They either destroy the vitamin content or make it unavailable. Examples are a substance in raw fish that destroys thiamin and one in soya beans that destroys vitamin A. Cooking will prevent these activities in many cases.

You should realise that it is normally only in cases where large amounts of one particular food are eaten that are there likely to be any noticeable nutritional ill-effects.

25 Food science

In this chapter we are going to have a look at how heat is transferred to food in the cooking process. First, however, we shall examine why food is cooked and what changes take place as a result of cooking.

25.1 Why food is cooked

The main reasons why food is cooked are because cooking can make the food more palatable and more digestible (though some foods are more palatable and more digestible when they are raw). Before we consider this in a little more detail, you ought to realise that cooking has other beneficial effects as well. For example, the smell of food cooking can be an added attraction for your customers, and adequate cooking will also make the possibility of food poisoning very much less likely (see page 179).

Palatability

Although a dictionary definition of palatability is 'being pleasant to the taste', most caterers would consider this to be too narrow a definition. We consider that we are concerned not only with the flavour but also with the smell, colour, texture, and general appearance of the food, both before and after it has been served. We would also be right to think that the hygiene of the kitchen, the staff, and the surroundings will contribute to our wider meaning of palatability.

Palatability is affected by cooking because of what happens to some of the components of food when it is heated. It is difficult to be precise about this, because certain things only happen above certain temperatures (see pages 158-9). It is not possible, or even necessary, to have a look at all the substances that foods might contain, but we shall consider those that have a particular effect on the palatability as well as the digestibility and the nutritional content of food.

Digestibility

Although our bodies are capable of breaking down food during digestion (see page 138), some cooking processes make the task less difficult for our digestive system. Perhaps the two most important processes involved are the gelatinisation (breaking down in the presence of heat and water) of starch granules (see page 157) and the 'softening' of the fibres that hold many plant materials together, especially cereals and vegetables (see page 193). If you were to try eating raw cereal grains, for example, by lengthy chewing you could eventually release some of the starch, which would be converted to a sugar in the mouth (by an enzyme in saliva – see page 139) and it would taste sweet. It would, however, take you an awfully long time. If the cereal is cooked first – like cornflakes, for example – the

25.2 Substances in food affected by cooking

digestive processes are speeded up and you don't need to spend most of the morning chewing your breakfast!

The components of food discussed here are water, sugars, starches, fats and oils, and proteins. In section 24.8 we looked at the effect of cooking on the nutritional value of these, but here we are going to consider its effects on palatability and digestibility. Vitamins and minerals were also mentioned in section 24.8, but they are not relevant here as cooking does not make them undergo any changes that are apparent to the consumer.

Water

Perhaps the most obvious property of water concerned with cooking is that it evaporates if you heat it. Actually it evaporates at any temperature, but the more you heat it, the quicker it evaporates until you reach boiling point (see page 164). This means that any food containing water will dry out unless it is surrounded by water or steam or unless steps are taken to prevent this happening. Using a cartouche (a circle of greaseproof paper) to cover vegetables when sweating them in a saucepan prevents the water from escaping, in the same way as storing food in a closed container stops it from drying out.

An example of water evaporating very quickly is when a potato chip is placed in hot fat. The water on the surface of the chip turns into steam so quickly that bubbles of water vapour are formed. This is why it 'fizzes'.

Sugars (see also page 153)

Sugars are, of course, added to food for their sweetening affect, but when sugar is heated with a small amount of water a brown substance called caramel is formed. This process is called *caramelisation*, and the caramel produced affects the colour and the flavour. Both of these will depend on how long the caramel is heated for. Heated for a short time it is pale brown with a sweet taste, but as heating continues it gradually darkens and becomes bitter-tasting.

Starches (see also page 154)

Starches are found in many vegetables and cereals. They occur in the form of starch granules, which are little 'packets' of starch that are not affected by cold water. If a starch, or a food containing a starch, is heated in the presence of water, the starch *gelatinises*. This is important in cookery, because it has the effect of thickening the watery liquid and increasing the digestibility (see page 156). What happens is that the granule starts to collapse as it absorbs the water, and as heating is continued the particles formed from the disintegrating starch granules mix with the water, making it more viscous (less 'runny'). If this thickened liquid is cooled, it may turn into a solid at room temperature.

Three examples will show what we mean:

- When making flour-based sauces, the wheat starch in the flour is gelatinised when the milk, stock or other water-containing liquid is

added to the roux (flour/fat mixture) which has been previously heated. The sauce then thickens as it is heated more.
- A blancmange may be made from cornflour, which contains maize starch. If the cornflour is mixed with cold milk (and some flavourings) and then heated, the mixture thickens. After it has been allowed to cool, it becomes solid.
- Many starch-containing foods also contain some water. When a potato, which contains potato starch and water, is boiled, the starch gelatinises inside the potato, giving it an improved texture and making it more digestible.

The effects of cooking on starch are mainly to do with heating in the presence of water, which we have just considered. But when starch is heated without any water being present (dry heat), starch *dextrinises*. The dextrins that are formed may be yellowish in colour, have a sweetish taste, and are more digestible. Toasted bread is a good example. Dextrins are also formed when you make a brown roux.

Fats and oils – lipids (see page 154)

Solid fats melt when they are heated. When foods containing solid fat (for example suet or other animal fat) are heated, the fat melts and escapes from the surrounding tissues. This is sometimes referred to as 'rendering'.

When fats and oils are heated to a higher temperature, they start to decompose and a blue smoke is given off. The temperature at which this happens is called the *smoke-point*. If they are heated to a still higher temperature, a vapour is given off which is flammable. At this temperature there is a danger that the vapour above the fat will catch fire and ignite the fat or oil in the pan. This temperature is called the *flash-point*. It is therefore dangerous to heat fats or oils above their smoke-point when cooking.

Proteins (see page 154)

The effect of heat on proteins is one of the most important in cooking. Cooking proteins can alter their palatability, due to changes in texture, flavour, and colour. Unless the food is grossly overcooked, the nutritional value of the protein will remain the same; but the digestibility may be improved. There are three types of change that may take place. It is necessary to realise that there are a large number of different proteins in food, so what might happen to one food might not happen to another.

(i) Proteins, like all other substances, are made up of very small particles. Many of the proteins that occur in food are composed of particles that change shape permanently when they are heated to temperatures above about 60° C (140° F). This change in shape is often followed by the particles clinging together – coagulating. This often results in a change of texture that is permanent – you just can't 'unboil' an egg!

This permanent change of shape caused by cooking is responsible for much of the firm structure that occurs in the final product. For example, the final structure in bread, cakes, and meringues is due to the special types of proteins in flour, milk, and eggs. Other examples would be soufflés, sponges, pastry, and pancakes. You can easily think of some more. If air or some other gas has been put into the food by beating, by chemical reactions, or by microbiological activity (see page 176), the gas will expand as it is heated and the protein will 'set' around the gas pocket, causing the cooked product to be *aerated*.

(ii) Some proteins – especially those in meat – contract or 'shrink' at normal cooking temperatures, causing some of the juices to be squeezed out. At higher cooking temperatures the shrinkage is considerable, causing a loss of weight and size as well as making the substance tough.

One of the proteins in connective tissue in raw meat and fish is called *collagen*. It is tough, insoluble, and difficult to digest. When it is cooked gently in the presence of water (moist heat), the collagen is converted to another protein called *gelatin*. Gelatin is soluble in water and easily digested. When meat containing a large amount of connective tissue (usually the cheaper cuts) is cooked slowly in moist heat, the product is much more tender than if it had been cooked quickly by a dry-heat method such as roasting or grilling.

(iii) When certain proteins and carbohydrates (mainly sugars) are heated together at temperatures above 100° C (212° F), a browning reaction takes place quite quickly. This reaction – known as the Maillard reaction – alters not only the colour but also the flavour and the aroma. Since many foods contain both protein and carbohydrate, it is probably this reaction that contributes more than any other to the differences in appearance, taste, and smell between foods cooked by dry heat and those cooked by moist heat. This reaction does not occur quickly enough at the temperatures of moist cooking to have any effect on food cooked by this method (see page 190).

Milk and egg contain sufficient protein and sugar to undergo this reaction. This is why you may well brush egg-wash on your sausage rolls to give then an attractive colour when cooked.

25.3 Cooking food by heat – heat transfer

Cooking involves putting some *energy* into a food. It is this energy that often changes the nature of the food. Heat is, of course, the commonest form of energy used in cooking, but there are others as we shall see later – microwave and induction cooking are two methods that use energy other than heat. If you put energy into an egg-white you can change it from a thick colourless liquid to a white solid, no matter whether the energy is heat energy from boiling water or a heated frying-pan or mechanical energy from a whisk. (The aeration produced by the whisk is a separate phenomenon.)

There are three methods of heat transfer that we have to consider when cooking foods by heat – conduction, convection, and radiation – but there are also two important additional points to note: first, that most cookery methods involve a mixture of two or three of these methods and, second, that heat can be transferred only if something is hotter than something else. You will never transfer any heat to a saucepan of potatoes (that is, cook them) if you place it on a cooker that has not been lit! To put it another way, heat transfer can occur only when there is a temperature differential.

Before we consider the methods of heat transfer, we shall look at how temperature is measured.

Thermometers

Temperature is measured by thermometers. There are two temperature scales still in use in kitchens: Celsius (or centigrade) and Fahrenheit. How you can convert from one to the other is shown on page 314.

Many thermometers depend on the fact that some liquids and some metals expand as they get hotter. Glass thermometers may contain mercury (silver in colour) or alcohol (usually coloured red, so that you can see it). These types of thermometer are not very useful in catering operations for two main reasons: the range of temperatures that they can be used for is not very large and, probably more importantly, they are easily broken (and mercury is very poisonous).

Bimetallic thermometers are much more useful in cooking, since there is little danger of them getting broken and no likelihood of them contaminating the food. If equal lengths of two different metals such as brass and invar (an alloy of steel and nickel) are joined together and one expands more (becomes longer) than the other, the bimetal strip will bend when heated. When one end is fixed and the other end is attached to a pointer (fig. 25.1), the temperature can be measured. (A similar principle is made use of in thermostats.) Bimetallic thermometers are rather slow to register changes in temperature, but for situations where this is not important – such as a meat thermometer – their use is perfectly satisfactory.

Fig. 25.1 A bimetal strip and its applications

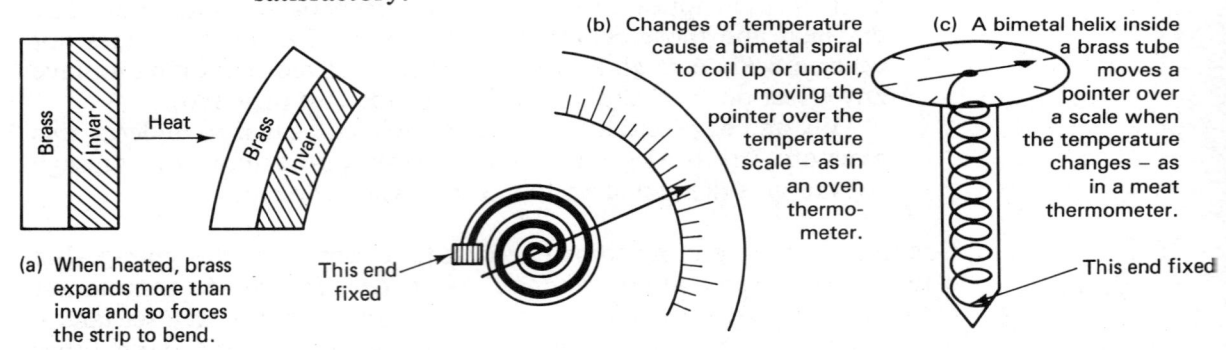

(a) When heated, brass expands more than invar and so forces the strip to bend.

(b) Changes of temperature cause a bimetal spiral to coil up or uncoil, moving the pointer over the temperature scale – as in an oven thermometer.

(c) A bimetal helix inside a brass tube moves a pointer over a scale when the temperature changes – as in a meat thermometer.

Thermocouples or electronic-probe thermometers make use of the fact that an electric current is produced if two different metals are joined at two points and one of these 'junctions' is heated (or cooled) so that it is at a different temperature than the other. This electric current can be measured by a sensitive meter and the results can be shown as temperature. These thermometers are not very expensive nowadays and are very useful for many cooking operations where temperature needs to be measured. They are very sensitive, they cover a wide temperature range, and they are quite robust.

Conduction

In things made of some solids – metals, for example – heat is transferred through the item very quickly. When one end of an object such as a metal spoon is placed on a hotplate or in a gas flame, the other end soon becomes too hot to handle. The spoon, like all solids, is made up of minute particles that are vibrating about a fixed point. The heat applied to the end of the spoon causes the particles it is made up of to vibrate more. Because the particles in the spoon are very close together, they jostle their neighbours and pass the vibrations along the spoon. It is this rapid vibration of the minute particles that we feel as heat (or, to put it in scientific terms, the particles have a greater kinetic energy – energy of movement).

Not all substances conduct heat to the same extent: some are much better at it than others, and it is these that we need to use as containers to put food in so that the heat is transferred to it when we are cooking. Metals are, generally speaking, good conductors of heat, but some metals are better conductors than others:

- *Silver* is a very good conductor (this is why putting a silver spoon in a glass into which you are going to pour boiling water is sometimes recommended to avoid cracking the glass) but it is much too expensive for use as saucepans.
- *Copper* is the best conductor of the metals normally used for cooking pans. As well as being fairly expensive, however, it may react with some of the substances in food, so it is usually coated on the inside with a metal which will not react, such as tin.
- *Aluminium* is quite good at conducting heat and is reasonably cheap. It is much less likely to react with the food or to suffer damage from careless handling. (Silver and copper are fairly soft metals and are easily dented.)
- *Iron* is a fairly good conductor, but pans made from iron are very heavy. They are useful for slow cooking.
- *Stainless steel*, although a metal, is not such a good conductor of heat as other metals. This means that if you put a stainless-steel pan on a gas ring or an electric ring, the heat from the gas jets or the electric element will not be conducted to all parts of the base of the pan quickly enough and you may get 'hot spots' where burning could occur.

Many solids and most liquids and gases are poor conductors of heat – for example, some plastics, some ceramics, wood, cork, water, and air. Some utensils used for cooking are made from relatively poor conductors of heat such as glass and pottery. Not only do they look attractive, they also stay hot longer, because they don't transfer heat very quickly, which means that they are very useful for serving straight from oven to table. They are also usually easy to clean.

When substances are not able to conduct heat to any extent they are called *insulators*. These also have their use in a kitchen – for example, the air trapped in the fibres of an oven-cloth, the wood of a pot stand, and the materials of which saucepan handles are made would be useless if they *did* conduct heat.

In cooking, conduction is the way in which most of the heat is transferred to the food in the following operations:

- shallow frying,

- griddle cooking,
- cooking in a pan on a solid-top cooker.

Other cooking methods make some use of conduction to transfer heat to the food.

CONDUCTION OF HEAT WITHIN FOOD

It is all very well to talk about how heat gets to the outside of the food, but what about how heat travels within the food? Since most food is solid, the heat is transferred by conduction. Food is not a very good conductor, so it will take time for the heat to travel through it. This means that the shape of food will affect how far the heat has to travel and, more importantly, how long the food will take to cook. For example, a leg of pork will take a lot longer to cook than the same weight of unrolled belly of pork.

Convection

The particles that make up liquids and gases are further apart than those in solids and they are free to move to a greater extent. When liquids and gases are heated, the heat gives these particles more energy and so they move further apart and the liquid or gas becomes lighter (less dense). Because the heated part becomes lighter, it rises and the cooler part sinks to take its place, causing what are called *convection currents*. These convection currents are always formed when a liquid or a gas is heated.

The following types of cooking procedures rely on convection to transfer most of the heat:

- cooking in an oven – where the hot air circulates (fig. 25.2);
- boiling – where convection currents are formed by heating the water;

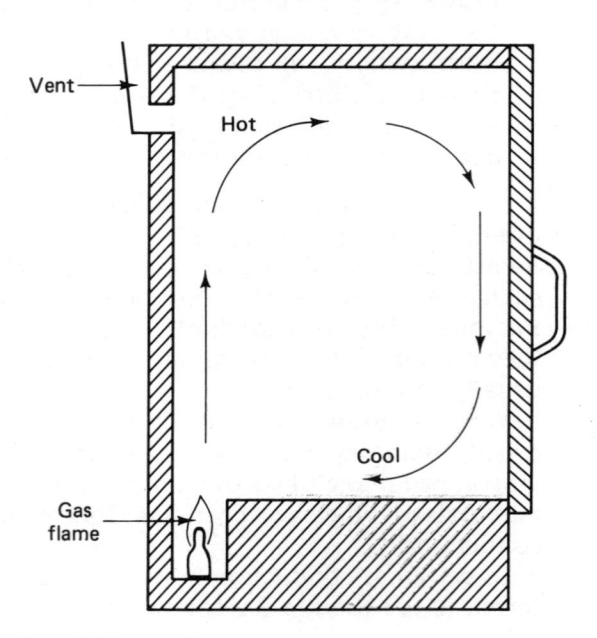

Fig. 25.2 Convection within an oven

- deep frying – where convection currents are formed in the oil or melted fat;
- steaming – where the steam produced from the boiling water is convected up to the food because it is being heated.

Convection is also the method by which heat is transferred within liquid foods such as soups and sauces.

Radiation

This method of heat transfer uses electromagnetic heat waves. These travel in a straight line and, unlike conduction and convection, they do not need a substance to be present in order for them to travel. In practice, however, in cooking processes the waves travel through the air. Since the waves of radiant heat travel in a straight line, food which is to be cooked must be placed in a position where the waves can strike it. Since these waves will lose energy the further they have to travel in air, the closer the food is to the radiant heat source the hotter the food will get. (Too close and it could burn!)

Most hot surfaces give out radiant heat to some extent, but the types of cooking equipment that rely very largely on radiant heat for cooking have areas which become red-hot. The heat may come from above (as in a salamander), from below (as from an under-fired grill), or from the sides (as in a toaster or in doner kebab equipment).

Since radiant heat waves do not penetrate the food to any extent, the inside of the food cooks by conduction.

Radiant heat consists of rays called infra-red rays. The radiant heat made use of in equipment such as regeneration cabinets in a cook–chill system and for browning in a microwave oven is sometimes referred to as infra-red heat.

We have considered the three methods of heat transfer separately, but you must remember that many cooking methods make use of more than one. Two examples will show what we mean:

Roasting a joint of meat in an oven

- The air is heated and the hot air conveys heat to the meat by *convection*.
- The sides of the oven will *radiate* heat when they become hot.
- The roasting tin will *conduct* heat to the meat when it becomes hot.

Boiling potatoes on a gas ring

- The heat is *conducted* to the water by the metal pan.
- The water *convects* the heat to the potatoes as it warms up and creates convection currents.

25.4 Substances used to transfer heat

We have talked about the methods of heat transfer: now let's have a look at the substances you may use to transfer heat when you are cooking. This is more important than you might think at first sight, because the end result of your efforts in the kitchen will depend on it.

Air

Hot air is used in ovens and similar equipment. Air can be heated to a very high temperature, so the food may be cooked at high temperatures. We have already seen that the effect of different temperatures on the components of food is important in the final product.

Water

Water is used to transfer heat in boiling, stewing, and similar situations, and in steaming. The water, even if it is in the form of steam, cannot get hotter than the boiling point of water (100° C (212° F)) unless it is under pressure. This means that the food cannot reach a higher temperature either. This will have an effect on the end product. (See section 28.1 – Boiling.)

An advantage of steam over boiling water is that it contains more heat (the energy used to convert it from water), not that it is at a higher temperature. In the special case of a pressure cooker, the temperature is higher than the normal boiling point of water because the boiling point goes up as the pressure is increased.

Oil or fat

Where oil or fat is used to transfer heat, a temperature much higher than that of boiling water can be reached. This is why deep-fried foods are so very different from the same foods if they are boiled.

Solids

Metals have already been mentioned for their ability to conduct heat and are commonly used in cooking-pots and pans.

Volcanic rock gives out radiant heat when it is heated – usually by gas or electricity – in the same way that metal plates give out radiant heat in a gas-fired grill. Volcanic rock is used in under-fired (flare) grills, and the characteristic flavours and appearance of food cooked in this way are due to the smoke and flames caused by fat dripping from the food on to the hot surface.

25.5 Other methods of cooking

While much of your cooking will be done by using methods that directly transfer heat (by conduction, convection, and radiation), you will also come across methods that transfer not heat but energy, which is converted to heat in the food. The commonest of these is microwave cooking. Less common, but increasingly being used, is induction cooking.

Microwave cooking

In this method of cooking, the energy is transferred by electromagnetic waves, rather like radiant heat; but in this case the waves carry not heat but a form of energy that agitates some of the small particles in the food, especially water particles. This agitation of the water particles causes them to get hot (see page 161), and this heat is transferred to the rest of the food by conduction.

Microwaves penetrate food to a far greater extent than do normal radiant heat or infra-red rays (see page 163). They will pass through some substances without having any heating effect – glass, some plastics, china, and paper, for example – but, like light waves, they can be reflected from some surfaces. Metals are particularly good at reflecting microwaves.

A basic microwave oven is shown in fig. 25.3.

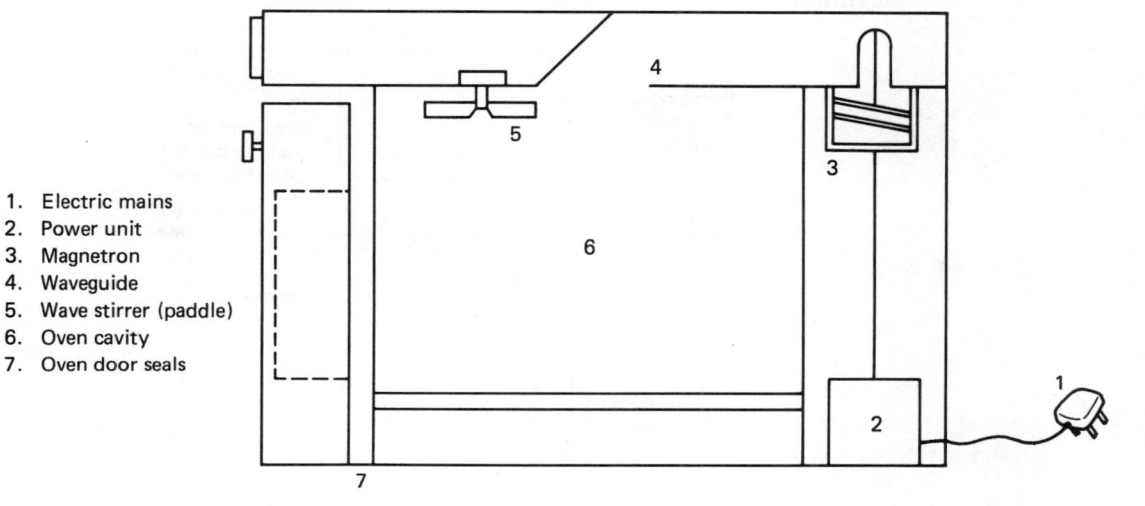

1. Electric mains
2. Power unit
3. Magnetron
4. Waveguide
5. Wave stirrer (paddle)
6. Oven cavity
7. Oven door seals

Fig. 25.3 A basic microwave oven. Electrical energy powers the magnetron (3) which generates microwaves. The microwaves are channelled into the oven cavity (6) by means of a waveguide (4) and distributed by a wave stirrer (paddle) (5). The oven cavity is lined with metal to reflect the microwaves. Special seals on the oven door (7) prevent microwaves escaping

The following important points will need to be considered every time you use a microwave oven (refer to chapter 41 on microwave cooking as a cookery method):

- Because it is the water particles that are heated first by the microwaves, the temperature in the food will not reach more than 100° C (212° F) unless the microwave has some additional form of heating (see pages 254–5). This means that microwave cooking is really a 'moist-heat' method of cooking (see page 190).
- The sort of containers you are likely to use in a microwave will not be heated up by the microwaves but they will eventually get hot by conduction from the hot food.
- If you use metal containers in many microwave ovens, you risk damaging the microwave source (the magnetron) by reflecting the waves back on to it.

Induction cooking

When a rapidly alternating electric current is passed through a helical metal coil it creates a rapidly changing magnetic field. If a pan made of a metal that is magnetic (cast iron or steel) is placed within this changing magnetic field, electric currents will flow in the pan and heat it up. Food placed in the pan will be heated up by conduction from the hot pan.

In practice, a ceramic plate is placed between the coil (called the inductor) and the pan (fig. 25.4). This plate itself is not heated up by the inductor because it is not made of magnetic material. This means that less energy is used than if a metal support were used, and also makes for easier cleaning.

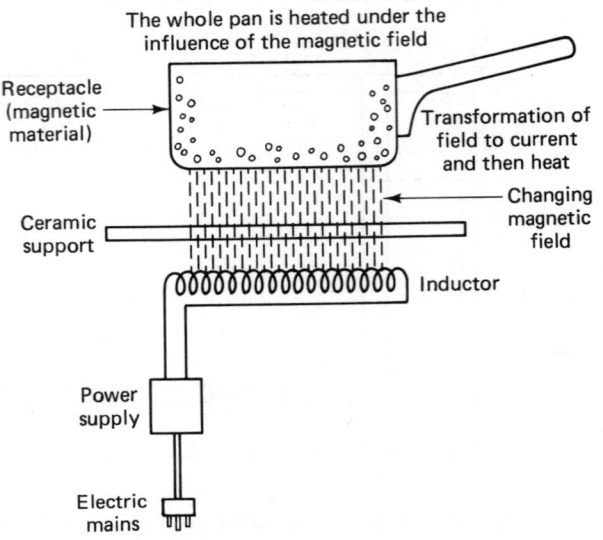

Fig. 25.4 The principle of the induction cooker

25.6 Energy in cooking

There are two important aspects of using energy (whether heat energy or some other form): these are cost and safety.

Some energy providers are called fuels. Although electricity and mains gas are the fuels that are most frequently used, solid fuels, bottled gas, and oil are also used in some kitchens.

The selection of the type of fuel you wish to use – if there is a choice available – should take account of the following:

- the cost of the fuel,
- the cost of equipment and its installation,
- the need for cleanliness and ventilation,
- the possible need for storage space for the fuel,
- whether fuel supplies are readily and constantly available,
- how quickly the heat is produced,
- safety factors.

Some of these will depend on the location and size of the kitchens, but for each fuel we can make some general points that will apply anywhere.

Electricity

This is the only fuel that arrives in the kitchen in the form of immediate energy. It does not take up any storage space, it does not need oxygen to 'burn' in, and it does not produce water vapour and carbon dioxide as other fuels do when they burn. The major disadvantage for many chefs is the time it takes for electric-heated equipment to heat up or cool down.

COST

The amount of electricity used is measured in *units*. A unit of electricity is consumed when one kilowatt (1000 watts) is used for one hour (this is why a unit is sometimes still called a kilowatt-hour). The price of electricity is quoted as so much per unit. Many electricity meters now have a dial which shows the number of units used. This means that you can keep an eye on how much is being used.

Since the unit of electricity involves time, equipment should always be switched off when not in use if it is possible to do so.

SAFETY

Well-maintained and correctly used electrical equipment does not represent a safety hazard. The main causes of accidents are likely to be due to overloading, bare or frayed wires or damaged equipment, lack of earthing, or trailing flex or cables.

When an electrical circuit carries more current than it is designed for, it is said to be *overloaded*. The danger then is that either the wires carrying the electricity to the equipment or the equipment itself will get hot and possibly catch fire or damage the equipment.

Your kitchen may well contain three separate circuits, each designed to carry a different maximum current (measured in amperes (A), or 'amps'). A lighting circuit is usually expected to carry up to 5 amps, a three-pin socket (power point) up to 15 amps, and a cooker circuit point either 30 or 45 amps. Since using electrical apparatus causes a current to flow through the circuit, using equipment which causes more current to flow than the circuit is designed for could prove dangerous. This is why equipment should not be plugged into sockets just because it will fit, regardless of how much current it takes.

Fuses are used to act as a safeguard against overloading. A fuse will 'blow' (that is, melt) if the current passing through it exceeds the fuse's 'rating'. When the fuse blows, the circuit is broken – preventing any further damage. In order for this to happen, the fuse should be appropriate to the circuit in use. It should not be *much* higher than the equipment requires, and no higher than the circuit is designed for. An electric mixer using about 2 amps (see below for calculation) would work on a 13 amp fuse, but a 5 amp or better still a 3 amp fuse would provide greater safety.

The current flowing when equipment is in use can easily be calculated from the following formula:

$$\text{current} = \frac{\text{wattage}}{\text{voltage}} \quad \text{or} \quad \text{amps} = \frac{\text{watts}}{\text{volts}}$$

Most equipment is labelled with the wattage (the power), and the standard voltage of mains electricity is 220 to 240 volts.

For an electric mixer having a power of 450 W (450 watts), the calculation is as follows:

$$\text{current} = \frac{\text{wattage}}{\text{voltage}} = \frac{450 \text{ W}}{240 \text{ V}} = 1.875 \text{ amps}$$

A 2 kilowatt (2000 watt) electric kettle would use 8.33 amps (2000 ÷ 240), so a 5 amp fuse would blow. A 13 amp fuse would be suitable.

A friture of 5.5 kilowatts (5500 watts) using 22.9 amps (5500 ÷ 240) would blow a 13 amp fuse and probably damage the usual power-point circuit. Equipment such as this would need to be wired into a special circuit where a 30 amp fuse would be suitable.

Bare or frayed wires or damaged equipment may cause a short circuit leading to a sudden surge of current that at best will blow the fuse or at worst will damage the equipment or the operator.

Some equipment needs to be *earthed*. An earth connection allows any electricity that may accumulate on the metal parts of faulty equipment to be carried away safely to the earth instead of travelling through any person who touches the equipment and causing an electric shock. If an earth connection is fitted to equipment it should always be used. Since a lighting circuit does not normally have an earth wire it is very dangerous to use light sockets for anything that requires earthing.

Some electrical installations have circuit breakers at the main inlet that will cut the whole of the power off if there is a current surge from the mains. Others have an earth-trip that will stop current flowing if it detects a faulty piece of equipment that sends a current along the earth wire. Some have both.

Trailing wires from equipment represent an unnecessary hazard to all users of the kitchen. It is very unwise to plug electrical equipment into a socket that is some distance from where it is to be used.

Gas

Mains gas is piped into the equipment from an external source. For it to produce heat, it must burn. This is a chemical reaction (unlike the use of electricity) and needs oxygen, which is contained in air. The reaction also produces water vapour and carbon dioxide, as well as some other gases if the equipment is not properly adjusted. Adequate ventilation is very important both for the safe use of gas burners and for the comfort of the kitchen staff.

No storage space is required for mains gas, and the heat is available immediately and readily controlled.

COST

Gas is sold in therms. One therm is 100 000 British thermal units (Btu). (One unit of electricity is 3142 Btu.) Gas meters measure the volume of gas used. If the number of therms provided by a certain volume of gas is known, then the number of therms can be calculated from the volume of gas used. As with electricity, gas which is 'turned on' will cost you money whether you are actually using it or not.

SAFETY

The two main aspects of safe use of gas are concerned with ventilation and operating procedures.

If sufficient ventilation is not provided the gas will not burn completely but will produce some poisonous gases. Even if sufficient oxygen is present, carbon dioxide is produced and, if not removed by proper ventilation, can cause discomfort to kitchen staff.

If gas equipment is maintained in good order, gas leaks are unlikely to occur unless the equipment has not been properly lighted or unless the pilot light has, for some reason, gone out. Burners and pilot lights should be checked frequently to make sure that they are still alight. Not only is gas poisonous: when mixed with air it is also highly explosive.

Other fuels

Oil, solid fuels, and bottled gas suffer from the disadvantage that they need storage space, which may not always be available, and that supplies depend on transport.

Solid fuels need more attention than other forms and tend to create more dust and fumes. The heat produced is not very easily controlled. Charcoal is a solid fuel used in flare-grills and barbecues.

COST

It is difficult to compare the operating costs of these fuels with any accuracy. This is partly due to the fluctuating costs of the various fuels and to their differing efficiencies at producing heat.

SAFETY

Adequate ventilation for burning oil and all solid fuels is necessary for the same reasons as it is for gas.

25.7 Refrigeration

We have so far looked at how heat is transferred *to* food. In refrigerating, the aim is to take heat *from* the food – that is, to make it colder – and to make sure that the heat does not get back into the food until we want it to. The walls and the door of a refrigerator or freezer must be good insulators (see page 161) and must not be opened unnecessarily. The heat-removing part of the equipment – the freezer – is at the top, so that convection currents (see page 162) are set up and the warmer air at the bottom rises to be cooled by the unit at the top. It is for this reason that the contents should not be so tightly packed that these convection currents cannot occur.

The heat that is taken out of the food by the refrigerating fluid (the refrigerant) flowing through the refrigerating unit is released outside the refrigerator when the fluid is compressed by an electric pump and passed through a condenser. This condenser should have a good flow of cold air around it to carry the heat away. This is why your refrigerator or freezer should not be placed next to an oven or very close to a wall at the back.

Use of refrigerators is discussed in more detail in section 26.11.

26 Microbiology and hygiene

26.1 Types of micro-organism

Microbiology is concerned with micro-organisms (or microbes) – minute living organisms that are not visible to the naked eye but that can be seen under a fairly high-powered microscope. You can sometimes detect them when they form large groups or colonies as on mouldy bread, but you can't see the individual micro-organisms.

There is a wide range of micro-organisms, but only two groups are of much interest to caterers: these are (i) bacteria and (ii) fungi (yeasts and moulds). In order of increasing size, the main groups of micro-organisms are as follows:

- *Viruses* Although these may be carried in food, viruses cannot multiply in food, because they can multiply only in living cells. Some viruses cause illness in humans, animals, and plants.
- *Bacteria* These can occur in food, can be carried in food, and can multiply in food. They can cause food poisoning and food spoilage, but some are used in food production.

    This group is very important to caterers, and we shall have a lot more to say about bacteria later in this chapter.
- *Fungi* These include moulds and yeasts. Moulds are important in food spoilage, and yeasts are used for aerating food and for producing alcoholic beverages. Some moulds are used in cheese-making.

    This group is also important to caterers, and we shall have a further look at fungi later.
- *Algae* These are plant-like single-celled micro-organisms that occur in water or very damp situations. They are sometimes used as a source of protein for animal feed, but they are not of any importance to practical caterers.
- *Protozoa* These are animal-like single-celled micro-organisms. You may have heard of amoebas. One type of amoeba can cause a particular type of food poisoning.

We tend to think that micro-organisms are harmful, but by far the majority are useful or harmless. A comparatively few cause illness or food spoilage.

26.2 Bacteria

(*Bacteria* is a plural word and should be used only when we talk about more than one. If we mean one, we should use the word *bacterium*, but you will find that lots of people who should know better don't. Bacteria are also sometimes called *germs*.)

Many of the problems associated with the proper storage, preparation, cooking, and service of food are caused by bacteria. To give an idea of their

Microbiology and hygiene

size (remember, you can't see them), about one million bacteria would fit on to the head of a pin!

Bacteria are found everywhere, so it is not surprising that most foods contain them, either on the surface of the food or inside the food. Most bacteria are not capable of causing illness, however. Bacteria that can cause illness are called *pathogens*. Many of the bacteria that are to be found in food can cause the food to deteriorate, if given the correct conditions (see pages 173-5), giving rise to food spoilage.

Bacteria are not only present in food – the human body is alive with them! They occur on the surface of the skin and in the hair and are present in very large numbers in the intestines. Many people also have them in the mouth and nasal passages.

If bacteria are present on the food brought into the kitchen and are carried by people who work in the kitchen, it is not surprising that they are also to be found on the work-surfaces and equipment in the kitchen. This is why *kitchen hygiene* is concerned with both *personal hygiene* and *hygienic work practices*.

Bacteria can be classified simply by their shape. Although you can see them only with the aid of a powerful microscope, the shape is often included in their name. A few examples will show what we mean.

- Rod-shaped bacteria are called bacilli (fig. 26.1(a)). One bacterium that causes food poisoning (especially from badly prepared rice dishes) is called *Bacillus cereus*. Other rod-shaped bacteria that can cause food poisoning are salmonellae and clostridia.
- Some rod-shaped bacteria are not straight rods, as the bacilli are, but curved or even spiral and they have special names – vibrios and spirillae (fig. 26.1(b) and (c)). These are not common sources of food poisoning.
- Round bacteria are called *cocci*. If they occur in long chains, they are known as streptococci (fig. 26.1(d)). *Streptococcus lactis* is a bacterium that is used in making some dairy products. Others can cause a sore throat and other illnesses. If they occur in groups they are called staphylococci (fig. 26.1(e)). *Staphylococcus aureus* is found in boils and other sores and sometimes causes food poisoning.

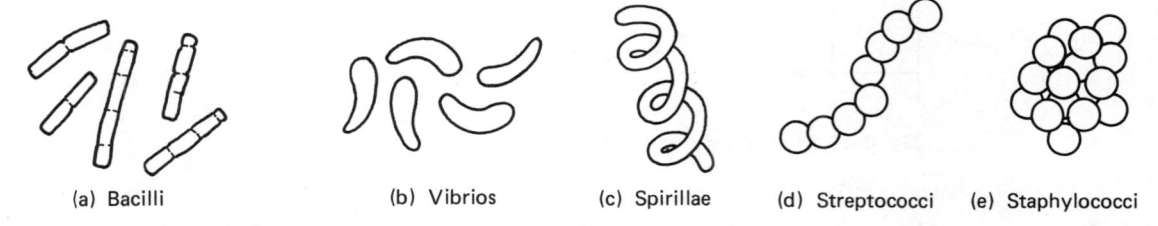

(a) Bacilli   (b) Vibrios   (c) Spirillae   (d) Streptococci   (e) Staphylococci

Fig. 26.1 Bacteria

Bacteria can also be classified by other characteristics. We have already said that bacteria are visible only under a microscope. If a very large number of them are present in the same place, they can form a colony of bacteria. You can see this if you deliberately encourage the growth of bacteria on a special agar jelly. These colonies have different shapes and colours. Only an expert bacteriologist could identify bacteria by the shape and colour of the colony, and even then some other tests would probably be needed to be quite sure. If you saw a colony that was a shiny golden colour you could say that it *might* be Staphylococcus aureus.

Some bacteria form protective *spores* when conditions are not to their liking (we'll have a look at the conditions that they need a little later on). These spores are more resistant to destruction than the bacteria in their non-spore form (the *vegetative* state). Some bacteria do not form spores – that is, they exist only as vegetative cells. Examples are salmonellae and staphylococci. Those that do form spores – such as some of the bacilli and the clostridia – can be very troublesome to the catering industry because they are much more difficult to destroy, especially by cooking, than the non-sporing bacteria.

Bacteria increase in number very easily, given the right conditions. The single cell splits in half and becomes two cells. Some of them can do this every 20 minutes given the best (or *optimum*) conditions. So a new generation of bacteria is produced every twenty minutes compared with a new generation of humans about every 25 years or so!

Imagine that you have a chess board in front of you and that you place one bacterium on the first square. Try to double the number on each square as you proceed along the line (fig. 26.2). If you have a pocket calculator, use this to double the number each time. How many squares can you complete before the number becomes too big for your calculator? Remember that a chess board contains 64 squares. Can you fill even half of these using your calculator? Each square represents only 20 minutes, so the whole chess board covers only about 21 hours. *You* started with only one bacterium, but food could easily start with several thousand per gram.

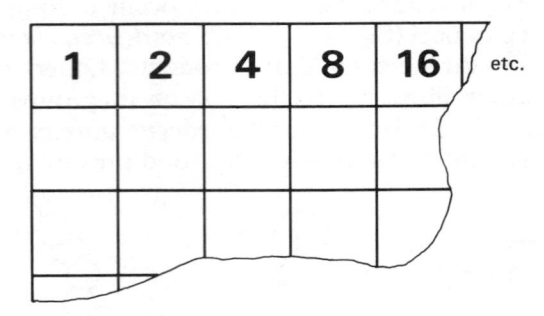

Fig. 26.2 Multiplication of bacteria

26.3 Moulds

You can actually see moulds. If you look at a piece of mouldy bread or at the blue veins in Gorgonzola cheese you are looking at a mould. What you are seeing is not a single mould, though, but a group of moulds growing together.

With a microscope or even a powerful hand lens you can see some of the individual threads that make up the mouldy growth (it looks rather like cotton wool). These threads or filaments penetrate the food so that the mould can obtain its nourishment. You might also be able to see the tiny

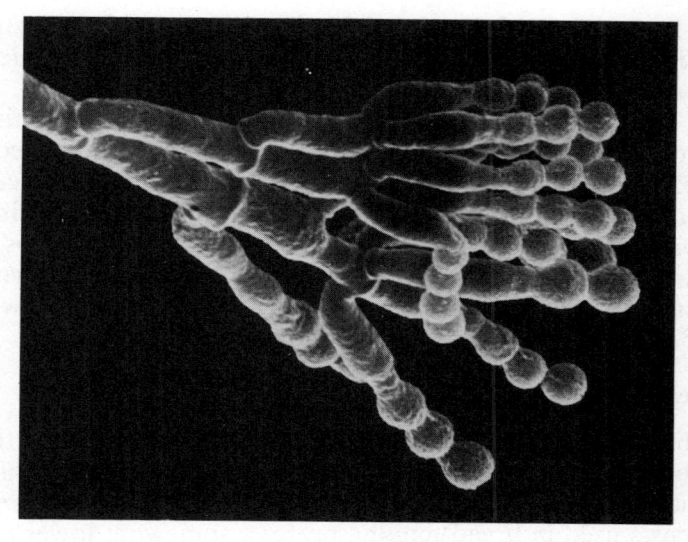

Fig. 26.3 A photomicrograph of *Penicillium* (magnified many times)

spores or spore cases that give the mould its colour – often grey, green, or blue, but they come in many colours. Two examples of moulds with coloured spores are *Penicillium* (fig. 26.3) (a type which is used to produce penicillin) and *Mucor* (which is often found on mouldy bread).

The spores that moulds produce are a means of reproduction. When the spore containers burst, they release vast numbers of minute spores which can travel through the air or in water until they reach a suitable site to start the mouldy process all over again. It is important to understand the different functions of bacterial spores (for protection) and mould spores (for reproduction).

26.4 Yeasts

Yeasts are single-celled micro-organisms but, although you cannot see the individual cells with the naked eye, they are larger than bacteria. They reproduce by a process called *budding*. A bud grows out of the parent cell and separates from it when large enough.

You will almost certainly have used fresh or dried yeast in your cooking, and you should always remember that the block of yeast and the little dried globules are both made up of living yeast cells. Other yeasts can cause food spoilage, and some are used for producing alcoholic drinks.

26.5 Conditions needed for the growth of micro-organisms

We have considered the range of micro-organisms that may be of some concern to caterers. Some are useful in producing food or drink; some are harmful in causing food poisoning or food spoilage. We shall have a closer look at all these aspects later on, but we must now consider the conditions that favour the growth of these microbes. If we know what conditions they like, then we can encourage them (in food and drink production) or discourage them (to prevent food poisoning and food spoilage). What follows applies more particularly to bacteria, but the principles also apply to other micro-organisms.

Bacterial multiplication – that is, the increase in the numbers of bacteria – is influenced by a number of factors, many of which are within the control of caterers.

Time is, of course, a very important factor, since time is needed for growth under any conditions. This is an important aspect over which you will have considerable control in your kitchen. As we discuss the conditions that favour microbial multiplication, it should be borne in mind that all the conditions need to be favourable at the same time. This means that if we can make one condition unfavourable we can slow down the growth. For example, if you put food in the refrigerator, you will slow down the growth of any bacteria which may be in the food.

Temperature

Microbes have a preferred temperature range in which they grow readily. Those bacteria that cause illness in humans – for example food-poisoning bacteria – like a temperature around body temperature (37° C (98° F)). Yeasts used in bread-making prefer a somewhat lower temperature.

At temperatures above 63° C (145° F) growth will not occur and the bacteria will be killed. This is why hot food should not be stored below this temperature and why certain foods need to be cooked thoroughly.

At lower temperatures the bacteria are not killed but little growth will occur, although the growth of *Listeria monocytogenes* is sufficient to cause food poisoning in certain cases. Food-spoilage bacteria may still grow slowly under conditions of refrigeration (1 to 5° C (34 to 41° F)). Bacterial spores are also resistant to deep-freeze temperatures (-18 to $-25°$ C (0 to $-13°$ F)) and start to grow again when the surroundings warm up.

Moisture

All living organisms need water to grow. Some foods will provide water for these micro-organisms, others will not. Dried foods do not contain enough water, but they will when reconstituted. Other foods may contain sufficient water but in a form in which the bacteria cannot use it – when the water is frozen, for example, or when it is attracted by sugar or salt in the food. All these factors are, of course, made use of in food preservation (see page 178).

As a general rule, moulds need less water than bacteria to grow well.

Food

There is a very wide range of materials that micro-organisms can use for food. Food-poisoning bacteria need most of the nutrients that we do, so they grow particularly well in meat and meat products, stocks, milk, and egg products. Yeasts grow well where there is sugar, and moulds can grow on a variety of foodstuffs. In all cases the microbial cell uses these nutrients to produce energy (a process called *respiration*) and to grow.

The micro-organisms may also produce waste products that are useful to us, such as alcohol or the flavourings in cheeses. This process is referred to as *fermentation*.

Oxygen

Air contains oxygen, and this is vital to many bacteria for their growth. These are called *aerobic* bacteria. All our cookery operations take place in air, and most food is stored in the air.

Some bacteria do not need oxygen, or even cannot grow in oxygen. These are the *anaerobic* bacteria. The number of anaerobic situations in catering is not as large as the number of aerobic ones, but there are probably more than you realise. Stock-pots and pâtés covered with a layer of solidified fat are examples. So are large joints of meat which have been rolled and cooked.

Acidity or alkalinity – pH

Acidity and alkalinity are measured on a scale called the *pH scale*. The scale goes from 0 to 14. Substances that have a pH of less than 7 are acid, and those with a pH of more than 7 are alkaline. Substances with a pH of 7 are neutral. Most foods are near the mid-point of the scale. Fruits tend to be acid. Figure 26.4 gives some examples.

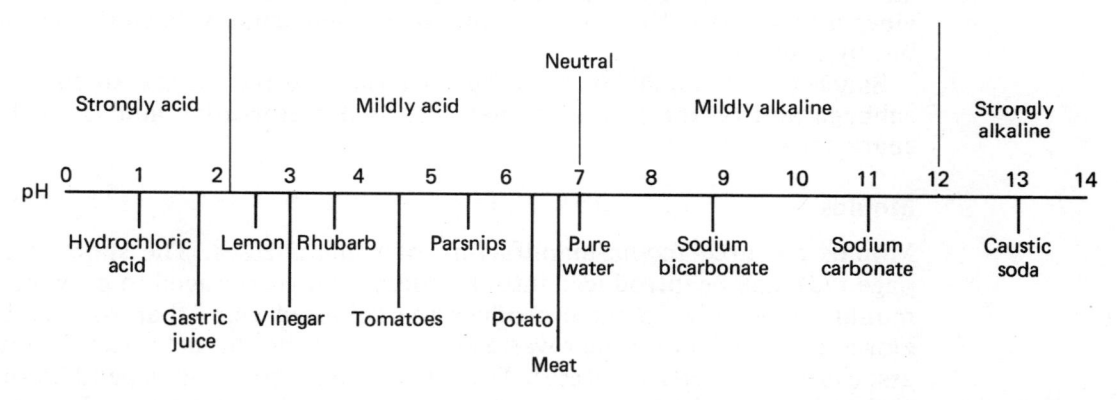

Fig. 26.4 The approximate pH of some common materials. (It must be borne in mind that solids will be acid or alkaline only in the presence of water.)

Most micro-organisms grow best in foods that are round about pH 7. Certainly the food-poisoning bacteria will not grow in vinegar, which has a pH of 3, which is why it can be used as a preservative.

26.6 Useful micro-organisms

Some micro-organisms are used in the production of food and drink. In the same way that harmful microbes can be controlled, so we control certain micro-organisms in food and drink by providing the situations that they thrive in.

Yeasts

Yeast produces alcohol and carbon dioxide when it breaks down food to provide energy for its growth. This *respiration* may be aerobic or anaerobic. If it is aerobic, carbon dioxide is produced; if it is anaerobic, alcohol and carbon dioxide are formed.

Yeast is used in baking bread because we want it to produce carbon dioxide to make the bread rise. The carbon dioxide is trapped in the elastic flour protein, gluten, which 'sets' when it is cooked. The yeast also contributes to the flavour.

When making alcoholic drinks using yeast, the air supply is eventually reduced or cut off to ensure that the yeast respires anaerobically and produces alcohol.

In both cases the yeast uses sugars, which are in the bread mix or in the extracts from which the drinks are made.

Bacteria

Many milk products depend on the action of bacteria for their production. Most of these bacteria produce acids, so the process is sometimes referred to as *acid fermentation*. The bacteria use sugar in the milk to start their fermentation. Cheese, butter, and yoghurt are examples of foods made by bacterial activity.

Vinegar (the proper stuff) is made from alcohol by bacteria that turn the alcohol to acetic acid. So wine vinegar is made from wine, and cider vinegar from cider. Non-brewed condiment is made not by bacterial action but by chemists.

Sauerkraut is made by allowing bacteria to grow on the surface of cabbage and produce an acid that acts as a preservative and gives the characteristic flavour.

Moulds

Moulds are used in the manufacture of some cheeses. The spores (see page 173) may be introduced into the cheese and encouraged to grow into moulds. Not only do these produce the coloured veins that you see in Gorgonzola or Stilton: their waste products give the characteristic flavour associated with certain cheeses. The flavour and colour will depend on the variety of mould used. Some cheeses such as Camembert or Brie are ripened from the outside by encouraging moulds on their surface.

26.7 Food spoilage and food preservation

Assuming that the chef doesn't spoil the food, there are a number of other ways in which the food may become unacceptable to the customer. The food may not be harmful, but its flavour, smell, and appearance may have changed to such an extent that it becomes uneatable.

Chemical changes

Many chemical changes occur in food over a period of time. These may be due to the fat content going rancid on exposure to air or other changes taking place which are encouraged by the enzymes present in many foods. If food is kept at a low temperature these changes occur more slowly. If fruit and vegetables are blanched before storage (see page 195), this will destroy some of the enzymes causing the spoilage.

Damage by pests

Tiny teethmarks in the cheese are not really acceptable any more than weevils in the flour. The answer is to keep commodities in suitable containers, rotate the stock, and observe the recommendations for prevention of pests given on pages 187–8.

Spoilage by micro-organisms

Bacteria, moulds, and yeasts can all cause food to deteriorate. This can only be prevented by

- making conditions unfavourable to them (see pages 173–5), or
- excluding them from food, or
- destroying them.

The way in which this is achieved is by *food preservation*. Cooking is one means of preserving food, but the effect is limited to a fairly short period of time, so we shall not consider this as a method of food preservation.

Methods of food preservation

The methods used can be classified under five headings: high temperature, low temperature, dehydration, chemical treatment, and irradiation.

HIGH TEMPERATURE

The micro-organisms are destroyed by heat, and the food is packed into containers that prevent any other microbes gaining access. There are two main techniques:

- *Pasteurisation* – heating to a fairly high temperature for a short period of time. This destroys the pathogenic bacteria and some of the spoilage organisms, but not all. The process is usually mild enough not to affect the flavour. Foods treated by pasteurisation include milk, eggs, ice-cream, and some canned drinks.
- *Sterilisation* – heating to a much higher temperature. This destroys nearly all the micro-organisms that cause spoilage, but the harsher treatment may affect the flavour. Foods treated by sterilisation include sterilised milk and many canned goods.

LOW TEMPERATURE

The temperatures can range from that of a cold-room to that of a deep-freeze (see page 182). You must remember that low temperatures do not destroy bacteria, so when the food thaws out it is at the same risk as fresh material. Further, if the thawing-out process is not carried out fully, the usual cooking time and temperature will not be sufficient to kill any bacteria that may have been in the food when it was frozen. This is why frozen poultry must be completely thawed before cooking begins.

Some commercial processes freeze food by subjecting it to much lower temperatures. These are sometimes referred to as *cryogenic* freezing methods and may use substances such as liquid nitrogen.

DEHYDRATION

Taking water away from micro-organisms will stop them from growing. There are quite a number of methods of doing this, ranging from traditional sun-drying to modern processes based on advanced technology. Some of the more recent processes use freeze-drying or accelerated freeze-drying (AFD). These turn the water to ice before it is removed, but they are *drying* processes and not freezing processes – it is easy to get confused by the name.

Another method of preventing the bacteria from having water available is to put something in the food which draws the water out of the bacteria. Sugar and salt are two examples. (The process is due to a phenomenon called *osmosis*, which you may have come across if you have studied biology.)

CHEMICAL TREATMENT

Many different types of chemical are added to food to preserve it. Vinegar, for example, contains acetic acid which makes the pH more acid than pathogenic bacteria can put up with (see page 175). The types of additive are strictly controlled by law. The law states the necessary purity of the additive, the maximum amount that can be used, and the foods in which it can be used.

IRRADIATION

Certain types of radiation are used to preserve foods. Ionising radiation (or irradiation) is able to kill micro-organisms in food and to delay the ripening and sprouting processes in some fruit and vegetables. The process is not thought to cause much change in the food itself. Although the process is used in many European countries and in the United States, its use in the UK is only now being permitted, subject to certain safeguards.

26.8 Food poisoning

The general symptoms of food poisoning are vomiting, diarrhoea, and abdominal pain. The effects generally occur between two hours and two days after eating the food causing the poisoning and may last from a few hours to a few days. The illness will vary in severity from a mild 'tummy upset' to severe pain, copious vomiting, and diarrhoea leading to dehydration.

The causes of food poisoning can be considered under three headings: bacterial food poisoning, chemical food poisoning, and poisonous foods. The food poisoning caused by bacteria is by far the most important to you as a caterer, but we'll leave that until we have said a word or two about the others.

Chemical food poisoning

Chemicals may accidentally enter food through their use in agricultural or manufacturing processes. Some of the chemicals used in a production kitchen are also poisonous. Disinfectants, some cleaning materials, and pesticides must be used with great care and be stored and used in accordance with any manufacturers' instructions.

Poisonous foods

Some plants – for example deady nightshade, rhubarb leaves, green potatoes, and certain toadstools – contain poison in sufficient quantities to cause poisoning if eaten. Occasionally a mould growing on a food can produce poisonous waste material in the food.

Bacterial food poisoning

This form of food poisoning is the most common and the one that caterers can do most about preventing. It is caused by eating large numbers of certain living bacteria or the poisonous waste products (*toxins*) that they make as a result of growing. (They don't produce these toxins out of spite – their waste products just happen to be poisonous to us!) So, for someone to develop food poisoning, the food must contain, or have contained, large numbers of bacteria. For this, the food needs to have been *contaminated* with bacteria that have been encouraged to produce large numbers by *multiplication*. In order to prevent food poisoning, then, we must try to prevent both contamination and multiplication. Doing this forms the basis of personal and kitchen hygiene.

The bacteria that most commonly cause food poisoning in the United Kingdom are *Salmonella, Clostridium perfringens (Clostridium welchii), Staphylococcus aureus, Bacillus cereus*, and, increasingly, a bacterium called *Campylobacter jejuni*. It is not really necessary to know where they all come from individually, but between them they can be transferred to food from human skin, nose and mouth, boils and cuts, and intestines. They also occur in soil, dust, pets, pests, animals, rubbish, and even food itself brought into the kitchen. You can see that it is going to be very difficult to prevent these bacteria from getting into food, and this is where both personal and kitchen hygiene are so important. We are aiming to prevent – or at least reduce – the risk of contamination. Even though the food may become contaminated, we can make sure that the bacteria cannot multiply sufficiently to cause food poisoning by storing the food either at low or at high temperatures and by cooking it sufficiently to destroy any bacteria, bacterial spores, or toxins that may be present.

Prevention of food poisoning

There are various regulations that control hygiene in food production kitchens. The most important are the Food Hygiene (1970) Regulations. In some outside catering situations, such as in marquees or delivery vans, separate regulations apply – the Food and Drugs (Control of Premises) Act 1976 and the Food Hygiene (Markets, Stalls and Delivery Vehicle) Regulations 1966. These are broadly similar to the Food Hygiene (1970) Regulations. These regulations are all administered by the local environmental health officer (EHO), who is normally most helpful and very happy to advise you on aspects of hygiene. However, if a caterer persists in not taking the EHO's advice on how to comply with the regulations, the business may be closed down until the necessary improvements are made so that either the building or the catering operation complies with the law. The regulations are quite complex, but we will mention some of them as we discuss hygiene in more detail. They concern both contamination by and multiplication of bacteria.

26.9 Personal hygiene

It is not going to be possible to keep a kitchen as clean as an operating theatre, or a chef as clean as a surgeon. However, it is true to say that one of the most likely sources of contamination in a kitchen is the people who work in it. A common possibility of contaminating food comes from the hands, mainly because the hand is the most likely part of the body to come into contact with food. It is for this reason that the regulations state that the kitchen must have a wash-basin with hot and cold water, soap, a nail-brush, and hand-drying facilities. The wash-basin must not be used for washing food or equipment. There should also be a hand basin in the toilets with a notice requesting users to wash their hands after using the toilets.

It is the caterer's responsibility to make sure that his or her hands stay as clean as possible. When would be appropriate times for washing hands? It is suggested that the following list of occasions is the minimum:

- when starting or re-starting work;
- after visiting the toilet;
- between handling different foods (especially between raw and cooked food, to avoid something that is sometimes referred to as *cross-contamination*);
- after blowing the nose;
- after handling refuse or waste.

Hand washing must be thorough, using hot water and a nail-brush. Many people carry staphylococci and other bacteria on their hands. Drying facilities should be disposable towels, hot air, or some other method which doesn't involve the possibility of picking up someone else's bacteria from a towel. Keeping the hands in good condition and the fingernails short will make the process of hand washing that much easier.

A way to reduce the possibility of contaminating food with bacteria from the hands is, of course, to handle the food as little as possible. Where it is possible to use tongs, greaseproof paper, foil, or other equipment instead of your fingers, it is advisable to do so – especially with cooked foods ready for service.

We have emphasised that hands are an important way in which bacteria are transmitted to food, but they are by no means the only way that bacteria can get from your body to the food. You may find the following list helpful. Some of the points are covered by the Food Hygiene Regulations, but it is *your* responsibility not to do anything which places food at risk from contamination by bacteria.

- Never smoke, take snuff, or spit in a kitchen. Most people carry staphylococci in their nose and throat, and these habits encourage the spread of these bacteria.
- Don't taste food with your fingers – use a clean spoon, and wash it after each use.
- Don't cough or sneeze over food. Many people's saliva contains bacteria.

- Don't pick your nose, poke around in your ears, or scratch yourself. Bacteria are normally present in the nose and ears and on the skin in large quantities.
- Always cover cuts, grazes, and boils with waterproof plasters, especially if they appear septic. It is useful if the plasters are coloured so that you can see them if they fall into any food (in which case you should throw the food away). Any skin abrasion is likely to contain very large numbers of staphylococci.
- Wash your hair regularly and keep it covered while you are in the kitchen. Long hair should be tied back. The scalp harbours many bacteria, and these are easily transmitted to food by falling hair or by scratching your head.
- Always report any illness to your supervisor, even if you have recovered. Upset stomach, sore throat, and some other illnesses are caused by bacteria that may be capable of causing food poisoning. Even if you have recovered from your illness, you may still be carrying those bacteria.
- Do not wear jewellery in the kitchen. The skin under jewellery is a common place for bacteria to live and grow.
- Always wear clean overclothing in the kitchen. This is important not only from a hygiene point of view but also for your own safety. Kitchen whites are designed to give you maximum protection from accidents, and it is easy to see if they are clean. Food-stained clothing can harbour and transmit bacteria.
- Keep your outdoor clothes in the lockers or cloakroom provided. Clothes and shoes can pick up bacterial spores from the dust and dirt outside and we can do without these spores in the kitchen.

A final point on personal hygiene: if you observe these 'rules' on hygiene, you will not only reduce the risk of giving your customers food poisoning but will also give them the image of a professional caterer who has their well-being at heart. That's good for trade!

26.10 Kitchen hygiene

The premises and equipment can play an important part in hygiene as well as the people working in the kitchen. The Food Hygiene Regulations expect certain minimum standards to be met. These are to do with the building itself, ventilation, lighting, and water supply. What they boil down to is that the kitchen and equipment must be clean and capable of being cleaned. Cracked floor tiles, badly sited equipment, and wooden work-surfaces are some of the things which made it difficult to keep up to the standards required.

As well as the general requirements, there are some additional points to mention:

- Provision must be made for storing outdoor clothing.
- First-aid boxes must be accessible and contain dressings, antiseptic, and waterproof plasters.
- Hand-wash basins must be provided.

(You will recall that all these points were mentioned when we talked about personal hygiene.)

26.11 Hygienic work practices

- There must be an efficient system of refuse disposal, and rubbish must not be allowed to accumulate in the kitchen.
- Steps must be taken to prevent the entry of pests (see section 26.12).

Avoiding cross-contamination

If cooked and stored properly, cooked foods will not contain enough bacteria to cause food poisoning as long as they are not contaminated again before service. The problem is that many raw foods contain bacteria, and if these foods are allowed to come into contact with cooked food, the bacteria that transfer to the cooked food will not be destroyed if this food is not going to be heated again before service.

There are a number of points that you need to observe to prevent this sort of contamination:

- Do not use the same equipment, knives, boards, etc. for raw and cooked food without cleaning them thoroughly in between.
- Wash your hands in between handling raw and cooked food.
- Do not store raw and cooked foods together. Having separate fridges for raw and cooked meats is a good idea. If this isn't possible, then store the cooked meat above the raw meat to avoid any contamination by the raw meat dripping on to the cooked meat.

Food storage

Care must be taken to reduce the risk of contamination from pests, from microbes in the air, and from dust. Food should be in covered containers and stored not less than 450 mm (18 inches) from the ground.

Certain foods that contain fair amounts of protein and water – meat, fish, eggs, stocks, and imitation cream for example – must be kept at temperatures at which either the bacteria will not grow or at which they will be killed. They must be kept either below 10° C (50° F) or above 62.7° C (145° F). The reason is, you will recall, that pathogenic bacteria can multiply readily between these temperatures. This means that any foods of this type must be kept in a refrigerator (1–5° C (34–41° F)), in a deep-freeze (below −18° C (0° F)), or in a hotplate or heated cupboard (above 63° C (145° F)). The temperature of a busy kitchen is probably at least 20° C (68° F), so you can see that leaving meat products lying around in the kitchen is not only unwise but may also be illegal.

Food on display should be protected by contamination by customers.

STORAGE TEMPERATURES

To keep food in good condition for the maximum period, it is important to be able accurately to set and maintain the internal temperature of refrigerated units. Regular checks are necessary to ensure that these temperatures are being maintained.

The key factors that affect the keeping qualities of food are

- the correct temperature setting to suit the food being stored (see Table 26.1);

Table 26.1 Food refrigeration temperatures

Food	Temperature
Dairy produce (milk, butter, cheese)	2 to 5° C (36 to 41° F)
Fresh cream	1 to 4° C (34 to 39° F)
Fresh fruit and vegetables	6 to 10° C (43 to 50° F)
Cooked pastry products	4 to 7° C (39 to 45° F)
Cooked meat and fish	2 to 4° C (36 to 39° F)
Cook-chill food	0 to 4° C (32 to 36° F)
Raw meat and dressed game	0 to 3° C (32 to 37° F)
Raw poultry	−1 to 2° C (30 to 36° F)
Raw fish	−2 to 1° C (28 to 34° F)
Freezer temperatures	
Frozen meat and fish	−20 to −16° C (−4 to 3°F)
Frozen foods (general)	−20 to −16° C (−4 to 3° F)
Ice-cream	−23 to −20° C (−9 to −4° F)

- the period of time that the food has spent in storage before being delivered (sometimes shown by the 'use by' date);
- the temperature of the food during delivery;
- the conditions under which the food was handled after delivery;
- the suitability and condition of the packaging when delivered;
- the type of container in which the food is stored after delivery or preparation. Rigid containers are best. Food that will be spoiled by evaporation should be covered with a close-fitting lid or a layer of clear film. Containers should be manufactured from materials that will not affect the flavour, smell, or colour of the food or contaminate the food with a harmful substance.

STORAGE HUMIDITY

To stay in the best condition in storage, different foods have different humidity requirements as well as ideal temperatures. For example, fish, soft fruits, and vegetables such as carrots and cabbage store best in conditions of high humidity; whereas fats, onions, cream, and milk need little or no humidity.

When storing a mixture of foods, the relative humidity requirements of different products tend to be less significant, since products should not be stored open but be kept in their own individual lidded containers or closed packages.

Some cabinets built for specialist storage (of fine cheeses, for example) employ built-in humidifier units to maintain extra-high humidity.

Use of refrigerators

Refrigerators should be sited in areas where the normal temperature does not exceed 32° C (90° F). If the area is poorly ventilated and likely to exceed this temperature, however, then purchase a model designed to work in temperatures up to 43° C (110° F).

The following types of refrigerator equipment are available:

- *Blast chillers* provide the most widely used method of rapid chilling for the caterer. They vary in size and capacity, but all work by circulating cold air over the hot food with the assistance of fans.
- *Blast freezers* are used to quickly reduce the internal temperature of cooked and uncooked foods to $-15°$ C (5° F) or lower. Air at high velocity is passed through refrigeration coils and then over the food products at an air temperature of $-32°$ C ($-26°$ F).
- *Counter or work-station cabinets* are designed with a work-surface on top of two or more refrigeration units. These cost more than upright cabinets of the same capacity but provide work preparation space as well as refrigeration space at the point of use. In a small kitchen these units will also make maximum use of available space.
- *Cold-rooms* usually serve as large walk-in larders or refrigerators, but they can be designed to suit any temperature band. Freezer versions are also available.
- *Display refrigeration* (fig. 26.5) is used to promote sales of cold food items. In most units the food stays in the cabinet for only a single service. Specifications often focus on external features like sneeze screens, colour trims, and front cladding, rather than storage performance. Good humidity control is important when displaying salad items and cheese.

Fig. 26.5 Refrigerated display unit

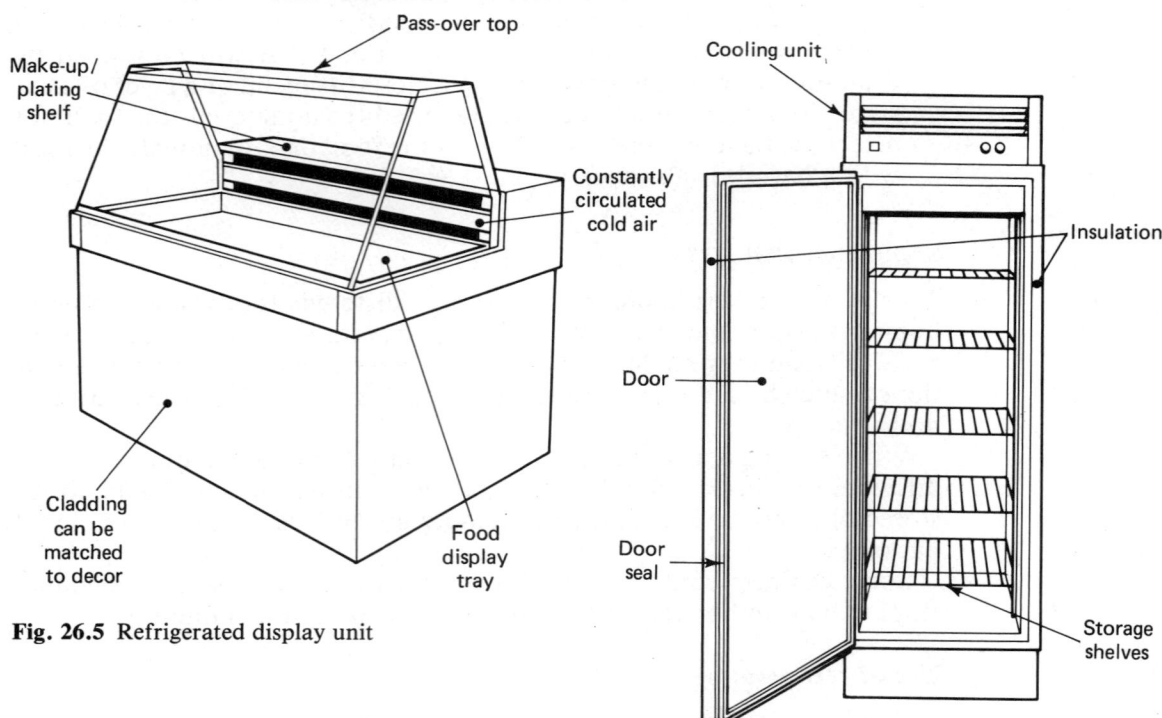

Fig. 26.6 Reach-in refrigerated cabinet

- *Dual-temperature refrigerators* are useful for the smaller caterer for storing different groups of commodities in separate compartments operating at different temperature settings.
- *Reach-in cabinets* (fig. 26.6) provide easy access and a quick visual check of food items in stock. Most cabinets have factory-set temperature and humidity levels to match the intended use. Both chill and freezer models are available.
- *Pass-through refrigerators* are cabinets with door access on both sides. These can reduce the amount of carrying needed to get food to the service point.
- *Storage freezers or chest freezers* provide freezer storage for already frozen foods where ready access is not of major importance. Access is via a hinged top lid. They are not designed to reduce the temperature of foods at cooking temperature or room temperature.
- *Ice-cream makers* are of two types. Soft-serve machines work by pumping air into a liquid or a powder–water mix as it freezes. Batch freezers use a continuous beating action to churn the mixture – this type of machine produces a harder type of ice-cream.
- *Ice makers* are available in a number of different types including hot-wire-grid machines, spray-type machines, prong machines, and auger machines.

Some points to be observed when using refrigerators

- Avoid operating refrigeration equipment in areas with high ambient temperatures, close to sources of heat, or beneath windows or skylights where there is excessive exposure to sunlight.
- Don't open doors any more than is necessary, and avoid leaving them open during protracted loading or unloading.
- Don't open doors by pulling the door seals.
- Always ensure that containers used to store liquids are sealed or covered (otherwise you'll overwork the evaporator).
- Don't block fans on fan-assisted models.
- Don't obstruct air circulation around compressors and condensers.
- Never place hot items straight into a cabinet intended for storage – let them cool in ambient conditions (or preferably a cool place) first.
- Don't use storage freezers for cooling down.
- Never use heaters to accelerate defrosting of a manual-defrost cabinet; instead, place containers of hot (not boiling) water inside the cabinet.
- Ensure that a regular cleaning and temperature-checking schedule is drawn up.
- Label each cabinet and cold-room door clearly with its correct operating temperature and a description of the type of stock to be stored.

Maintenance and cleaning

A clean, well-maintained kitchen is a more attractive and hygienic place in which to work as well as presenting a better image. Undamaged floors, walls, and work-surfaces are easier to clean and to keep clean. Always clean down at the end of each service. In addition there should be a cleaning routine or cleaning schedules in operation where some items are cleaned daily, some weekly or monthly, and perhaps also an annual cleaning programme.

The following are examples of areas that should receive regular cleaning:

- *Daily* Work-surfaces, sinks and drainers, floors, preparation equipment, tiled splashbacks, splash and drip trays.
- *Weekly* Refrigeration units (routine defrost and clean), deep-fat fryers, ovens, shelving units, storage cupboards.
- *Monthly* Walls, ceilings, canopies.

Washing-up must ensure that all crockery, cutlery, and kitchen utensils are thoroughly cleaned between each use. Many kitchens have dishwashing machines, but some of the following recommended stages may have to be done by hand:

- *Pre-wash* Scrape off food particles and rinse the item in hot water.
- *Main wash* Wash in hot water (50–60° C (122–140° F)) with detergent. Frequent changes of water are needed to ensure that the correct temperature is maintained.
- *Rinse* Use a separate sink containing water at about 80° C (176° F). This will kill any remaining bacteria, remove the detergent, and be hot enough to allow the items to be air-dried.
- *Drying* If air-drying is not possible, use disposable paper towels to dry the items. Cloth towels should be used only if they are properly cleaned between each session.

Cleaning may involve the use not only of detergents (which help to remove the grease) but also of other materials that will reduce the numbers of micro-organisms. In fact some detergents have an effect on bacteria. These substances that destroy bacteria and other microbes go under a variety of names. *Biocides* and *bactericides* kill bacteria. Those that are used on humans (and animals) are called *antiseptics*; those used on inanimate objects are called *disinfectants*. If you put it down the drain to clean it, it is a disinfectant; if you put it on your skin it is an antiseptic.

Cleaning refrigerators

Each day, check for spillage and clean it up immediately – particularly on door seals. A thorough cleaning operation for each cabinet should be carried out at least once every two months and should include the following:

- Switch off power and defrost if necessary before cleaning.
- Transfer stock to a suitable short-term holding area.
- Strip shelves, grilles, etc. and wash in a sink.
- Wipe over interior surfaces with lukewarm water containing a small quantity of mild, perfume-free detergent. Pay particular attention to corners, runners, and door seals (fig. 26.7). Rinse with a suitable disinfectant, then finish with a dry cloth.

Microbiology and hygiene

Fig. 26.7 Cleaning refrigerator door seals

Fig. 26.8 Cleaning behind a refrigerator

- Remove dust and debris from the rear of the cabinet and the motor bay using a brush or vacuum cleaner (fig. 26.8), taking great care not to damage condenser fins.
- Switch on and wait until the correct operating temperature is reached before refilling.

Timing of operations

Many situations that increase the risk of food poisoning result from poor kitchen practices involving bad timing. It may be convenient or even traditional to prepare certain dishes or components of dishes long before they are needed. This is fine, provided that they are then stored at temperatures below 10° C (50° F), but often they are left in the kitchen until they are required. A little thought given to the order in which you do things in a kitchen can sometimes make all the difference.

26.12 Pests

The four main common kitchen pests are rats, mice, cockroaches, and flies. If the first three are a problem in your kitchen, it would be a good idea to ask for professional advice from a pest-control specialist. All pests are likely to carry bacteria that are capable of causing food poisoning.

Rats and mice

Apart from damaging packaging by chewing through it, rats and mice also carry salmonellae which are excreted in their droppings. Look out for droppings and footprints in food as well as signs of gnawed food containers or woodwork. Rats and mice can produce several litters a year, and the infestation can soon become serious. It is recommended that you seek expert advice if there is any sign of their presence.

To prevent them becoming a problem, rats and mice should be prevented from gaining access to

- the kitchen – make sure that buildings are in good order and pipes

entering or leaving the building are sealed where they pass through the walls;
- food – store food off the ground in vermin-proof containers, and make sure that no scraps of food are left on the floor;
- water – avoid dripping taps, spillages on the floor, and sinks that don't drain properly.

Cockroaches

Cockroaches, like many other insects, have a hard bodyshell that helps them to conserve water and enables them to live in warm, dry conditions. Since their body is flattened, they can live in very narrow cracks. They are also nocturnal – that is they come out only at night. It is possible to have a heavy infestation of cockroaches in a kitchen without knowing it, unless you happen to switch the light on in the middle of the night. If cockroaches are present, your cleaning routines should find their droppings by skirting boards and behind ovens. If you do have an infestation, you must seek professional help, as several treatments may be necessary since cockroach eggs do not hatch for several months.

Measures for preventing cockroaches from infesting your kitchen are similar to those for rats and mice (see above).

Flies

The fly is a menace to health at all times but especially so in warm weather as it breeds so quickly. A fly can transmit bacteria to food just by landing on it. These bacteria will have been picked up as the fly feeds on refuse and rubbish – a good reason why kitchen refuse should be stored in properly covered containers. The fly has some other disgusting habits such as 'spitting' on food and depositing its waste products on food and surfaces. These processes will also transmit bacteria.

Keeping flies out of a kitchen is difficult, but you can take some measures which will help to reduce their numbers:

- Kitchen waste and rubbish should be kept in containers with well-fitting lids.
- Food should be kept in a fly-proof room or kept covered.
- Fly-screens can be fitted to doors or windows.

Control of flies can be achieved by

- fly-sprays – but do not use near food or direct the spray on to crockery or equipment;
- ultra-violet fly electrocutors – the blue light that they give out attracts the flies to a metal mesh which has an electric current flowing through it. The flies are electrocuted and fall on to a collecting tray beneath.

PART FOUR
Food preparation and cooking

The following eighteen chapters are concerned with cookery methods and the use and care of equipment needed for the preparation and cooking of food. At the end of each method, the major items of equipment used will be discussed. (The details given are only a general guide, however – actual specifications will vary from one manufacturer to another). Information on small utensils will be found in chapter 46.

The main reasons why food is prepared and cooked are as follows:

- to improve palatability;
- to improve digestibility;
- to improve appearance;
- to enable the caterer to combine different types of commodities, giving a wider range of dishes;
- to kill bacteria and other micro-organisms that may be harmful to the customer;
- to extend the keeping properties of some perishable items.

An understanding of the basic principles of cooking methods and the use of equipment will enable you to produce the wide range of dishes expected of today's professional chef. The ability to memorise recipes and methods will come with experience and practice, but the basic principles can easily be applied where new trends have been introduced (such as cuisine nouvelle) or where any other trends may occur in the future.

27 Introduction to food preparation and cooking

27.1 Methods of cooking

Cooking almost always involves transfering heat to food (see section 25.3). The changes that take place when the food is cooked will affect its structure, colour, and taste. The changes will to some extent be affected by the temperature at which the food is cooked and by how the heat is transferred to it, as well as by how long it is cooked for. Cooking methods are frequently divided into two groups: *moist heat* and *dry heat*. The differences in the properties of the food produced by each method are due, very largely, to the temperature at which cooking takes place. (Have a look at chapter 25). You have only to think about the difference between a chipped potato (cooked in oil at about 180° C (356° F)) and a boiled potato (cooked in boiling water at 100°C (212°F)) to realise this.

Moist-heat methods

The methods of cooking that are usually grouped under this heading are those where a large quantity of water is present, either on its own or as a major constituent of some other liquid such as milk, stock, or wine. In these cases the temperature at which cooking takes place does not exceed the boiling point of water.

An additional point is that the final dish may make use of the liquid in which the food has been cooked, as in stewing, poaching, and braising, for example.

Dry-heat methods

With dry-heat methods, no additional watery (aqueous) liquid is present. This is not to say that the recipe may not include water or milk, but water is not used to transfer the heat, that is to 'cook' the food. Since there is not much water present, the temperature can go up considerably, and cooking takes place at much higher temperatures than with moist-heat methods.

It is possible to classify methods of cooking as either moist-heat or dry-heat, although there are some occasions where a mixture of cookery methods is used: for example fish en papillote (cooked in an envelope of greased grease-proof paper in an oven) involves a combination of several methods.

This next twelve chapters consider the following cooking methods, which can be classified as shown:

Moist heat	Dry heat
Boiling	Deep frying
Poaching	Shallow frying
Stewing	Baking
Braising	Grilling
Steaming	Sauté
	Roasting
	Poêlé cooking

Batch cookery

Batch cooking, which we shall discuss in more detail in chapter 42, is not so much a method of cooking as a system. It has been developed because of the need, in certain circumstances, to produce a high output of some dishes over an extended service period and to reduce the bulk cooking that would otherwise be necessary. As will be seen later on, bulk cooking of some items, especially vegetables, can lead to the products being less acceptable. Batch cooking will ensure a ready supply of the required commodities at any time, and there is now a range of equipment especially designed to meet this requirement.

Production systems

Although this part of the book concerns itself with cookery *methods*, we shall be looking at some of the important centralised cookery production systems such as cook–chill and cook–freeze and their advantages and applications (chapter 44), and at sous-vide cooking (chapter 43).

27.2 Basic preparatory tasks

Before any of the cooking methods can be started, some basic preparation will need to be done. This will involve preparing not only the commodities and the equipment but also yourself. If you are properly dressed for the operation you are going to perform and in the correct frame of mind, you will find that the tasks present less difficulty. In addition, of course, the hygiene and safety factors will, to some extent, be taken care of automatically.

The menu will form the basis of your cookery operations. From this you will be able to organise the commodities required, the methods of cooking to be used, and the equipment needed. The menu will also enable you to plan the sequence of the tasks that you are going to carry out. This can also lead to a more efficient use of time, energy used by cooking equipment, and commodities – all of which can help to keep the costs down (and the profits up !).

You will use the menu, as well as the selling price and the style of operation in which you are working, to discover what commodities are going to be needed (whether fresh or convenience foods will be used) and to see what preparatory work needs to be done on the commodities (does the fish need filleting, or have the potatoes got to be cut into special shapes?). You may see that food needs marinading or that some basic stock needs to be prepared. Having got as much information as you can from the menu, you can then set about organising your commodities, your equipment, and yourself.

192 Food preparation and cooking

By making sure that your equipment is clean, safe, and in good working order, that the commodities are the most suitable for the dish you are going to prepare, and that your hygiene standards are of the highest order (don't lick your finger and dip it in the custard to see if you remembered to put sugar in it), you will produce food that customers will want to eat as well as giving yourself greater job satisfaction.

27.3 Basic procedures and equipment

Although this is not a practical cookery book, Table 27.1 lists some of the common procedures and equipment used in preparing food. (See also chapter 46.)

Table 27.1 Basic procedures and equipment

Technique	Equipment	Function
Peeling	7.5cm (3 inch) cooks' knife Vegetable peeler	To remove outer skin or layer from fruit and vegetables.
Whipping	Whisks of various shapes and sizes	To incorporate air into a food to increase the volume and sometimes to thicken it.
Slicing	Large cooks' knife	To cut raw or cooked food items into uniformly thin pieces or portions.
Dicing	Large cooks' knife	To cut raw or cooked food items into even-sized dice. The dice can be small or large.
Shredding	Large cooks' knife	To cut food items into long thin slivers.
Mincing	Electric or hand mincer	To reduce food items into small particles. Tough meat can be made more tender by cutting the connective tissue and muscle fibres.
Crushing or grinding	Large cooks' knife Pestle and mortar	To reduce dry food products to a powder or to rupture the cell walls of fruit and vegetables.
Stirring and mixing	Wooden spoon Spatula Electric mixer	To blend or mix ingredients – liquid, solid, or both.
Straining	Chinois Strainer	To strain out lumps and large pieces from a liquid.
Filleting	15 cm (6 inch) fish filleting knife	To remove the flesh from either flat or round fish and produce fillets.
Puréeing	Electric blender Food processor Cooks' sieve	To convert food to a smooth pulp or paste-like consistency.
Blending	Electric blender Food processor Hand whisk	To mix together a number of ingredients to produce a single identity and flavour.
Spreading	Palette knife Flexible scraper	To spread a soft food product over the surface of another food.

28 Boiling

28.1 General principles

Boiling is the cooking of food items in an aqueous liquid at boiling point. An aqueous liquid is a liquid with a high water content, such as water itself, stock, milk, aromatic cooking liquors, or a blanc (see page 196). Depending on its type, the food item may be placed in cold liquid or boiling liquid before being brought (back) to the boil.

The commodities being boiled must be covered in the aqueous liquid for the whole of the cooking period and be kept boiling. This does not mean that it is necessary to keep the liquid boiling rapidly all the time that cooking is proceeding: even when the liquid is just simmering, it is still at boiling point. The advantages of simmering are that less evaporation of the water will take place and that less damage will be done to the structure of the food by the movement of the water.

Since the boiling point of water is lower than the temperature of some other cooking methods, such as roasting, frying, grilling, or baking, food that has been boiled will in many cases differ from food cooked by these other methods. Some of the effects of boiling are as follows:

- The food may be more tender and digestible. The fibre that makes up the structure of vegetables is softened. It is not broken down, but the fibres are not so well 'stuck together' and the food becomes soft. Overcooking of vegetables can result in them becoming mushy; on the other hand, no amount of boiling will make really stringy beans acceptable.
- The starch becomes gelatinised (see page 157). This makes it more digestible, as the starch granules are broken down. In foods with a high starch content, such as rice or pasta, the food absorbs a considerable amount of water and swells up.
- Some of the protein in the food will be denatured at the boiling temperature (see page 158) and will coagulate and turn solid, for example egg-white. This makes it more acceptable to most people as well as making it easier to digest, as it stays in the stomach for a longer time. The effect of long slow boiling on the collagen connective tissue in meat – especially the older, tougher cuts – is to convert it to gelatin (see page 154). Gelatin is soluble in water so, in addition to the meat becoming more tender, the cooking liquor may be capable of forming a jelly when cold.

In addition to these effects, boiling may alter the colour and the flavour, especially if the cooking liquid contains salt, sugar, or aromatic flavourings. These may all make the food more palatable.

Boiling food may also make it safer to eat. Bacteria are destroyed at temperatures below boiling point if they are in their vegetative form (see page 172), but many bacterial spores and bacterial toxins are destroyed only by boiling for quite long periods of time. For example, if you reheat a casserole, by bringing it to the boil you may kill the food-poisoning bacteria, but to destroy the spores and the toxins that could also cause food poisoning you will need to boil it for a longer time.

The heat is transferred to the food by convection when it is boiled (see page 162); however, if the food being cooked is solid, the heat is transferred within the food by conduction (see page 162), which takes quite a long time as the solid components of food are not good conductors of heat. A medium-sized potato, for example, will reach an internal temperature of only about 80° C (176° F) after a half-an-hour's boiling. This is why it is so important to boil large joints for long enough for the internal temperature to become sufficiently high to kill any bacteria. If large joints are to be boiled, it may be better to divide the joint into smaller portions.

Boiling can have an effect on the nutritional value of food. Since a large volume of water is present, it follows that any substance in the food that is soluble in water is likely to be dissolved out into the cooking liquid. The most significant nutrient lost in this way is vitamin C, which is very soluble in water. Some of the other water-soluble vitamins and minerals are also removed from the food, but this is less important from a nutritional point of view of as there are other sources in our diet, whereas most of our vitamin C is gained from fruit and vegetables, many of which are normally boiled before being eaten.

Some foods may gain nutrients by boiling: fruits may increase their sugar content if cooked in a sugar solution, and you can taste the salt (sodium chloride, see page 144) in many foods that have had salt added to the water in which they are boiled. Foods boiled in very hard water, which contains dissolved calcium compounds, may have an increased calcium content (see page 143).

28.2 Boiling vegetables

Nearly all vegetables can be cooked by boiling. Vegetables where we eat the part that grows above the ground – sometimes referred to as 'green' vegetables – are often treated differently from those whose edible part grows below the ground – 'root' vegetables. In all cases, overcooking can cause the texture to become unacceptable – most people like their vegetables to have 'bite' rather than be soggy.

When some vegetables are boiled (swedes, for example) a scum rises to the surface as cooking proceeds. This needs to be removed before the items have finished cooking, especially if the vegetables are to be puréed.

Green vegetables (see page 97)

These are always placed into boiling salted water and are quickly brought back to the boil with the lid on. Boiling is then continued fairly rapidly with the lid off until the vegetables are just cooked. (Removing the lid helps preserve the colour.) If they are not to be served immediately, they are best refreshed under cold running water until completely cold, then drained and refrigerated in trays. They can then be reheated before service (see page 196). All types of cabbage, kale, and sprouting broccoli are best served immediately after cooking instead of being refreshed. If the vegetables are required over a long service period, batch cooking is a more appropriate method (see chapter 42).

When large amounts of green vegetables have to be boiled, these are best added in smallish portions and the salted water brought back to the boil before the next batch is added. Delicate structures such as asparagus, broccoli, and cauliflower need to be boiled very gently, otherwise the movement of rapidly boiling water will damage them.

The advantages of cooking in water that is already boiling are that the enzymes in the vegetable that would otherwise destroy the vitamin C are immediately inactivated and that the colour is improved.

Adding bicarbonate of soda (cooking soda) may improve the colour, but it has the effect of destroying the vitamin C as well as breaking up the plant structure, making the cooked vegetable 'mushy'.

Sometimes vegetables are placed into boiling water for a short time to *blanch* them before other processes. This inactivates the enzymes near the surface that could affect the colour and the flavour.

Root vegetables

With the exception of new potatoes, which are treated like green vegetables, root vegetables are normally cooked by being placed into cold salted water and brought to the boil. Unlike green vegetables, root vegetables are not usually refreshed but are drained when cooked and are allowed to dry by their own heat immediately before service. If they are not required for use straightaway, they can be cooled and refrigerated for future use.

The advantages of cooking vegetables by this method are that the longer cooking period may help to improve the texture and that there is less likelihood of personal injury through placing large quantities of vegetables into rapidly boiling water. A disadvantage is that the enzymes that affect the vitamin C will not be destroyed until a fairly high temperature is reached. In fact, while the temperature of the water is increasing from cold, the enzymes will become more active for a while, thus encouraging more loss of vitamin C.

Puréed vegetables

Root vegetables that are to be puréed are boiled until tender and then drained in a colander. They are then returned to the saucepan in which they were cooked and carefully dried out over a low heat until all the excess moisture has been evaporated. The vegetables are then processed in a food processor or rubbed through a sieve.

Potatoes, swedes, and carrots are often puréed. When spinach is puréed, it is drained and refreshed before having the excess moisture physically squeezed out.

Glazed vegetables

Carrots and turnips are sometimes cooked in this way. The vegetable is placed in a pan with a small amount of water, some sugar, and some butter. A cartouche (a circle of greaseproof paper) is placed over the surface of the contents and the water is brought to the boil. After a few minutes boiling, the cartouche is removed and much of the water is allowed to evaporate. The butter and the sugar (plus a small amount of water that remains) form a glaze in which the vegetables are gently turned.

These vegetables may appear on the menu as follows:

Carottes glacées (glazed carrots)
Navets glacés (glazed turnips)

Reheating vegetables

Reheating commonly applies to green vegetables such as beans, peas, and (less satisfactorily) broccoli. They can be placed in a suitable serving dish, seasoned as necessary with salt and milled pepper, sprinkled with melted butter, and covered with a clear film before being reheated in a microwave oven for a short time. Alternatively, they can be put into a wire basket and carefully lowered into a pan of gently boiling water. If you use this method, you will need to drain them thoroughly before placing them on to the service dish.

If the vegetables are to be served 'au beurre', they will be sprinkled or brushed with melted butter, or tossed in a sauteuse with butter.

Cooking vegetables in a blanc

A blanc is made by mixing 60 grams (2 oz) of flour in 4.5 litres (1 gallon) of cold water to which has been added the juice of one lemon and some salt.

The blanc helps to prevent the discoloration which occurs with some vegetables and is used for globe and Jerusalem artichokes, salsify, and cardoons.

Cooking frozen vegetables

The manufacturer's instructions should be followed when cooking frozen vegetables. This usually involves cooking the vegetables straight from the freezer in boiling salted water. Green vegetables not required for immediate use should be refreshed as for fresh green vegetables (see above).

Vegetables suitable for boiling

- *Tubers* Old and new potatoes, Jerusalem artichokes, sweet potatoes.
- *Flower heads* Asparagus, broccoli, cauliflower, sprouting broccoli, globe artichokes.
- *Legumes* Peas, broad beans, French beans, runner beans.
- *Leafy green* Cabbage, spinach, Swiss chard, leaf beet, spring greens, brussel sprouts, kale.
- *Roots* Carrots, swede, turnips, salsify, parsnips, kohlrabi, beetroot.
- *Bulbs* Onions.
- *Stems* Leeks.

28.3 Boiling fish

Because of its rather delicate structure, which could be damaged by the movement of the liquid as it is boiling, fish is usually cooked at

28.4 Boiling meats and poultry

temperatures just below boiling point. This is called 'poaching' (see chapter 29).

Boiling is suitable for the older, tougher, and coarser cuts or joints of meat. The process will make them more tender (see page 193) as well as producing a stock that can be served with the meat.

If you are using salted meat, you must soak it in cold water to remove the excess salt before you put it on to boil. This may take 2 to 3 hours for a small joint or overnight for a large joint.

Fresh meats are usually placed in boiling salted water, but salted meats are put into cold water and brought to the boil. This gives an additional chance for surplus salt to be dissolved out of the meat. As with vegetables, once boiling has been reached the heat can be turned down to keep the liquid simmering. Any scum that rises to the surface should be skimmed off.

The effect of boiling on the meat will be to alter the colour, the flavour, and the texture. Because no coating is formed as in some other cooking methods, some of the water-soluble juices of the meat pass into the cooking liquor, adding to its flavour. At boiling point, some of the fat in the meat will melt and rise to the surface of the cooking liquid. This will need to be removed.

All boiled meats need to be cooked thoroughly (read page 194 about the dangers of food poisoning from undercooked large joints of boiled meat). Table 28.1 gives typical cooking times.

Table 28.1 Typical boiling times for meats and poultry

Joint/cut	Approximate cooking times
Silverside of beef	25 min per 500 g (1 lb) and 25 min over
Thin flank/brisket	30 min per 500 g (1 lb) and 30 min over
Ox tongue	3½ hours
Lamb's tongue	1½ hours
Gammon	25 min per 500 g (1 lb) and 25 min over
Bacon joint	25 min per 500 g (1 lb) and 25 min over
Chicken – large	15 min per 500 g (1 lb) and 15 min over
Boiling fowl	2½ to 3 hours
Pork – leg	25 min per 500 g (1 lb) and 25 min over

28.5 Boiling eggs

Eggs should be carefully lowered into gently boiling water and allowed to return to the boil. Since the protein in both the egg-white and the yolk will be eventually coagulated by the boiling (see page 158), the cooking time will depend on the texture that is required. The following cooking times are for general guidance, but will vary with the size of the egg and whether or not it has come straight out of the fridge:

- Soft-boiled breakfast eggs   3–5 min
- Eggs mollet, for serving hot at lunch with a garnish   6–7 min
- Hard-boiled eggs   10–12 min

28.6 Boiling rice

Rice is added to boiling salted water and brought back to the boil. The amount of water and the cooking time will depend on the type of rice. Rice contains a lot of starch granules, and a fair amount of water will be absorbed by these as the starch is gelatinised (see page 157). As the rice grains cook, so they will swell up. Some manufacturers make recommendations about the amount of water to be used and how long the rice should be cooked for. It is only sensible that you follow these instructions if they are given.

Rice not required for immediate use can be refreshed thoroughly to remove the surface starch that has gelatinised and become sticky, drained well, stored until required, and then reheated. Boiled rice can be reheated in a microwave oven, a hot-water bath, a steamer, or covered and heated in an oven.

28.7 Boiling pulses

All pulses can be cooked by boiling. The material should be washed well in cold water before cooking. Most pulses are soaked in cold water before boiling in fresh water. The cooking time will depend on the type of pulse that is being cooked. Red kidney beans must be boiled rapidly for at least 10 minutes.

28.8 Boiling pasta

Both fresh and dried pasta are cooked by being placed into gently boiling salted water to which has been added a small amount of oil. The oil stops the pieces of pasta from sticking to each other as they would otherwise do because of the gelatinised starch on the surface (see page 157). Fresh pasta cooks more quickly than dried pasta, but both of them are cooked until they are tender but still have 'bite' (*al dente*).

If not required for immediate use, pasta products are refreshed in cold water and either drained, lightly oiled, and stored or stored in cold water until required for reheating.

28.9 Some points to be observed when boiling

- Choose a container appropriate to the size of the material you are boiling. Do not use more water than is necessary to cover the item(s). Top up with additional water if necessary.
- Be careful when moving large containers of boiling liquids on a stove top and when items are put into or removed from boiling liquids.
- Cook green vegetables by placing them in boiling salted water.
- Do not put too many green vegetables into a small saucepan, as this will increase the cooking time and spoil the colour.
- Do not leave the lid on when cooking green vegetables, as this spoils the colour.
- Unless green vegetables are to be served straightaway, always refresh them in cold running water, drain them, and store them in a refrigerator.
- Always drain all vegetables thoroughly before service.
- Do not refresh root vegetables or potatoes.
- Remove any scum that rises to the surface when boiling meat or vegetables.
- Vegetables should never be overcooked or soggy: they should be firm but tender.
- Place fresh meats into boiling water. This helps to retain the flavour.
- To test if meats are cooked, pierce the thickest part with a larding

needle. The juices that run out should be clear and should run freely.
- Salted meats should be soaked in cold water to leach out excess salt before boiling.
- Adding aromatic vegetables or herbs during boiling will improve the flavour.
- To retain more vitamin C, new potatoes are started in boiling salted water.
- Do not add bicarbonate of soda to retain the colour when cooking green vegetables.
- To maintain a regular supply of vegetables for service, cook in small batches rather than one large one.

28.10 Equipment used for boiling

In addition to a selection of saucepans and lids, boiling pans, tilting kettles, boiling tables, Bratt pans (see section 30.4), and induction hobs (see section 25.5) are used.

Boiling pans

Boiling pans are of two types: single-purpose and dual-purpose. They may be heated by either gas or electricity.

- Single-purpose pans are best suited to heating water for cooking vegetables etc. Where vegetable baskets or containers are used, these should be placed on the strainer plate fitted in the bottom of the pan.
- Dual-purpose pans have a lift-out inner pan in which the food to be cooked is placed. The inner pan is fitted and clamped into an outer pan or jacket containing heated water and so is heated indirectly – this reduces the risk of burning or sticking when cooking thick soups, milk dishes, etc.

The boiling pan shown in fig. 28.1 has a lift-off cover that can be stored in the rack at the rear of the hob when not in use. A swivel tap is fitted for filling the pan with cold water. (Dual-purpose pans also have a filler pot on the hob for filling the jacket space with water.)

Fig. 28.1 A boiling pan

Using the boiling pan

- Do not heat the pan when it is empty.
- Do not overfill the pan.
- As a general guide, a boiling pan will take about one hour to reach boiling from cold when filled to capacity with water.
- Always switch off the electricity or turn off the gas before emptying the contents of the boiling pan.
- The contents of the pan should not be drained immediately after switching off – wait until boiling stops.
- When removing the cover from a hot pan with a lift-off lid, grasp the centre handle and raise the rear edge first – this will allow steam to be directed away from you. Lift the cover to a vertical position to allow condensation to drip back into the pan, then store the cover in its rack. Ladle out cooked food from the inner pan.

Cleaning

Regular cleaning is of course essential with an appliance of this type, and boiling pans are designed with emphasis on ease of cleaning – dirt-retaining crevices being eliminated and smooth, curved surfaces being used wherever possible.

- Before cleaning an electrically heated pan, *switch off at the mains switch*.
- After draining the pan, wash the interior with warm water and detergent, afterwards thoroughly rinsing out. Avoid the use of harsh scouring powders, nylon scrubbers, etc. which may scratch the stainless-steel surface.
- *Do not wash down the front of an electrical appliance*, as water may enter the electrical control compartment – if cleaning is necessary, use a dry or slightly damp cloth.

Tilting kettles

These consist of a pan heated by a jacket fed with steam from a gas- or electric-powered boiler in the base of the pan unit. A swivel tap is fitted for filling both the pan and the boiler. An overheat cut-off operates when there is insufficient water in the boiler and when the pan is tilted to remove its contents.

The unit shown in fig. 28.2 is tilted by means of a handwheel and has a cover hinged to one of the support pedestals. Smaller table-top units are tilted by means of a simple lever and have a fully removable lid.

Boiling tables

There are two types of boiling table:

- the open-top type, with a number of separate gas rings or heating elements (fig. 28.3(a));
- the solid-top type, which has a single large cooking area with different parts of it being at different temperatures (fig. 28.3(b)).

Fig. 28.2 A tilting kettle

To save energy, it is recommended that the solid top should not be left unused with the gas or electricity on the 'full' setting. If it is necessary to keep the top hot for any length of time, the control should be turned down to the 'low' setting.

Fig. 28.3 Boiling tables. *Left* Open top. *Right* Solid top

29 Poaching

29.1 General principles

Poaching is the gentle cooking of prepared items of food – usually small items – by covering or partially covering them with an aqueous liquid that is kept at a temperature just below boiling point.

The effects of poaching on food are almost identical to those produced by boiling (see section 28.1). In poaching, however, the liquid must *not* be allowed to boil. The movement of the liquid when it boils causes the food to move. If food of a fragile nature is boiled, then there is a danger of it breaking up. Since poaching is carried out at temperatures of between 92 and 96° C (205–208° F), the cooked product will have the characteristics of moist-heat cooking rather than dry-heat cooking (see section 27.1).

Poaching is suitable for a wide range of commodities that are naturally tender and do not need much cooking. The poaching liquid can be used as the basis for a finished sauce. If this is to be the case, you should use just sufficient liquid in the smallest container that will conveniently hold the food. If you use a large pan you will need more liquid, and this will take longer to reduce if you use it to flavour the sauce. Poaching is best done in shallow trays or pans. The liquid must never be allowed to boil, as it may well break up the food. Even when poaching eggs, the acidified water will break up the egg-white if allowed to boil and will distort the shape of the egg.

The liquid that you use for poaching depends on what you are cooking. Possible liquids include stock syrup, court-bouillon, chicken or fish stock, acidified water, and milk, all of which may have had various flavourings added to them. Some of these will be described later on in this chapter.

Whole fish and meat cooked by this method are referred to as being deep-poached (see page 203). In this case the fish is poached in a larger volume of liquid in a deep-sided container such as a fish-kettle. It is important that the liquid is not allowed to boil.

Food items to be poached can be placed either into liquid that is already at the cooking temperature or into cold liquid and then brought to the cooking temperature. This is usually done quickly.

Cooking in a bain-marie (a hot-water bath) is sometimes referred to as poaching. This style of cooking is used to moisten the dry heat of the oven when cooking sweet and savoury custards, creams, pâtés, etc. in moulds. When cooking with a bain-marie, several thicknesses of paper should be placed into the bottom of a tray and the filled moulds placed on top. Paper, being a good insulator, will stop the custards and creams from boiling. To make sure that cooking starts immediately it is placed into the oven, the bain-marie should be filled with hot water.

29.2 Poaching fish

Fish contains much less connective tissue than meat, most of which is collagen and very little if any elastin (see page 159). Since collagen is converted to soluble gelatin by moist heat, fish that has been poached is tender with flakes that are easily separated.

Shallow poaching

This method is used for small cuts of fish prepared from fish with a close texture (see pages 69–72). Fish with a more open texture with large flakes, such as whiting and cod, are not really suitable for poaching. The cooking liquid is always used to flavour the finished sauce and usually consists of white wine, fish stock, and a little lemon juice. The cooking process is carried out in a shallow tray or pan that is started on top of the stove and continued in the oven under a lid or a cartouche.

The pan or tray that you have chosen should be buttered, seasoned with salt and white pepper, and sprinkled with finely chopped shallots. The prepared fish is folded (if required – presentation side out), arranged neatly on the shallots, and partly covered with the poaching liquid. The pan is brought to poaching temperature on top of the stove. The pan is then covered and placed into a moderate oven for the cooking to be completed. Once cooked, the fish is removed and drained on a clean dry cloth. The poaching liquid is reduced to one-third and added to the accompanying sauce. Cream and butter can be added to improve the quality.

If the finished dish is to be glazed under a salamander, a glazing agent such as sabayon, hollandaise sauce, or lightly whipped cream is needed.

Some garnishes, for example tomates concassées and mushrooms, can be poached with the fish: others such as fleurons (cooked puff-pastry crescents) need separate cooking and are placed on to the dish when it is served.

Deep poaching

This method is used for poaching whole salmon, turbot, and salmon trout; darnes of salmon; tronçons of turbot; lobsters, crabs, and crayfish; etc. The fish are completely covered with the cooking liquid, which could be salted water, court-bouillon (see below), or a mixture of milk and water with a dash of lemon juice.

Oily fish are best poached in a court-bouillon:

4 litres (7 pints)	Water
0.5 litre (⅞ pint)	Vinegar
0.5 kg (1 lb)	Aromatic vegetables (onion, carrot, celery, leek)
	Bouquet garni
	Salt

White fish, with a more delicate flavour, are best poached in salted water. Tronçons of turbot can be deep-poached in milk and salted water. The flesh of fish cooked in a court-bouillon is firmer than fish cooked in salted water. Whole fish is best cooked in a fish-kettle of suitable size and shape.

If the poached fish is to be displayed whole on a cold buffet table, it should be placed into *cold* cooking liquid and then slowly brought to the poaching temperature. This prevents the skin and flesh from contracting suddenly, which might make the fish split and look less than perfect.

Cuts of fish (darnes and tronçons) are placed into *hot* cooking liquid so that the surface protein is immediately coagulated (see page 158). This prevents the protein from the inside seeping out and coagulating in dribs and drabs, giving it a cotton-wool appearance.

If the fish is required cold, it can be left to cool in the cooking liquid. Cuts of fish and small whole fish served hot can be placed on the warmed serving dish and moistened with some of the cooking liquid.

Live shellfish must always be placed into rapidly boiling liquid to kill them instantly before reducing the heat to poaching temperature for the rest of the cooking time.

Table 29.1 lists suitable cooking liquids for deep poaching fish.

Table 29.1 Suitable cooking liquids for deep poaching fish

Fish	Cooking liquid
Lobster	Court-bouillon
Crayfish	Court-bouillon
Crawfish	Court-bouillon
Crabs	Salted water
Prawns and shrimps	Salted water
Salmon (whole or darnes)	Court-bouillon
Trout	Court-bouillon
Salmon trout	Court-bouillon
Mackerel	Salted water or court-bouillon
Turbot (whole)	Salted water
Turbot (tronçons)	Milk and salted water or salted water
Brill (whole)	Salted water
Brill (darnes)	Milk and salted water or salted water
Cod (darnes)	Salted water
Smoked haddock	Seasoned milk or milk and salted water
Fresh haddock	Salted water

29.3 Poaching meats

There are a few meats that are sometimes poached. These are chicken (whole or suprêmes), fillet of beef, and loin of lamb. The meat is deep-poached in white stock or salted water. It is placed into the hot cooking liquid and brought back to poaching temperature until it is cooked. When cooked, the meat is drained and the cooking liquid may be used as it is or reduced to make the sauce.

29.4 Poaching fruit

Most fruits can be poached in stock syrup (a mixture of lightly boiled sugar and water) and served chilled as a compote. The fruit is cooked by covering with hot stock syrup and heating until the syrup is nearly boiling. The fruit is then allowed to poach gently off the heat until it is soft. Fruits that have a tendency to float must be held under the surface by a clean plate. Soft fruit only needs to be covered with the hot syrup off the heat and allowed to cool.

Poached fruit can also be used for flans, coupes, condés, etc.

Pears, apples, rhubarb, apricots, peaches, gooseberries, raspberries, plums, and red and black currants are all suitable for poaching.

29.5 Poaching eggs

Only fresh eggs should be used for poaching – stale eggs do not retain their shape well when poached.

The eggs should be broken into a container and then gently transferred to salted water at a temperature slightly higher than that normally used for poaching. If you add a little acid such as vinegar, this will help retain the shape, especially if the eggs are not absolutely fresh. (The acid causes the protein to coagulate more quickly.) Poaching is continued for 3 or 4 minutes. The eggs are then removed from the water with a slotted or a perforated spoon and drained well before use. Poached eggs intended for use later on should be refreshed in iced water. They can be reheated in hot water.

29.6 Some points to be observed when poaching

- The cooking liquid must never be allowed to boil – poaching should be done at a temperature of 92–96° C (205–208° F).
- Shallow pans or trays are best for poaching: they allow the food items to be arranged in single layers.
- Eggs are poached at a higher temperature than other items.
- Where the poaching liquid is used to improve the flavour of the finished sauce, the cooking liquid must be kept to a minimum.
- Poached items that are served with a sauce should be well drained before dressing, to prevent the formation of a water line at the edge of the serving dish.
- A little of the finished sauce placed into the warmed service dish before the food item is placed in it will prevent the food from sticking to the dish.
  (These last two points are particularly important for poached fish.)
- When folding a fish fillet, make sure that the presentation side is facing outwards. (The non-presentation side is the side from which the skin has been removed.)
- Except in the case of some fish where the cooking liquor is to be used as part of the sauce, the item being poached must be completely covered by the cooking liquid.
- Whole fish for a cold buffet must be started in a cold liquid and then brought to the cooking temperature, to prevent the fish from splitting.
- Very large or tough food items are not suitable for poaching.

29.7 Equipment used for poaching

Equipment for poaching, such as shallow pans and trays and fish-kettles, is discussed in chapter 46. Bratt pans (see section 30.4) can also be used.

30 Stewing

30.1 General principles

Stewing is the slow cooking of small pieces of food – usually meat, poultry, or game – in a minimum amount of aqueous liquid with suitable flavourings under a cover. The cooking liquid forms part of the finished dish.

The changes that take place are similar to those resulting from other moist-heat cooking methods such as boiling (see chapter 28). Stewing is particularly useful for the tougher cuts of meat, as the long slow cooking converts the tough collagen connective tissue into soluble gelatin (see page 159). The slow cooking also helps to develop the flavour. Since the cooking liquid is also part of the dish, any nutrients that dissolve out of the meat will be eaten rather than being thrown away.

Unlike braising (see chapter 31), the meat is not usually marinaded before cooking. (An exception to this is a traditional French daube.) The meat is cut into small pieces and seared before stewing. Meats for a white stew are sometimes 'set up' in oil or clarified butter – gently heated to stiffen the surface, but without colouring them – whereas those items for a brown stew are coloured by frying rapidly in hot oil or dripping. Once the meat has been seared it is placed in a suitable container with the liquid, vegetables, and flavourings and brought quickly to the boil on top of the stove. Cooking can then be continued under a cover in the oven until the meat is tender. Only sufficient liquid should be used to just cover the ingredients – if you use too much liquid, the flavour will be diluted.

The cooking liquids for stewing meats are normally based on a white or brown stock. Sometimes the stock is thickened into a sauce before it is added to the meat. In some cases the thickening is due to the flour used for *singeing* the meat (coating with flour which is then browned in a hot oven) at the beginning. Sometimes the stock is unthickened.

For service, the meat is presented with the accompanying cooking liquid and a suitable garnish. This liquid may be refined by passing through a chinois or be served as it is.

Joints of meat suitable for stewing

- *Beef* Thick flank, topside, thin flank, brisket, shin, chuck rib, clod.
- *Veal* Knuckle, thick flank, neck end, shoulder, breast.
- *Lamb* Middle neck, shoulder, breast.
- *Poultry* 1.5 kg (3½ lb) broiler, for curry or fricassée.
- *Game* Mature game birds and cuts of venison, hare, and wild rabbit.

30.2 Types of stew

Coloured stews

- *Ragoût* Brown, well-flavoured; made from beef, veal, lamb, and game.
- *Navarin* Reddish-brown, well-flavoured; made from lamb, with a definite flavour of tomatoes.
- *Goulash* Reddish-brown; made from veal or beef, flavoured with paprika and tomato.
- *Carbonnade* Brown; portion-size slices of beef cooked in beer and stock with onions.
- *Jugged hare* Brown, made from jointed hare. The blood is used to thicken the sauce.

White stews

- *Irish stew* Made from lamb and sliced white vegetables.
- *Hotpot* Slices of lamb, with layers of potatoes and onions.
- *Fricassée* ⎫ Thick white stews, made from lamb, veal, or chicken with
- *Blanquette* ⎭ a velouté sauce.

30.3 Some points to be observed when stewing

- Second-quality joints or cuts can be used – these have a more pronounced flavour, and the cooking process makes the meat tender.
- Cut the meat into even-sized pieces to allow even cooking.
- Remove all excess fat from the meat. Fat left on the meat will render during the cooking process and make the finished product greasy.
- Season the meat before searing.
- Searing the meat improves the flavour.
- Do not brown the meat for a white stew.
- The main colour for a brown stew is from the meat and vegetables that have been browned when searing.
- Do not use more stock than is necessary to cook the meat.
- Do not allow the stew to boil rapidly, as this may harden the meat.
- Always cover the stew while it is cooking, to stop the cooking liquid from evaporating.
- Serve the meat and the cooking liquid together.

30.4 Equipment used for stewing

Small items for stewing such as casseroles and stewing pans are considered in chapter 46.

A Bratt pan can be used for stewing.

Bratt pans

Bratt pans are large, shallow, heated pans that can be tilted by means of a handwheel (fig. 30.1) or, in some models, a push-button or foot-pedal. The pan itself may be made of stainless steel or of cast iron, which gives more even temperatures and has good heat-retaining properties. Cold water should *never* be poured directly into a hot cast-iron pan, as this could cause the casting to crack. The exterior of the appliance is usually stainless steel.

Bratt pans may be heated by either gas or electricity. As well as

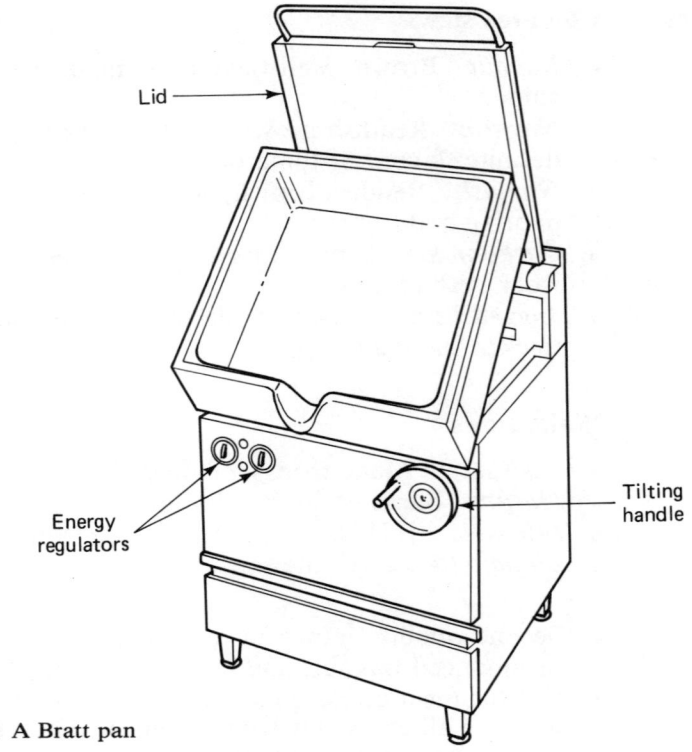

Fig. 30.1 A Bratt pan

thermostat and simmerstat controls, a tilt-switch is fitted that cuts off the energy supply if the pan is moved even slightly from the fully lowered position.

Cooking uses

A Bratt pan can be used for a wide variety of cooking processes, though care must be taken not to overfill it:

- Medium frying – oil depth 40–50 mm (1½–2 inches).
- Shallow frying – oil depth 6 mm (¼ inch) and less.
- Boiling, poaching, stewing, braising – liquid depth not more than 75 mm (3 inches).

Cleaning

- After use at the end of each day, fill the pan with warm water and bring it to the boil. Empty out the water and rinse with clean warm water. Finally, lightly brush cast-iron pans with a good-quality vegetable oil.
- Before cleaning the exterior of the appliance, *turn off the energy supply to the appliance*.
- Clean the exterior of the appliance with soapy water as often as possible. Rinse with clean cold water and dry off. Remove grease with fine steel wool or proprietary cleaning pads, rubbing in the direction of the 'grain' of the stainless steel to retain its finish.

31 Braising

31.1 General principles

Braising is the cooking of prepared commodities, which have been previously seared or blanched, in a covered vessel with an appropriate quantity of liquid or sauce. The commodities are usually larger than for stewing. Some meats are marinaded before cooking. This may sound terribly complicated, but in fact it isn't. You could almost consider it to be a mixture of roasting and stewing.

Meat and vegetables are braised. The effects of braising on the foods are similar to those produced by stewing. Braising is a moist-heat method of cooking and the process will tenderise the connective tissues in meat and the cell structure in vegetables (see page 159). Since the liquid in which the commodities are cooked is usually part of the finished dish, the loss of water-soluble nutrients is not great. The cooking liquid is flavoured, and this will affect the flavour of the braised product.

31.2 Braising meat

Braising, like stewing, tends to be used for the coarser, tougher, and cheaper cuts of meat, poultry, and game. Meats are often marinaded in a 'pickle' before cooking. This not only adds flavour but also begins to tenderise the connective tissue even before cooking takes place. The type of liquid used for pickling will depend on the type of meat being braised. A robust red-wine pickle is suitable for beef or game. If a marinade is used for veal, the wine should be white wine. Meats are usually marinaded for 12–24 hours; red meats need longer than white meats. If the meat is very lean after trimming and removing the excess fat, it can be larded (see page 240) before marinading.

Red meat for braising is usually cooked whole and portioned for service. Once the marinading is finished, the meat is taken from the pickle, carefully dried, and roasted in a hot oven for about 30 minutes to sear it and colour it. It is then put into a deep-sided braising pan with the *aromates* (a mixtures of aromatic vegetables, herbs, and spices), the marinade (reduced to one-third), and sufficient brown stock and demi-glace to half-cover the meat. Cooking is then carried out in a moderate oven with the braising liquid just simmering and the lid on. Towards the end of cooking, the lid can be removed and the meat basted regularly with the braising liquid to glaze the meat.

White meats (except sweetbreads) are improved by being 'set up' and lightly coloured before braising. Sweetbreads are washed and blanched before braising, to keep the colour and flavour of the sauce. The cooking method is very similar to that used for red meats, but the red wine and demi-glace are omitted. The meat is braised in good-quality stock and white wine or reduced marinade. The sauce is made from the lightly reduced braising liquid thickened with arrowroot.

Braised steaks are prepared from second-quality joints, such as thick flank or topside, which are cut into portion-sized slices. These are seared and coloured by frying quickly in hot dripping, placed into a braising pan with the liquid, and cooked slowly in the oven with the lid on. Steaks for braising are not normally marinaded before cooking. Most offal (other than sweetbreads and tongue) is treated similarly.

Meat, offal, poultry, and game suitable for braising

- *Beef* Topside, thick flank, rump, fore rib, middle rib.
- *Veal* Shoulder, saddle, cushion, under-cushion, small whole leg.
- *Offal* Beef – tongue, liver, heart, kidney, oxtail.
  Lamb – tongue, heart, sweetbread.
  Veal – sweetbread.
- *Poultry* Duck, duckling, guinea-fowl, large capon-type chicken.
- *Game* Mature grouse, pheasant, partridge, wild duck, wood pigeon.
- *Venison* Haunch, best end, and shoulder.

31.3 Braising vegetables

Vegetables are usually braised on a bed of sweated aromatic vegetables flavoured with bacon scraps and a bouquet garni. The vegetables are washed, trimmed, blanched in boiling water, and drained before being arranged on the bed of aromates. The vegetables may need to be folded before you arrange them neatly in shallow trays and half-cover them with white beef stock. They are then covered with greased greaseproof paper and cooked in a moderate oven.

For service, the cooked vegetables are removed from the aromates, drained, and accompanied by a suitable sauce. If the braising liquid is not too highly flavoured, it can be reduced and added to the sauce, which is usually a jus-lié (brown veal stock flavoured with tomato and thickened with diluted arrowroot).

Vegetables suitable for braising

- Onions, leeks.
- Chicory, cos lettuce.
- Celery, fennel.
- Peppers stuffed with rice, cooked minced meat, tomatoes, etc.
- Cabbage stuffed with sausage meat, breadcrumbs, etc.

31.4 Some points to be observed when braising

- Braising utilises the tougher cuts of meat, poultry, and game.
- The meat is not usually sliced until cooked and ready for service.
- The braising liquid nearly always forms part of the finished sauce, served with the dish.
- Most meats benefit from marinading before cooking. (Offal is not marinaded before cooking.)
- The meat is seared and coloured before braising, to enrich the sauce.

- Sweetbreads and tongue are washed and blanched before braising: they are not fried and coloured.
- The items being braised should only be partly covered with the liquid.
- The size of the braising pan should be appropriate to the size of the items being braised.
- The container should have a tightly fitting lid, to prevent the braising liquid evaporating and the food drying up.
- Meat that is lean and likely to dry during cooking should be larded with strips of pork fat before marinading and braising.
- Many vegetables are blanched before braising.

31.5 Equipment used for braising

Equipment used for braising includes casseroles, braising pans, and stewpans (see chapter 46). A Bratt pan can also be used (see section 30.4).

32 Steaming

32.1 General principles

Steaming is a method of cooking in which the food is cooked by the heat given out by steam (water vapour) as it condenses. The steam may come into contact either directly with the food or with the container holding the food. If the steam is at normal atmospheric pressure, the temperature will be 100° C (212° F); if the pressure is increased the temperature will go up. The higher the pressure, the greater the increase in temperature.

In addition to the steamers that operate at normal atmospheric pressure and those that operate at a higher pressure, there is a third type which has a convection fan to circulate steam that is at atmospheric (normal) pressure. Unfortunately this is sometimes referred to as a pressureless convection steamer, which is, of course, not true since it operates at atmospheric pressure. The fact that the steam is made to circulate helps to speed up the cooking process.

Although the steam doesn't necessarily come into contact with the food, steaming is usually classified as a moist-heat method of cooking. This is because the temperatures reached, even under high pressure, are still nothing like as hot as those when you fry or roast (see page 190). This means that the changes of colour, texture, and flavour that occur with steaming are much more like those produced when food is boiled or stewed. The effect on the food is similar to that produced by other moist-heat methods, in that the connective tissue in meat and fish is made more tender and the fibrous material in vegetables is softened. Because the food is never immersed in water, the loss of water-soluble nutrients is quite small.

The advantage of using steam at high pressure is that cooking or reheating takes place more quickly. At lower pressures, or at atmospheric pressure, there is less chance of the protein being overcooked or the vegetables becoming soft and difficult to handle.

Steaming has a wide range of applications and is used to cook white fish, tougher cuts of meat or poultry, vegetables, and sweet or savoury puddings.

Steaming is a method of cooking that requires little direct supervision and so is useful in large-scale operations. Care must be taken that high-pressure (or high-compression) steamers are not allowed to overcook the food because of the higher temperatures that are reached.

In the simplest form of steaming, food items are cooked by placing them over a pan of boiling water, either between two plates or in a perforated container with a tight-fitting lid. The more complicated pieces of equipment are described in section 32.6.

Steamers are equipped with both perforated and solid-bottomed trays. Perforated trays are suitable for vegetables, puddings, etc., where the steam is required to come into direct contact with the food or its container without collecting in the bottom of the tray. Meat, poultry, and fish items are best cooked in solid trays that can collect the escaping juices, which you can then serve with the food or use to make the accompanying sauce.

32.2 Steaming sweet and savoury puddings

To keep out the steam, puddings need to be covered with greaseproof paper, which can be pleated down the midde to allow for expansion. If steam is allowed to penetrate the pudding, the sponge or suet paste will become soggy. Specially made steaming sleeves are available for steamed jam roll etc., as well as pudding basins with tightly fitting lids.

32.3 Steaming vegetables

Most kinds of vegetable are suitable for steaming. Batch cooking of vegetables (see chapter 42) using high-pressure steam ovens has become a popular method of supplying the dining-room with a steady supply of freshly cooked vegetables. Potatoes cooked in their skins for sauté potatoes are often cooked by this method.

32.4 Steaming fish and poultry

The prepared pieces of fish or poultry are seasoned and placed in solid-bottomed trays, sprinkled with appropriate flavourings, covered with greaseproof or moisture-proof paper, and steamed until cooked. Fish and poultry cooked by this method are moist and tender, and, of course, the fish doesn't break up.

32.5 Some points to be observed when steaming

- Select the appropriate type and size of tray.
- Cover all puddings with pleated greaseproof paper, foil, or greaseproof paper and a tightly fitting lid.
- Green vegetables quickly lose their colour if overcooked.

32.6 Equipment used for steaming

An atmospheric steamer, a high-pressure steamer, or a convection steamer may be used for steaming. We will discuss the first of these here: the other two will be discussed in chapter 42 on batch cooking.

Atmospheric steamers

An atmospheric steamer (fig. 32.1) consists of a stainless-steel oven compartment with a side-hinged door and a heated water well at the bottom of the compartment, to generate the steam. Water flows into the well from a cistern at the rear of the appliance, the correct level being automatically controlled by a ball valve in the cistern.

A steam vent is fitted at the top of the oven and a drain valve at the bottom. A small drip cock is fitted to drain the condensate that collects in the drip trough on the front panel when the door is opened.

Heating up

The well may be heated by gas or electricity. Check that it is full of water before the oven is turned on. Allow the oven to heat up with the energy supply full on for 20–30 minutes, until steam is escaping from the top vent.

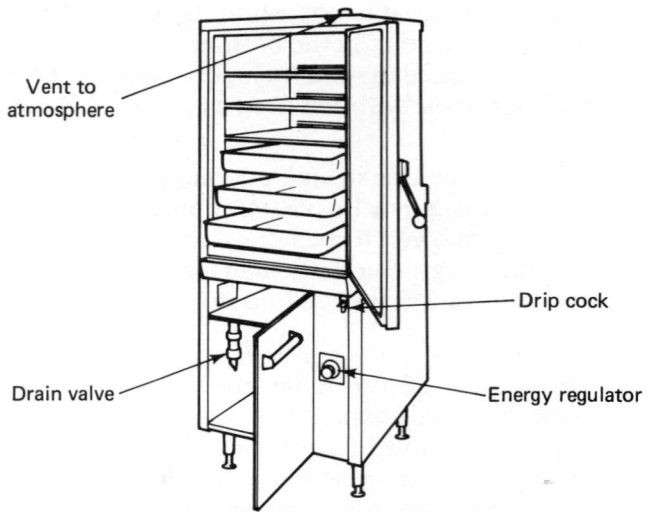

Fig. 32.1 An atmospheric steaming oven

(With gas-heated models, the burners should be lit before the oven door is closed.)

Cooking

- Load with food as required – it is preferable to spread the load over several shelves rather than concentrate it on one shelf. The maximum loading will depend on the capacity of the steamer.
- Close the oven door and turn the energy supply full on.
- When steam is again escaping rapidly from the top vent, turn the energy supply down to maintain cooking without undue waste of steam.

Cleaning

The oven compartment should be cleaned daily, immediately after completion of work, while the unit is still warm.

- Turn off the energy supply (and the pilot light in gas-heated models).
- Turn off the stopcock controlling the water supply to the appliance.
- Open the lower door of the cabinet and drain the oven well and the cistern into a bucket under the drain valve.
- Remove the wire baskets and hangers from the oven compartment and clean the compartment using a suitable detergent. Rinse with a clean cloth and warm water.
- Close the drain valve, turn on the water supply, refill the cistern and well, and drain off again. Dry the interior with a clean cloth.
- Drain and clean out the front-panel trough.

Safety points to be observed when steaming

- Make sure that the door is properly shut after placing items in the steamer.
- Regularly check the water level in the well and the ball-valve efficiency in an atmospheric steamer.

33 Deep frying

33.1 General principles

Deep frying is the cooking of food by immersing it completely in preheated fat or oil. (We shall usually refer just to 'oil' throughout this chapter, but what we say applies to fat too). The method is suitable for many food items, including meat and poultry, fish, vegetables, and fruit and sweet products. Many of these can be deep-fried straight from the frozen state.

Deep frying is a dry-heat process (see section 27.1) and so the cooked items have different characteristics from those cooked by moist-heat methods. The colour, texture, and flavour are different even if no coating is used on the food when it is deep-fried. The nutritional content will be different as well. The cooking process will 'seal in' some of the nutrients, but the food has a higher energy content because of the fat it contains. The deep-frying process also means less loss of water-soluble vitamins, because there is no water for them to dissolve in. Chipped potatoes contain more vitamin C than boiled potatoes.

Conventional deep frying can be of two types. In one type the food is completely cooked in one stage; in the other, the cooking is done in two stages, the first stage of which is called *blanching*.

Foods with a naturally high starch content – such as potatoes and choux pastry – can be fried without a coating, but many items are coated with a protein-containing food such as egg and breadcrumbs or milk and seasoned flour before deep frying. This protein coagulates rapidly at a high temperature to form a protective layer (see page 158).

The advantages of using a coating are

- it prevents searing of the surface of the food,
- it reduces the amount of oil that is absorbed,
- it improves the appearance,
- it provides a pleasant flavour and texture,
- it makes the food less likely to break up when you handle it after cooking.

Table 33.1 describes three common protective coatings. Other coatings may include oatmeal, nibbed or flaked almonds, broken vermicelli, and cornflour.

If the oil is not hot enough to form the coating into a protective layer quickly, some of it will be absorbed, causing the product to be greasy and soggy, and some of the coating may flake off. The lower temperature will also result in a paler colour and lack of flavour because the starch has not dextrinised to any extent and the Maillard reaction has not taken place sufficiently (see page 159).

Table 33.1 Types of protective coating

Type	Contents	Used for
À l'anglaise	Seasoned flour, egg-wash, and breadcrumbs	Fish cakes, croquette potatoes, suprêmes of chicken.
À la française	Milk and seasoned flour	Whitebait, french-fried onion rings.
À l'Orly	Seasoned flour and fermented yeast batter	Cauliflower, fish fillets.

Blanching

Items of food that need a longer cooking period are usually blanched at a lower temperature, to make sure that the centre of the food is cooked before the outside is over-coloured. Chipped potatoes, whole fish (plaice, whiting, and sole), and chicken drumsticks and suprêmes are examples of items that need blanching. The process is as follows:

- Prepare the food and dry it if necessary.
- Lower the food into preheated oil at 165–175° C (329–347° F) until it is cooked through.
- Remove the food and drain it on absorbent kitchen paper.
- Before service, immerse the food in oil at 185° C (365° F) for the final colouring and crisping.

This process is very useful for large-scale catering or where there is a large demand over a short period of time. The blanched items need only a short final cooking time.

Pressure frying

The same principle that we mentioned for pressure steaming (see section 32.1) applies to pressure frying. The oil heated under pressure reaches a higher temperature than it would at atmospheric pressure. As a result of this higher temperature the food cooks more quickly and, because the container is sealed to obtain the increased pressure, fewer fumes and smells escape into the air.

33.2 Suitable frying fats or oils

Any fat or oil used must be free from odour and taste, to avoid tainting the food. It must be capable of being heated to at least 185° C (365° F) without smoking (see page 158). The most commonly used fats and oils are lard and oils derived from plants. Any oil (or fat) you use will deteriorate with repeated use, because the temperature to which you can heat it before it smokes will gradually go down. However, there are a number of steps you can take to make the oil in your friture last longer:

- Do not keep the oil hot for any longer than you have to. Each time you heat the oil, the smoke-point goes down.
- Try to keep the oil away from air as much as possible. Deep-frying equipment should be designed to trap a layer of steam over the hot oil to

keep out the air to some extent. The oil should be kept covered when not in use. Stored oil should be kept in well-filled, closed containers.
- Do not use copper equipment in a deep-fat fryer. Minute traces of copper cause the oil to deteriorate.
- Where possible, dry the food before cooking.
- Always strain the oil at the end of a frying run, to remove food particles. In left, these particles become charred and will cause the oil to darken and deteriorate more quickly. Deep fryers with a cool zone help to prevent this by allowing the residue to sink from the main cooking area.

33.3 Selection of foods for deep frying

Only foods that are tender and small are suitable for deep frying. Large items will not be cooked in the centre before the outside is browned, even if they are blanched. Some small items are *not* suitable for deep frying, however – for example, oily fish (except whitebait) and close-textured vegetables such as carrots. Suitable foods include:

- *Potatoes* Chipped, croquette, dauphin.
- *Vegetables* Onion, courgette, aubergine, cauliflower (par-boiled).
- *Whole fish* Small sole, whiting, plaice, whitebait.
- *Cuts of white fish* Fillets of codling, haddock, sole, or plaice.
- *Poultry* Drumstick, suprêmes.
- *Meats* Kromeskies, Durham cutlets, rissoles.
- *Dessert items* Fruit beignets (fritters), soufflé beignets, doughnuts.

Deep frying frozen foods

Food manufacturers have produced a wide range of foods that can be cooked directly from the frozen-food cabinet. These are very useful for the caterer in controlling wastage, as only those items needed for immediate cooking need be taken from storage. The most important point with cooking these is to read and follow the manufacturer's instructions regarding temperatures and cooking times.

There is a danger of overloading the fryer with frozen material. If you put too many items in at any one time, you are likely to lower the temperature of the oil and prevent satisfactory cooking from taking place.

33.4 Presentation of deep-fried foods

All deep-fried items are prepared and presented for service in a similar manner:

- Remove the frying basket from the hot oil and hang it on the basket rail.
- Carefully lift the cooked item out of the frying basket.
- Drain it on clean absorbent paper.
- Sprinkle lightly with salt or sugar as appropriate.
- Place on to a warmed service platter lined with a dish-paper.
- Serve with the appropriate accompaniments.

Extra care must be taken with draining if the item is to be placed directly on to the customer's plate.

Deep-fried items should not be sprinkled with salt or sugar over the frying basket, as salt or sugar will speed up the deterioration of the oil.

218 *Food preparation and cooking*

33.5 Some points to be observed when deep frying

- Do not overload the fryer.
- Do not place wet items in the hot oil.
- Use a fat or oil with a suitably high smoke-point.
- Choose the most suitable temperature for what you are cooking.
- Do not put too much oil in the fryer – follow the manufacturer's instructions.
- Wait until the oil has reached the required temperature each time before you put the food in. This is particularly important in batch cookery (see chapter 42).
- Blanch food items that need a longer cooking time.
- Lower the foods into the hot oil slowly.
- Remove items carefully from the frying basket.
- Drain cooked items before service.
- Sprinkle savoury items with salt and sweet items with plain or flavoured sugar before serving.
- Drain the fryer after use, having checked that the storage reservoir is empty.
- Switch off the appliance when not in use.

33.6 Equipment used for deep frying

As well as specialised deep-fat fryers, Bratt pans can also be used for medium frying (see section 30.4).

Deep-fat fryers

Deep-fat fryers may be heated by either gas or electricity. In some fryers the oil is heated at a point above the bottom of the pan, so that there is a

Fig. 33.1 A deep-fat fryer

relatively cool zone below the heaters in which sediment can collect without charring.

The fryer shown in fig. 33.1 is fitted with two mesh chip baskets which can be hung from the rail on the back screen for draining etc. A lift-off dust cover is provided to cover the full area of the pan when it is not in use. Some models have a pan strainer in the cool zone in the bottom of the pan to collect sediment during the frying operation.

A thermostat ensures that the frying medium is kept at the temperature selected for the items being cooked.

Frying medium

A good-quality vegetable oil should be used. Solid fats are not recommended for fryers having immersion elements, as they may cause the elements to overheat while heating up.

Using the fryer

- Ensure that the drain valve is closed and fill the fryer with oil to the level marked on the back of the pan.
- Turn on the energy supply, set the thermostat to the desired frying temperature, and leave the oil to heat up. *Never* heat up the fryer unless it is filled with oil or water. Electric fryers and some gas models are fitted with an indicator lamp that shows when the selected temperature has been reached.

Frying chips

Chipped potatoes may be fried by the following methods:

- *Raw to finish* Set the thermostat at 185° C (365° F), load each basket with raw chips, and cook for 8–10 minutes according to the size and the variety of potato.
- *Blanching* This method is used when large quantities of chipped potatoes are required at peak periods. It consists of pre-frying at 180° C (356° F) for 8–10 minutes and finishing off up to 3 hours later at a temperature of 190° C (374° F) for 1–2 minutes. The chips should then be served immediately, avoiding further storage if possible.

Frying fish

Fish or fillets of fish are best fried directly on the base grid – not in the chip baskets. The temperature and time will depend on the type and size of fish. When cooked, remove the fish with the aid of a fish-lifter.

Cleaning

Before any cleaning is undertaken, turn off the energy supply.

- *Daily cleaning* Turn off the energy supply and allow the contents of the pan to cool to a safe temperature. Drain the pan through a strainer and close the drain valve. If the fryer has stainless-steel exterior surfaces, wipe them down with a cloth wrung out in hot water and detergent. Finish with clean water, then wipe dry. Stubborn stains etc. can be removed with a nylon scourer – *do not* use caustic or abrasive cleaners. Refill with oil.

- *Weekly cleaning* Carry out the normal daily cleaning. Remove the false bottom and strainer from the pan (if fitted) and clean them separately. Fill the pan to just above the normal oil-level mark with low-sudsing detergent and hot water and allow to soak – overnight if necessary. Drain off the detergent water and rinse thoroughly with clean water, then wipe dry. Close the drain top. Replace the strainer and false bottom then refill the pan with oil.

34 Shallow frying

34.1 General principles

Shallow frying is the fast cooking of small tender food items in a shallow pan or on a metal griddle plate in a small amount of pre-heated fat or oil, at a temperature of 150–170° C (302–338° F). Foods to be shallow-fried need to be in small pieces, tender, and of good quality. If the suitable food is large, it should be cut into smaller pieces before it is shallow-fried.

Shallow frying is a dry-heat method of cooking (see section 27.1) and the effects on the food will be similar to those produced by other dry-heat methods. The energy content may go up because the food is cooked in fat or oil, but, provided that the items are not overcooked, the amino-acid content will remain the same, even though the protein shrinks. There is likely to be a loss of some B-group vitamins. Shallow frying is unsuitable for coarser cuts of meat, which need a moist-heat method of cooking.

Shallow frying is carried out in thick-based shallow pans or on griddle plates. A deep-sided pan tends to trap the steam and makes turning over the food more difficult. The type of fat or oil used depends on what you are cooking – for example, you shouldn't use beef dripping for cooking fish! A whole range of fats and oils can be used for shallow frying, including dripping, lard, butter, olive oil, soya oil, sunflower oil, peanut oil, and blended vegetable oil. Clarified butter and olive oil are considered the best because they contribute flavour to the finished product, but these are fairly expensive and have a low smoke-point. A blended vegetable oil is suitable for general use.

There are many items that can be shallow-fried and a number of variations in the methods used. Suitable items include fresh or frozen small whole fish or cuts of fish, some fresh vegetables, reconstituted meat dishes, bacon and egg, egg dishes, and certain fruits. Some of the items may be coated (see 'Deep frying', page 215). We shall look at some general guidelines and then in a little more detail at the meunière, stir-fry, and flambé method. Sautéing is dealt with separately in the next chapter.

Cooking should always begin in hot oil (or fat). If you put the food into warm oil it may stick to the pan and absorb too much oil, and any coating you have put on will probably flake off the food. The heat can be reduced once the outside has formed a crisp exterior.

It is usual for items to be turned only once during the cooking. For this reason, the side that is going to be visible to the customer – the 'presentation' side – is cooked first, to make sure that it has no burnt food particles on it. The presentation side for whole fish is the side with the best appearance – for fillets of fish, it is the side that was cut away from the bone, not the side with the skin on.

Savoury items should be seasoned before cooking begins.

After each batch of food has been cooked, the pan should be cleaned with absorbent kitchen paper and new oil should be put in and heated ready for the next batch.

The cooked food must be well drained on absorbent paper before being placed on to a warmed serving dish.

34.2 Shallow-fried fish – meunière

The term 'meunière' is used to describe a particular style of shallow frying fish. The finished dish can be varied by altering the garnishes. Not all shallow-fried fish is served meunière – for example, fish that has been coated with egg and breadcrumbs appears on the menu as 'à l'anglaise' or 'in the English style'.

The following general procedure applies to all fish cooked in the meunière style:

- Wash and dry the fish and pass it through seasoned flour. Shake off surplus flour.
- Place the fish carefully into hot fat or oil, presentation side first.
- Reduce the heat once the presentation side has become crisp and lightly coloured.
- Turn the fish and cook the other side, adjusting the heat as necessary.
- Remove the fish from the pan, drain it, and place it (presentation side up) on a warmed service dish.
- Heat some butter in a separate small pan until it turns a deep golden brown – this stage is reached when the foaming stops and the butter gives off a smell of toasted hazelnuts.
- Add a small amount of lemon juice to flavour the butter and to stop it from browning any more.
- Decorate the fish with thin slices of peeled lemon, pour over the nut-brown butter, and sprinkle with chopped parsley.
- Wipe the edges of the dish and serve.

The frying can be done in oil, clarified butter, or a mixture of the two.

34.3 Stir-frying

This is a traditional Chinese method of cooking, using a wok. The method has much in common with shallow frying and is suitable for very tender foods that will retain their shape after cooking. Unless the food is small, it is cut into slices or batons and cooked in a very small amount of oil over a fierce heat, with frequent stirring. Vegetables cooked by this method should not be coloured and should have a 'bite'.

34.4 Flambé method

Tender cuts of meat, poultry, and fish and certain types of fruit such as bananas and tinned cherries and peaches are suitable for processing into flambé dishes, which are prepared in the restaurant. The technique is similar in some respects to shallow frying, the main difference being that the food is flamed with an appropriate spirit after having been shallow-fried in unsalted butter. Cream and other ingredients are added to the flambé pan to produce a sauce.

34.5 Commodities suitable for shallow frying

Fish

- Dover sole – whole or fillets.
- Lemon sole – whole or fillets.
- Torbay sole – whole or fillets.
- Plaice – whole or fillets.
- Flounders – whole or fillets.
- Dabs – whole.
- Herring – whole or fillets.
- Mackerel – small whole or fillets.
- Sprats – whole.
- Sardines – whole.
- Whiting – fillets.
- Cod/codling – fillets, suprêmes.
- Haddock – small fillets, suprêmes.
- Trout – whole or fillets.
- Brill – suprêmes.
- Red mullet – whole.
- Grey mullet – fillets.

Meat

- Pork – chops, cutlets, pork fillet.
- Lamb – chops, cutlets, noisettes, fillet mignon.
- Beef – beef steaks from the sirloin and fillet.
- Veal – escalopes, escalopines, cutlets.
- Chicken – suprêmes.
- Turkey – escalopes, escalopines cut from breast.
- Offal – lamb, calf, and pig's liver and kidney; lamb and veal sweetbreads (after blanching).
- Miscellaneous – bacon, gammon steaks, beefburgers, sausages, pojarski of veal and chicken, bitoks of beef, epigrammes of lamb, Vienna steak, fishcakes.

Vegetables

Onions, mushrooms, tomatoes, aubergines, courgettes.

Fruit

Bananas, tinned peaches and cherries.

34.6 Some points to be observed when shallow frying

- Always pre-heat the pan or griddle.
- Select a suitable oil or fat for the item being cooked.
- Avoid fats with a low smoke-point, such as unclarified butter.
- Use the minimum amount of oil or fat – just enough to prevent the food from sticking to the pan.
- All items must be thoroughly dried before flouring or cooking.
- Flour food items immediately before you fry them. If you leave moist items coated in flour, they will become sticky.
- Season all savoury items before cooking.

224 *Food preparation and cooking*

- Cook the presentation side first.
- Wipe out the pan and heat fresh oil or fat for each batch.
- Only reduce the heat when the presentation side has formed a crisp outside.
- Drain cooked items on absorbent paper before placing on a heated service dish.
- If a sauce is to be served with an egg-and-breadcrumbed item, flood the service dish with the sauce and place the cooked food on top.
- Turn foods only once; avoid moving them about.

34.7 Equipment used for shallow frying

In addition to assorted frying pans (see chapter 46), a fryplate, a griddle, or a Bratt pan (see section 30.4) can be used.

Fryplates and griddles

Fryplates and griddles are solid plates heated from below by either gas or electricity. They are used for the fast or continuous frying of eggs, bacon, liver, steak, chops, beefburgers, pancakes, etc. Although fryplates and griddles are basically the same thing, manufacturers tend to use the word 'fryplate' for units that are incorporated into a boiling table (fig. 34.1) and 'griddle' for self-contained units (fig. 34.2).

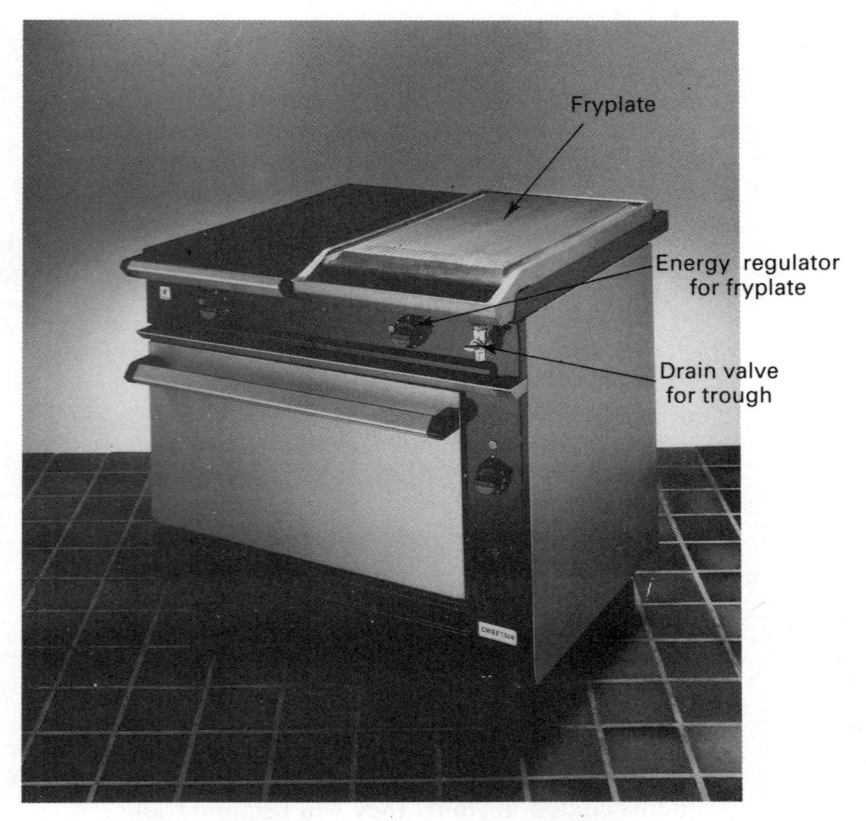

Fig. 34.1 A general-purpose oven incorporating a fryplate

Shallow frying 225

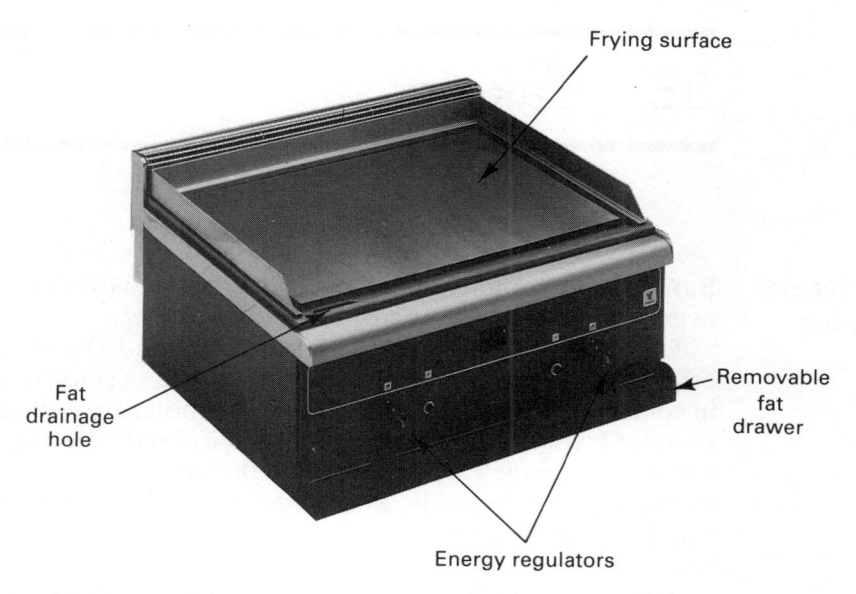

Fig. 34.2 A griddle

Getting the best out of a fryplate or griddle is largely a matter of experience, coupled with the needs of the particular task in hand:

- Adjust the surface temperature of the plate to suit the food being cooked – for example, fried eggs need a low temperature, whereas steaks, chops, beefburgers, and other meats need a much higher temperature for successful results.
- As food absorbs heat from the plate, a higher gas or electricity setting may be needed when continuously cooking large quantities than when cooking small batches.
- The fryplate or griddle should not be left with the gas or electricity turned full on when not actually cooking. If the plate has to be kept hot, use of the 'simmer' setting will save fuel and prevent overheating.
- From cold, allow about 35 minutes pre-heating at the maximum setting to get the plate ready for high-temperature cooking. The plate temperature will then be about 260° C (500° F).
- Allow about 15 minutes pre-heating from cold at the maximum setting to get the plate ready for low-temperature cooking. The 'simmer' or low heat setting will then maintain a plate temperature of about 190° C (375° F).

Surplus fat etc. produced during cooking is drained off into a trough at the front of the fryplate or a drawer underneath the griddle. Take care not to let this overflow.

A wide metal scraper should be used to remove heavy deposits from the surface of the plate. Regular cleaning will prevent the build-up of burnt-on fat and food particles.

35 Baking

35.1 General principles

Baking is the cooking of prepared food items in the dry environment of an oven without the addition of extra fat or water.

The effects of baking on the food are similar to those produced by some other dry-heat methods (see section 27.1) but, because there is no fat added in cooking the food, the energy content is not increased as it is with deep or shallow frying. The surface may be crisp and coloured by the Maillard reaction (see page 159) and have the flavour associated with foods cooked by the dry-heat methods. Provided that the food is not overcooked, there will be little loss of nutrients, except, perhaps, some of the B-group vitamins.

Baking is used for cooking most yeast and pastry goods and a large number of sweet dishes, including meringues, baked apples, and rice and semolina puddings. It is also used to cook some meat, fish, and other items. Some sweets and pastry items need to be cooked on top of the stove for a while before they are put into the oven to finish cooking – for example, choux pastry for éclairs, choux buns, and profiteroles.

Although the atmosphere in the oven starts off by being dry, water that evaporates from the food during cooking will gradually build up to make the air in the oven more moist. This is often an advantage because it prevents the crust from forming until the food item has risen well. Indeed, in some cases extra moisture may be introduced deliberately by sprinkling the baking tray with warm water before putting it in the oven. This may also be achieved by using special ovens that are capable of injecting steam. An oven that is fully loaded with food will generate more moisture than one with only a few items in. If you fill the oven with choux-pastry items of a similar size, you will find that they will rise more than if you put just one tray in.

Although ovens have a thermostat to control the temperature, you must realise that this is not necessarily very accurate for all shelves in an oven. You may have to adjust the shelf position for the best result. In a fan-assisted or forced-air-convection oven, all the shelves are more likely to be at about the same temperature. For baked flour products, the temperature needs to be much more carefully controlled than in many other cooking methods.

Approximate baking temperatures are shown in Table 35.1.

35.2 Baking cakes, pastries, and bread

We have just said that the temperature needs to be carefully controlled: well, so does the recipe. Once you have added the liquid there is not much you can do to alter the texture to any extent. Assuming that you have got the ingredients, the method, and the temperature right, the items are put into the pre-heated oven at the appropriate temperature. The oven temperature is sometimes lowered towards the end of cooking to allow the

Table 35.1 Approximate baking temperatures

Product	Temperature
Short pastry	200–210° C (392–410° F)
Sugar pastry	200–220° C (392–428° F)
Puff pastry	210–225° C (410–437° F)
Choux pastry	225–245° C (437–476° F)
Scones	200–210° C (392–410° F)
Genoese sponge	200° C (392° F)
Victoria sponge	230–250° C (446–482° F)
Fatless sponge	225–230° C (437–446° F)
Madeira cake	160–175° C (320–347° F)
Rich fruit cake	120–150° C (248–302° F)
Bread rolls	240–260° C (464–500° F)
Tin loaf	235–250° C (455–482° F)
Yeast buns	230–240° C (446–464° F)
Savarin paste	235–245° C (455–476° F)
Rum baba	235–245° C (455–473° F)

items to dry out. If the temperature is too hot, the outside will colour and burn before the inside is cooked. The last area to cook in a moulded item such as a cake or a sponge is just below the 'crown', through which the steam passes to escape. This area is the most moist part of the finished item.

If the oven temperature is too low, the food will not rise to its full volume. Bread is cooked at a high temperature to give the final increase in volume and to kill the yeast.

After baking, these items are lifted off the baking sheet and placed on to wire-mesh cooling racks. Fruit cakes and other items cooked in moulds are cooled before being removed from the moulds.

35.3 Cooking in a bain-marie in an oven

We have mentioned the use of this method for some items under Poaching (see section 29.1). In some cases the top of the mould is left uncovered, in which case the surface of the item becomes brown and forms a crust – for example, baked egg custard and crème caramel.

35.4 Baking fish

Round white fish are occasionally stuffed with forcemeat or flavoured breadcrumbs and baked in the oven. Trout and other small whole fish may be wrapped in foil with butter and lemon juice etc. for baking.

35.5 Baking en croûte

Small to medium-sized pieces of meat, poultry, or fish can be wrapped in pastry and baked in an oven. Meat and poultry are first coloured in a little hot fat in a frying pan or an oven. Fish is usually deep-poached (see section 29.2). Before wrapping in the pastry, the pieces of food are cooled and sometimes spread with a suitable stuffing.

35.6 Baking vegetables

A few varieties of vegetables are baked – the most common are potatoes and tomatoes. The skin of potatoes is cleaned and scored with the point of a sharp knife before baking.

35.7 Baking fruit

Baking is a popular method of cooking apples. The apple is left whole with the skin on. The core is removed and the skin is scored. The hole left by removing the core is often filled with a mixture of dried fruit, brown sugar, and spices before baking.

35.8 Some points to be observed when baking

- Always pre-heat the oven to the required temperature before beginning the cooking.
- Collect all the ingredients and equipment before you start preparation and cooking.
- Make sure that the recipe balance is correct and that the ingredients are carefully measured or weighed.
- Do not try to cook items that need different cooking temperatures at the same time, in the same oven.
- Do not open the oven door more than is absolutely necessary.
- Do not lower the oven temperature to dry the items out before they have risen and formed a crust.
- Yeast goods require baking at a higher temperature.
- Don't forget that the temperature in some ovens will vary from shelf to shelf. This is not so noticeable in a convection oven.

35.9 Equipment used for baking

Ovens suitable for baking include conventional ovens (see section 38.5), convection ovens, and baking ovens.

Convection ovens

In forced-convection ovens (fig. 35.1), an electric fan draws air from the oven and over gas or electric heating elements before returning it to the oven. This results in the required temperature being reached in a shorter time than would be the case with a conventional oven relying on natural convection. Also, because an even temperature is maintained throughout the oven, shelf manipulation is unnecessary, the full capacity of the oven can be used, and cooking times are reduced, so the output is much higher than that of a conventional oven of the same size.

Irrespective of the temperature setting, the oven should be allowed to heat up for at least 30 minutes from cold before use. The food should then be inserted as quickly as possible and the doors closed firmly.

- *Cook-only timer* The timer knob is marked in minutes and should be set to the required cooking time when the food is placed in the oven. A manual 'on' position is also provided, which switches the oven on without a time setting.
- *Cook-and-hold timer* For roasting meats, the oven shown in fig. 35.1 has a cook-and-hold facility. The cooking temperature and time are selected, and at the end of the cooking time the oven automatically switches to the 'hold' condition in which the meat is kept at a constant temperature controlled by a separate thermostat until required for carving. Indicator lamps show whether the oven is cooking or holding.

The oven may also be used for holding only, to keep food warm that has been cooked elsewhere. Remember to allow the oven to heat up before inserting the food to be kept warm.

Fig. 35.1 A convection oven

Fig. 35.2 A three-deck baking oven

Cleaning

Before any cleaning is undertaken, *switch off at the mains switch*.

- Remove light staining and spillage deposits by washing with a slightly damp cloth and soap detergent, wiping off with a soft cloth rinsed in fresh water and squeezed free of excess water. Doing this daily will prevent build-up of stubborn baked-on deposits.
- Use nylon scouring pans or spray-on oven cleaners to remove any stubborn stains and baked-on deposits that do develop. Do *not* use steel-wool scourers on enamel surfaces or these will be scratched and local rusting could take place.
- Use proprietary spray-on cleaners to clean the glass panel in the oven door. Do not apply cold water to the glass panel when it is hot, as this may cause the toughened glass to crack.
- Oven shelves and support grids can be removed for cleaning and to facilitate cleaning the oven walls.

Some internal areas of the oven around the fan cannot be reached by kitchen staff but should periodically be cleaned by specialist personnel, otherwise deposits in these regions may build up and impair the performance of the oven.

Baking ovens

These are basically shallow ovens heated from both top and bottom and arranged one above the other (fig. 35.2). Each oven can be individually controlled, and some of them can have automatic steam injection for various types of bread, such as French bread.

36 Grilling

36.1 General principles

Grilling is the cooking of small items of food, on oiled grill bars or trays, by radiated heat. The items for grilling should be tender and suitable for fast cooking at high temperatures.

Grilling is a dry-heat method of cooking, and the effects on the food will be similar to those produced by other dry-heat methods. Fat present in the food will render and drip out of the food, thus reducing the energy content. The protein will only be damaged if drastically overcooked, but some B-group vitamins will be lost. The flavour is characteristic of foods cooked by dry heat.

There are three different types of grill:

- the heat coming from above the grill, as in a salamander;
- the heat coming from below the grill, as in a flare grill or a barbecue unit;
- the heat coming from both above and below, as in an infra-red grill (or from both sides as in a toaster).

With the first two types of grill it is easy to keep an eye on the food. The additional effect of flare grills or barbecues is that the hot fat dripping from the food as it is cooking catches fire when it comes into contact with the hot grill or charcoal in the barbecue. This burning fat gives additional flavour to the food cooking above it.

Meat, fish, and some vegetables are suitable for grilling.

Meat for grilling should be cut into small pieces not more than 5 cm (2 inches) thick. Tender cuts of meat containing a fair amount of marbled fat are ideal, as they do not dry out too much. Veal, pork, and chicken need to be basted regularly with oil or clarified butter during cooking. These meats and white fish are sometimes marinaded before grilling. If the marinade contains oil, it can be used for basting. Oily fish do not need basting.

Before any food is placed on it, the grill should be heated to a fairly high temperature. This has two advantages: first, the food is less likely to stick to the grill, and second the high temperature will sear the food and improve the quality. If necessary, the grill temperature can be lowered a little after the initial searing.

You may need to treat some food items very gently when grilling, as they may quickly lose their shape and some of their natural 'juices', so affecting the finished article.

If a salamander is used for cooking small items of food – whether they are pieces of food such as fish portions or whole foods such as sprats – it is sometimes better if you place the food into shallow trays to grill it. Do make sure that the tray has a rim around the edge to prevent fat running off the tray. By using a tray you will find that it is easier to handle and turn foods that have a delicate structure – some cuts of fish for example.

Place the food items on to lightly oiled trays, brush the top of the food with melted butter or oil, and season with salt and pepper. Slices of bread for toast, sausages, and rashers of bacon are placed on a clean tray before being placed under the salamander. Fish is passed through seasoned flour before being brushed with melted butter.

If a ribbed grill tray or 'brander' is used, pieces of meat can be laid on to the pre-heated tray after they have been brushed with oil and seasoned with salt and pepper. On cooking, the ribbing of the tray will give the meat the appearance of having been cooked on a flare grill.

A salamander is also used to glaze and colour a large number of dishes before the final presentation – for example, glazed fish dishes, cauliflower au gratin, and gnocchi and pasta dishes.

36.2 Commodities suitable for grilling

Fish

- Small whole fish – oily fish such as trout, herrings, sprats, and sardines; white fish such as plaice, lemon sole, and dover sole.
- Cuts from larger fish – fillets of plaice, lemon and dover soles, whiting, and haddock; darnes of cod and occasionally salmon.
- Smoked fish – cod, haddock, kippers, bloaters.

Beef

Small slices from prime-quality joints:

- Boned, trimmed sirloin – sirloin steak, minute steak.
- Whole sirloin including the fillet – T-bone steak, porterhouse steak.
- Fillet: head or rump end – chateaubriand;
  middle cut or saddle – fillet steak, tournedos steak;
  tail – fillet mignon.
- Rump – rump steak, point steak.

Also beef sausages and beef burgers.

Lamb

Small slices or cuts from prime-quality joints:

- Saddle of lamb – crown chop (Barnsley chop).
- Loin of lamb – chump chop, loin or lamb chop.
- Best end of lamb – single and double lamb cutlets.

Pork

- Loin – cutlets, chops.
- Various cuts – belly slices, leg slices, spare-rib chops.
- Pork sausages.
- Gammon steaks and bacon rashers.

Chicken

- Poussins – whole, split spatchcock style.
- Broiler birds – whole, 675 g – 1.25 kg (1½–3 lb), spatchcock style or portions.

Offal

- Lambs' liver and kidney.
- Calves' liver and kidney.
- Pigs' kidney.

Kebabs

Lamb, pork, chicken, fish, fruit, vegetables.

Vegetables

Those with a loose cellulose structure are suitable. Mushrooms and tomatoes are the most popular.

Convenience items for grilling can be bought frozen. These are grilled straight from the freezer. Examples include steaklets, barbecued spareribs, and rissoles.

36.3 Degree of cooking for grilled foods

The temperature at which food is cooked and the time it is cooked for can be very easily controlled. Many customers have preference for some grilled food to be cooked to a particular degree. Perhaps the most usual is beef steak, but some people prefer their lamb or liver 'pink' – that is, slightly underdone.

The terms for the various degrees of cooking are as follows:

- *Very rare* (*au bleu*)   The meat is cooked just long enough to brown and sear the outside. When pressed, the meat will feel soft and spongy. Inside, the meat will appear red and raw.
- *Rare* (*saignant*)   The meat is cooked when drops of blood appear on the surface. It is spongy and offers little resistance when pressed. Inside, the meat is a deep reddish-pink.
- *Medium* (*à point*)   The meat is cooked when drops of clear juice are visible on the surface. It is firm and offers some resistance if you press it. The meat inside has a rosy pink colour.
- *Well done* (*bien cuit*)   The meat is cooked completely through to the centre. It is very firm and inside the meat has an even brown colour.

The above terms may be applied to the following items:

- Very rare – beef steaks.
- Rare – beef steaks, game, kidney, and occasionally lamb.
- Medium – beef steaks, lamb, kidney, liver, and duck.
- Well done – pork, turkey, chicken, veal, and fish.

Grilling 233

36.4 Some points to be observed when grilling

- Leave meat and fish at room temperature for 30 minutes before grilling.
- Allow 150–200 g (5–7 oz) per portion of meat and fish – this may need to be doubled if the food contains a lot of bone.
- Cut away excess fat before grilling; otherwise the fat will render during grilling, causing the grill to flare and smoke excessively.
- A small quantity of fat will improve the flavour and prevent the food from drying out.
- Do not place food on to cold grill bars. Hot grill bars prevent the food from sticking (brushing food items with oil or clarified butter will also help).
- Cook the presentation side first.
- Sear the outside of the food as quickly as possible.
- Do not move the food until it has formed a 'crust': doing so may cause the food to stick and damage the surface and spoil the shape.
- Avoid piercing meat with a carving fork or the tip of a knife during grilling, as this encourages the juices to escape.
- Meats are best turned with long-handled tongs.
- Fish must be turned very carefully with a fish-slice or a palette knife during cooking, to prevent damaging the structure.
- Large pieces of meat or fish should be moved to a cooler part of the cooking area after searing.
- Grilled foods quickly spoil by overcooking or burning – you will need to keep an eye on the food while you are grilling.
- Never grill foods a long time before service – they are best served straight from the grill.

36.5 Equipment used for grilling

As well as an overhead or underfired grill, small items such as long-handled tongs, assorted thick-based trays, and brushes for basting are required.

Overhead grills

Overhead grills, or 'salamanders', may be heated by gas or electric elements above the food to be cooked. The model shown in fig. 36.1 features

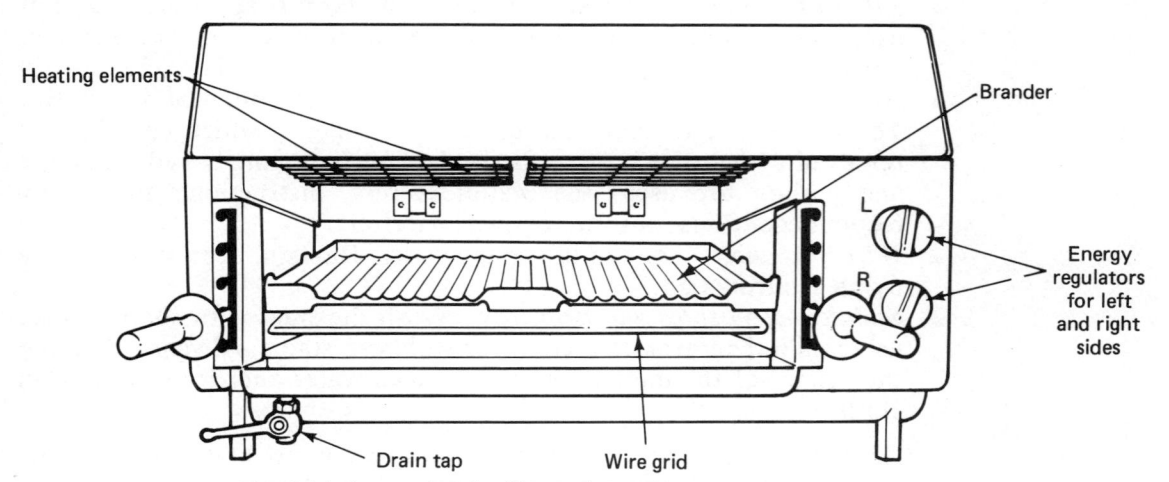

Fig. 36.1 An overhead grill or salamander

- a wire-grid shelf that can be used in several support positions and will not tilt when pulled forward;
- a drip tray at the bottom of the compartment to catch grease and crumbs etc. during grilling or toasting – the trough at the front of the tray has a tap so that melted grease can be drained off with the tray still in position;
- a double-sided brander plate supported by the wire grid in any of the support positions available. If batches of steaks are to be cooked to the same degree, the brander can be inserted level. If, however, steaks within a batch are to be cooked to different degrees at the same time, the brander can be made to slope from a high position at the rear to a lower position at the front so that the distance from the heating elements varies (see Table 36.1).

Table 36.1 Cooking guide using the brander plate in a central position

Food	Approx. cooking time (minutes)*	Position on sloping brander plate
Steak		
rare	1½–3	Rear
medium	3–5	Centre
well done	5–7	Front
Beefburger	2–3	Centre
Sausage	4–6	Centre

* Steak cooking times are only approximate – actual cooking times will depend on the thickness of the steak and the cut of meat.

Cleaning

Clean the appliance after every working session – preferably while it is still warm. Mop up any spillages immediately, to avoid the build-up of stubborn stains. Once a week, clean the appliance thoroughly:

- *Vitreous enamel* Wash thoroughly with warm soapy water. Do not use caustic abrasives as these can seriously discolour the surface, especially when hot.
- *Aluminium brander* Leave the brander under the full heat of the grill. The heat will eventually carbonise any spillages, which can then be removed with a wire brush. If materials for removing baked-on grease and carbon are used, the manufacturers' instructions and safety recommendations must be followed carefully.
- *Wire-grid shelf* Soak in hot soapy water. Rub stubborn stains with a nylon scouring pad.
- *Stainless-steel sides and drip tray* Wash the sides with soapy water, using mild detergent on a cloth for stubborn stains. Always rub along the 'grain' of the metal. Rinse with clean water and dry with a clean cloth.

Clean all fat and debris out of the drip tray before soaking it in hot soapy water. Rinse in clean water and dry with a clean cloth.

More persistent grease and stains should be removed with a proprietary detergent or, for hardened stains, cleaning pads.

Underfired grills

Figure 36.2 shows an underfired simulated-charcoal grill. Lava rocks on cast-iron grids are heated by gas burners. The food is cooked on brander bars above the hot rocks and is given additional flavour by hot fat dripping from the food flaring up on the rocks, as in a traditional charcoal barbecue.

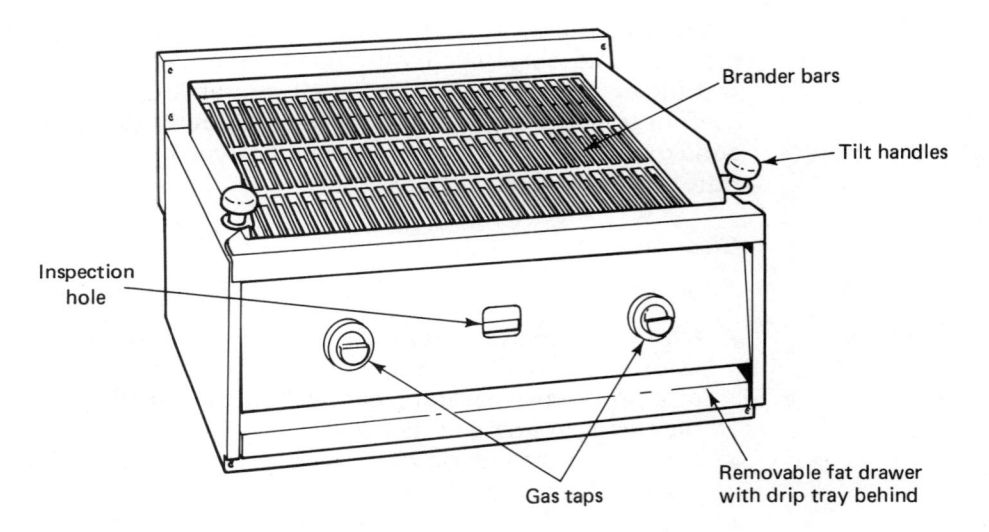

Fig. 36.2 An underfired grill with brander

The brander bars making up the cooking surface can be independently positioned by means of the tilt handles. During cooking, excess fat drains into a removable fat drawer at the bottom front of the appliance, and behind the fat drawer there is a removable full-area drip tray to collect remnants of rock, charred food particles, etc.

Cooking on the grill

- Before cooking, allow the grill to heat up from cold for about 30 minutes with the burners full on. The lava rock and the brander bars are at the correct working temperature when the rocks show a red glow at the bottom. (The rocks need not glow red throughout.) They are then giving off the infra-red heat required for fast cooking. The gas can then be turned down, so long as the red glow in the rocks is maintained.
- The temperature varies across the depth of the brander bars, being hottest at the rear and cooler towards the front.
- Thick cuts of meat require a longer cooking time at a lower temperature than thinner cuts, to avoid burning, and so should be cooked nearer the front of the bars.

- Steak or chops should be seared (branded) on both sides to retain their juices and then be cooked as required with as few turns as possible. 'Rare' cooking should be done at the rear of the cooking area, where the outside of the food will be cooked more quickly.
- Attractive 'branding' is produced on the food by the searing action of the edges of the hot brander bars. To obtain a criss-cross pattern, turn the food through 90° part-way through the cooking process.
- If excessive flaring occurs when cooking fattier meats, some underfired grills have branders with drainage channels which can be lowered to run off excess fat.

Cooking times vary considerably according to the type and thickness of the food and customer requirements, but experience will soon produce satisfactory results. For general guidance, 100 g high-meat-content beefburgers can be cooked in about 6 minutes (3 minutes each side) and good quality steaks 20 mm (¾ inch) thick can be cooked in about 4 minutes (rare) to 12 minutes (well done).

Cleaning

Allow the appliance to cool before cleaning or removing parts.

- Clean the stainless-steel external body of the appliance with soapy water as often as possible, rinse, and dry. Remove grease with fine steel wool or a proprietary cleaning pad, rubbing in the direction of the 'grain' of the metal to preserve its finish.
- Remove the brander bars daily for cleaning with a wire brush to remove carbon deposits and keep the drain channels clear.
- Clean the burners at least once a week to maintain maximum performance.

37 Sautéing

37.1 General principles

Sautéing involves rapid cooking of small pieces of meat, poultry, game, or vegetables in oil or clarified butter in a shallow pan. The difference between this method and shallow frying is that the items are often turned or tossed during sautéing, whereas, you will remember, in shallow frying the food is usually only turned once.

Sautéing is a dry-heat method of cooking (see section 27.1) and is used only for commodities that are young and tender. The effects are very similar to those produced by shallow frying (see section 34.1).

The food items are started in hot oil. Red meat (beef) should be cooked over a fiercer heat than poultry and light meats (veal, lamb, and pork). After the initial searing, the pan is drawn to one side and cooking is continued more slowly. For larger joints of chicken the pan can be covered or put into the oven for the later stages of cooking. Beef should never be treated like this but always cooked quickly without being covered. The length of cooking will depend on the thickness of the food item.

With all meat sautés, the cooking pan is swilled out with stock or wine to lift off the hardened meat sediments on the base of the pan. The swilled pan juices can be reduced and added to the sauce, or some demi-glace, velouté, or cream can be added to the pan to make a sauce. A pan only slightly larger than the item(s) being cooked should be used, otherwise the sediment will burn, making swilling difficult. The cooked items should be placed back into the pan with the sauce for a few minutes to warm them through immediately before service. Meat must not be overcooked by this method or else the protein will become hard and tough.

Sauté potatoes are slices of cooked potato tossed over a fierce heat in oil and clarified butter in a thick-bottomed sauté pan. Potatoes for sauté are cooked but left slightly firm by steaming or boiling in their skins. These are best peeled warm but sliced cold. Sauté potatoes need to be served immediately they have been cooked, otherwise they become tough and unpalatable.

37.2 Commodities suitable for sautéing

- *Beef* Tournedos, strips of fillet for beef Stroganoff, sirloin steak, fillet mignon.
- *Lamb* Noisettes, cutlets, kidneys.
- *Veal* Cutlets, escalopes, escalopines, sweetbreads, kidneys.
- *Pork* Escalopes, escalopines.
- *Chicken* 1.5 kg (3–3½ lb) chickens cut for sauté, suprêmes, livers.
- *Duck* Small ducks cut for sauté, suprêmes.
- *Pigeon* Breasts only.
- *Fish* Scampi.
- *Potatoes*

37.3 Special points to be observed when sautéing

- Only use prime commodities.
- Always sear items quickly in hot oil or butter at the beginning of cooking.
- Continue cooking at as high a temperature as you can without spoiling the food.
- A copper plat à sauter is best for all items except potatoes (see chapter 46).
- Try to lay items flat in the pan for rapid searing.
- Never cook the meat in the sauce – only bring the two together at the end of cooking.
- Potatoes for sauté must not be overcooked, otherwise they will tend to disintegrate when browning.
- Never sauté meat and vegetables together – the vegetables lose some of their water into the pan and prevent the meat from frying.

37.4 Equipment used for sautéing

Sauté pans are described in section 46.3.

38 Roasting

38.1 General principles

Roasting is the cooking of food items in the dry heat of an oven or on a spit in the presence of fat or oil. In a traditional (general-purpose) oven the food is cooked by a combination of convection, conduction, and radiation. In some of the more recent ovens, use is made of forced air convection, steam convection, and microwaves. The oven may also have an automatic revolving spit. Roasting is used for cooking tender joints and cuts of meat, poultry, game, and some vegetables.

Whatever the type of oven used, the effect on the food is typical of dry-heat methods (see section 27.1). The flavour, colour, and texture are due to cooking at a high temperature. The changes that take place in the nutritional content are the loss of fat, which will reduce the energy content (unless the fat is included in the sauce), and the destruction of some of the B-group vitamins. Although the protein shrinks, it has the same protein value as the raw meat, as long as it is not hopelessly overcooked.

38.2 Roasting meat, poultry, and game

Items chosen for roasting should be tender, have little connective tissue, and contain sufficient internal fat (marbling) and external fat to prevent the food from drying out during cooking. For those with little fat, larding or barding may be used (see later). The joints or carcasses used will usually come from young domesticated birds and animals. Older animals and birds are cooked by one of the moist-heat methods.

The food is placed into a hot oven (227–235° C (440–455° F)) to sear the surface and provide some of the flavour and colour. It may be placed on a trivet (see below). After about twenty minutes, you must turn the temperature down so that the meat can be cooked through to the centre. If you don't lower the heat, the outside will be overdone before the middle is cooked. How much you reduce the heat will depend on the shape and size of the item being cooked.

The cooking time depends on the size and shape of what you are roasting. A 5 kg (11 lb) piece of meat that is compact will require longer cooking than the same weight that is flattened or elongated. A loin of pork, for example, will cook in a shorter time than a leg of pork weighing the same amount. You will also have to take your customers' wishes into account – some people prefer meat that is underdone to that which is well done. Table 38.1 gives some approximate cooking times for guidance.

The meat should be basted regularly by spooning the hot fat from the bottom of the tray over the meat. To test how well it is cooked, press or pierce the thickest part of the meat to make some juice run out. If the juice is clear, the meat is cooked through.

Table 38.1 Approximate cooking times for roast meats

Meat	Time per 500 g (1 lb)	Degree of cooking
Beef	15 min and 15 min over	Underdone
Pork	25 min and 25 min over	Very well done
Lamb	15–20 min and 15–20 min over	Pink to cooked through
Veal	25 min and 25 min over	Just done
Chicken		
1.5–2 kg (3–4 lb)	15 min and 15 min over	Well done
Above 2 kg (4 lb)	15–20 min and 20 min over	Well done
Duck	25 min and 25 min over	Pink to just done
Turkey		
4–7 kg (9–15 lb)	25 min and 25 min over	Well done
7–13.5 kg (15–30 lb)	15–20 min and 20 min over	Well done
Pheasant	30–40 min, no extra	Pink to cooked through
Grouse	20–25 min, no extra	Pink to cooked through
Hare (râble)	18–20 min, no extra	Pink to cooked through
Venison	15–20 min and 20 min over	Pink to cooked through

Use of a trivet in roasting

A trivet is used to stop the meat from lying in the fat in the bottom of the tray and frying. If this is allowed to happen, the part that is actually in the fat may become hard and tough. A trivet can be made from large cut aromatic vegetables (such as onions, carrots, celery, and leeks), small pieces of bone, or a perforated metal tray can be used. If either vegetables or bones are used, the colour and flavour of the roast gravy will be improved. The gravy is made by adding brown stock to the sediments in the roasting tray after the meat has been taken out.

Larding and barding

One of these techniques is necessary when the item to be roasted does not contain enough internal or external fat to prevent it from drying out during cooking. The fat used is usually pork back fat, which does not affect the flavour of the meat being roasted.

- *Larding* For this process the pork fat is cut into long strips and inserted, with the aid of a larding needle, into the lean flesh of fillets of beef, joints of veal, or furred game. The fat renders on cooking and has the effect of basting the meat.
- *Barding* In this case, the fat is cut into thin slices and is wrapped over the piece of meat before roasting. It is commonly used when roasting game.

Sometimes both larding and barding are used at the same time, particularly when roasting saddles of venison or râbles of hare.

Traditional accompaniments to roast joints

Roast beef Yorkshire pudding, horseradish sauce, roast gravy.

Roasting

- *Roast lamb* Mint sauce or jelly, roast gravy. Red-currant jelly can also be served.
- *Roast pork* Apple sauce, sage-and-onion stuffing, roast gravy.
- *Roast chicken* Bread sauce, game chips, thyme-and-parsley stuffing, bacon rolls, chipolatas, and roast gravy.
- *Roast turkey* Cranberry sauce, game chips, chestnut stuffing, bacon rolls, chipolatas, and roast gravy. Bread sauce can also be offered.
- *Roast duck* Apple sauce, sage-and-onion stuffing, roast gravy.
- *Roast pheasant* Fried breadcrumbs, bread croûtes spread with game pâté, game chips, and roast gravy. Bread sauce can also be offered.

Carveries

Some restaurants offer their customers a variety of hot roasted joints from which they can choose. The joints are displayed on a heated display unit and carved by a chef to the customers' requirements. The customers may then help themselves to vegetables. Table service is usual for the starter, sweet, and coffee.

38.3 Roasting vegetables

Potatoes and parsnips are the vegetables that are most commonly roasted.

Potatoes are sometimes shaped into barrels before they are cooked. They are drained and placed into hot fat on top of the stove to crisp the surface before being finally cooked in the oven.

Parsnips are treated in a similar way, but are blanched in boiling salted water before being roasted.

Roast vegetables need to be well drained of fat before service.

38.4 Some points to be observed when roasting

- Select only best-quality joints.
- Increase the fat content if the meat is very lean.
- Cut away excessive amounts of fat.
- Boning and rolling will make carving easier.
- Season the meat before cooking.
- Always start roasting in a hot oven.
- Regular basting prevents excessive searing and drying during the cooking.
- Use a trivet to prevent the bottom of the joint from spoiling.
- Allow the meat to 'rest' for 15 minutes when cooked, to make carving and portion-control easier.
- A long, thin, sharp carving knife with a fairly flexible blade will make carving easier.

38.5 Equipment used for roasting

Roasting may be carried out in conventional ovens, in convection ovens (see section 35.9), or in steam convection ovens (fig. 42.2).

Ovens

Conventional (general-purpose) ovens may be heated by either gas or electricity. Figure 38.1 shows single-tier and double-tier arrangements.

As it is heated by natural convection, the temperature will vary within the oven, being hotter at the top and cooler at the bottom, but approximate

242 Food preparation and cooking

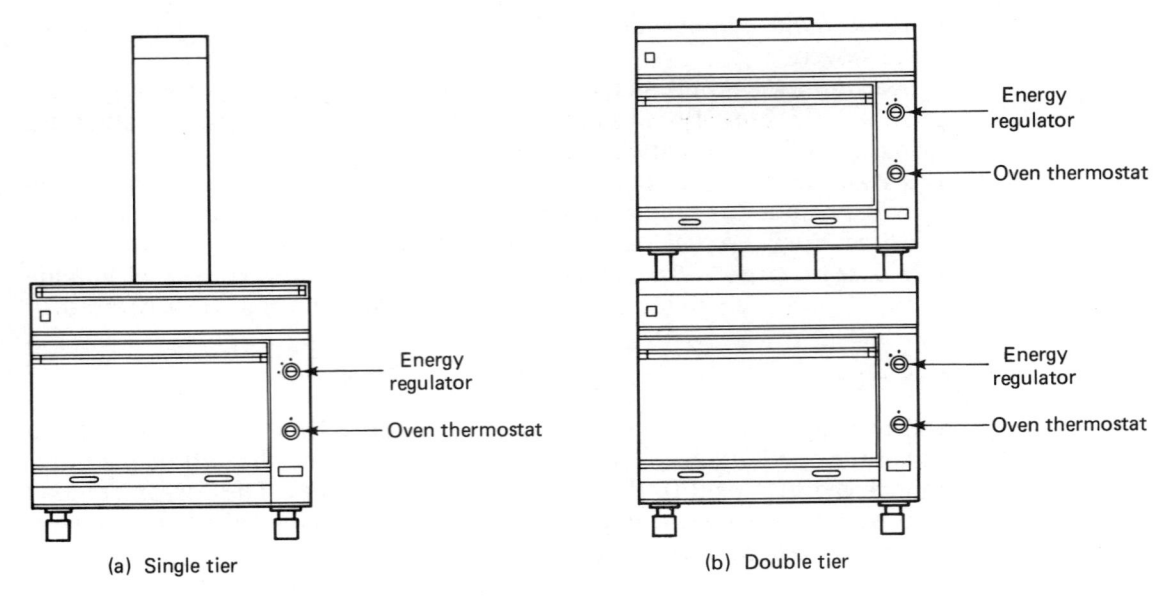

Fig. 38.1 General-purpose ovens

(a) Single tier

(b) Double tier

centre-oven temperatures for each temperature setting are shown in Table 38.2.

The oven should be allowed to heat up from cold for at least 45 minutes before loading with food. The food should then be put in quickly, to minimise heat losses, and the door should be closed firmly.

Table 38.2 Centre-oven temperatures for conventional ovens

Gas Mark	Description	Temperature °C	°F
¼	Slow	120	248
½	Slow	135	275
1	Slow	150	302
2	Moderate	165	329
3	Moderate	180	355
4	Fairly hot	195	383
5	Fairly hot	210	410
6	Hot	227	440
7	Hot	243	470
8	Very hot	258	496
9	Very hot	272	522

Cooking hints for roasting and baking (see section 35.9)

- High-temperature (quick) roasting is suitable only for good-quality meat. The cooking time will depend on the quality and shape of the meat and on personal tastes.

- Low-temperature (slow) roasting is preferable for tougher joints and old birds. Longer cooking times are required but there is less weight loss and cooking is more even.
- When cooking two trays of small cakes, scones, etc. the upper tray will be cooked first. This should then be removed from the oven and the low tray raised to the upper position.
- When cooking Yorkshire puddings etc. in baking-tins on two shelves, the upper and lower tins should be interchanged about half-way through the cooking process.
- When cooking fruit cakes in large tins, the cooking time will vary considerably according to the weight of the cake and the richness and depth of the mixture. When cooking on two shelves, the upper and lower tins should be interchanged about half-way through the cooking process.

Cleaning

- Clean the range daily after use, using hot soapy water, rinse, and dry. Remove grease with fine steel wool or proprietary cleaning pads – but take care if using nylon pad scrubbers, especially when new, as they may scratch enamelled surfaces.
- Wipe down the vitreous enamelled oven linings with a soapy cloth while still warm.

39 Poêlé cooking

39.1 General principles

Poêlé cooking, or pot-roasting, is the cooking of prime-quality meat, poultry, or game with butter and aromatic vegetables in an enclosed container in an oven. It should not be confused with casseroling, which is similar to stewing and is used only for the coarser cuts of meat.

Poêlé cooking is used for the smaller cuts of meat, because of the size limit of suitable containers. The containers should be deep-sided, with a tight-fitting lid to prevent the moisture from escaping during cooking, and can be made of metal or earthenware.

The meat is trimmed, tied, seasoned, and placed into a lightly buttered container on a bed of aromatic vegetables, parsley stalks, bay leaves, crushed peppercorns, and rubbed thyme. It is smeared with a little more butter, and placed into a hot oven (185–210° C (365–410° F)) with a lid on. Regular basting with the cooking juices is necessary to make sure that the dish is moist and tender. The cooking temperature and time depend on the type and size of the item being cooked. To give colour to the dish, the lid is taken off for the last half-hour or so of the cooking time. The accompanying gravy is produced by swilling out the cooking pot with brown stock and thickening the liquid with diluted arrowroot.

Poêlé meats are usually served with a vegetable garnish.

39.2 Items suitable for poêlé cooking

- *Beef* Larded fillet, contrefilet, wing rib.
- *Lamb* Saddle, loin, best end.
- *Veal* Larded saddle, loin, best end.
- *Poultry* Duckling; small turkey; chicken – poussin, broiler birds from 750 g to 2.25 kg (1½–5 lb).
- *Game* Young grouse, partridge, pheasant, woodcock, snipe. Râble of hare, saddle or loin of venison.

39.3 Equipment used for poêlé cooking

Assorted containers with lids are required for poêlé cooking – see chapter 46.

40 Cold preparations

The term 'cold preparations' refers to cold food commodities brought together for the purpose of presentation in a particular style. The foods may be raw or cooked, and the presentation may range from a simple ham sandwich to a decorated whole salmon. The main aim in producing cold preparations, however simple or complex, is to make the items as visually appealing as possible, while at the same time making them palatable and of a suitable eating quality. Since, in many cases, raw foods are used, the nutritional value of the food may well be very good. For example, the vitamin-C content in salads, raw vegetables, and fresh fruit is much higher than if the same materials were cooked. Raw fruit and vegetables also provide a crunchy texture that may be missing from dishes composed entirely of cooked items.

Many different commodities – fresh, frozen, preserved, cooked, or convenience items – can be used in the preparation of cold dishes. Cold dishes can be eaten as a meal in themselves (cold buffet), at the start of a meal as an hors-d'oeuvre, as an accompaniment to a hot fish or meat dish, or as a snack at any time. We shall have a look at some of these.

40.1 Decorated cold-buffet dishes

Many cooked items of fish, meat, poultry and game can be displayed on a decorated cold buffet. These items are sometimes covered with a coating of chaud-froid sauce before being decorated and given a final coating of aspic jelly. The decorations can be prepared from a wide range of edible materials. Truffles, mushrooms, turned vegetables, cucumber peelings, tomatoes, hard-boiled egg-white, and piped butter are some examples. Designs can be made with edible marking pastes, which are available from suppliers. The process should make the items look exceedingly attractive and appetising. The aspic coating has the added benefit of preventing the decorated item from drying out too quickly and looking dull and unattractive.

You will need a certain amount of practice and experience before you can guarantee to produce a cold-buffet masterpiece. Care must be taken with the temperature of the food being coated and the thickness of the sauces you are using. It is very easy to get an uneven coating on the food. Both chaud-froid sauce and aspic jelly are available as convenience products.

Many items of food that are served as part of a cold buffet have only a simple garnish, for example slices of smoked salmon or wedges of melon. The purpose is the same as for the elaborately decorated items – that is, to make the food visually attractive.

40.2 Hors-d'oeuvres

These are served early in a meal and portions should be small, light in texture, attractive, and pleasant-tasting in order to stimulate the appetite for the rest of the meal.

An hors-d'oeuvre may consist very largely of one food that is garnished and served with an accompaniment or of many different items.

Single-food hors-d'oeuvres

These may include a sauce or a dressing and be accompanied by buttered toast or brown bread and butter.

Foods used include smoked salmon, smoked trout, smoked eel, sliced cured meats, parma ham, pâté, oysters, dressed crab, prawn cocktail, caviar, melon, grapefruit, avocado pear, stuffed eggs, egg mayonnaise, and quail's eggs.

Assorted hors-d'oeuvres

These are prepared from many different commodities and can be presented to the customer on an hors-d'oeuvres trolley or display unit or individually plated where the customer has no choice. Assorted hors-d'oeuvres often make use of left-over cooked meat and fish as well as fresh and preserved commodities.

Foods used include sardines, anchovy fillets, buckling, roll-mop herrings, gherkins, olives, radishes, salad onions, tomato salad, beetroot salad, potato salad, and coleslaw.

40.3 Salads

Salads can be divided into two groups: simple and compound.

Simple salads

These are usually prepared from raw ingredients, seasoned and dressed with vinaigrette. Examples include lettuce, cucumber, endive, chicory, beetroot, celery, pepper, and tomato.

Compound salads

These are sometimes referred to as mixed salads, because they are made from a mixture of ingredients which are usually bound or dressed with mayonnaise, vinaigrette, or acidulated cream. The ingredients may include fish, meat, poultry, vegetables, fruit, and nuts. Here are some examples:

- *Fish*   Monte Carlo salad, Françillon salad
- *Meat*   Opéra salad, Bagration salad
- *Vegetable*   American salad, oriental rice salad, Russian salad
- *Fruit*   Alice salad, Florida salad, Japanese salad

A range of fully prepared compound salads, salad dressings, mayonnaise, and other types of cold sauces ready for serving is available from food manufacturers. A smaller number of specialists also supply a range of fresh salads, sauces, and dressings ready for service. These are often vacuum-packed, which means that they keep longer.

Cold preparations 247

40.4 Sandwiches and filled rolls

These will vary both in type and size with the time of day and the type of service. If eaten as part of a main meal they need to be fairly substantial, filling, and nutritious. Afternoon tea and finger-buffet sandwiches are normally much smaller and far less substantial. The possibilities for variety in sandwiches are almost endless. Both the bread and the filling are capable of being varied, as well as the number of layers and the shape.

Fillings may include:

- *Meat* Sliced ham, tongue, roast beef, lamb, pork, chicken, turkey, or sliced chicken or turkey roll, grilled bacon rashers, meat paste or pâté.
- *Fish* Tinned sardines, fish or shellfish paste, sliced smoked fish, flaked salmon, fresh prawns or crab.
- *Salad* Cucumber, lettuce, tomato, watercress, mustard and cress, sliced onion.
- *Dairy produce* Grated or sliced cheese, sliced hard-boiled egg.

To make the fillings interesting and to provide variety, any combination of commodities is possible, although some are more appealing than others. Sandwiches should be well-seasoned and, if appropriate, a choice of pickles, mustards, mayonnaise, or relishes can be offered to the customer.

40.5 Some points to be observed when making cold preparations

- Always maintain a very high standard of hygiene. (This is very important, as the food will not be heated again to kill any harmful bacteria which may have been introduced during your preparation – see page 182.)
- Keep the equipment and serving dishes spotlessly clean.
- Use only food that is really fresh.
- Make the items in small quantities and frequently. Do not make in bulk that may take several days to use up.
- Provide the most appropriate storage conditions for each item. Once the food has been prepared it must be stored appropriately. Do not leave it on the work-bench in a kitchen to get warm and spoil.
- Cool hot food quickly. Refrigerate roast meats and salads for later use.
- If the food is on display to the customers, it should be stored under cool conditions. If none are available, the food should not be kept on display for any longer than is absolutely necessary.
- If you are at all doubtful about the freshness of any food items, they must be discarded.

41 Microwave cooking

41.1 General principles

Microwave cooking is cooking with the energy transferred to food by microwaves. This is explained in a little more detail in section 25.5, but the point is that the waves are of energy rather than heat and the energy in these waves causes some of the particles in the food – especially the water particles – to vibrate. The vibration of the water particles creates heat, which is transferred to the other components of the food by conduction.

Microwave equipment is suitable for cooking, reheating, and rapid defrosting. When operated correctly, microwave cookers are fast and efficient, saving up to 75% of the time taken by some other cooking procedures and consequently using less energy. Their cost-effectiveness is particularly marked where small quantities of food items are being dealt with at any one time.

Cooking by microwave alone (not in combination with other methods) is really a moist-heat method of cooking (see section 27.1), since it is the water content that is heated. The temperature will not go much higher than 100 °C (212 °F). This means that only certain foods are suitable for cooking by this method and that the effects of the higher temperatures reached in frying and grilling, for example, will not be produced. Since a high temperature is not reached and since the food is not in contact with water, the loss of nutrients is very small.

A wide range of dishes can make use of microwave cooking, either as the sole cooking process or as part of the cooking process in combination with other heat-transfer methods such as convection. For a production system that makes use of fully prepared menu items that are made elsewhere, a microwave cooker is very fast and efficient. This type of product allows the caterer to offer a wide range of menu dishes without the need for highly skilled staff or expensive equipment.

In some batch cooking (see chapter 42), where only relatively small quantities of food are cooked at any one time, a microwave cooker is very useful. This is also the case if you find that you need a few more portions quickly towards the end of a service. In fact a microwave oven, on its own or in combination, can prove to be a very useful item of cooking equipment in almost any kitchen, as long as you remember what it can't do!

41.2 Points to be observed when cooking by microwave

- Always avoid operating an empty oven. A bowl of water can be placed inside to prevent this happening.
- The cooking time will be different for different types of food and for different amounts of the same food.
- Food items should not be more than 3-4 cm (1-1½ inches) thick. Shallow trays are more suitable than deep trays.
- Don't use trays that are much larger than the food – these will get hot and conduct heat away from the food.

- When heating or reheating plated food, spread the food out as evenly as you can.
- Overloading the oven with too much food slows down the heating of the contents.
- Read the manufacturer's instructions carefully before using the oven for the first time. The cooking time will depend on the output of the oven. Be careful not to overestimate the cooking time needed.
- Always switch on the oven to allow it to become operational before you actually use it.
- Metallic plates and containers should not be used in some microwave ovens, as they reflect rather than absorb the microwaves. These reflected rays may damage the equipment.
- Most foods are best covered with film (not foil!) before heating, as this reduces the loss of water.
- Only use the microwave cooker for the appropriate foods. (Deep-fried and other types of food with a crisp surface, such as pizzas, are unsuitable.)
- Ensure that the microwave cooker is serviced regularly, to lessen the chance of radiation leaks.
- Clean the cooker inside and outside at the end of each period of use. Wipe up any spillages inside the oven as they happen.

42 Batch cooking

42.1 General principles

Batch cooking is a technique by means of which freshly cooked food is supplied in limited quantities throughout a service period. This method is very useful in situations where freshly cooked items are needed over an extended service. The alternative is to cook all the menu items in advance of service and store them in hot cabinets or bains-marie until required. However, many food items deteriorate in colour, flavour, and texture if kept hot for long periods. This is especially true of green vegetables. There is also a considerable loss of vitamin C. Batch cooking means that the quality of the product will be as good for your last customer as for your first.

Batch cooking involves cooking smaller quantities – often on specially designed equipment – immediately before they are served. This goes on during the whole of the service period, which in the case of some operations is for quite a long time. You will find it helpful if you have a good idea of the likely demand for certain items at peak periods, and this can often be the case in particular situations such as industrial canteens and cafeterias.

Not all menu items are suitable for batch cooking – particularly those that take a long time to cook, such as stewed or braised meats or steamed savoury puddings. Items that are especially suitable are those deteriorate fairly quickly after cooking – green vegetables; grilled, shallow-fried, and deep-fried foods; and hot egg dishes. The technique can also be used for frozen items. These should be regenerated in small quantities to meet the expected demand.

You must make sure that the batch-cooked products are used in the correct sequence. Care must be taken that the last items of one batch are competely used up before you start serving the first of the next batch. Some companies issue guidelines telling staff how long certain cooked food items can be left on display before they must be replaced by a freshly cooked batch.

We mention elsewhere the idea of keeping records to help forecast demand. Batch cooking is a good example of how the expected demand can be based on previous sales with some degree of accuracy.

The work of the kitchen staff in preparing the raw commodities for cooking is not affected by batch cooking.

Batch cooking should not be confused with the style of production used for à la carte service, where the demand for certain dishes is very unpredictable. An à la carte menu (see page 288) is designed in a way that allows a small number of portions of dishes on the menu to be cooked to order in a reasonably short time.

42.2 Equipment used for batch cooking

Equipment used for batch cooking could include microwave ovens (see chapter 41), steam convection ovens, high-pressure steamers, and combination ovens.

Steam convection ovens

These are multi-purpose forced-convection ovens which cook with hot air, steam from a built-in boiler, or a combination of both. A fan circulates hot air or steam around the oven to give an even temperature within the oven and so avoid the need for shelf manipulation.

When the door of the oven shown in fig. 42.1 is opened, a concealed switch stops the fan and cuts off power to the oven and boiler elements. The door catch operates in two stages: the first stage allows the door to open slightly for steam to escape safely; the second stage allows the door to open fully.

Fig. 42.1 A steam convection oven

A rapid-cooling feature is incorporated. An automatic filling system maintains the correct water level in the boiler, which can be drained at the touch of a switch.

Cooking modes

- *Hot air* Air is drawn from the oven by the fan, blown over heating elements, and returned to the oven. This mode is suitable for cooking processes normally carried out in a conventional oven – baking, dry roasting, regenerating frozen foods, etc. The temperature of the oven shown in fig. 42.1 can be set at up to 250° C (482° F) in this mode.
- *Steam* Steam from the boiler is circulated around the oven by the fan. This mode is suitable for cooking food normally cooked in steamers – fresh or frozen vegetables, fish, etc. The oven will run at about 100° C (212° F) in this mode.

- *Combination* This is a combination of the two previous modes, the oven being supplied alternately with hot air or steam. This mode is suitable for all roasts etc. where shrinkage reduction is desirable, and the oven temperature can be set at up to 250° C (482° F).
- *Controlled steam* The oven temperature is controlled by steam being delivered to the oven as required. This mode is suitable for sous-vide and other delicate steaming, and the oven temperature can be set at up to 100° C (212° F).

In the hot-air or combination modes, the oven should be allowed to heat up for at least 30 minutes from cold before use, irrespective of the temperature setting.

In the steam or controlled-steam modes the oven is suitable for use once steam is being produced.

Use of the oven

The shelf arrangement will depend on the food being cooked and the size of container used. All shelf positions may be used at the same time if the food and container size permit. Normally manipulation of food on the shelves is unnecessary.

The oven should be loaded as quickly as possible, to avoid loss of heat.

The oven is fitted with a meat probe for automatic control of the cooking time, using the temperature of the centre of the meat to shut down the oven.

Cleaning

- The interior of the oven should be cleaned daily using a spray-on oven cleaner. The oven should be cooled to about 60° C (140° F) and sprayed with the cleaner. After 15–30 minutes the oven should then be switched on and set to 'steam' for 10–20 minutes. The oven should then be switched off and the interior rinsed with plenty of water.
- Stubborn stains and baked-on deposits are best removed by the use of nylon scouring pads or spray-on oven cleaners. Do *not* use steel-wool scourers, otherwise the surfaces will be scratched and localised rusting could develop.

Regenerating frozen food in an oven

When using any oven to heat up frozen food, there must be a good circulation of air around the frozen packs so that the oven can do its job properly. Overloading the oven may result in some parts of the food being inadequately cooked, with potentially serious consequences.

- Never pack a shelf with cartons pushed together so that air cannot circulate between them – fig. 42.2(a).
- Never pack a shelf with one carton on top of another so that air cannot circulate between them – fig. 42.2(b).
- Always allow space between cartons – fig. 42.2(c) – so that air can circulate freely and allow the product to cook through.

The greater part of the regenerating process, in terms of time and

(a) Overloading   (b) No air space   (c) Air allowed to circulate

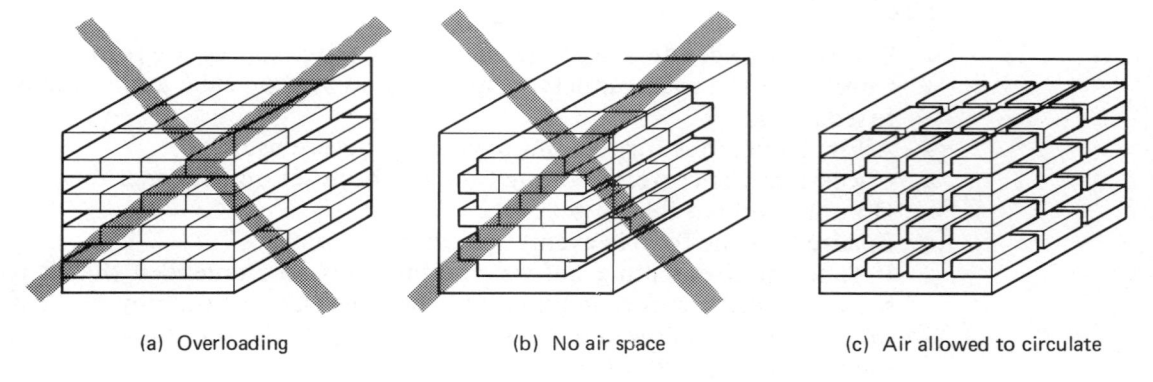

Fig. 42.2 Regenerating frozen food in an oven

temperature, is that required to thaw out the product. When this has been done, the food will heat quickly to a safe eating temperature (70° C (158° F)).

The total cooking time will depend on the food and the manufacturer's recommendations.

High-pressure steamers

The high-presure steamer (fig. 42.3) is a compact unit, heated by gas or electricity, which can rapidly cook fresh or frozen meat, poultry, fish, and vegetables at a high pressure of 0.55 bar (8 p.s.i.). Sponge puddings are best cooked at a low pressure of 0.17 bar (2.5 p.s.i.).

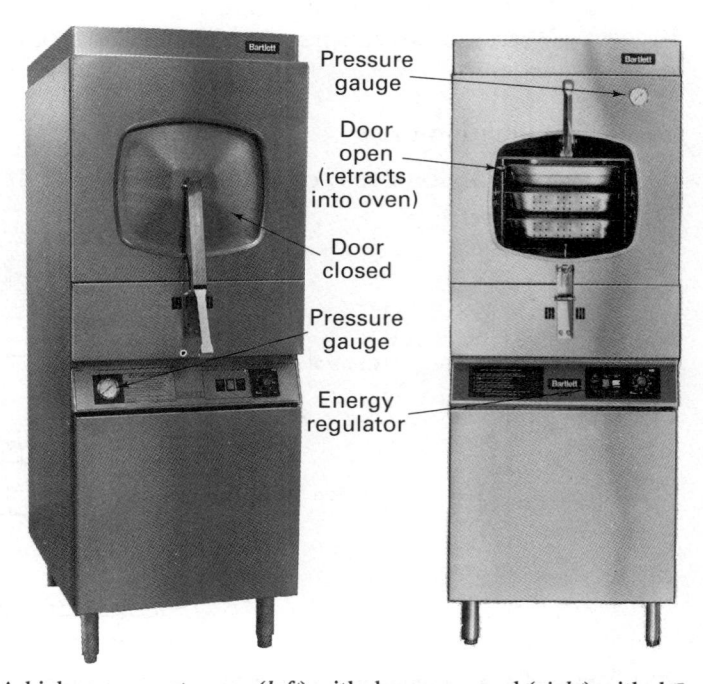

Fig. 42.3 A high-pressure steamer (*left*) with door open and (*right*) with door closed

254 *Food preparation and cooking*

Cooking hints

- Before starting, check that the energy and water supply are turned on.
- Check that the rack runners, drip tray, and syphon tube are correctly fitted.
- Allow 30 minutes for the unit to heat up before using.
- Check that the correct cooking time has been set on the timer dial.
- Do not overload the trays.
- Ensure that the food is evenly spread in the trays.
- If food requires salting before cooking, it is recommended that it is soaked in brine before loading into the oven. Corrosion may result if salt crystals are allowed to stick to the casting of the cooking chamber, the door fittings, and the tray runners.
- Cooking times will depend on the type of food and the quantity of food being cooked; for example, 2.25 kg (5 lb) of frozen peas will cook in 4–5 minutes, 6.5 kg (14 lb) of frozen peas will cook in 11–13 minutes.
- Take great care when opening the door after cooking.

Cleaning

The cooker should be cleaned every day after use. Before cleaning, turn off the electricity at the mains and allow the cooker to cool down.

- Remove the trays, syphon tube, drip tray, and side runners and clean with detergent and warm water.
- Wash off any food residue from the internal casing.
- Remove any scale from the bottom and check the spray jets for blockages.
- Rinse with clean water and dry.
- Wipe the exterior panels with a damp cloth – do not clean with a jet of water.

Combination oven

A combination oven, or 'micro-air', (fig. 42.4) uses forced air convection

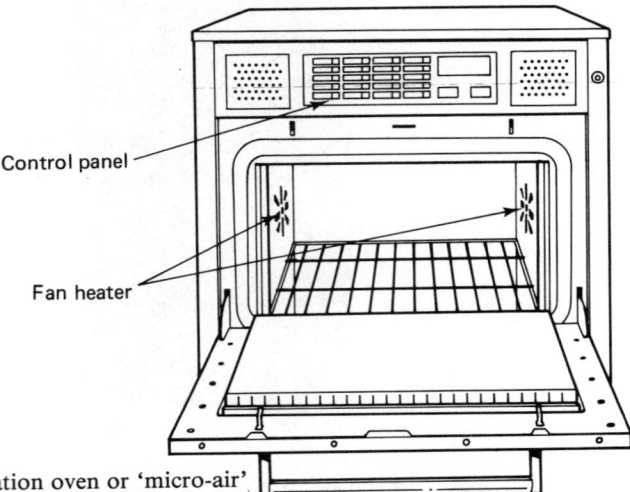

Fig. 42.4 A combination oven or 'micro-air'

and microwaves together to roast, bake, poach, or boil in a much reduced cooking time. With the addition of hot pans and grills, frying and grilling can also be achieved.

Additional source of heat

To increase the range of dishes that the micro-air can cook, a solid or open-top range is required to heat the frying pans and grill trays. These are used to sear and colour the pieces of food, which are then placed into the micro-air to cook through.

Pot and pans

All normal cooking utensils may be used in the micro-air cooker, whether of metal, earthenware, Pyrex, or other heat-resistant materials, but not pans with plastic, bakelite, or wooden handles. It is not advisable to use high-sided metal saucepans, since reflection of microwaves by the metal will reduce effective penetration.

Roasting

Choose roasting trays, of either steel or aluminium, preferably not deeper than 3–5 cm (1½–2 inches). A trivet is not always essential but can be used if required. Small joints can be cooked in small black iron pans. For all roast meats and poultry a low microwave power setting is advised – a better finish can sometimes be achieved by using hot air only.

Baking

Use black mild-steel baking-trays, as these absorb a certain amount of heat and help to colour the baked goods. You will find that pies are best made in individual portions, rather than multi-portion pie dishes which have to be portioned after cooking. When cooking from raw, turn the microwave down to half power.

Frying

All types of frying pan can be used in the cooker, provided that they can withstand heating to 260° C (500° F). Pans with plastic or wooden handles are not suitable. The pan and the fat must first be heated before searing the pieces of food. The food is then transferred to the micro-air. This will greatly reduce the cooking times.

Grilling

Branders and skillets made of cast iron produce the best results.

Sautéing

The classic sauté pan can be used, provided it is used without a lid.

Boiling

This is best done in earthenware dishes, the size depending on the quantity of food being cooked. Ovenproof glass or Pyrex can also be used. Small portions of food and some frozen vegetables will require very little water. Frozen spinach can be cooked without any extra water.

No exact times can be given for the boiling of meat and poultry – much will depend on the size and quality of the food.

Poaching

This can be done quickly in any dish, using the minimum amount of liquid and following all the normal rules (see chapter 29).

Stewing and braising

These can be carried out in all types of dish – the size will depend on the quantity of food to be cooked. Five portions of braised steak can be cooked in a small earthenware casserole, whereas braised steak for fifty portions would be better in a large aluminium tray.

It is recommended that up to a third more liquid is added than for stewing or braising in a conventional oven, to allow for the reduction that occurs in a micro-air.

Reheating

This can be successfully carried out in most types of dish. For vegetables use earthenware, which will give a slightly quicker and better result, especially if using a lid. If reheating in a metal dish, cover the food with a piece of damp or buttered greaseproof paper or (for microwave only) plain clingfilm.

Defrosting

This is best carried out in a shallow tray on a low microwave setting.

Cleaning the micro-air

The cooker will work more efficiently if you clean if regularly, using hot soapy water with a clean cloth or a nylon pad. More stubborn deposits can be removed using a proprietary brand of oven-cleaner. Do not, however, use a cleaner containing caustic soda or made of wire wool. The cooker will be easiest to clean while still warm – aim for a temperature of 50–60° C (122–140° F). The microwave-absorbing material around the door should be checked regularly for any sign of wear.

43 Sous-vide cooking

43.1 General principles

Sous-vide cooking is a method of food preparation where the prepared food is cooked in a sealed plastic pouch from which all or much of the air has been removed to prevent oxidation of the food. This is different from the preparation of 'boil in the bag' products, which are cooked and portioned *before* being sealed in plastic bags.

Although the term sous-vide means literally 'under a vacuum', this is not strictly true of this method of cooking. What happens is that some of the air surrounding the food is removed, creating a 'modified atmosphere'. Some manufacturers of vacuum equipment prefer this term.

The fresh food is prepared and, if necessary, par-cooked under very strict hygienic conditions and placed into a specially designed plastic pouch. Air is removed from the pouch by a specially designed vacuum-packing machine. Once this has been done, the neck of the pouch is heat-sealed. Very delicate foods that might be damaged by the removal of too much air, such as fish or some fruits, are flushed with a gas such as carbon dioxide or nitrogen that will not react with the food.

Cooking is done in a steam convection oven at a controlled temperature between 70 and 100 °C (158–212 °F). Generally, white meat is cooked at a lower temperature than red meat. Because of the low temperature involved, cooking times are up to 2.5 times longer than those for conventional cooking methods. Lower cooking temperatures also result in less shrinkage of food and less damage to food structure. Some meats are reported to lose only about 5% in shrinkage, compared with 35% by some roasting methods. We can assume that the nutritional losses will also be low, because of the absence of air (oxygen), provided that any juices escaping into the bag are used in the finished dish. Some users of the system claim that meats cooked by sous-vide have a better flavour and are more tender.

If the food is not to be eaten straight away, it must be rapidly chilled to a temperature of 0–3° C (32–37° F) and be stored at or below those temperatures.

Sous-vide cooking is suitable for most areas of catering. It can be used in an à la carte restaurant to spread the preparation over a longer period. Hospitals, trains, and in-flight catering have also shown an interest in this method. A small number of specialist companies now offer a range of sous-vide dishes for the caterer to purchase.

The food is regenerated (reheated) by the use of a steamer, a pan of boiling water, or a microwave oven.

43.2 Some points about sous-vide cooking

- Uses low temperatures for cooking (70–100° C (158–212° F)).
- Reduces food shrinkage caused by some methods of cooking.
- Vegetables and garnishes can be added before the pouch is sealed.
- Food can be served immediately it is cooked or be chilled for later use.
- Cooked foods can be stored for up to 5 days at 0–3° C (32–37° F).
- Little nutrient loss during cooking.
- Food is cooked in its natural juices, with little loss of flavour. Less use of herbs, spices, and flavourings is needed.
- The absence of air (oxygen) surrounding the food in the pouch means that less food spoilage will take place, whether due to micro-organisms or chemical changes (see pages 176 and 177).
- Very strict hygiene is vitally important in the preparation stages. A number of food-poisoning micro-organisms can live very happily in vacuum packs and at the temperature of a refrigerator.

43.3 Vacuum packing

Many caterers who do not prepare sous-vide dishes use vacuum-packing before or after conventional cooking. The process actually uses a modified atmosphere rather than a true vacuum. If a caterer uses a vacuum-packer to extend the storage life of fresh or cooked foods, it is claimed that they can be kept for 21 days, provided that the hygienic practices used in preparation and packaging are of the highest standard.

44 Centralised production

44.1 General principles

It is not unusual nowadays for some of the food-production work for a number of kitchens or other outlets to be done in a central unit. As equipment becomes increasingly expensive and skilled catering staff harder to find, many organisations are using a central kitchen with the latest equipment and skilled staff to prepare food items that can be transported for sale elsewhere, in either a finished or a partly finished state.

Very frequently the dishes or food items are frozen or chilled before being distributed. A cook–chill or cook–freeze system (see sections 44.2 and 44.3) operates in many hospitals and other large institutions.

Within a single hotel, you may find that the main kitchen will supply prepared food items to several other outlets within that hotel, for example:

- the main hotel restaurant;
- other restaurants, possibly with a special feature;
- a coffee shop;
- functions, banqueting;
- floor or room service;
- a staff dining area.

In some cases, a finishing kitchen is necessary to provide any additional menu items and to assemble and garnish those dishes supplied by the central kitchen. Even where a finishing kitchen is necessary, this does not mean that all the staff and equipment of the main kitchen have to be duplicated in the finishing kitchen: both the staff and the equipment in a finishing kitchen will need different skills and capabilities from those in the central kitchen.

44.2 Cook–chill operation

This is a food-production system based on traditional methods of preparing and cooking foods, using the normal items of equipment.

Once the dishes are cooked, they are rapidly cooled to 0–3° C (32–37° F). The chilled dishes can be stored at this temperature for a maximum period of 5 days. Immediately before they are needed, the dishes are reheated (regenerated). A finishing kitchen running entirely on a cook–chill system would need only semi-skilled staff and a minimum of equipment. A number of manufacturers specialise in the necessary equipment for such systems.

The following catering operations can successfully utilise a cook–chill system:

- banqueting and function work;
- in-flight catering and train catering;
- hospitals, day centres, and meals on wheels;

260 Food preparation and cooking

- industrial catering;
- school meals.

In each of these situations the demand for meals is either fairly constant or highly predictable. A cook–chill system is not a good idea where the demand may be small or unpredictable, for example in a kitchen producing meals for an à la carte menu (see page 288).

Recommendations for a cook–chill cycle of food production

Preparation

- Suppliers of ready-prepared food to be incorporated into a cook–chill system must have their premises inspected by a competent person (an environmental health inspector).
- Raw food items should be prepared in an area physically separated from the cooking and after-cooking areas.
- Frozen cooked food and cooked food should be prepared separately from raw food materials.
- Electrical preparation equipment, utensils, and knives used for the preparation of raw food items must not be used to further process cooked food.

Equipment

- The use of specialised rapid-thaw equipment is compulsory.
- Standard microwave ovens are considered suitable for reheating food only if the doors are fitted with an interlock to prevent food being removed before the correct pre-set time has elapsed.
- Care must be taken to ensure that the food has reheated evenly when using a microwave oven.
- Automatic controls and temperature-sensing equipment are required on all reheating equipment.

Cooking

- The food should be cooked at a sufficiently high temperature to kill any possible pathogenic micro-organisms (see page 174).
- Disposable gloves for handling cooked food before chilling can be worn, but only if the operator's gloved hands are washed at frequent intervals.

Storage

- Cooked food should be stored at a temperature of 0–3° C (32–37° F).
- Cooked food should be stored not longer than 5 days, including the day of production and the day the food is consumed.
- Bought-in food products that may have a longer shelf life must be consumed within the 5 day period.

- If the storage temperature rises above 5° C (41° F) but remains below 10° C (50° F) the food must be consumed within 12 hours.
- If the storage temperature rises above 10° C (50° F), the food must be discarded.
- The volume of rapid-chill capacity must be equal to the maximum output of the production area.
- Storage chillers specially designed for cook–chill food must be used. These are recommended to include sophisticated temperature-monitoring devices with alarms and remote recording equipment.

Chilling

- Chilling should start within 30 minutes of the food being cooked.
- The food should be chilled to an internal temperature of 0–3° C (32–37° F) within 90 minutes of the start of chilling.
- Food labels should show the day of production and the expiry date of the food.

Reheating

- The internal temperature of the food should reach a minimum of 70° C (158° F) for not less than 2 minutes.
- Reheating should take place as soon as possible after removal from chilled storage close to the consumer for prompt consumption.
- Food not reheated within 30 minutes of removal from chilled storage must be discarded.

Distribution

- Cooked food should be stored at the recommended temperatures (see above) during distribution.
- Insulated containers are allowed where distribution times are short.
- The maximum distribution time for hot food is restricted to 15 minutes.
- Food to be eaten cold or at room temperature should be eaten within 30 minutes of removal from chilled storage.
- Cold plating at hospitals must be completed in an air temperature that does not exceed 10° C (50° F).

Central production unit

Figure 44.1 illustrates what happens to the raw material from the point of entry (stores reception) to the point of exit (distribution to the finishing kitchen).

The equipment used for preparation and cooking should be of a large capacity and a heavy-duty design and consist of the following types: mincers, mixers, bowl cutters, gravity-feed slicers, convection ovens, Bratt pans, steaming ovens, boiling units, tilting kettles, baking ovens, etc.

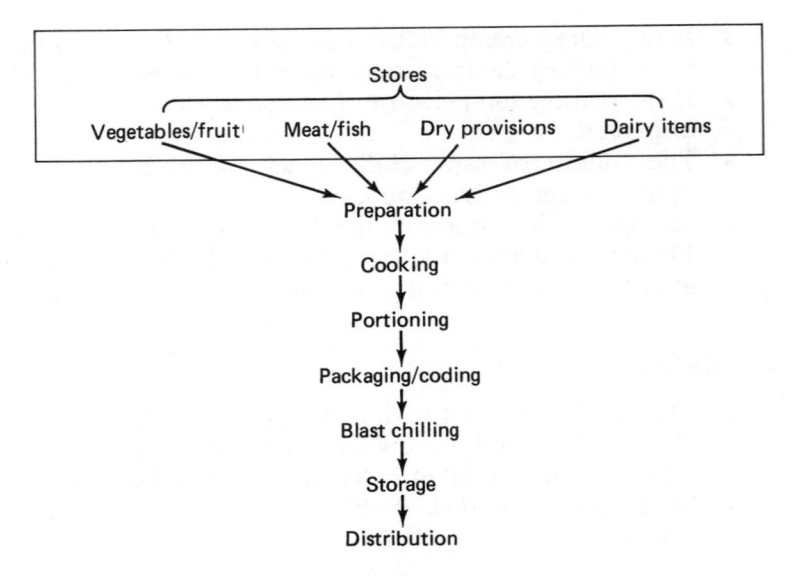

```
              Stores
   ┌─────────────┴─────────────┐
Vegetables/fruit  Meat/fish  Dry provisions  Dairy items
   └─────────────┬─────────────┘
            Preparation
                ↓
             Cooking
                ↓
            Portioning
                ↓
         Packaging/coding
                ↓
           Blast chilling
                ↓
             Storage
                ↓
           Distribution
```

Fig. 44.1 Flow diagram of a central production unit

Advantages of a cook–chill system

- Allows equipment and staff to be used to their full potential.
- Avoids the peaks and troughs associated with traditional kitchen production.
- Energy-saving. Only those items of equipment that it is known are going to be used are switched on.
- Increases output with a planned production, using skilled staff and expensive equipment to the best effect. The increased efficiency should soon repay the cost of the initial outlay on equipment.

In some systems, such as the Regetherm system, the meals are pre-plated into specially designed trays for regeneration. The final reheating then needs no skill other than placing the loaded trolley into the pre-programmed oven unit.

44.3 Cook-freeze operation

This type of system operates along similar lines to the cook–chill system, except that the food is frozen after portioning instead of being chilled. The temperatures required are much lower and the equipment for freezing, storing, and transporting the frozen food is more expensive. The frozen food items or complete dishes have a much longer storage life than cook–chill items, but the high cost of the equipment needed and of running the system have made it less popular than cook–chill.

45 Stocks, thickening agents, and sauces

45.1 Stocks

Stocks are well-flavoured liquid preparations that are used as a basis for sauces, soups, stews, gravies, glazes, and other dishes. Stocks are made from bones, aromatic vegetables, herbs or spices, and water.

The flavour and the colour will depend on the ingredients and how you cook them. Stocks are classified as 'white' or 'brown' and have different uses, as you will have noticed in your cookery book. Fresh stocks are easy to make, although they do take a bit of time. Care should be taken that you end up with a clear, well-flavoured product of the colour you need, without any apparent fat on the surface. If you have made a good stock, it will enhance the favour and appearance of the dish you are going to use it in. If you have not made a good job of it, you may spoil the dish.

Convenience stocks can be produced from a variety of commercially available preparations and are widely used in the catering industry. They come in many forms, such as cubes, granules, or extracts, and in different flavours: meat, fish, and vegetable. These convenience stocks can be used instead of fresh stocks or can be added to dishes to improve the flavour of the finished article. They have some advantages and some disadvantages (Table 45.1), and whether you use them or not will depend on the situation in which you are working.

Table 45.1 Convenience stocks

Advantages	Disadvantages
• Readily available. • No special storage facilities needed. • Long shelf life. • Can be prepared quickly. • Do not 'tie up' equipment for long periods. • Not much equipment needed. • Cheap to produce in small quantities • Do not need skilled staff to supervise their preparation.	• Not the same flavour as fresh stock. • Inclined to be salty. • Care must be taken not to add too much salt. • Unsuitable for making glazes. • Limited range of flavours. • Strongly flavoured or coloured convenience stocks can overpower a light, delicate dish.

45.2 Glazes

Glazes are made from brown, white, or fish stock by boiling for long enough to reduce the liquid to a gelatinous consistency with a concentrated flavour (without the lid on the pan, of course.). In classical cookery they are used to enhance the flavour of some dishes, to decorate sauces, or as a basis for sauces with the addition of butter and cream.

45.3 Thickening agents

Thickening agents are added to liquids such as soups, sauces, and stews to give 'body'. Only enough thickening agent should be added to make the product of the required consistency.

Sauces and soups in recent years have tended to be thinner in consistency and lighter in texture than they used to be – probably as a result of the interest in the new, lighter style of cooking. This often means that less thickening agent is used in the recipe.

Most thickening agents fall into two broad categories: those based on starch and those based on protein.

Starch-based thickening agents

These depend on the fact that starch, in the presence of water and heat, gelatinises to form a viscous liquid (see page 157).

ROUX

A roux is a mixture of flour and fat, gently cooked together in a thick-based pan over a low heat. The roux may be cooked to one of three stages: white, blond, or brown. To produce a sauce or a soup from this, an aqueous liquid is added and the mixture is cooked (see Table 45.2). To make the product smooth and to avoid being scalded by steam, the roux should be cooled a little before the hot liquid is added. If you cool the roux too much, the fat will turn solid and make mixing very difficult.

BEURRE MANIÉ

This is a mixture of three parts butter to two parts flour. These are kneaded together in a basin until a smooth soft consistency is reached. The mixture is then whisked or stirred vigorously into the hot liquid that is being used to prepare the soup or sauce and is then simmered for a few minutes.

Beurre manié is sometimes referred to as cold roux or pounded butter.

In using both of the above types of thickening agent, you should not use aluminium pans or whisks as these may discolour the sauce.

STARCHES

Cornflour, arrowroot, potato flour, rice flour, and barley flour are all used as thickening agents, although cornflour and arrowroot are the two most commonly used. The starch is mixed with the cold liquid – which might be milk, stock, water, or fruit juice – and then added to the boiling liquid with constant stirring. The whole of the liquid then needs to be cooked for a short time to complete the gelatinisation of the starch.

The type of starch used will depend on the effect that is required – for example, arrowroot gives a translucent product and is suitable for a fruit glaze.

Table 45.2 Preparation of basic sauces using a roux

Type of roux	White roux	Blond roux	Brown roux
Type of sauce	Béchamel sauce	Velouté sauce	Sauce espagnole
Ingredients	Equal quantities of flour and margarine or butter	Equal quantities of flour and margarine or butter	4 parts dripping or lard to 5 parts flour
Quantities for 1 litre	50 g flour 50 g butter/margarine (Increase these quantities if thicker sauce required.)	50 g flour 50 g butter/margarine (Increase these quantities if thicker sauce required.)	40 g lard 50 g flour (Increase these quantities if thicker sauce required.)
Cooked out for	2–3 minutes – sandy texture similar to damp sand	3–5 minutes – sandy texture similar to damp sand	10–15 minutes – soft moist texture and a deep brown colour
	Cool off the heat.	Cool off the heat.	Cool and stir in tomato purée.
Type of liquid	Milk infused with shredded onion, cloves, and bay leaf	White stock – fish, chicken, veal	Brown beef stock
	Gradually add the milk, stir to the boil, and cover with a buttered cartouche.	Gradually add the required stock, stir to the boil, adding any recipe flavourings.	Stir to the boil, add browned drained aromatic vegetables, bacon trimmings, and bouquet garni.
Simmer, stirring regularly for	20 minutes	30 minutes	4–6 hours – skim off impurities.
	Strain through a chinois at the end of cooking.	Strain through a chinois at the end of cooking.	Strain through a chinois at the end of cooking.
Other uses for roux	White vegetable soups – onion, cauliflower, celery, leek	Velouté soups, tomato soup and sauce, white stews	Brown soups – kidney, oxtail, game

Protein-based thickening agents

These depend on the protein coagulating (see page 158) or forming an emulsion for the thickening effect.

EGG-YOLKS

These used in a number of ways to thicken liquids:

- Whisked with oil, mustard, salt, and vinegar to form an emulsion – mayonnaise sauce.
- Mixed with cream to form a liaison to thicken and enrich soups, sauces, and stews at the end of the normal cooking period. The liquid must not be allowed to boil once the liaison has been added.
- Cooked to a sabayon with a wine and vinegar reduction. This is then used to emulsify clarified butter for hollandaise sauce.
- Mixed with sugar, vanilla essence, and hot milk and cooked over a gentle heat without boiling to make custard sauce.
- Mixed with sugar, vanilla essence, and warm milk; poured into a mould; and cooked in the oven in a bain-marie to make baked egg custard.

Further information on the use of eggs in making sauces will be found in Table 45.3.

Table 45.3 Preparation of basic sauces using egg-yolk

Sauce mayonnaise	Sauce hollandaise
• Place the ingredients into a stainless-steel, glass, or earthenware bowl: 4 egg-yolks 2 g salt 15 ml white-wine vinegar 5 g English mustard • Whisk together for 10 seconds with a fine wire stainless-steel sauce whisk. • Add 500 ml oil gradually in a thin stream, whisking vigorously and continuously. • Correct the seasoning and adjust the flavour with lemon-juice if necessary.	• Place the ingredients into a tinned copper or stainless-steel sauteuse: 60 ml white wine 30 ml white-wine vinegar 8 crushed peppercorns 30 g finely chopped shallots • Reduce to one-quarter over heat. • Arrest and reconstitute with a little warm water. Cool. • Melt 500 g butter, skim off impurities, and pour off the clear butterfat, leaving behind the opaque water and solids. • Make the sabayon by adding 4 egg-yolks to the reduction and whisking over a low heat until thick and creamy in consistency. • Remove from the heat and whisk until cool. • Add the warm butterfat gradually in a thin stream whisking vigorously and continuously. • Correct the seasoning and adjust the flavour with lemon-juice if necessary. • Pass through muslin into a pre-warmed bowl, cover, and keep warm.

BLOOD

This is used to thicken and provide the characteristic flavour of jugged hare and coq au vin. The blood is collected and is added to the sauce at the end of the cooking. Once the blood has been added, the sauce should not be allowed to boil.

Miscellaneous thickening agents

Butter (which contains no starch and hardly any protein) is also used as a thickening agent for many types of sauce. Soft butter is shaken or whisked into a reduced stock away from the heat until a smooth consistency is obtained. Sauces thickened by this method are not suitable for long storage and are best made to order and stored for a short time in a warm position.

Many fish and savoury sauces have a small quantity of butter added just before they are served. You will find that this improves the flavour and gives the sauce 'shine'.

Other sauces are made from vegetables or fruit simmered with a liquid and puréed to provide the thickness that is required.

45.4 Sauces

Sauces are hot or cold flavoured liquids that have been thickened, usually by including one of the thickening agents discussed in section 45.3.

Sauces are still very important in food preparation, although the style of some sauces is changing. In days when transport and refrigeration were difficult or non-existent, rich and highly flavoured sauces were in some cases used to mask the poor quality of the foods. Nowadays this is not necessary, so the trend is towards lighter, more delicate sauces which allow the flavour of the food to be appreciated. Some customers are also wanting to get away from the rich sauces, which contain substantial amounts of saturated fat (as in butter or cream), for health reasons.

Sauces are incorporated into or served with prepared dishes for a number of reasons:

- to enchance the flavour of the main ingredient – for example, curry sauce;
- to complement the flavour of the main ingredient – for example suprême sauce with a chicken dish;
- to enchance the flavour of high-quality food – for example, truffle sauce with tournedos steak;
- to counteract the fatty nature of food – for example, apple sauce with roast duck;
- to provide extra moisture with dry foods – for example, tomato sauce with white haricot beans;
- to increase or improve the flavour of bland foods – for example, sauces served with pasta and gnocchi dishes;
- to increase the selection of available menu dishes.

There are a number of basic sauces (sometimes called 'mother' sauces) from which other sauces (called 'derivatives') are made, by the addition of wines, herbs, garnishes, vinegar reductions, etc. In addition, there are some sauces that do not fit into any of these categories – these are referred to as miscellaneous sauces.

Basic sauces

The five basic sauces are espagnole, béchamel, velouté, hollandaise, and mayonnaise. We give an outline of their preparation in Tables 45.2 and 45.3, to show their different components and methods of preparation.

Sauces that are derivatives

A look at your cookery book will show you the enormous range of sauces that are still in quite common use in catering in fairly modest establishments. A number are made from each of the basic sauces described earlier.

Miscellaneous sauces

These sauces are not made from any of the basic sauces. In some cases the taste, texture, and appearance are unique to that particular sauce. Examples are mint sauce, horseradish sauce, cranberry sauce, apple sauce, and bread sauce.

46 Cooking utensils and small equipment

46.1 Materials used in cooking equipment

This chapter covers the chefs' hand tools, moulds, and bowls used in the preparation of the menu dishes and the items of equipment that the chef will use for cooking. These can be produced from a variety of different materials (Table 46.1).

Table 46.1 Materials used in cooking equipment

Material	Description	Uses	Cleaning
Copper	Copper is a good conductor of heat and transfers heat to the food quickly and evenly. It does not rust or pit but tarnishes quickly. For most uses, copper saucepans are lined with tin, which needs replacing when the copper shows through. Copper items are expensive to purchase and to have professionally retinned. They are traditionally used in hotel/restaurant kitchens. Where possible, avoid the use of metal hand tools, which scratch the soft tin lining.	Unlined copper bowls – whisking egg-whites. Saucepans of various types – sauteuse, plat à sauter, rondeau, braisière, etc. Moulds – dariole, charlotte, bombes, etc. Sugar boiler – unlined.	Avoid excessive heat when the pan is empty, as this softens the tin. Wash with soap and hot water – never scour the inside of a tinned pan. Soak burnt-on food residue to soften it before washing off. Clean the outside with either salt and vinegar mixed together or a suitable commercial cleaner.
Aluminium	Aluminium is cheaper than copper and, although not as good a conductor of heat, it conducts heat reasonably well. It is durable, hardwearing, and non-corrosive, but is not suitable for the preparation of white sauces. Thin metal saucepans will warp and produce hot spots; those	Suitable for the manufacture of plats à sauter, saucepans of various shapes and sizes, fish-kettles, trays, baking-sheets, etc.	Will not rust. Wash with soap and hot water. Burnt-on food residue can be removed with a scouring pad.

Table 46.1 Materials used in cooking equipment (*continued*)

Material	Description	Uses	Cleaning
	with a solid thick base are more suitable for commercial use.		
Cast iron	A poor conductor of heat, but durable and hard-wearing, holding the heat well after being removed from the stove. Cast iron is inclined to rust, so is best used where fat or oil is a feature of the method of cooking.	Shallow saucepans; omelette, crêpe, and frying pans; heavy-duty roasting trays. New pans need to be seasoned before use – heat a layer of oil in the pan until it is smoking, empty out the oil, and wipe the pan with a soft, dry cloth.	Wash with soap and hot water. Burnt-on food residue can be removed with a hard bristle brush. Dry well and oil very lightly.
Black/plain steel	A good conductor of heat, durable, and hard-wearing. It is best used for methods of cooking involving fat or oil, because it rusts quickly if not throughly dried after washing.	Omelette, crêpe, and frying pans; pizza pans; paella pans. New pans need to be seasoned before use (see above).	Pans are best wiped out with an oily cloth. Burnt-on food residue can be removed as for cast iron.
Stainless steel	A very poor conductor of heat – copper is often incorporated into the base of stainless-steel saucepans to improve this. Thin stainless-steel pans will produce hot spots. Stainless-steel items are durable and do not pit or rust. Although expensive, stainless-steel equipment is easy to maintain and always looks attractive.	Knives, cleavers, meat saws, bowls and trays of various types and sizes, flan rings, egg-whisks, ladles, perforated spoons, fish-slices, chip scoops, conical strainers, mandolin cutters.	Wash with soap and hot water. After soaking, burnt-on food residue can be removed with a hard bristle brush. Using a scouring pad will dull the surface shine.
Silver plate	An excellent conductor of heat, but too expensive for the manufacture of cooking utensils. It tarnishes quickly and so requires constant maintenance.	Serving dishes, sauce-boats, cutlery, cruet sets, etc.	Cutlery – Silver Dip. Dishes, sauce-boats, etc. – burnishing machine or a commercial cleaner.
Vitreous enamel coatings	Poor conductors of heat, but retain heat well after being removed from the stove. Enamel chips easily, so must be handled carefully. Traditionally	Oven-to-table casseroles, gratin dishes, saucepans, bowls, terrines, colanders, jugs.	Wash with soap and hot water. Burnt-on food residue can be removed with a hard bristle brush or a soft abrasive pad after soaking.

Table 46.1 Materials used in cooking equipment (*continued*)

Material	Description	Uses	Cleaning
	used more for domestic kitchens than industrial.		
Tinned ware	This equipment damages easily, so must be handled carefully. It does not pit or rust.	Colanders, conical strainers, frying baskets, ladles, skimmers, cooling racks, spoons, trays, flan rings, whisks, etc. Moulds and cases – charlotte, dariole, savarin, pie/pâté, cake tins, brioche, tartlet, barquette cases.	Wash with soap and hot water.
Wood	Items made of wood are porous and unhygienic when not properly cleaned. Wood burns and warps if exposed to high temperatures. It is durable and not easily broken under normal use.	Rolling pins, butchers' blocks, sieve surrounds, salt-boxes, spoons, spatulas, mushrooms, knife handles, meat/steak hammers, marzipan wheels, pastry-brush handles, etc.	Wash in soap and fairly hot water, rinse, and dry well. If necessary, scrub well with a stiff bristle brush. Never soak. Butchers' blocks are scraped with a metal scraper, sprinkled with salt, and scrubbed with a wire brush in one direction only.
Plastic	Plastic is not suitable for use at high temperatures. It is cheap to purchase, durable, light, and hygienic but is of only limited use in an industrial kitchen.	Pudding bowls, storage bowls and trays, plastic scrapers, measuring jugs, ice-trays, microwave cooking utensils, chopping boards (may be colour-coded to prevent cross-contamination between raw and cooked foods).	Wash in soap and hot water. Rinse and drain/dry.
Earthenware	Earthenware heats up slowly, but retains the heat for a long time once removed from the oven. It is easily broken, so must be handled carefully. If left unglazed it is liable to affect the flavour of food.	Casseroles, bowls, storage jars.	Wash with soap and hot water. Burnt-on food residue can be removed with a stiff bristle brush or scouring pad after soaking.

Other materials such as glass and marble are occasionally used for making items of kitchen equipment.

272 *Food preparation and cooking*

46.2 Small items of kitchen equipment

Small items of kitchen equipment can be classified according to use into the following groups. (Figures 46.1 to 46.3 show some items in these groups.)

Cutting/chopping

Assorted cooks' knives, potato peeler, canelle knife, butter curler, ball-cutters, oyster knife, lemon zester, aspic cutter, pastry cutter, dough cutter,

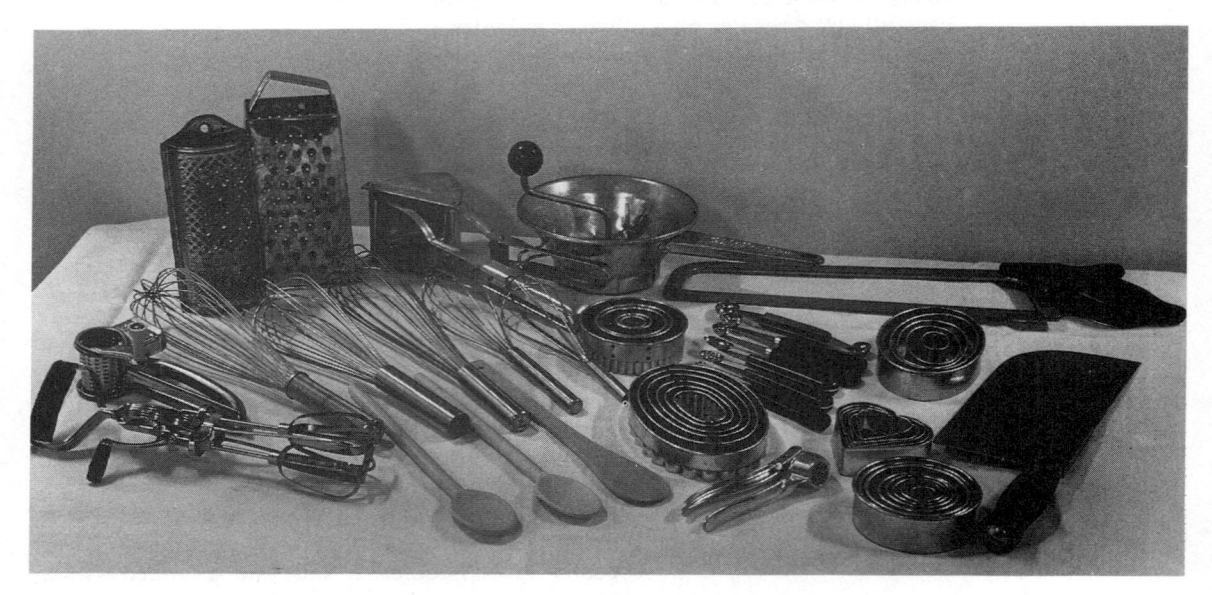

Fig. 46.1 Some tools for cutting, chopping, grating, whisking, and stirring

Fig. 46.2 Some tools for straining and draining

croissant cutter, egg slicer, ravioli cutters, food mills, mandolin, garlic press, cherry/olive stoner, cheese grater, nutmeg grater, fish-scissors, poultry secateurs, butchers' bone-saw, single/multi-bladed parsley choppers (hachoirs), cleaver, cheese-wire.

Straining/draining

Colander, chinois, cooks'/drum sieve, perforated spoon/ladle, long-handled skimmer, fish-lifter, straining spoon, wire ladle, boiling baskets, spaghetti baskets, salad basket, bowl strainer, sauce strainer.

Whisking/beating/stirring

Whisks (sauce, egg, balloon, batter, coil), wooden spoons, spatulas, basting spoons, Cutlet bat, meat hammer.

Moulds

Brioche, charlotte, savarin, pie/pâté mould, bombe, dariole, fancy patisserie (petit four, chocolate), confectionery, pie moulds, terrines, ravioli mould/tray.

Fig. 46.3 Some moulds

Trays/sheets/tins

Trays – roasting, butchers'/storage.
Baking-sheets – lipped, plain.
Flan rings – deep, shallow, adjustable, plain, fluted.
Flan frames – petal, oblong, heart, muffin/egg rings.
Tins – Swiss roll, shallow cake, bun, tartlet, sponge/sandwich tins, loaf, barquette, madeleine.
Cake tins – round, square, heart, hexagonal, etc.

Bowls

Hand bowls, mixing bowls (round and tapered), pudding basins, flour scoop.

Service equipment

Oval meat/fish flats, vegetable dishes, sauceboats, round trays, toast-racks, asparagus dish, avocado dish, oyster plate, shell dishes, sur-le-plat dish, oval sole dishes, ravier dish, ramekin dish, petit-marmite, cocotte dish, soufflé dishes, flan/cake slice, salad tongs, ice-cream scoop, tongs, kebab skewers, lemon-slice squeezer, snail tongs, fork, and dish.

Measuring

Ladles, sauce ladles, jugs, weighing scales, ice-cream scoop.

Wooden items

Mushroom, pestle, chopping boards, rolling-pins, pastry brushes, pepper/salt mills, salt-box, marzipan wheel.

Miscellaneous items

Long-handled grill tongs, fish-slice, cooling racks, potato ricer, can opener, flour/sugar dredger, meat hook, grill scrapers, butchers' block brush, piping bags and assorted tubes, plastic bowl scrapers, cake turntables, cake boards larding/trussing needles, skewers.

46.3 Pots and pans

The best-quality pots and pans available should be obtained, selecting the correct pan for the selected task (Table 46.2), of the right size, and manufactured from the most appropriate materials. Many pots and pans can be used for a number of different functions, but only the one basic design is suitable for some dishes such as omelettes, crêpes, sauté potatoes, etc.

Cheap, light pots/pans produced from thin metal will not conduct heat evenly but will develop hot spots. They will also quickly dent and buckle and become unsuitable for anything other than boiling vegetables.

Heavy, thick-based pots/pans with flat bottoms will conduct heat evenly and last for many years with thoughtful use. Handles should be stoutly constructed, be angled away from the heat source, offer a good grip, and preferably be riveted to the pot/pan. For those pots that have a lid, ensure that the lid lies flat, is unlikely to buckle when heated, and is well-fitting.

46.4 Professional cooks' knives

These are the most important hand tools that the chef uses. Each one must be carefully selected for the task(s) that it is to perform. Whenever possible, purchase only the best quality – the purchase of inferior-quality knives may prove more expensive in the long run.

Knives are available in either stainless steel or carbon steel. Although more expensive, stainless-steel knives are nearly always the first choice of the professional chef. They are easier to clean and attractive in appearance. Stainless-steel knives do not rust, stain, or impart off-flavours and colours to food items. If purchased from a reputable manufacturer of professional

Table 46.2 Pots and pans

Type	Description
Sauteuse (*sauteuse*)	Shallow pan with sloping sides, slightly rounded where the sides join the base. Used for reductions and sauces.
Sauté pan (*plat à sauter/sautoir*)	Shallow pan with straight sides used for the cooking of sauté and shallow-fried foods.
Saucepan (*russe*)	General-purpose saucepans are available in a range of shapes and sizes and often sold under a variety of names, such as stewpan, boiling pan, etc.
Stockpot (*marmite*)	Tall, upright pan with straight sides. Some models are fitted with a tap to drain off the contents. The shape helps to reduce evaporation.
Braising pan (*braisière*)	Round or rectangular in shape with a closely fitting lid.
Turbot kettle (*turbotière*)	Diamond-shaped pan with a lift-out perforated plate – used for deep poaching large, whole flat fish.
Salmon kettle (*saumonière*)	Long, narrow pan with a lift-out perforated plate – used for deep poaching salmon and other large round fish.
Rondeau (*rondeau*)	A large, deep-sided, round saucepan.
Asparagus kettle	Narrow vertical pot with a lift-out perforated inner sleeve for cooking fresh asparagus.
Omelette pan (*poêle à omelettes*)	Small, heavy, round pan with shallow sloping sides.
Pancake pan (*poêle à crêpes*)	Small flat pan with very shallow angled sides.
Frying-pan (*poêle*)	General-purpose pans have shallow sloping sides, and are available in a variety of sizes.
Sugar boiler	Straight-sided unlined copper pan, with a round, hollow, tapering handle.

Other types of pans used in the kitchen include oval fish-pans, grill pans, paella pans, pizza pans, double saucepans, and preserving pans.

cooks' knives and carefully looked after, stainless-steel or carbon-steel knives will last for many years.

Knives should be kept sharp at all times – blunt or poor-quality knives cannot be expected to perform efficiently. Knives that have the tang (the continuation of the sharpened blade) and the handle riveted together are preferable to those where the tang is only pushed into the handle and inevitably works loose. A knife ought to feel balanced with the blade slightly heavier than the handle, which should fit comfortably into the hand, offering a secure grip. Knife handles are made either from wood or from non-slip moulded polypropylene.

Knives that are intended for chopping and cutting should feel heavy and be of stout construction. Each knife is designed for a particular purpose and should not be used for other tasks. After use, all knives must be carefully washed in warm soapy water, thoroughly dried, and carefully put away.

Details of a typical set of chefs' knives are given in Table 46.3.

Table 46.3 A typical set of chefs' knives (see fig. 46.4)

Knife	Uses
25 cm (10 inch) cooks' knife	Slicing/cutting vegetables, chopping parsley.
20 cm (8 inch) cooks' knife	General-purpose knife for slicing and cutting.
10 cm (4 inch) cooks' knife	Peeling thick-skinned vegetables, trimming vegetables/fruit, coring apples and pears, trimming mushrooms.
15 cm (6 inch) boning knife	Boning meat, poultry, and game.
6 cm (2½ inch) turning/paring knife	Turning vegetables.
15 cm (6 inch) fish filleting knife	Filleting and skinning fish.
25.0–30.5 cm (10–12 inch) butchers' steak knife	Cutting steaks, dicing pie meat, slicing escalopes, etc.
30.5–35.5 cm (12–14 inch) carving knife, plain or serrated blade	Carving roast meats, cold ham, tongue. Slicing bread.
30.5 cm (12 inch) cooks' meat fork, including handle	Assisting with carving joints, testing for the stage of cooking of roast joints.
10 cm (4 inch) and 20 cm (8 inch) palette knives	Numerous uses in the preparation of cold and hot savoury dishes and sweet and pastry dishes.
Lemon zester	Preparation of julienne of orange and lemon zest.
Ball-cutters, assorted sizes	Preparation of melon, potato, and vegetable balls for decorative/garnish purposes.
Potato peeler	Peeling potatoes, thin-skinned vegetables, and hard fruit.
Cannelle cutter	Decorating oranges, lemons, carrots, courgettes, etc.
30.5–35.5 cm (12–14 inch) fine steel	Not strictly a knife but indispensable to the chef for maintaining the edge on all knives. For the best-quality, high-carbon, stainless-steel knives a very hard fine steel will be required.

46.5 Electrical food-preparation equipment

The introduction of electrical food-preparation equipment has indirectly resulted in the reduction of the number of staff employed in the food-preparation area. Machines' ability to perform many tasks quicker and more efficiently has a number of advantages to offer the caterer. The use of such equipment

- increases job interest by eliminating repetitive, uninteresting manual tasks such as peeling potatoes and shredding vegetables;
- helps reduce the volume of heavy work such as mixing bread dough and whisking egg-whites;
- allows experienced staff to be used more effectively – many tasks once done by skilled staff, such as slicing cold meat and preparing mousselines, can now be carried out by semi-skilled staff;

Cooking utensils and small equipment 277

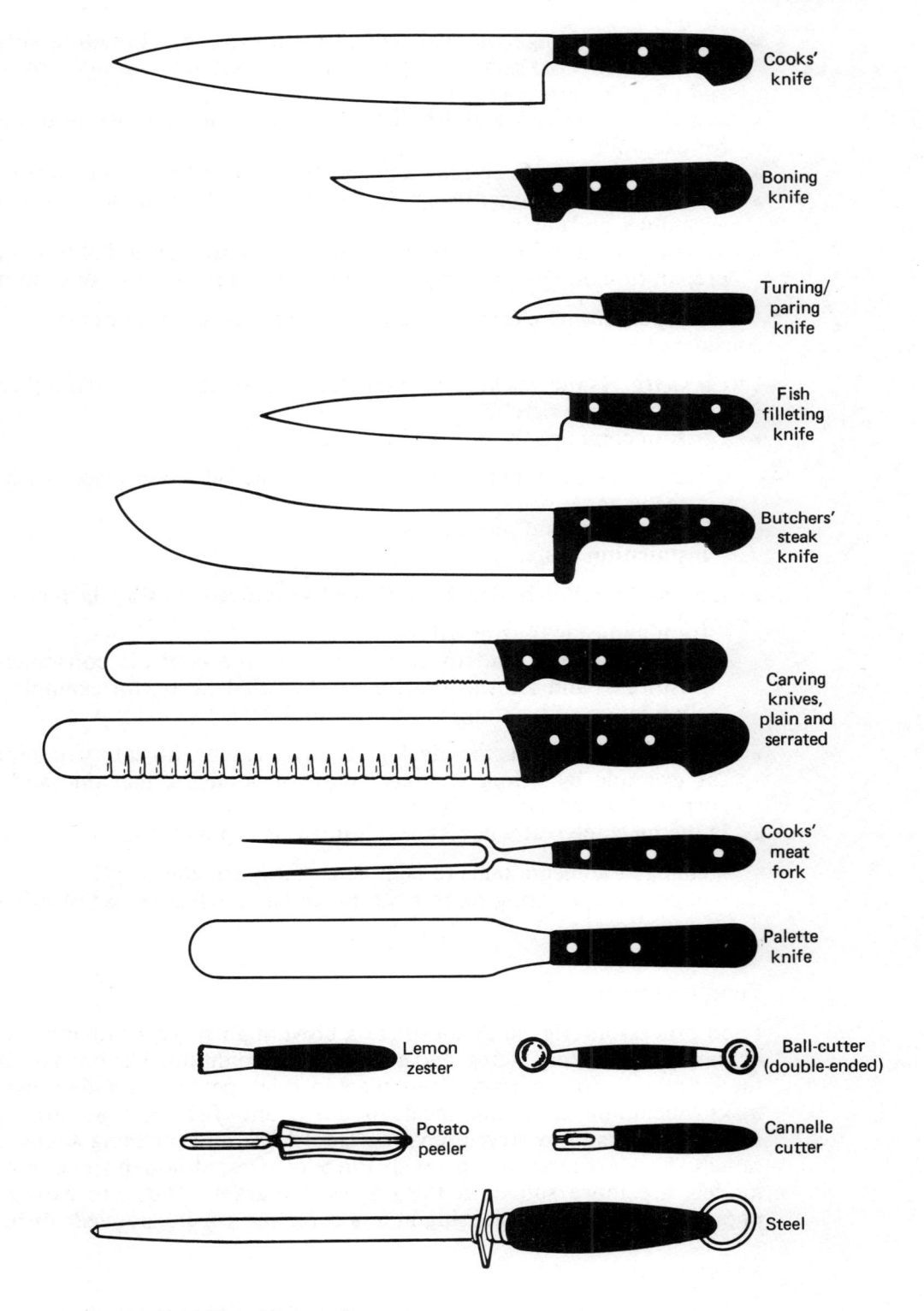

Fig. 46.4 Chefs' knives

- increases the range of available menu dishes, by shredding/slicing vegetables for cold salads and preparing mousselines, savoury mousses, and pâté, for example;
- assists in portion control, by slicing cold meats on a gravity-feed slicer, for example;
- allows the caterer to employ a proportion of less highly skilled staff;
- helps maintain consistency in product standards, in shredding vegetables and slicing cold meats, for example;
- allows many jobs/tasks to be completed in a shorter period of time – the preparation of pâté, savoury pie fillings, and mousselines, for example.

When purchasing electrical equipment, the following points should be considered:

- *Capacity*   Is the machine big enough to process the required number of portions in one batch?
- *Costs* in comparison to a similar model:
  - additional costs not included in the basic purchase price, such as attachments;
  - maintenance and service costs;
  - installation costs.
- *Ease of operation* or degree of difficulty involved in using the machine:
  - training needs for operatives;
  - does the design lead to easy use – are the controls conveniently positioned and can the attachments be fitted easily, for example?
  - elimination of bending, reaching, and lifting.
- *Safety features*   Has the machine been designed with safety in mind – for example by fitting a safety guard on a slicing machine and incorporating fail-safe mechanisms?
- Is the machine really necessary? Instead, is it possible to
  - change the menu items to eliminate that particular need?
  - change the working patterns to make more effective use of existing appliances?

Food processors

Food processors (fig. 46.5) consist of a bowl, high-speed revolving blades or slicing and grating plates, and a lift-off watertight lid. The bowl and/or the lid may be transparent. These machines can perform a wide range of tasks, including chopping meat, poultry, and fish; slicing/shredding vegetables; mixing pastry; preparing emulsions; and puréeing soups and sauces. They are available in a wide range of sizes, although some smaller models are more suited to the domestic market. They are extremely popular in kitchens specialising in à la carte and cuisine nouvelle dishes.

Safety points

- Never try to use or clean the machine without proper training.
- Never push material down the feed tube by hand – always use a pusher.

Cooking utensils and small equipment 279

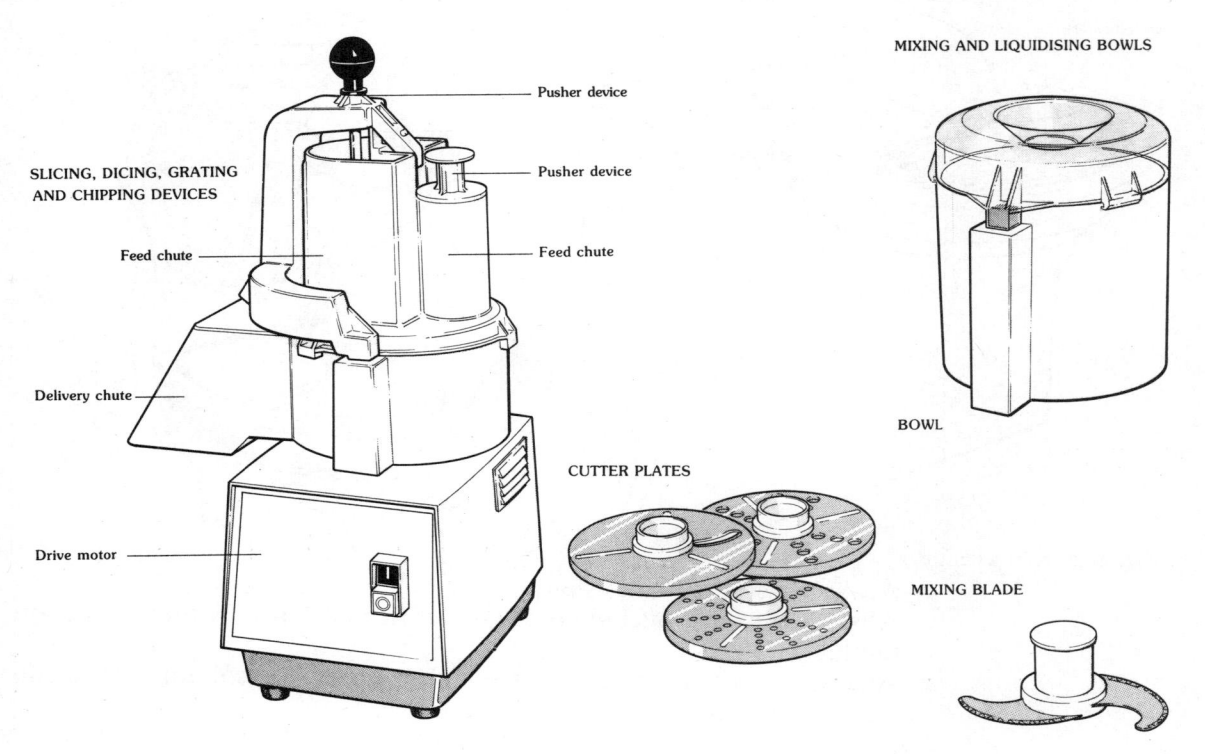

Fig. 46.5 A food processor

- Never use a machine with a broken bowl lid, feed chute, or electrical interlock.
- Never overfill the bowl with hot ingredients.

Vertical bowl choppers

These can perform a similar range of tasks to food processors, but on a larger scale. A vertical bowl chopper consists of a large enclosed upright bowl fitted with high-speed rotating blades. The appliance is free-standing and is designed to allow the bowl to be tipped for ease of emptying.

Bowl cutters

A bowl cutter (fig. 46.6) is used for finely chopping food and consists of a revolving bowl which carries food items past two rotating stainless-steel blades located in the rear section. Bowl cutters are suitable only for dry or moist foods.

Safety points

- Never try to use or clean the machine without proper training.
- Never reach under the blade guard.
- Never use the machine if the interlock between the blade cover and the blade drive motor is not working.
- Do not use the machine unless it is fully guarded.

280 *Food preparation and cooking*

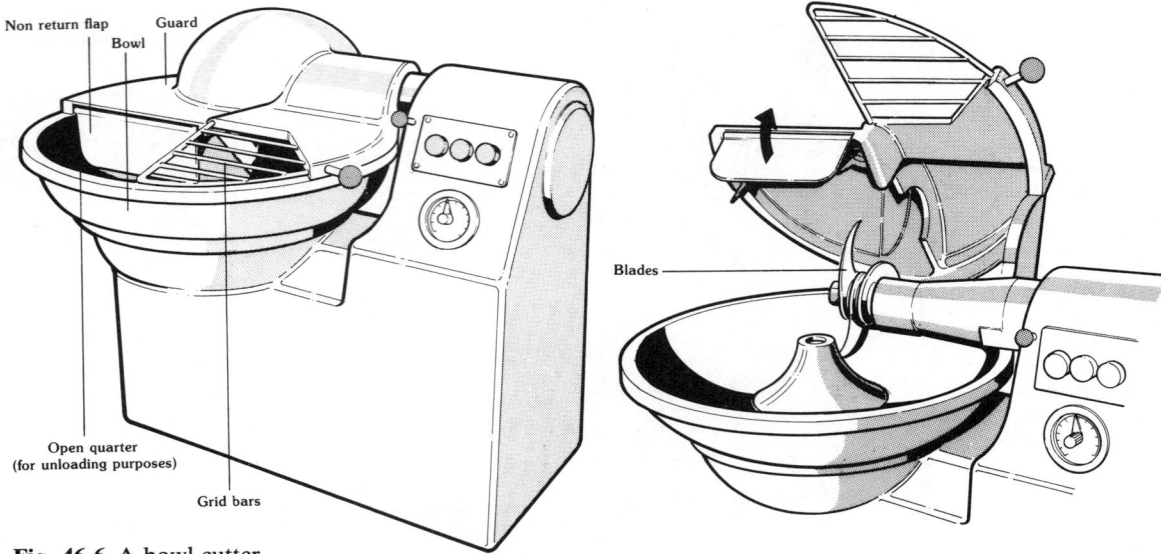

Fig. 46.6 A bowl cutter

- Always keep the blades sharp.
- Always keep the machine properly lubricated – follow the instruction manual.
- Always unplug the machine or switch it off at the isolator before you start to clean it.

Slicing machines

These have a revolving circular blade and either a horizontal platform (fig. 46.7) or an angled platform (on gravity-feed machines) on which the

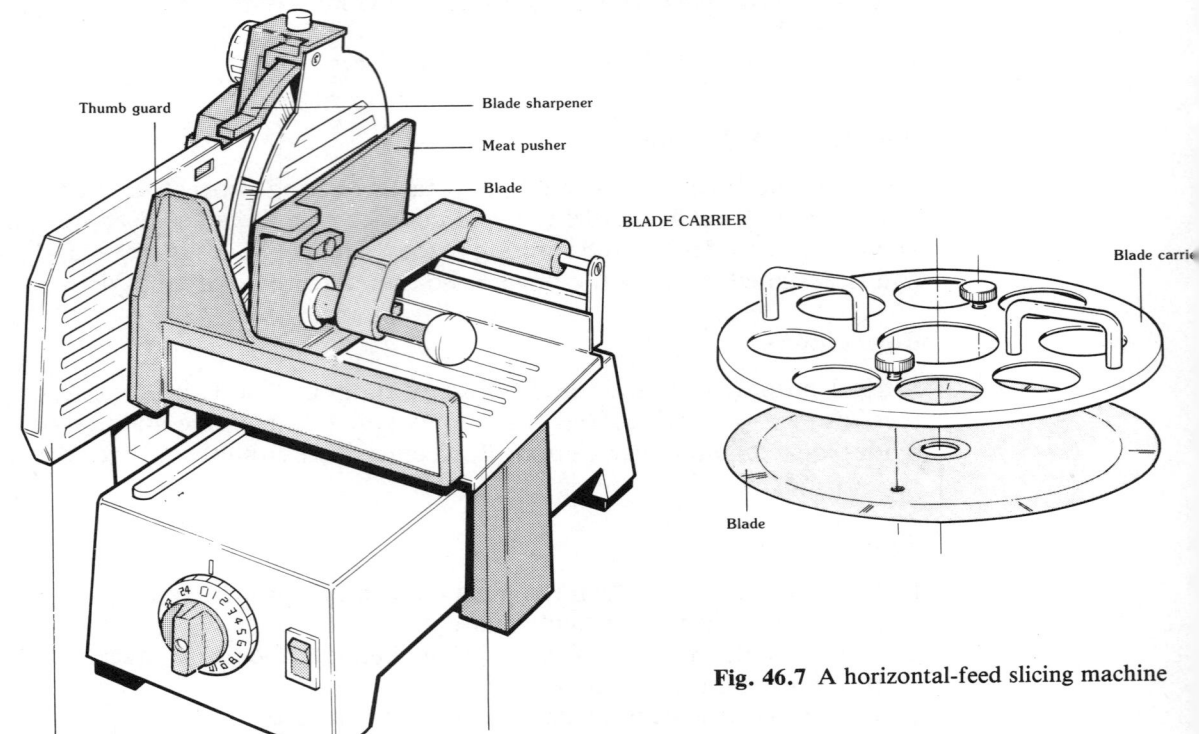

Fig. 46.7 A horizontal-feed slicing machine

Cooking utensils and small equipment 281

food items intended for slicing are placed to bring them into contact with the blade. The thickness of the cut is controlled by a simple knob. If not cleaned thoroughly after use, this type of machine can become a health hazard.

Safety points

- Never try to use or clean this machine unless you have been properly trained.
- Never slice slippery, small, or unevenly shaped food that cannot be securely held on the carriage.
- Always push the carriage by the handle on the meat pusher, never by holding the food.
- Always keep the blade sharp.
- Never use the machine unless all guards are in position
- Never try to clean a moving blade.
- Never try to remove the blade without using a blade carrier.
- Before you start to clean the machine, always unplug it or switch it off at the isolator.

Food mixers

Food mixers (fig. 46.8) can perform a wide range of tasks requiring beating, mixing, and whisking. They are supplied with a range of attachments including a bowl extender, whip/whisk, dough hook, and spade (for

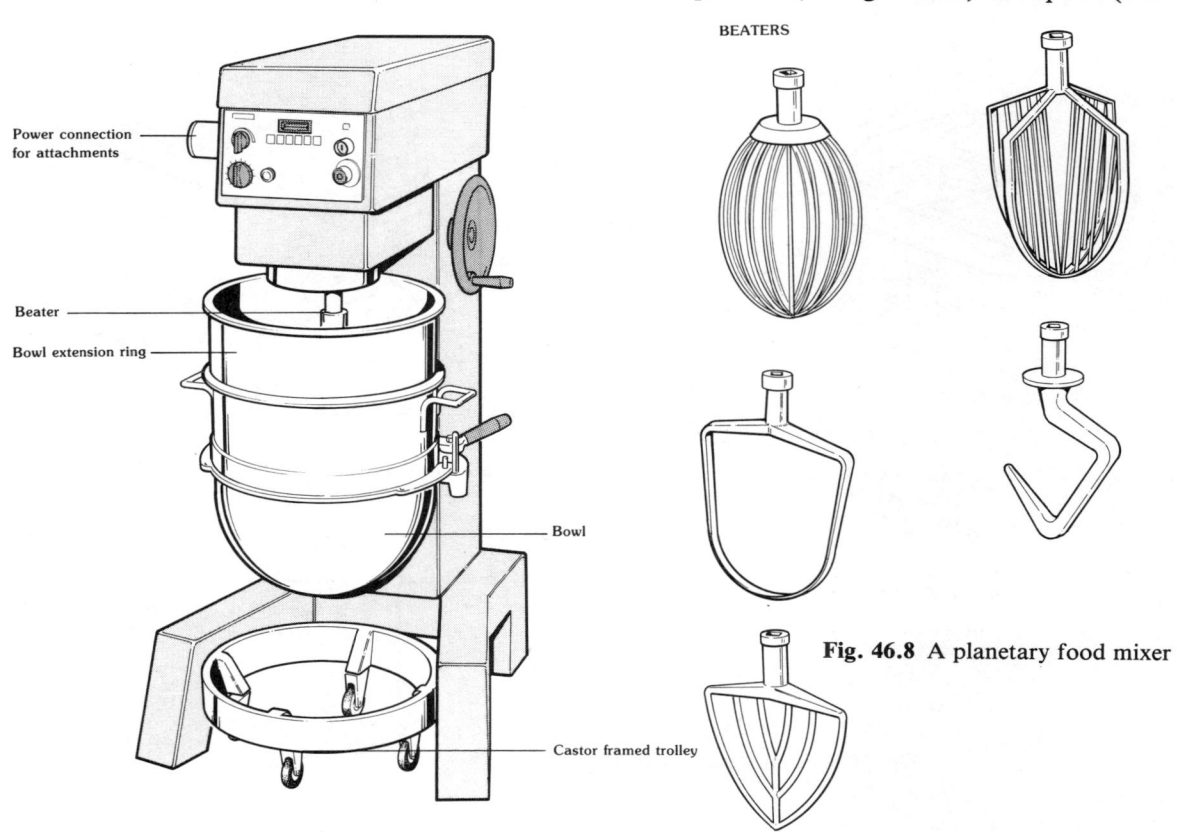

Fig. 46.8 A planetary food mixer

282 *Food preparation and cooking*

general mixing/blending). Mixers usually operate at three different speeds. They are available in both floor-mounted and bench-mounted models and are normally designed with a hub to which a further range of attachments can be fitted, including a mincer and a vegetable slicer for shredding and grating.

Safety points

- Never try to use or clean the machine without proper training.
- When the machine is running:
  - never try to feel the mix,
  - never try to scrape down the bowl,
  - never reach into the bowl when adding ingredients.
- Always use a bowl extension ring whenever possible.
- Make sure that the gear or clutch lever cannot fall or be knocked into gear.
- Always unplug the machine or switch it off at the isolator before you start to clean it.

Mincing machines

Specialist large-capacity bench-mounted mincers (fig. 46.9) are available for use in the butchery department.

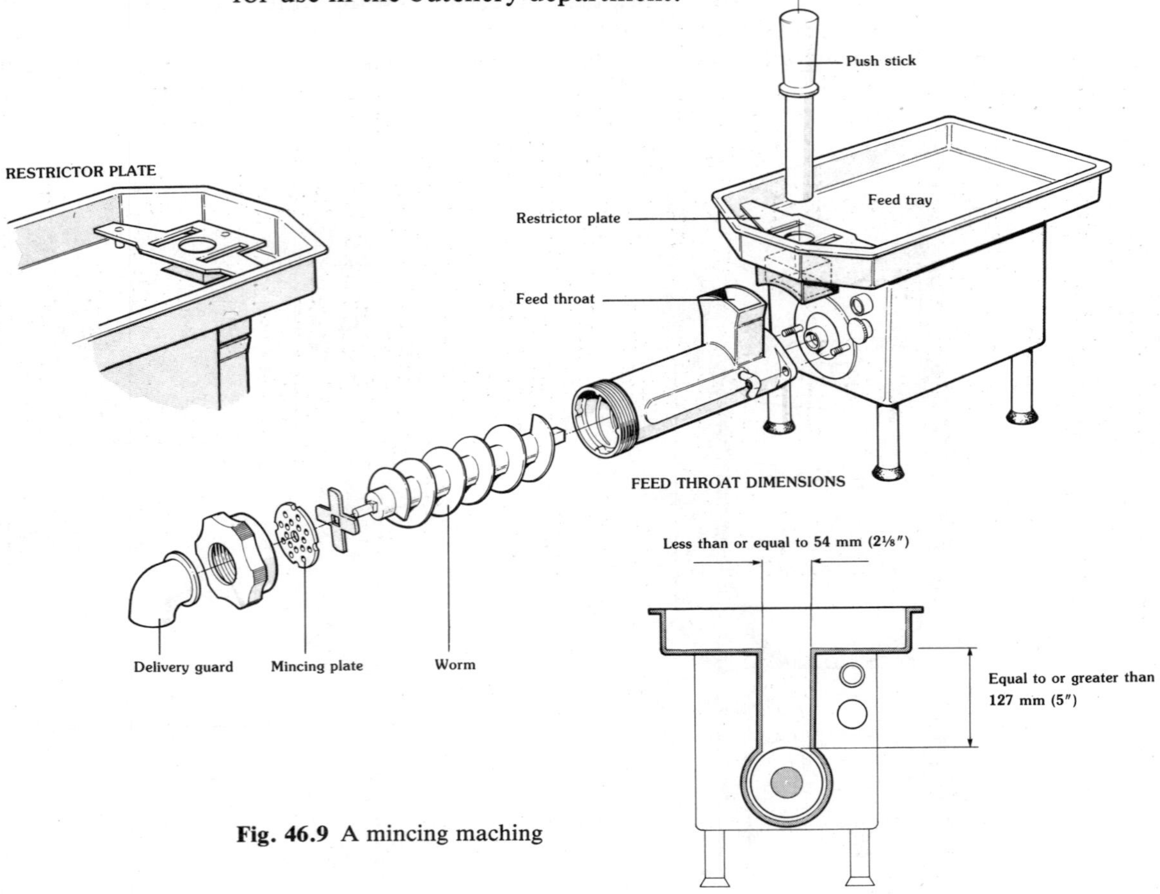

Fig. 46.9 A mincing maching

Safety points

- Never try to use or clean the machine without proper training.
- Never try to reach any part of the worm while the machine is in use.
- Never overload the machine.
- Do not use the machine if the restrictor plate is loose, bent, or missing.
- Never run the machine without the feed tray in the correct position.
- Always use the push-stick to force meat down the feed throat, never your fingers.
- Always unplug the machine or switch it off at the isolator before you start to clean it.

Potato peeler

This is an essential item of equipment in any kitchen, for peeling potatoes and root vegetables. It consists of a peeling chamber with a watertight door and a revolving contoured base disc covered with rough carborundum. The sides are also lined with the same material. When operating, the revolving disc pushes the potatoes against the rough sides of the peeling chamber, scraping off the outer skin of the potatoes. A cold-water supply is required to feed water into the peeling chamber to wash the dirt and scrapings out of the chamber and into the drain. Smaller bench-mounted models can be sited so that the scrapings are washed into the vegetable preparation sinks.

Other mechanised items of equipment used in the food-preparation area include vegetable shredders, chippers, liquidisers, pastry rollers, toasters, and air whips.

46.6 Dishwashers

The most efficient way to wash soiled food-service crockery, cutlery, and dishes is to use a specially designed dishwasher. Dishwashers are manufactured in a range of sizes and designs to suit the type and size of operation. A dishwasher will reduce the need for washing-up staff and provide an efficient method of supplying the food-service outlet(s) with a continuous supply of clean, sparkling tableware.

No matter what type of dishwasher is used, the following operations will take place:

- *Scraping* – to remove food scraps from the plates, dishes, etc.
- *Pre-wash rinsing* – to help remove the food residue still remaining on the plates.
- *Washing* – carried out at a temperature range of 68–71° C (154–160° F).
- *Rinsing* – to wash away the dirty main-wash water from the surface of the plates, bowls, cutlery, etc. Rinse water will be heated to a maximum temperature of 82° C (180° F).
- *Air drying* – some items, in particular glasses and stainless-steel tableware, will require a final polish with a soft cloth.
- *Recycling* – items are now ready to be put back into the system for further use. This might involve stacking in the hotplate or storing in the waiters' pantry.

Types of dishwasher

MANUAL SPRAY TYPE

Suitable for small to medium-size operations. The soiled cutlery/crockery is stacked into plastic racks after scraping. If a pre-wash rinse is necessary, this will be carried out manually in a sink using hot water. The operator pushes the filled racks into the dishwasher, where the contents will be sprayed with hot water containing a detergent through high-pressure jets for a pre-set period. Washing is followed automatically by rinsing. This type of dishwasher is fitted with two separate water tanks – one for the washing water, the other for the rinse. Once the wash/rinse cycle is complete, the clean items can be removed manually by the operator.

Racks can be varied in design to suit the needs of the different items that will require washing. Some small units have a single built-in tray in which the different items will be placed for washing.

AUTOMATIC SPRAY TYPE

Designed for large operations, this type of dishwasher reduces the need for labour and the amount of handling. After scraping and stacking, the racks are placed on to a conveyor belt that takes the soiled item through the dishwasher. Unlike the manual spray type, this type of dishwasher is designed with two separate sections – one for washing and the other for rinsing.

FLIGHT TYPE

A variation on the automatic spray type of dishwasher. This type of machine eliminates the need for racks, except for cutlery and cups. The soiled items are placed directly on to a pegged conveyor belt which moves the soiled tableware through the dishwasher.

Hot-air driers can be incorporated into some designs to speed up the drying process.

46.7 Hotplates and heated cupboards

Hotplates

These are basically heated cupboards with a heated table/counter top. They are available in a range of designs and sizes to suit the style of operation and the available space. They may be heated by gas, electricity, or live steam. Some caterers have a preference for electrically heated models, as these tend to provide a more even heat, eliminating hot spots. A thermostat will also help to maintain an even heat.

Hotplates are used to warm service equipment/crockery and to retain hot food items at service temperature over a relatively short period. Hotplates must be sufficiently hot to prevent the growth of bacteria. Cooked items left in the hotplate for too long will dry out and look unappetising. The doors should be well-fitting to provide easy opening and closing. For cleaning it is an advantage if the doors can be lifted out. The best models are constructed with an insulated stainless-steel exterior with the shelves made from a suitable non-corrosive metal.

Where a hotplate is purchased with a built-in bain-marie well, this can be of either the water-filled or the dry hot-air type. Both have proved acceptable and efficient.

To prevent the accumulation of dirt and food residue, hotplates are supplied either with adjustable legs or with a skirt that fits flush with the floor, under which dirt cannot penetrate. Electrically heated mobile models are also available.

Heated cupboards

Most of what has been written about hotplates applies to heated cupboards too. The main difference between a hotplate and a heated cupboard is that the heated cupboard will not have a service-counter top.

Heated cupboards are available as either static or mobile units. Static models can be stacked above each other.

PART FIVE
The business of catering

This last part of the book relates the content of the earlier chapters to the practicalities of running a business. You personally might not necessarily deal with money or customers, but your activities in the kitchen should nevertheless be geared towards meeting criteria such as making a profit, keeping within a budget, meeting the demands of customers, and so on.

The menu and its very important role in running a catering business is examined at some length in chapter 47. We look at the factors that need to be taken into account in producing a menu – from its type and content to its implications for staffing, equipment, and kitchen planning.

The final chapter shows the sort of records which need to be kept and the calculations which may need to be done. It is hoped that this will help you to realise the importance of control in running a catering operation successfully. We also give examples of how much of this can now be done by using computers.

47 The menu and the organisation

We pointed out in chapter 27 that the driving force behind a catering operation is the menu. Not only does the menu affect the commodities you use and what you do with them: it also affects the staffing, the planning of a kitchen, the organisation of the staff, and their duties. The other purpose of a menu is to advertise what it is you are trying to sell. The menu (or bill of fare, as it is sometimes called) plays a large part in marketing your product.

47.1 Types of menu

You will come across a number of terms describing menus. These don't actually tell you what the menu contains or how it is presented, but they do give information that may be important to you and to your customers, if they understand what the terms mean.

Table d'hôte menu

This menu shows a set number of courses with a very limited number of choices at each course. The price quoted is usually how much the meal will cost if the customer has one dish from each course. There should be little waiting by the customer, since the kitchen will have based its preparation and cooking of some dishes in advance on an expected number of customers for each dish.

À la carte menu

This type of menu can have a very large number and a wide selection of dishes. Each dish is individually priced, and customers can make up their meals by choosing any combination of dishes that they fancy. With an à la carte menu the kitchen cannot have the dishes in the state of readiness that it can with a table d'hôte menu, even though some of the basic preparations will have been done. Customers are usually prepared to wait to have their dishes individually cooked or finished.

Plat du jour (dish of the day)

This often consists of a large joint of meat – roasted or braised – that is offered as an alternative to the set main-course menu items. This dish lets the chef take advantage of seasonally available foods and special offers from suppliers. Steak and kidney pie, baked ham, or boiled beef and dumplings might also be available as the plat du jour.

The 'Chef's special' is something similar, but may refer to any course of the menu.

Special function menu

This will be arranged by the establishment in consultation with the organiser of the function. The number of courses, the type of service, and the cost can be adjusted to the customer's requirements (within certain limits). Function menus sometimes need to take into account the traditions of a special occasion such as a wedding reception or a new year's party.

Buffet menu

For a very large function the food service may be restricted to a finger or fork buffet. Although the caterer must know what the menu is, it is not usually issued to the guests. It may consist of hot and/or cold items.

Banquet menus

Banquets are usually dinners, although they may occasionally be lunches. Although the guests are usually given a menu, they are not in fact given a choice. This means that, however elaborate the menu and important the occasion, the chef's task is made easier by knowing how many portions of a limited number of items are required to be ready at a particular time. The problems may come with the actual service of a large number of people at the same time.

47.2 Course content of different menus

Although the menu may stay the same for the whole of the opening period in some restaurants, in others the menu will be changed for different times of the day: breakfast, lunch, tea, and dinner (or supper).

Breakfast

Breakfast is available as full English breakfast or Continental breakfast. Some kitchens have to prepare one or the other; some have to prepare both.

The English breakfast consists of several courses, with a choice of items for each course. It is frequently a table d'hôte menu, and would probably contain some of the following:

- fresh fruit, fruit juices;
- porridge, cereals;
- smoked fish, kedgeree;
- eggs cooked in a variety of ways, bacon, sausages, tomatoes, mushrooms;
- toast, rolls, croissants served with preserves;
- coffee or tea.

The Continental breakfast is a much simpler affair and does not usually contain any hot dishes. The most basic menu is table d'hôte with the following on offer:

- fruit juice;
- rolls, croissants, and preserves;
- coffee or tea.

Some Continental breakfasts include cold meats and cheeses, as are actually served in some Continental countries.

Lunch

The eating pattern of many people has changed during the last twenty or thirty years. Most people do not eat their main meal at lunchtime nowadays, so the catering industry has to provide a range of lunch options – from a light snack for someone in a hurry to a more formal meal for people who are using the meal for business or pleasure.

A traditional lunch menu might include the following courses:

- starter – soup, fruit juice, hors-d'oeuvres, pasta, egg dish;
- fish – poached, glazed, grilled, or shallow- or deep-fried;
- main – roast, braised, boiled, sautéed, or grilled meat or poultry – cut or joint – served with vegetables;
- sweet – hot or cold desserts;
- cheese – a selection of cheeses and biscuits;
- coffee.

The items on the menu will depend on the type of menu – à la carte, table d'hôte, buffet, etc. (see page 288).

Tea – afternoon tea

As we said when we were discussing lunch, people's eating patterns have changed. Tea is no longer an essential part of many people's lives, but afternoon teas are still required for special occasions.

A really traditional afternoon tea menu might look something like this:

- small sandwiches with savoury fillings,
- white and brown bread and butter with preserves,
- pastries and gateaux,
- fruit and ices,
- tea – Indian, China, etc.

Variations on this could transform the tea into a strawberry tea, which would include strawberries and cream; a high tea, which would include a hot snack; and so on.

Dinner

This tends to be the most substantial meal of the day for most people, and is also frequently used for celebrating special occasions. The menu can be of any type, and the contents and number of the courses are open to considerable variation.

A table d'hôte menu might contain the following:

- hors-d'oeuvres;
- soup – consommé, velouté;
- fish – shellfish, poached, grilled, or shallow-fried fish;
- main course – roast or braised meat or poultry or sautéed or fried cuts of meat or poultry or offal, served with vegetables (meat dishes served with a sauce are sometimes referred to as *entrées*);
- sweet course – hot or cold sweets;
- cheese board;
- coffee.

47.3 Factors to be taken into account in compiling a menu

These factors can be divided into two groups: those that depend on the caterer and those that depend on the customer. Of course the two are bound to overlap to some extent, but it you can match what you are providing with what the customer is looking for, you are in business.

The caterer will want to take the following into account:

- type of catering establishment (see section 1.2),
- time of year,
- time of day,
- capabilities of food-preparation and food-service staff,
- availability of equipment,
- skill level of staff,
- size of premises,
- location of premises,
- availability of commodities,
- number and type of expected customers,
- selling price,
- sales mix.

The customer may want you to take the following into account when you design your menu:

- *Age* The expectations and requirements of prospective customers may well depend on their age group.
- *Occupation* People whose job involves heavy physical work may need a meal with a high energy intake (see section 24.5).
- *Health* More and more people are interested in the nutritional aspects of what they eat. 'Healthy eating' may not be to everyone's taste, but if that is what the customer wants then you should consider offering it.
  Special diets for people with medical conditions (therapeutic diets) would not normally be your responsibility, but would be specified by a dietitian if you were working in a hospital or nursing home.
- *Culture and belief* It is usual for people with strict beliefs relating to the origin and preparation of certain foods to use special restaurants – for example, kosher foods and dishes. Where no specialist expertise is needed, however, the caterer may be able to please the customer – as is the case with vegetarians.

To comply with the Food Act 1984, the Trade Descriptions Act 1968, and the Sale of Goods Act 1979, the food provided must be of the nature, substance, and quality demanded by the customer and not injurious to health.

Our aim is, of course, to make a profit – or in some case to stay within our budget. If we can keep records of sales, the popular and unpopular dishes, the numbers of customers, the time of day at which peaks and troughs occur, and so on, we can use this information to ensure that the menu meets the needs of the potential customers. The technical name for this is *forecasting*.

Sales mix

To ensure profitability, it is important to take into consideration the food costs and the likely sales for items on a fixed-price menu. When writing a menu, it is necessary to consider what proportion of total food costs should be allocated to each of the courses included on the menu. The main course consisting of meat, poultry, and fish dishes will probably require between 45% and 60% of the total amount of money allowed for food costs. Too much money spent on this course may mean that the other courses will suffer from a loss of quality.

Where a number of dishes are offered at each course, each dish should fall within the allowed percentage range. If one menu dish has a much greater appeal to the customer because of higher food costs and the subsequent increase in quality, this will seriously affect the overall profitability of the menu. You must ensure that all customers have a meal of similar value and quality, regardless of their choice from the menu.

Sales mix can also be used to express the number of sales for each menu dish as a percentage of the total number of dishes sold.

Having looked at many of the factors that affect the design of a menu, it is obvious that, since many of them are constantly changing, we need to be flexible in our approach. Changing trends in customer requirements must be met with the appropriate changes in our menu.

When all these factors have been taken into account, we still need to have a menu which gives a balanced meal. We are not here considering nutritional balance, but other things:

- The predominant colour of each course should be different.
- A commodity should not appear as a major component in more than one course.
- Avoid masking delicate flavours with stronger ones.
- Methods of cooking should vary between the courses.
- The texture of dishes and within dishes should be varied.

47.4 The use of computers in menu planning

Computer programs are available that help you to plan a menu. They can be designed so that cost, portion control, and nutritional content are linked to yield, preparation time, holding time, and seasonal availability – see section 48.11.

47.5 Examples of menus for a variety of operations and customer requirements

The traditional idea of classifying menus as either à la carte or table d'hôte is becoming less satisfactory to describe the range of menus which are now commonplace. For example, many fast-food menus use the à la carte principle — that is, you make a choice from the menu and pay for each item — but we can't really call them à la carte menus. In the same way, although some school meals and staff restaurants use the table d'hôte idea — that is, you pay for a set meal and choose one dish from each course — they are not really accepted as traditional table d'hôte menus.

A fixed menu with a limited choice is becoming popular with caterers for a number of reasons:

- it can be prepared by less-skilled staff once production methods have been learned;
- it requires fewer food items to be held in stock;
- it will reduce food wastage, as not so much food will have to be prepared in advance;
- it will help to maintain the required standard of food production – the chef will find it easier to supervise a smaller number of dishes.

This type of menu can be changed as required – daily, weekly, or after longer periods.

A traditional table d'hôte menu used in many hotels and restaurants is a fixed menu with a fixed price. The customer selects one dish from each course. Figure 47.1 shows an example.

Terrine de poulet aux fines herbes
Chicken terrine with fresh herbs

Moules Rochelaise
Mussels stuffed with thyme

Crème cressonière
Cream of watercress soup

*

Truite hollandaise
Poached trout with hollandaise sauce

Aiguilletté de caneton a l'orange
Breast of duck with orange sauce

Entrecôte grillée au beurre maître d'hôtel
Grilled sirloin steak with parsley butter

Escalope de veau cordon-bleu
Escalope of veal stuffed with ham and cheese

*

Pommes au four et croquettes
Jacket and croquette potatoes

Mange-tout au beurre
Mange-tout with butter

Purée de panais à l'oseille
Parsnip purée with sorrel

*

Gâteau moka
Coffee gateau

Crème caramel
Cream caramel

Charlotte aux pommes
Apple charlotte

Bavarois au chocolat
Chocolate bavarois

Fig. 47.1 A traditional table d'hôte menu

Fixed menus can also be used in other areas of catering – for example, staff restaurants, coffee shops, breakfast menus, and afternoon tea menus. Figure 47.2 shows an example of a staff catering menu suitable for office workers. A large proportion of foods that have been fully or partly prepared by a food manufacturer would be used to cook and serve this type of menu. This allows the chef to offer a wide choice of dishes without increasing the kitchen staff. The menu features dishes to suit many people's tastes and allows customers flexibility – for example, the jacket potato could be chosen to accompany a meat dish or a salad, or be eaten as a snack with a filling.

Another type of fixed menu is the cyclic menu. Here, a set menu runs for a number of days. This may be for a week, a fortnight, or a longer period. In some cases the same menu appears on the same day of the week at weekly, fortnightly, or monthly intervals. This type of menu helps the chef with ordering, as the menu dishes will always be known in advance. It will also reduce waste and mean that kitchen staff do not need to learn new dishes. Figure 47.3 shows part of a menu of this type used in a hospital.

Function menus can be written in many different styles, depending on the occasion and the type of service. Formal functions usually require a number of courses with little, if any, choice – fig. 47.4 shows an example.

Vegetable soup with wholemeal roll
Grapefruit and orange segments

*

Roast leg of lamb with mint sauce
Casserole of beef and herb dumplings
Vegetable pizza
Stir-fry chicken with savoury rice
Jacket potato with a choice of fillings

*

Roast and creamed potatoes
Buttered carrots
Green beans

*

Selection of salads from the bar

*

Fresh fruit
Assorted yoghurt
Cheesecake
Fruit and nut crumble with custard

*

Coffee, tea, or hot chocolate
Assorted fruit juices
Carbonated drinks

Fig. 47.2 A staff catering menu for office workers

Points d'asperges sauce mousseline

*

Consommé aux diablotins

*

Tournedos fleuriste
Pommes nouvelles à la menthe
Broccoli au beurre
Concombres farcis au gratin

*

Vacherin aux fraises

*

Café et petits fours

Fig. 47.4 A formal dinner menu for a function in early summer

The menu and the organisation 295

WEEK NO 4 — BREAKFAST

NAME..........
WARD..........
WEDNESDAY....DAY

SMALL ☐

1. ☐ Fruit Juice
2. ☐ Porridge
3. ☐ Cornflakes
4. ☐ High Fibre Cereal
5. ☐ Cold Ham & Tomato HP.
6. ☐ Boiled Egg HP.LR.
7. ☐ White or Brown Bread, Butter, Marmalade
8. ☐ Toast, Butter, Marmalade
9. ☐ Brown Roll, Butter, Marmalade

1. Please put an "X" in the box beside the item you would like to have. Any other indications will be disregarded.
2. If you would like less than the normal helping, please put a cross in the box for the meal concerned.
3. If a cooked breakfast is ordered only fruit juice or cereal or porridge, may be ordered as a starter.

WEEK NO 4 — DINNER

NAME..........
WARD..........
TUESDAY.....DAY

SMALL ☐

1. ☐ Scotch Broth
2. ☐ Corned Beef Hash HP.
3. ☐ Fish Fingers HP.
4. ☐ Cheese & Tomato Sandwich HP.
5. ☐ Spinach
6. ☐
7. ☐ Creamed Potatoes
8. ☐
9. ☐ Vanilla Bavaroise & Fruit Puree
10. ☐
11. ☐

THIS HOSPITAL OBSERVES
A HEALTHY EATING POLICY

WEEK NO 4 — LUNCH

NAME..........
WARD..........
TUESDAY......DAY

HP – HIGH PROTEIN
LR – LOW RESIDUE

SMALL ☐

1. ☐ Sausage & Bacon Pie HP.
2. ☐ Curried Chicken HP.
3. ☐ Tuna Fish Salad HP.
4. ☐ Swedes
5. ☐ Cabbage
6. ☐ Rice
7. ☐ Creamed Potatoes
8. ☐ Castle Sponge & Custard HP.
9. ☐ Pineapples & Custard HP.
10. ☐ Semolina Pudding HP.LR.
11. ☐
12. ☐

Fig. 47.3 Part of a cyclical menu used in a hospital

Most buffet menus offer a choice. The following might be offered at a finger buffet including hot and cold eats:

Sandwiches

- Rolled in brown bread: asparagus, smoked salmon
- Buffet sandwiches: ham, tongue, egg and tomato

Cold eats

- Smoked-haddock and leek quiche
- Ham cornets filled with liver pâté mousse
- Celery boats filled with Stilton cheese
- Seafood barquettes

Hot eats

- Goujons of plaice with tartare sauce
- Curried-prawn and almond patties
- Chicken and mushroom bouchées
- Mini barbecued spare-ribs of pork with chilli dip
- Mini lamb kebabs with spicy yoghurt dip
- Vegetable samosa with mint jelly

Assorted pastries

- Cream horns, éclairs, fruit tartlets, palmiers, and mokatines

Coffee or tea

Other types of buffet might include fork buffets and carved buffets.

In figs 47.5 and 47.6 we give two examples of menus based on à la carte principles. As you can see, one is an accepted à la carte menu and the other is for a mass-market food outlet. In both cases the customer makes a selection from a wide choice range and pays for each item.

47.6 Presenting and selling the menu

We have looked at the individual factors that need to be taken into account in compiling a menu. However, we must also consider the menu in the context of selling *food* to *customers*.

Our first aim must be to give customer satisfaction. This must include making customers feel welcome, making them feel at home, and making them feel that they are getting value for money. Customers who have enjoyed their visit to your operation are more likely to come again and to recommend you to other people. Much of this customer satisfaction will depend on the menu, your expertise, and the quality of the food service: but some will also depend on the surroundings in which the meal is eaten. The decor and ambience of the restaurant should be appropriate to the menu you are offering. The pace at which the meal is to be served should also feature in your considerations – a menu for a leisurely evening out ought to be different from a hurried snack at midday!

Having decided on the menu, you must then think about how you are going to bring your very desirable products to the attention of your possible customers. There are a number of ways in which menus are presented, and we shall have a look at some of them. If the menu is changed

Pour Commencer

Panier de Champignons Sauvages aux Pointes Vertes et aux Agrumes
A crispy vegetable basket, filled with a warm salad of wild mushrooms from the Surrey woods, garnished with tips of green asparagus, and a citrus fruit and pistachio nut oil dressing
£12.80

Lasagne de Saumon tiede au Fenouil et sa Vinaigrette de Tomates au Coriandre
Warm marinated salmon layered with thinly sliced fennel in a tomato and coriander vinaigrette
£9.50

Petite Tourte de Homard, et sa Gelee Salade aux fines herbes
Scottish lobster baked in a pastry shell, served with a delicate lobster jelly and garnished with a fine herb salad
£16.80

Croustade de Fromage D'Appenzell, Petite Salade Quercinoise
Appenzell cheese souffle baked in a fillo shell served with a salad of truffles, home made duck ham and autumn leaves
£13.50

Gateau de Gibier au Foie Gras et ses Truffes fraiches
Pressed layers of game, goose liver, fresh perigord truffles and wild mushrooms served with a truffled vinaigrette, mache salad and boulangere potatoes
£18.60

Salade de Crustaces tiedes et son Foie Gras d'Oie Grille
Lobster in caviar butter, Pacific oyster in its own jelly, Maryland crab fritter on a mustard sauce and a slice of grilled goose liver on a young dandelion salad
£18.50

Ragout de Legumes verts aux Morilles, Pointes d'Asperges a la Vinaigrette de Racines
Tender young green vegetables in a creamed morelle mushroom sauce with asparagus tips and root vegetable dressing
£8.40

Bisque de Tourteaux et ses Raviolis, Creme de Caviar
Raviolis of crab in its bisque and a cloud of caviar cream
£8.50

Soufflé d'Aiglefin Fume a l'Oeuf de Caille Poche, Sauce a la Moutarde
Smoked haddock souffle with chives and a poached quail egg served on a pool of grain mustard sauce
£8.50

Crevettes a la Vapeur, Vinaigrette tiede aux Agrumes

Poissons et les Crustacés

Feuillantines de Saumon et Turbot a l'Oseille
A fan of salmon, turbot and crisp potato wafers on a sorrel and vermouth sauce
£14.50

Filet de Rouget grille et sa Croustade de Moelle
Grilled red mullet fillet with a puff pastry case of glazed bone marrow, garnished with dandelion and baby spinach salad and a vegetable vinaigrette
£14.50

Supreme de Turbot a la Vapeur, Beurre rouge
Steamed fillet of turbot on a bed of sliced new potatoes with a red wine butter sauce, garnished with vegetable noodles
£16.80

Sole Soufflee Homardine a la Creme d'Oursins
Poached boneless slip sole with lobster mousse in a sea urchin cream sauce vegetable solferinos, garnished with oscietre caviar
£18.50

Eventail de Poissons a la Fondue de Legumes, Beurre Nantais
Steamed salmon, seabass, turbot and red mullet on a vegetable and chive butter sauce
£15.20

Croustillant de Loup de mer et Saumon aux Pistils de Safran et Basilic
Sauted pirouettes of seabass and salmon on a saffron and basil sauce with crisp potato slices
£16.50

Entrées

Cotelettes de Pigeonneau sur choucroute de Navets
Braised culets of squab pigeon on pickled turnips with young carrots, bacon, button mushrooms and cocotte potatoes
£15.20

Noisettes de Chevreuil "Saint Hubert"
Marinated fillets of venison in an Armagnac flavoured cream sauce, served on a bed of leek and bacon, garnished with gnocchi, winter vegetables and a "rose de sable"
£18.50

Canon d'Agneau marine aux herbes aromatiques
Herb marinated fillet of lamb sauted with a touch of garlic, garnished with a ragout of green vegetables, baby spinach and soufflé potatoes
£16.50

Fig. 47.5 A traditional à la carte menu – part of an actual menu from the Inter-Continental Hotel, Park Lane, London, W1

Appetisers

PRAWN COCKTAIL £1.85
Peeled prawns on a bed of crisp lettuce topped with Thousand Island dressing and served with brown bread and butter.

COUNTRY STYLE PATE £1.45
Traditional smooth pâté served with French toast and butter, or Flora.

New CONTINENTAL MEAT £1.65
A combination of three smoked continental meats served with a side salad of coleslaw, crisp lettuce, red cabbage and half a tomato.

BOWL OF CHILLI £1.75
A bowl of spicy chilli con carne with a sprinkling of natural Cheddar Cheese and accompanied with tortilla corn chips.

MIXED SALAD BOWL 95p
Crisp iceberg lettuce, crunchy coleslaw, grated carrot, tomato, cucumber and red cabbage sprinkled with croutons and served with your choice of dressing – Thousand Island, Blue Cheese, Classic French.

SOUP OF THE DAY 48p
Served piping hot and sprinkled with croutons. Please ask your waitress for today's choice.

MINIATURE LOAF – BROWN OR WHITE 33p
Served with butter or Flora.

PURE CHILLED ORANGE JUICE 65p

American Style Hamburgers

All our ground beef hamburgers are ¼ lb uncooked weight. Served with a fresh garnish of crisp lettuce, red cabbage, a half tomato and your choice of American Style Hamburger Relishes – Sweet Corn, Onion and Tangy Tomato.

9. **STRAIGHT AND SIMPLE** .... ¼ lb single £2.40
   Quarter Pounder or Half Pounder served straight in ½ lb double £3.30
   a toasted bun with French Fries.

11. **CHEDDAR GORGE** .... ¼ lb single £2.60
    Quarter Pounder or Half Pounder with melted ½ lb double £3.60
    natural Cheddar Cheese in a toasted bun and served with French Fries.

Over The Top Half Pounders

14. **CARIBBEAN PINEAPPLE ISLAND** £3.70
    Double burger served open and topped over with an exotic combination of pineapple rings and coleslaw served with French Fries.

16. **SUMMER SMOKEY BARBEQUE** £3.70
    Double burger served open and topped over with a blanket of hickory smoked barbeque sauce served with French Fries.

18. **MEXICAN CHILLI SOMBRERO** £3.70
    Double burger served open and topped over with hot and spicy chilli con carne, sprinkled with natural Cheddar Cheese and served with French Fries.

19. **MIXED SALAD BOWL** 95p
    A delicious side order to accompany your burger.

We will be pleased to serve
OUR QUARTER POUND VEGETARIAN BURGER
as an alternative to our American Style Hamburger.

Main

All Main Choice meals are serve
we will be pleased to substitute

1. **HALF A TENDER ROAST CHICKEN** £3.95
   Half a tender young chicken, oven roasted and served with garden peas and savoury gravy.

2. **SIRLOIN STEAK** £4.95
   Prime Sirloin cooked to your order – rare, medium or well done and served with fried onion rings, garden peas and tomato.

3. **PRIME GAMMON STEAK** £3.95
   A traditional cut prime gammon steak griddled to perfection, topped with a ring of pineapple and tomato and served with garden peas.

New DEEP FRIED SCAMPI TAILS £4.25
Succulent golden breaded scampi, served with tender garden peas and a wedge of lemon.

4. **FILLET OF PLAICE** £3.30
   Fillet of plaice in golden breadcrumbs deep fried and served with garden peas and a wedge of lemon.

Side Orders

May we recommend an add

MIXED SALAD BOWL 95p
Crisp iceberg lettuce, crunchy coleslaw, grated carrot, tomato, cucumber, and red cabbage sprinkled with croutons and served with your choice of tangy dressings – Thousand Island, Blue Cheese, Classic French.

Fig. 47.6 An à la carte menu for a mass-market food outlet

daily, the type of menu presentation may be different from a menu which remains the same for longer periods of time. If you are trying to keep your costs to an absolute minimum, the menu could well be different from that for a special occasion where the price is not of particular concern to your customer.

The Salad Bar

Choose a delicious fresh salad. All our Main Choice Salads are served with crispy iceberg lettuce, crunchy coleslaw, tomato, cucumber, grated carrot and red cabbage.
To complement your salad, choose one of our salad dressings. Thousand Island, Blue Cheese, Classic French or Salad Cream.

New **FLAKED POACHED SALMON AND PRAWN** £4.25
Flaked salmon bound with mayonnaise and served with juicy peeled prawns.

22. **PRAWN AND THOUSAND ISLAND** £3.95
Juicy peeled prawns with your choice of Thousand Island or other dressings.

23. **BROCCOLI AND CHEESE WHOLEMEAL FLAN** £2.95
An individual oven baked flan, served cold.

24. **COTTAGE CHEESE AND PINEAPPLE** £2.95

New **SMOKED MEAT AND SALAMI** £2.95

25. **CHEDDAR CHEESE GRATE** £2.95
Simply natural grated Cheddar cheese, with a twist of pineapple.

Choice

d with French Fries. However, aked Jacket Potato on request.

5. **TRADITIONAL FISH AND CHIPS** £3.25
Fillet of cod coated in crispy batter, served with garden peas and a wedge of lemon.

6. **MIXED GRILL** £3.75
Ground beef hamburger (¼ lb), fried egg, back bacon rasher and sausage garnished with buttered fresh mushrooms and a half tomato.

7. **STEAK AND KIDNEY PIE** £2.95
Short-crust steak and kidney pie topped with savoury gravy and served with garden peas.

8. **LIVER AND BACON** £3.35
Griddled liver topped with savoury gravy, served with a rasher of bacon, garden peas, fried onion rings and a half tomato.

New **ALL DAY FARMHOUSE BREAKFAST** £2.95
Two griddled rashers of prime back bacon, two sausages, two fried eggs, buttered fresh mushrooms, a whole tomato and crispy fried bread.

& Vegetables

ition to your main choice –

FRESH MUSHROOMS Freshly cooked with butter and lemon juice 60p
ONION RINGS Six deep fried rings in golden batter 55p
BAKED BEANS Served in tomato sauce 45p

Lighter Meals

20. **THE "LIGHT DIET" BURGER** £2.60
Ground beef hamburger (¼lb) topped with a generous portion of Cottage Cheese and served with a crisp salad of lettuce and tomato, grated carrot, cucumber, red cabbage and crunchy coleslaw.

27. **BROCCOLI AND CHEESE WHOLEMEAL FLAN** £2.10
An individual oven baked flan served hot with garden peas and french fries.

New **CONTINENTAL MEAT** £1.65
A combination of three smoked continental meats served with a side salad of coleslaw, crisp lettuce, red cabbage and half a tomato.

28. **BOWL OF CHILLI** £1.75
A bowl of spicy chilli con carne with a sprinkling of natural cheddar cheese and accompanied with tortilla corn chips.

29. **BAKED JACKET POTATO** £1.85
Served with a side salad of coleslaw, crisp lettuce, red cabbage and half a tomato with your choice of topping –
SPICY CHILLI CON CARNE – BAKED BEANS –
COTTAGE CHEESE OR GRATED NATURAL
CHEDDAR CHEESE.

31. **HAPPY EATER BRUNCH** £2.50
Three sausages, baked beans, fried egg and french fries.

32. **HOT CHEESE AND SWEET PICKLE SANDWICH** £1.85
Butter griddled combination of natural cheddar cheese and sweet pickle served with a side salad of coleslaw, crisp lettuce, red cabbage and half a tomato.

Fig. 47.6 An à la carte menu for a mass-market food outlet (continued)

As with any other publicity, there are certain things that need to be taken into account. The menu needs to be

- readily available and attractively presented;
- clearly written so that the customers understand what you are selling, with the dishes described in a way that whets the appetite;
- priced in a way that does not confuse your customers

There are several different methods of menu presentation:

Blackboard and chalk

These allow for very frequent change of dishes and prices and are frequently used by bars, bistros, and Continental cafés. Since it is portable, the blackboard can be placed outside the premises to attract attention.

Pinboard-back display

Often used in cafeteria-type operations. Customers approaching the service points can see at a glance what is on offer. It is quite easy to change the list of items and prices.

Individual menus

- *Wipe-clean cards* These are suitable where the menu is not changed very often and where there is a high throughput of customers. Many motorway restaurants and well-known franchise operators use this type of menu. The menu is often attractively produced, with pictures of what the food offered is going to look like.
- *Individual bound covers* This type of presentation is used where there is a change of menu at each meal. The menu may be printed, typed, or hand-written and is inserted into a cover which may contain information about additional services offered, such as wine, accommodation, and other catering facilities available.

47.7 The language of the menu

Many traditional establishments use French on their menus. Whatever language is used on a menu, it must convey information and be correct in respect of spelling and grammar. Incorrect language on a menu may convey to customers a lack of attention to detail, and they may worry that this also applies to the food.

Some of the more common things to keep an eye on when using French are as follows:

- Commodities must be given the correct gender (masculine or feminine – see the note on page 16).
- Any description of a commodity must agree with the commodity's gender.
- The order in which a dish is written is: the cut, then the type, then the cooking method, then the garnish – for example, *carré d'agneau rôti persillé*.

If you have to write a menu in French and you are not sure of your spelling, you should check it in a standard reference book such as *Le Répertoire de la Cuisine*. If you have to write a menu in English and you are not sure of your spelling, use a dictionary!

47.8 Producing new dishes

It can be an interesting challenge to both the experienced chef and the trainee chef to produce a new dish. It is not easy to produce a completely new dish, but many interesting menu dishes can be made by varying the available ingredients. Many chefs are influenced by the cooking of other countries in obtaining ideas as a basis for a new creation. Exotic or unusual commodities can be used to provide a different flavour or an eye-catching garnish.

It is important, however, to follow good kitchen practice and the basic rules appropriate to each selected method of preparation, cooking, and storage. The recipe must be capable of being repeated accurately each time the dish is made. The new dish must appeal to the eye and the palate. It is not always necessary to use expensive or unusual ingredients – many interesting dishes can be prepared that make use of locally available fresh produce in season.

Naming a new dish

A number of methods can be used to name a new dish – but remember that it needs to have a name that will invite the customer to order it. The name needs to be informative or to promote interest. The following are just some possibilities:

- The name lists the ingredients involved.
- The name gives the main ingredients and the method of preparation.
- The name includes the area in which the main ingredient is produced.
- The name reflects the style of cooking used to prepare the dish.
- The name includes a reference to the establishment in which the dish was produced.
- The name includes the event or person that the dish was invented for.

47.9 Design of the premises in relation to the menu

Before designing the kitchen area, the type of menu and the style of operation of the establishment must be decided as well as the type of customer expected. If the kitchen can be designed from scratch, it is easier than adapting premises which were originally designed for a different purpose. No kitchen can be designed to meet all the special features required by the many different styles of operation.

Foremost in the planner's mind will be the size and style of operation that the finished kitchen will be used for. However, consideration should also be given to flexibility and possible changes that might be required at some later date.

Knowledge of food purchasing policy will also be required. Will the caterer be preparing the menu dishes from raw commodities or purchasing them in a prepared, ready-to-cook, or ready-to-serve form? The difference this will make can be seen from the example given in Table 47.1 for preparing and serving chipped potatoes.

When the style of operation etc. has been decided, the correct amount of space needs to be allocated to provide for the maximum catering activity that the establishment anticipates. The kitchen should be sited close to the dining areas, to avoid unnecessary delays between cooking and service. The kitchen also needs good access for the delivery of regular supplies.

Building standards and codes of practice give guidance as to the total space that needs to be available. Their recommendations are based on two general ideas: either that the floor space in the kitchen should be half of that allowed for customers in the restaurant or that a basic floor space of 90

Table 47.1 Preparing and cooking chipped potatoes – an example of the different requirements when using raw commodities and ready-to-cook foods

	Using raw potato	Using frozen chipped potatoes
Storage	Vegetable store	Deep-freeze cabinet.
Preparation	Peeling Eyeing Chipping Blanching	Space and equipment will not be required for these stages.
Cooking	Reheating and browning for service	Cooked straight from the freezer.

square metres (1000 square feet) should be allowed for the first 50 covers and increased by 9 square metres (100 square feet) for every three staff working within the kitchen after this.

The original layout of the premises will affect the final design. So, of course will cost and space. For a traditional style of food production, the following is a logical layout based on the flow of work:

- *Goods reception* To receive and check deliveries for quantity and quality.
- *Food stores* Separated into dry stores, freezer stores, vegetable stores, meat stores, and fish stores.
- *Preparation areas* Larder (including wet fish, meat, poultry, and game) and vegetable preparation. These should be placed in the coolest part of the kitchen, within easy reach of the stores. This reduces the carrying of heavy loads over long distances.
- *Pastry* Often equipped with its own ovens, for the preparation of pastry and sweet dishes.
- *Main cooking area* For cooking the prepared meat, fish, and vegetable items for the menu dishes.
- *Service area* Equipped for the final portioning and temporary holding of hot and cold dishes for service.
- *Still room* For preparation of hot and cold non-alcoholic beverages, breakfast toast, and sometimes afternoon tea sandwiches.

For the smooth running of the kitchen, additional supporting areas are needed. These include a pot and plate wash area, a chef's office, staff toilets, and changing rooms.

Work flow

The final layout should be based on a good flow of commodities from the goods reception, through the preparation and cooking areas, to the service area. Careful positioning of preparation equipment and work-surfaces, sinks, and cooking equipment reduces the distance that staff and food have to travel. The benefits to staff comfort and safety are obvious.

A perfect kitchen, then, is one where raw and cooked foods items are not moved unnecessarily and travel a particular route only once. Careful planning and good work flow reduce the risk of accidents caused by bottlenecks and congestion, but planning your work is not always easy if you and your colleagues are preparing a large number of dishes at the same time. A compact design that allows easy access to all areas of the kitchen will allow a good work flow to operate.

The layout for the hot cooking equipment will be another important decision. The total output and the available space will affect the positioning, but two popular arrangements are line grouping and island grouping.

- *Line grouping* Items of equipment are placed against a wall to prevent access from behind. This layout is popular in snack bars and self-service restaurants. Work-surfaces for holding raw and cooked food are placed between the items of cooking equipment or immediately in front.
- *Island grouping* The cooking equipment is placed back-to-back in a central position with easy access. Gaps between the equipment are covered with stainless-steel plates to prevent food waste from dropping behind. Work-surfaces for holding raw and cooked foods are placed immediately in front. This arrangement is suitable for medium or large kitchens.

If you are involved in designing or redesigning your own kitchen, you will find it useful to used squared paper and standard symbols (see fig. 47.7) to represent items of equipment. Give careful thought to the height of the work-surfaces and to the width of the gangways.

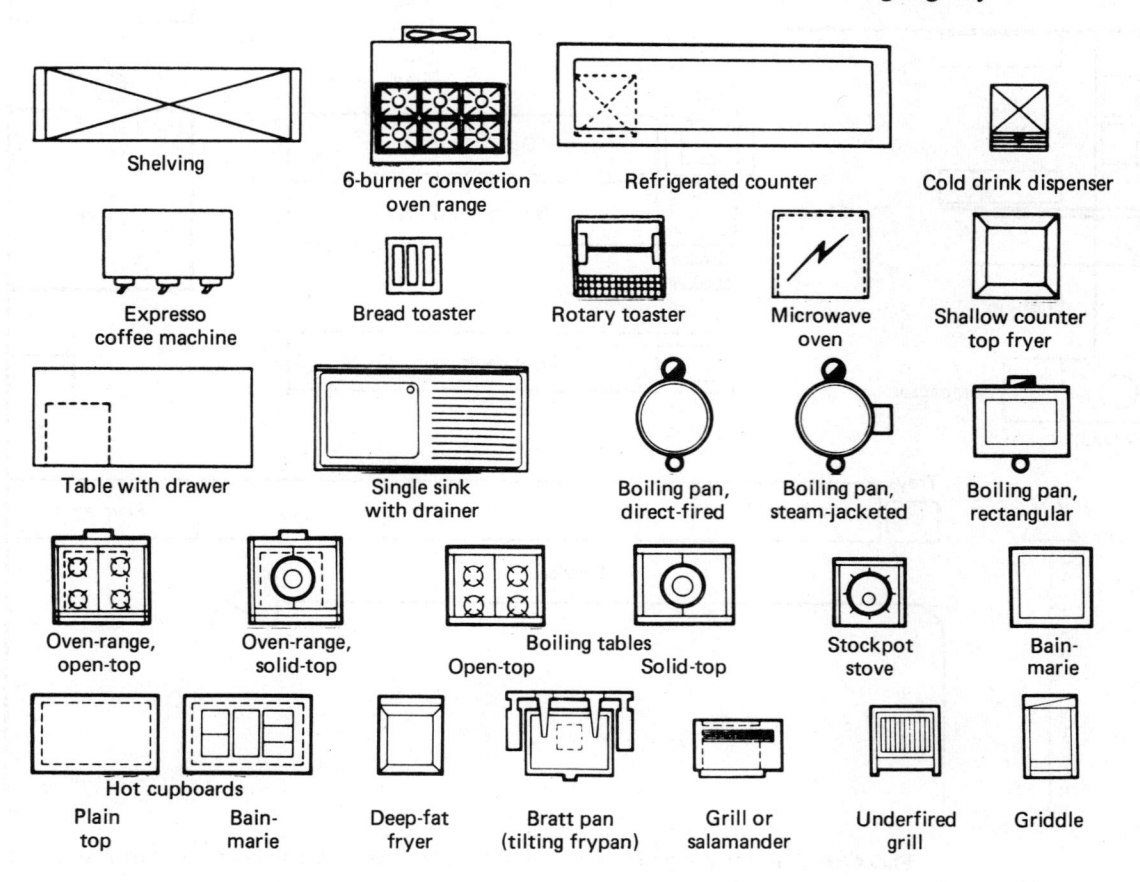

Fig. 47.7 Standard symbols for kitchen equipment

304   *The business of catering*

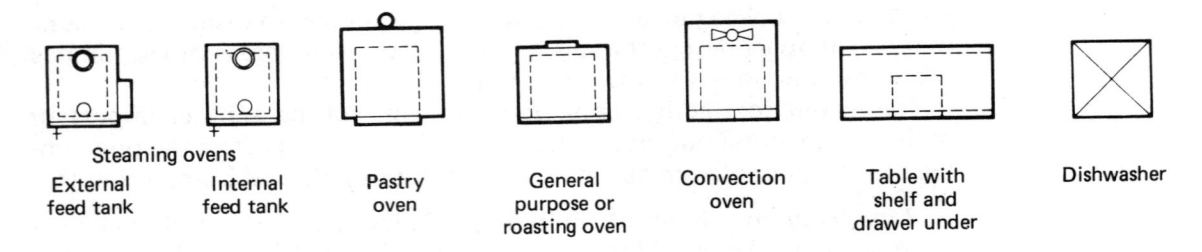

Steaming ovens
External feed tank | Internal feed tank | Pastry oven | General purpose or roasting oven | Convection oven | Table with shelf and drawer under | Dishwasher

Fig. 47.7 Standard symbols for kitchen equipment (*continued*)

Examples of plans for three different types of operation are given in figs 47.8 to 47.10.

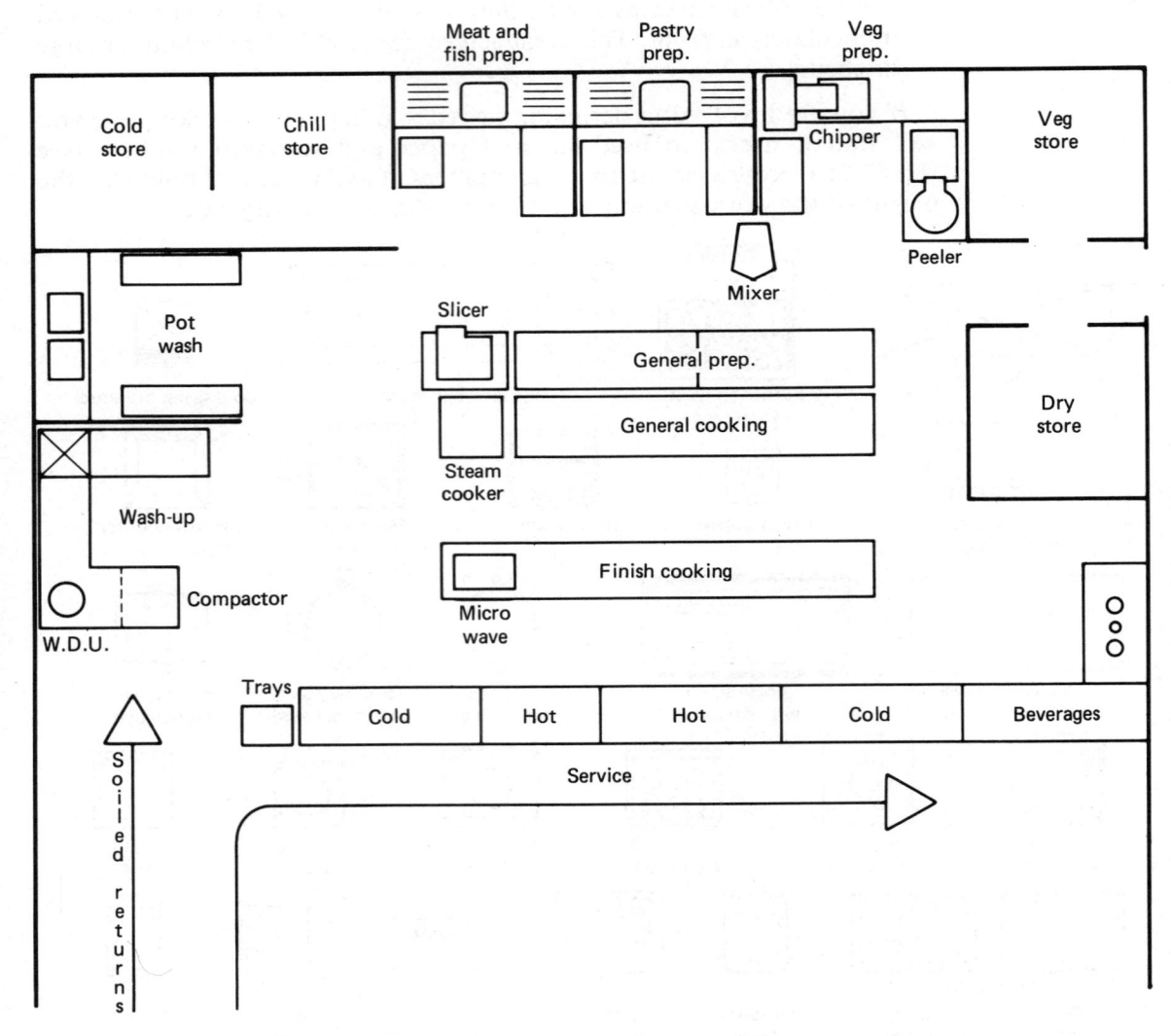

Fig. 47.8 Plan for a kitchen serving 150 to 250 lunches in a self-service staff restaurant

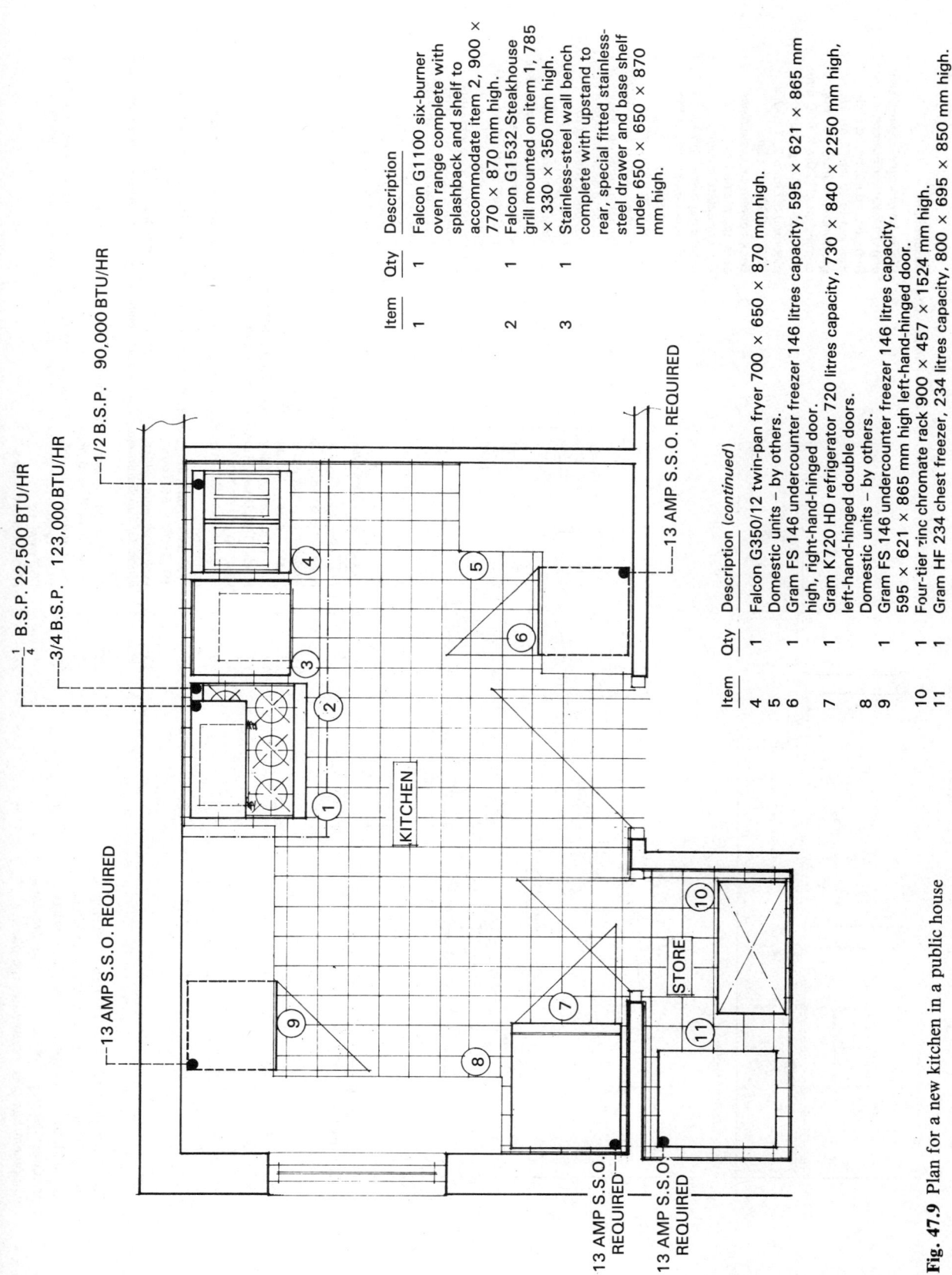

Item	Qty	Description
1	1	Falcon G1100 six-burner oven range complete with splashback and shelf to accommodate item 2, 900 × 770 × 870 mm high.
2	1	Falcon G1532 Steakhouse grill mounted on item 1, 785 × 330 × 350 mm high.
3	1	Stainless-steel wall bench complete with upstand to rear, special fitted stainless-steel drawer and base shelf under 650 × 650 × 870 mm high.

Item	Qty	Description (continued)
4	1	Falcon G350/12 twin-pan fryer 700 × 650 × 870 mm high.
5		Domestic units – by others.
6	1	Gram FS 146 undercounter freezer 146 litres capacity, 595 × 621 × 865 mm high, right-hand-hinged door.
7	1	Gram K720 HD refrigerator 720 litres capacity, 730 × 840 × 2250 mm high, left-hand-hinged double doors.
8		Domestic units – by others.
9	1	Gram FS 146 undercounter freezer 146 litres capacity, 595 × 621 × 865 mm high left-hand-hinged door.
10	1	Four-tier zinc chromate rack 900 × 457 × 1524 mm high.
11	1	Gram HF 234 chest freezer, 234 litres capacity, 800 × 695 × 850 mm high.

Fig. 47.9 Plan for a new kitchen in a public house

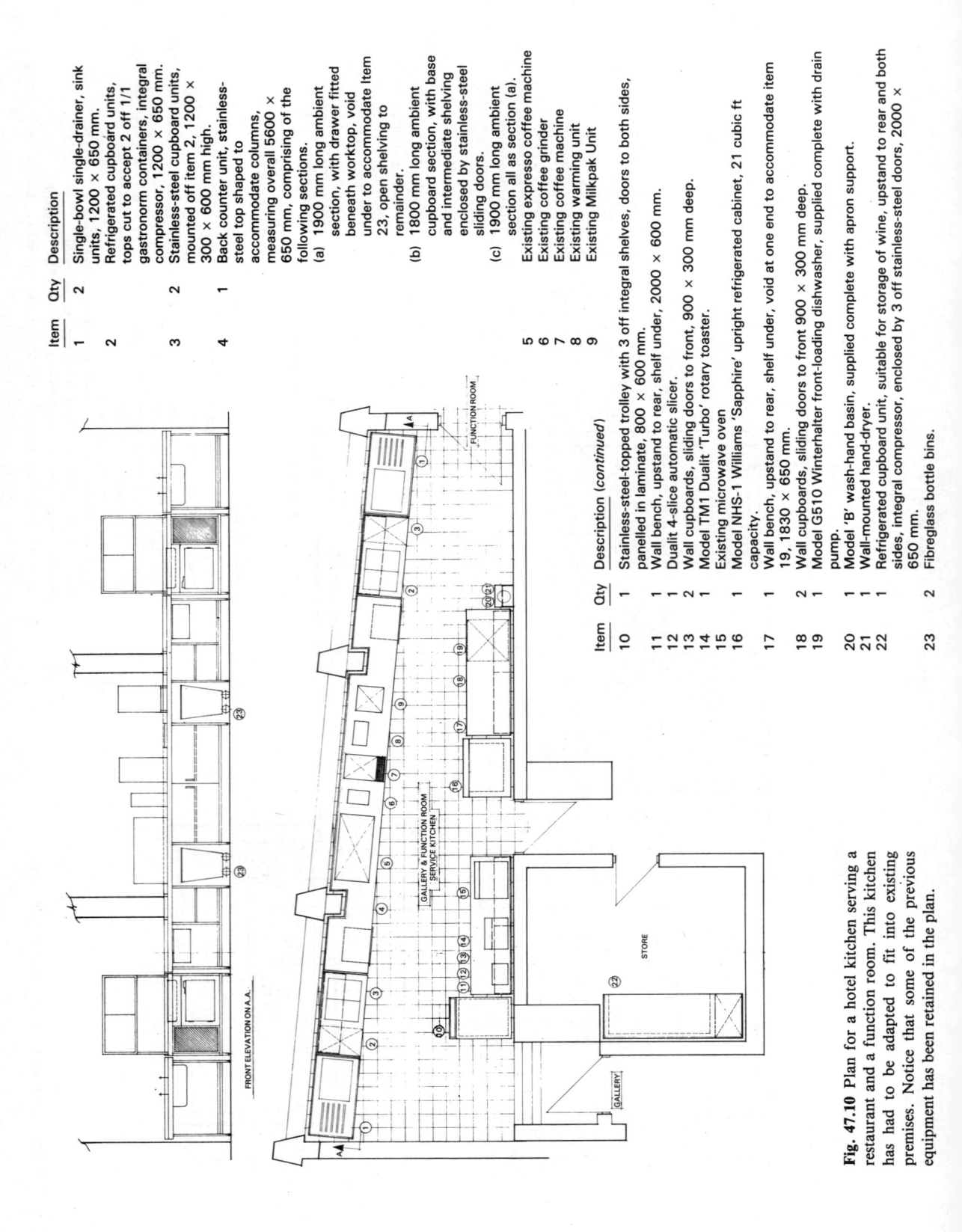

Item	Qty	Description
1	2	Single-bowl single-drainer, sink units, 1200 × 650 mm.
2	2	Refrigerated cupboard units, tops cut to accept 2 off 1/1 gastronorm containers, integral compressor. 1200 × 650 mm.
3	2	Stainless-steel cupboard units, mounted off item 2, 1200 × 300 × 600 mm high.
4	1	Back counter unit, stainless-steel top shaped to accommodate columns, measuring overall 5600 × 650 mm, comprising of the following sections.
		(a) 1900 mm long ambient section, with drawer fitted beneath worktop, void under to accommodate Item 23, open shelving to remainder.
		(b) 1800 mm long ambient cupboard section, with base and intermediate shelving enclosed by stainless-steel sliding doors.
		(c) 1900 mm long ambient section all as section (a).
5		Existing expresso coffee machine
6		Existing coffee grinder
7		Existing coffee machine
8		Existing warming unit
9		Existing Milkpak Unit

Item	Qty	Description (*continued*)
10	1	Stainless-steel-topped trolley with 3 off integral shelves, panelled in laminate, 800 × 600 mm.
11	1	Wall bench, upstand to rear, shelf under, 2000 × 600 mm.
12	1	Dualit 4-slice automatic slicer.
13	2	Wall cupboards, sliding doors to front, 900 × 300 mm deep.
14	1	Model TM1 Dualit 'Turbo' rotary toaster.
15		Existing microwave oven
16	1	Model NHS-1 Williams 'Sapphire' upright refrigerated cabinet, 21 cubic ft capacity.
17	1	Wall bench, upstand to rear, shelf under, void at one end to accommodate item 19, 1830 × 650 mm.
18	2	Wall cupboards, sliding doors to front 900 × 300 mm deep.
19	1	Model G510 Winterhalter front-loading dishwasher, supplied complete with drain pump.
20	1	Model 'B' wash-hand basin, supplied complete with apron support.
21	1	Wall-mounted hand-dryer.
22	1	Refrigerated cupboard unit, suitable for storage of wine, upstand to rear and both sides, integral compressor, enclosed by 3 off stainless-steel doors, 2000 × 650 mm.
23	2	Fibreglass bottle bins.

Fig. 47.10 Plan for a hotel kitchen serving a restaurant and a function room. This kitchen has had to be adapted to fit into existing premises. Notice that some of the previous equipment has been retained in the plan.

47.10 Kitchen organisation

We have dealt with the organisation of space and equipment in the kitchen earlier in this chapter, and some aspects of health and safety in chapter 2. Now we need to concern ourselves with the organisation of kitchen staff.

As we have said many times before, the menu is the driving force in the operation. Once the menu has been defined, the essential features of the catering operation have been decided. Once the essential features have been identified, the staffing can be organised to suit the various activities that are required.

In most cases nowadays, the need to be flexible is all-important. The traditional *partie system* may still be in use in very large up-market hotels, and we shall describe it briefly, but its relevance to the majority of modern catering operations is very limited. Any system chosen should be capable of being personalised to suit the particular operation concerned. We give below an example of a possible staffing structure for one type of establishment, but you should remember that a structure is only a possibility to which adjustments can be made to 'fine tune' it to a particular situation.

An example of the staffing structure and job responsibilities for a typical fast-food unit offering both an in-house eating facility and take-away service

Menu

(Notice how we start with the menu!)

- Various burgers in buns with an assortment of sauces and garnishes
- French fries
- Coffee
- Milk shakes
- Minerals

Staffing structure

- *Area manager* Responsible for a number of units in a geographical area; also responsible for seeing that company policy is carried out.
- *Unit manager* Has overall control for the profitability, organisation, and running of the unit; responsible for maintenance of standards of performance and cleanliness.
- *Assistant unit manager* Assists and deputises for the unit manager.
- *Floor manager* Responsible for the daily organisation of either the front or rear area of the unit.
- *Senior crew members* Experienced crew members with the added responsibility of providing assistance and guidance to new or inexperienced crew members.
- *Crew members* Operatives who perform a range of practical activities, including cooking, cashier duties, food and counter service, and clearing tables.

Equipment needs

- Griddle(s)
- Toasters
- Deep-fat fryer(s)
- Coffee machine(s)
- Drinks dispensers
- Heated display unit(s)
- Ambient display unit(s)
- Service counter
- Refrigeration unit(s)
- Deep-freeze unit(s)
- Cash register

Methods of displaying menu

- Overhead counter display
- Visual display using large colour photographs
- Wipe-clean display cards

Special points

- Located in a town centre or other area with good pedestrian flow.
- The kitchen area is an extension of the service area.
- Menu items are dispensed in disposable containers. (These containers must conform to the Materials and Articles in Contact with Food Regulations 1978, which require that the containers shall not affect the taste, appearance, and quality of the food or make it injurious to health.)
- The business relies on a large volume of sales.
- Customers eating in-house are not expected to remain seated once the menu items have been consumed.

Two further examples of staffing structures are given below, but with not quite so much detail.

A traditional partie system would probably be used to organise staff preparing formal menus. This type of staffing structure is still used in many hotels and restaurants, and its main personnel are as follows:

- *Chef de cuisine* (head chef)   In overall control of the kitchen – responsible for maintaining standards and profit margins.
- *Sous chef* (second chef)   Deputises for the head chef, but will be more closely involved with the daily running of the kitchen.
- *Chef de partie* (section head)   Supervises the daily running of one of the sections of the kitchen – these include the sauce, larder, patisserie, and roast sections.
- *Commis chef* (assistant chef)   A trained chef seeking further experience.
- *Trainee chef*   A trainee, following a training programme which may include part-time attendance at a local college.

- *Kitchen porter*   Responsible for the general cleaning of the kitchen and the washing of dirty cooking equipment, cutlery, and crockery.

A different staffing structure would be necessary to operate a staff restaurant. Here are some examples of personnel grades that you might expect to find:

- *Catering manager*   In control of the unit – responsible for keeping the costs within the budget limits, for cleanliness, and for standards of performance.
- *Chef supervisor*   In charge of the daily running of the kitchen and of ensuring the standards are maintained.
- *Leading cook*   Responsible for the preparation and cooking of the menu dishes. May have special duties in a particular area of the kitchen.
- *Assistant cook*   Helps with the preparation and cooking of the menu dishes under the supervision of the leading cook.
- *General assistant*   Covers a range of duties, including general cleaning, helping with simple food preparation, assisting with the service, and clearing tables.

47.11 Professional attitudes and behaviour of staff

In a well-run establishment, staff are motivated to complete their tasks effectively. The motivation will, of course, be partly financial reward, but there are many other factors that can contribute to job satisfaction at whatever level you are employed.

The staffing structure should be such that every employee knows who he or she is responsible to and gains recognition for tasks well done. Good staff relations depend on all members of staff behaving in a professional and responsible manner. (You are advised to consult the Hotel and Catering Training Board publication entitled *Employee Relations* for details of legislation and official terms commonly used when discussing this topic.)

These are a few of the more important general points:

- *Your behaviour towards other members of staff* – for example, courtesy, tact, patience, and respecting confidences; not rudeness, arrogance, or impatience.
- *Your responsibilities to the operation* – for example, efficiency, a good image to the customers, and contribution to profitability.
- *Your contribution as part of the team* – for example, doing your job conscientiously and helping others where possible or necessary.
- *Your duty to your employer* – for example, being punctual and notifying proposed or unavoidable absence so that cover can be arranged.
- *Your duty to yourself* – for example, making the most of any opportunities you may have to improve your skills and knowledge, following instructions designed to help you, and responding sensibly to constructive criticism.

Many employers prefer staff who are able to work in all areas of the kitchen as well as help out in the food service area. This requires each member of staff to possess a number of different skills. This flexibility helps the head chef or supervisor when preparing the work schedules.

The skills required for the food service area include selling and merchandising. Even if your main duties are in the food preparation area, you should realise the importance of persuading customers to buy something – and preferably something that will make a profit. The persuasion may be created by the menu (see page 296), the display of dishes, or your personal recommendation. Whatever method or combination of methods you use, the result should be that the customers have purchased something that they wanted and enjoyed and feel that they have had value for money.

The reasons for persuading a customer to buy a certain dish may relate to profitability, the need to reduce stock of a certain commodity, or the introduction of new items. Provided that your client leaves as a satisfied customer, you have done a good job of selling.

The skills required at a personal level are

- interpersonal skills – your relationship with the customer,
- technical competence in serving food,
- knowledge of the products you are selling.

From time to time it will be necessary for the head chef or supervisor to review staff work schedules and levels of responsibilities. This review will tell the head chef if the amount of work and the degree of skill required to complete the work are appropriate for each staff member. As you become more experienced you will be able to complete a larger number of tasks as well as being able to take on extra responsibilities such as checking the work of someone with less experience than yourself. This may be shown on the revised schedules.

Periodic reviewing and flexible work schedules will assist in the smooth, efficient running of the kitchen, as will effective liaison with other areas of the operation involved in the provision of food and beverages. As well as the dining areas, these may include the stores, reception, housekeeping department, and bars.

48 Catering calculations and costing

In this chapter we shall have a look at aspects of the catering industry that must be understood if any catering business is to be profitable. Remember that your goods and services have to be paid for, either directly by a customer or indirectly as in a hospital. In both cases you will have to ensure that you contribute profitably to the operation. You may have all the technical skills necessary to produce marvellous food, but you won't last very long if you run out of money in the process of producing it, whether you are working for yourself or for somebody else.

We shall consider units of measurement used in catering and simple calculations concerned with these. We shall also look at food costing and how control procedures can contribute to running a profitable operation.

48.1 Measurement systems

Although metric (or SI) units are now in common use, the imperial system still finds some place in catering. Some equipment and books use imperial units of measurement, and you will come across many commodities that are sold by the pound. It is therefore necessary for you to understand both systems and to be able to convert from one to the other.

The metric system

WEIGHT

The metric units of weight used in the catering industry are the kilogram (kg) and the gram (g).

$$1 \text{ kilogram} = 1000 \text{ grams}$$

Amounts other than whole kilograms may be shown by using a decimal point. For example,

$$1200 \text{ grams} = 1.2 \text{ kilograms}$$

which means $1\frac{2}{10}$ kg. Similarly,

$$1.2 \text{ kg} - 500 \text{ g} = 1.2 \text{ kg} - 0.5 \text{ kg}$$
$$= 0.7 \text{ kg} \quad \text{or} \quad 700 \text{ g}$$

CAPACITY

The main units used are the litre (l) and the millilitre (ml).

$$1 \text{ litre} = 1000 \text{ millilitres}$$

Thus $10\,600 \text{ ml} = 10.6 \text{ l}$

LENGTH

The main units are the metre (m), the centimetre (cm), and the millimetre (mm).

$$1 \text{ metre} = 100 \text{ centimetres}$$
$$= 1000 \text{ millimetres}$$

Thus 500 mm = 50 cm = 0.5 m

and 6.2 m = 620 cm = 6200 mm

TEMPERATURE

The Celsius (or centigrade) scale is based on 0 degrees (written as 0° C) as the freezing point and 100 degrees as the boiling point of water.

The imperial system

WEIGHT

The main units are the pound (lb), the ounce (oz), and the hundredweight (cwt).

$$1 \text{ hundredweight} = 112 \text{ pounds}$$
$$1 \text{ pound} = 16 \text{ ounces}$$

Thus 3½ cwt = 3.5 × 112 lb = 392 lb

2¾ lb = 2.75 × 16 oz = 44 oz

CAPACITY

The main units are the gallon (gal), the quart (qt), the pint (pt), and the fluid ounce (fl oz).

$$1 \text{ gallon} = 8 \text{ pints}$$
$$1 \text{ quart} = 2 \text{ pints}$$
$$1 \text{ pint} = 20 \text{ fluid ounces}$$

Thus 6 gal = 6 × 8 pt = 48 pt

= 48 × ½ qt = 24 qt

¾ pt = ¾ × 20 fl oz = 15 fl oz

LENGTH

The main units are the yard (yd), the foot (ft), and the inch (in).

$$1 \text{ yard} = 3 \text{ feet}$$
$$1 \text{ foot} = 12 \text{ inches}$$

Thus 2½ yards = 2.5 × 3 ft = 7.5 ft

= 7.5 × 12 in = 90 in

TEMPERATURE

The Fahrenheit scale is based on 32 degrees (written as 32°F) as the freezing point and 212 degrees as the boiling point of water.

Conversion between the two systems

You may well find that, although a recipe states the quantities required in metric quantities, the ingredients are actually sold in imperial quantities, or vice versa. It is therefore necessary to convert one of the quantities so that the correct amount is purchased or used.

Tables 48.1 and 48.2 give the conversion factors needed when converting the main units of measurement from metric to imperial or vice versa.

Table 48.1 Metric to imperial equivalents

Metric units	Imperial units
1 kilogram	= 2.2 lb
100 grams	= 3.52 ounces
1 litre	= 1.76 pints
100 millilitres	= 0.176 pints
1 metre	= 39.37 inches
1 centimetre	= 0.394 inches
1 millimetre	= 0.039 inches

Table 48.2 Imperial to metric equivalents

Imperial units	Metric units
1 pound	= 454 grams
1 ounce	= 28.35 grams
1 gallon	= 4.54 litres
1 quart	= 1.136 litres
1 pint	= 0.568 litres
1 yard	= 0.914 metres
1 foot	= 0.304 metres
1 inch	= 2.54 centimetres

Examples of conversion

$$6\tfrac{1}{2} \text{ kg} = 6.5 \times 2.2 \text{ lb} = 14.3 \text{ lb}$$

$$15 \text{ pt} = 15 \times 0.568 \text{ litres} = 8.52 \text{ litres}$$

$$4\tfrac{1}{2} \text{ gallons} = 4.5 \times 4.54 \text{ litres} = 20.43 \text{ litres}$$

$$16\tfrac{3}{4} \text{ litres} = 16.75 \times 1.76 \text{ pt} = 29.48 \text{ pt}$$

$$200 \text{ g} = 200 \times \frac{3.52}{100} \text{ oz} = 7.04 \text{ oz}$$

$$750 \text{ ml} = 750 \times \frac{0.176}{100} \text{ pt} = 1.32 \text{ pt}$$

Conversion of temperature

To change degrees Fahrenheit to degrees Celsius the formula is:

(i) subtract 32,
(ii) multiply by 5,
(iii) divide by 9.

To change degrees Celsius to degrees Fahrenheit the formula is:

(i) multiply by 9,
(ii) divide by 5,
(iii) add 32.

Examples of temperature conversion

Convert 54° F to °C.

(i) $54 - 32 = 22$

(ii) $22 \times 5 = 110$

(iii) $110 \div 9 = 12.2$

$\therefore \quad 54°F = 12.2°C$

Convert 43° C to °F.

(i) $43 \times 9 = 387$

(ii) $387 \div 5 = 77.4$

(iii) $77.4 + 32 = 109.4$

$\therefore \quad 43°C = 109.4°F$

Be careful with minus temperatures:

Convert $-18°$ C to °F.

(i) $-18 \times 9 = -162$

(ii) $-162 \div 5 = -32.4$

(iii) $-32.4 + 32 = -0.4$

$\therefore \quad -18°C = -0.4°F$ (recommended temperature of a deep-freeze)

48.2 Applied calculations

This section assumes that you are reasonably competent in the four basic arithmetic operations of addition, subtraction, multiplication, and division and deals with the application of these principles to the caterer.

Percentages

It is sometimes necessary to express one item as a percentage of another:

EXAMPLE 1

If the total sales of a restaurant in a certain week were £1325 and in that same week the sales value of meat dishes was £830, the £830 could be expressed as a percentage of the £1325 thus:

$$\frac{830}{1325} \times 100\% = 62.64\%$$

This enables comparison with a previous week's figures, budgets, or other targets to be made much more easily, as they will all be calculated on the same basis.

EXAMPLE 2

What percentage of a bag of potatoes which weighed 25 kg when full has been used when only 11 kg remains?

Amount used = 25 kg − 11 kg = 14 kg

$$\text{Percentage used} = \frac{14}{25} \times 100\% = 56\%$$

EXAMPLE 3

If the sales target for a week was £920 and the actual sales achieved were £825, what percentage of the target was achieved?

$$\frac{825}{920} \times 100\% = 89.67\%$$

Discounts

Most suppliers offer discounts to their customers.

Cash discounts are offered to customers who pay their accounts promptly, within an agreed time limit. For example, a supplier might offer a customer '2% cash discount 7 days'. This means that, if the account is paid within 7 days from the date of the invoice, 2% may be deducted from the bill before it is paid.

Discounts are also offered to customers who buy large quantities or who agree to buy certain quantities regularly – say every two weeks or every month. If a business agreed to buy all its cleaning materials from one supplier, then that supplier might agree to give it a discount of 5%. This has the effect of reducing the prices by 5%.

EXAMPLE

You purchase a consignment of tinned goods with a basic price of £320. The supplier agrees to allow you a discount of 5% in view of the large quantity and also offers a cash discount of 3% if the bill is paid within 10 days. The amount you will have to pay is

		Cost	£320.00	
less	Trade discount 5%		16.00	$(320 \times \frac{5}{100})$
			304.00	

$$\begin{array}{llr} \textit{less} & \text{Cash discount 3\%} & 9.12 \quad (304 \times \tfrac{3}{100}) \\ & & \overline{£294.88} \end{array}$$

If the account is not paid within the 10 day limit then £304 will have to be paid – you will lose the cash discount.

Service charges

As an incentive to staff to increase the sales of a business, a service charge is made as an addition to the charge on the customer's bill and this is understood to be passed to the staff concerned. (Unfortunately, it is not *always* the case that this *is* given to the staff concerned.) If customers are pleased with the service received, they will consider returning and the staff will receive more service charges and the business will benefit from the sales made. Service charges are normally expressed as a percentage of the total bill.

EXAMPLE

Suppose a customer's bill in a restaurant totalled £16.20 before a service charge of 8% was added. The customer would have to pay £17.50:

$$£16.20 \times \frac{8}{100} = £1.30$$

$$£16.20 + £1.30 = £17.50$$

Wastage

It is nearly always inevitable that some wastage will occur in the cooking and preparation of food. However, if a business is to make a profit, this wastage must be controlled. It is normal therefore to calculate the percentage wastage expected.

EXAMPLE

Suppose you purchase 40 kg of meat and actually serve 30 kg of this to the customers. You have obviously lost as wastage 40 kg − 30 kg = 10 kg of the total originally purchased, or

$$\frac{10}{40} \times 100\% = 25\%$$

Thus 25% of the meat purchased was lost through wastage in the preparation and cooking processes and was not able to be sold to the customer.

Wastage and purchasing

As a certain amount of any food purchased will probably be wasted before it can be sold to the customers, it is essential that this loss is taken into account when calculating the amount to be purchased.

EXAMPLE 1

Suppose your restaurant expects to serve 50 portions of meat each weighing 125 g. The total it will serve will weigh $50 \times 125\,g = 6250\,g$ or 6.25 kg. If, however, it is known that 28% of meat purchased is normally lost in preparation and cooking, then if you purchased only 6.25 kg you would not have enough remaining to serve the required number of portions. You therefore need to calculate the amount you need to purchase to allow for the expected wastage. The way to do this is as follows:

(i) If the wastage expected is 28% of the amount purchased, then the portions sold to the customers must represent $100\% - 28\% = 72\%$ of the amount purchased.

(ii) It is known that the amount sold to the customers must be 6.25 kg and, as stated in (i) above, this will represent 72% of the total purchased.

Since $72\% = 6.25\,kg$

then $1\% = \dfrac{6.25\,kg}{72} = 0.0868\,kg$

(iii) If 1% of the amount purchased is 0.0868 kg, then the total amount purchased (100%) must be

$$0.0868\,kg \times 100 = 8.68\,kg$$

EXAMPLE 2

Using the three steps detailed in example 1 above, it is possible to calculate the total amount needed to be purchased to serve 60 portions, each 110 g, assuming a wastage of 38%.

(i) Total served $= 100\% - 38\% = 62\%$

(ii) $1\% = \dfrac{60 \times 110\,g}{62} = 106.5\,g$

(iii) $100\% = 106.5\,g \times 100 = 10\,650\,g = 10.65\,kg$

Thus if 10.65 kg is purchased there will be enough to serve the 60 portions after 38% has been wasted.

Calculations using the metric system

EXAMPLE 1

What is the cost of 125 g of sugar at £20 for 10 kg?

$10\,kg = 10 \times 1000\,g = 10\,000\,g$

Since 10 000 g costs £20, 125 g will cost

$$\dfrac{£20}{10\,000} \times 125 = \dfrac{2000\,p}{10\,000} \times 125 = 25\,p$$

EXAMPLE 2

What is the cost of 675 ml of cooking oil at £9 per 5 litres?

$$5 \text{ litres} = 5 \times 1000 \text{ ml} = 5000 \text{ ml}$$

The cost is therefore $675 \times \dfrac{£9}{5000} = £1.22$

EXAMPLE 3

What is the cost of 2.25 kg of peppers at 40 p per 125 g?

125 g costs 40 p

$$\therefore \quad 1000 \text{ g} (= 1 \text{ kg}) \text{ costs } \dfrac{40 \text{ p}}{125} \times 1000 = 320 \text{ p}$$
$$= £3.20$$

$\therefore$ 2.25 kg costs £3.20 × 2.25 = £7.20

48.3 Food costing

Any business must know what an item being sold has cost and what price that item is now being sold for. It is essential to realise that, while cost is normally known, the selling price has to be fixed at a level that the customer will accept, that is comparable with that being charged by competitors, and that will produce a profit.

The total costs of a catering business are normally broken down into three main areas:

> Total costs = food costs
> + labour costs (wages, holiday pay, overtime pay, pension costs, etc.)
> + overhead expenses (rent, electricity, gas, insurance, advertising, etc.)

Thus the price charged for a meal must be sufficient to cover both the cost of the food used and also a share of the other costs.

All businesses need to develop a system that collects and analyses costs correctly. Accuracy is most important, because decisions will be made on the figures that such a system reveals.

Accurate food costing is helped by carrying out yield tests for the major commodities such as meat, fish, poultry, game, and vegetables. Yield tests will show you the amount lost during trimming, the percentage left for the intended dish, and the real cost of the commodity. If you have a standard yield for all or some of the important commodities, it will assist in your purchasing by showing you which size or weight of a particular item is best for you to buy. The information from a yield test can be used to check the number of portions achieved against the predicted portion numbers. It may be necessary to reweigh or remeasure portion sizes to ensure that any discrepancies are not being caused by incorrect portion sizes (see 'Portion control' – page 330).

In the catering industry it is normal practice to calculate the selling price using the following method.

Suppose the accounts for a restaurant for a year show the following information:

	Sales	£100 000
Food costs	40 000 }	75 000
All other costs	35 000 }	
	Profit	£ 25 000

The management have considered these accounts and have decided that the amount of profit is satisfactory and that they wish to achieve similar results next year. It has already been stated that the prices chosen must recover the food costs and a share of the other costs. In the illustration given above it can be seen that the food costs represent 40% of the sales $\left(\frac{40\,000}{100\,000} \times 100\%\right)$. Therefore the profit and other costs represent 60% of the sales (100% − 40%). To achieve similar profits, each selling price must therefore be calculated so that, after the food costs have been paid, a 'gross profit' of 60% of the selling price remains available to pay the other costs and give some real profit. In calculating a selling price, then, there are two known factors: the food costs and the gross profit (mark-up) needed, that is, the 60%.

Thus it is now possible to calculate what selling price is needed to achieve the desired profit.

Suppose the food cost of a meal is £1.50 and the required gross profit as in the example above is 60%. The selling price will then be calculated using the formula

$$\text{selling price} = \frac{\text{food cost}}{100 - \text{required gross profit}} \times 100$$

So $\text{selling price} = \frac{£1.50}{40} \times 100 = £3.75$

It is essential that the formula for selling price is learned.

Another calculation linked to this which is frequently used is the *food cost percentage* – also called the *kitchen percentage*. This calculation expresses the food cost as a percentage of the selling price, using the formula

$$\text{kitchen percentage} = \frac{\text{food cost}}{\text{selling price}} \times 100\%$$

Thus if the food cost of a dish is £1.50 and the selling price is £2.50, the kitchen percentage will be

$$\frac{£1.50}{£2.50} \times 100\% = 60\%$$

Price-fixing is an extremely important task for any business. If the prices are set too high, customers may go elsewhere; if they are set too low they may not cover costs. In both of these situations a business will soon find itself in considerable difficulties. However, it is not possible for one

320 The business of catering

business to set prices in isolation – it would be ridiculous for a business to fix prices which were double those of a local competitor for meals which were very similar. Discussion of these matters – which are in the realms of marketing and economics – are outside the scope of this book, but these simple facts should be remembered.

48.4 Standard recipes

While it is quite common for a chef to vary a recipe sometimes when using it, the business needs to know that its costs, profits, cash forecasts, etc. will be maintained. This is why standard recipes should be prepared and used on all occasions whenever they are available. Whatever chef prepares the dish, the quality and cost should then remain the same.

A standard recipe should always state

- the name and quantity of all ingredients,
- the method of production and service instructions,
- the expected yield from that quantity of ingredients.

Figure 48.1 shows an example of a standard recipe card.

The standard recipe card may also give details of the equipment to be used – the size of baking-tins, for example.

Thus the chefs in an establishment that uses a menu that repeats itself fairly regularly will work to the instructions laid down by the standard recipe card. The management can then be sure that they should achieve their target profits, as the food used by the chefs will be as detailed on the costing sheet (see below) and its value will have been included in the selling-price calculation together with the appropriate mark-up to cover all other costs and profit.

48.5 The cost of sales

The costing sheets show the standard amounts of ingredients that should have been used for each recipe, with the cost of each ingredient. At the end of each month, the total of the ingredients *actually* used will need to be calculated. In any business there will always be stocks remaining at the end of each day, and the method used to find the cost of the food used needs to take these into account. The basic principle is

$$\frac{\text{food}}{\text{used}} = \frac{\text{opening}}{\text{stock}} + \text{purchases} - \frac{\text{closing}}{\text{stock}}$$

Imagine that the only item in stock was eggs. At the start of the month there were 16 eggs (this is called the opening stock). During the month 242 were purchased, and at the end of the month there were 26 left (this is the closing stock). Thus the number of eggs used in the month must have been:

	Number in stock at the start of the month	16
plus	Number purchased	242
	Number available for use	258
less	Those left in stock at the end of the month	26
	Number actually used	232

This same method is used to calculate the *cost* of the actual food used, called *the cost of sales*. The total food in stock is priced and then the calculation is carried out as shown above for the eggs:

	Value of opening stock	£ 642
plus	Total cost of goods purchased	1794
	Value of stock available to use	2436
less	Value of closing stock	522
	Value of food used (cost of sales)	£1914

Suprême of chicken stuffed with cheese and ham

Recipe number 84

Yield required (200 g portions):	10	30	50
Item	Quantity	Quantity	Quantity
Fresh suprêmes of chicken	10 × 125 g	30 × 125 g	50 × 125 g
Mozarella cheese	250 g	750 g	1250 g
Thin slices of ham (tinned shoulder)	5 × 50 g	15 × 50 g	25 × 50 g
White breadcrumbs	250 g	750 g	1250 g
Eggs (grade 2) } mix lightly	3	9	15
Milk } together	100 ml	300 ml	500 ml
Plain flour	250 g	750 g	1250 g
Salt	20 g	60 g	100 g
Pepper	10 g	30 g	50 g
Watercress	2 bunches	6 bunches	10 bunches
Straw potatoes (recipe No. 27)	250 g	750 g	1250 g
Cutlet frills	10	30	50

Method of preparation

- Trim suprêmes of chicken, remove fillet, and gently flatten the fillet and the suprême using a cutlet bat and clear polythene.
- Trim ham and cut each slice in half. Cut cheese into even-sized batons and wrap each in half a slice of ham.
- Place a cheese baton on to each seasoned flattened suprême, cover with the flattened fillet, and roll up neatly.
- Refrigerate for 30 minutes. Remove and coat with the flour, egg-wash and breadcrumbs. Reshape and flatten lightly.
- Place into a frying basket and lower gently into hot oil at 180°C (365°F) for 8–10 minutes.
- Remove from the oil, drain well on absorbent paper, and serve on a dishpaper.

Service instructions

Place the cooked chicken on to a pre-warmed stainless-steel flat on an oval dish-paper. Arrange the watercress sprigs and straw potatoes neatly at each end of the flat and place a cutlet frill on the wing of each suprême.

Fig. 48.1 A standard recipe card

48.6 Gross profit and net profit

A business measures its profit at two levels. The first is called the *gross profit* and is calculated by deducting the cost of sales (that is the value of the stocks of raw material used) from the total value of the sales made in the same period:

gross profit = sales − cost of sales

Thus if the total sales made by a restaurant for the month of July were £16 420 and the cost of sales was £9746, the gross profit would have been £16 420 − £9746 = £6674.

The other level of profit calculated is the *net profit*. This is the amount that is left after all the costs of the business, other than the cost of sales, have been deducted from the gross profit. These costs will include the cost of labour plus all the expenses of the business such as electricity, bank interest, insurance, advertising, rent, stationery, etc.

net profit = gross profit − all costs except cost of sales

= sales − all costs

If the total of these other costs for July was £3296, a profit statement can be prepared as follows:

Profit statement for July

	Sales	£16 420
less	Cost of sales	9 746
	Gross profit	6 674
less	All other costs	3 296
	Net profit	£ 3 378

The amount of any profit or loss is determined by the amount of sales made and the level of costs. It is important to prepare forecasts of what the sales and costs are expected to be in future periods and regularly compare the actual results with these forecasts. Action must be taken if sales are below forecast or expenses above, as either of these factors will cause the actual profit to be lower than that forecast.

Cost behaviour

Not all costs increase or decrease for the same reason or by the same amount. Costs are usually classified as:

- *Variable costs* – those costs that vary in direct proportion to changes in the level of activity, for example the cost of food. The greater the number of meals served, the higher the food cost.
- *Fixed costs* – those costs that are unaffected by changes in the level of activity, for example the rent of restaurant premises. No matter how many meals are served, the rent will remain the same.

While you cannot normally influence the amount of fixed costs that a business incurs, you can affect the total of variable costs by working efficiently and in accordance with the standard recipes and other instructions.

48.7 Value added tax

Practically all goods and services sold in the UK must have value added tax (VAT) added to their selling price.

The VAT charge is a percentage of the value of the goods or services supplied. The standard rate is at present 15%. This rate applies to all transactions except those that fall within two categories:

- some goods and services are *exempt* from VAT – these include those supplied by small businesses with a taxable turnover of less than £25 400 per year (at present), insurance, and financial services;
- some goods and services are *zero-rated* – these include some foods (see below), books, newspapers, fuel, and power.

The difference between these is that traders in exempt categories cannot claim back the VAT that they themselves have paid on goods and services supplied in connection with their business, whereas suppliers of zero-rated and standard-rated goods and services can recover the VAT that they have paid – which is why a VAT receipt must always be obtained for all VAT-able goods bought for your business.

VAT and the catering industry

Special VAT regulations apply to the hotel and catering industry, and leaflets detailing these can be obtained from any VAT office. (VAT offices can be found in the telephone directory under 'Customs & Excise Department'.)

VAT is chargeable at the standard rate on food and drink supplied in a restaurant. Where food is supplied on a 'take-away' basis, VAT is charged at the standard rate on items that have been 'heated for consumption', such as fish and chips. Food sold by a take-away that has not been heated, such as a cold sausage roll, is zero-rated. Certain items are always standard-rated in whatever circumstances they are supplied. Items falling into this category include ice-cream, alcoholic drinks, crisps, and confectionery.

Details of the appropriate rate of VAT to be charged on any item or service sold are given in leaflets issued by the Customs & Excise Department, which may be obtained on request from their offices.

Examples of VAT transactions

1. Four dinners at £12 each   £48.00
   Standard-rate VAT added at 15%   £ 7.20
   Total charged to customer   £55.20

2. Six cold pork pies sold at a take-away at 40 p each   £2.40
   Zero-rate VAT, i.e. 0%   –
   Total charged to customer   £2.40

3. Four portions of chips sold at a take-away at 45 p each   £1.80
   Standard-rate VAT added at 15%   £0.27
   Total charged to customer   £2.07

324 *The business of catering*

It must be remembered that the prices advertised to a customer include the VAT charge, so for analysis purposes the total sales made will have to be broken down into the total charged as VAT and the total charged as income of the business.

For example, if it is known that the total standard-rated sales made for a week total £1270 including the VAT at 15%, this may then be broken down as follows:

$$\text{Sales income} = £1270 \times \frac{100}{115} = £1104.35$$
$$\text{VAT} = £1270 - £1104.35 = £165.65$$
$$\text{Total sales value}   £1270.00$$

Figures 48.9 to 48.11 show the VAT element in the price of various recipes stored in a computer.

The VAT charged to customers by a business has to be paid to the Customs & Excise at the end of each quarter. The business is therefore simply acting as a tax collector for the government. Before paying the VAT collected from the customers to the Customs & Excise, the business will deduct any VAT which it has been charged, for example on telephone bills, repair charges, equipment, stationery, etc.

48.8 Business documents

In order to understand the next sections on stock control and food control it is necessary to consider the documents used in commerce. The documents shown in figs 48.2 to 48.5 are simple illustrations of forms that a business might use, but it should be remembered that all businesses will have their own requirements and ideas about the size and layout of their forms and no two businesses will ever use identical documentation.

Purchase order

Figure 48.2 shows a typical purchase order

```
                    PURCHASE ORDER
                    The Elite Hotel       Order No.  6432
                        Norwich
                    Tel. No. 934567       Date ...... 15.7.90

TO: Ted Cole & Co.
    Birmingham                VAT No. 714137926

Please supply:
```

Quantity	Unit size	Description	Unit price
4 bags	10 kg	White sugar	£6.00
8 bags	5 kg	Plain flour	£1.60
6 bottles	850 g	Tomato sauce	0.75p

Signed ....   Delivery required ...... 10 days

Fig. 48.2 A purchase order

All purchase orders must be prepared in duplicate, and any orders placed by telephone must be confirmed by a purchase order. The unit price is important as, by demanding that this is filled in, the management are in fact checking to see that the buying clerk has obtained prices before ordering and so is able to choose the cheapest supplier. The signature must be that of a responsible manager and not that of the buying clerk. The manager must make certain that the order has been correctly prepared and that the goods ordered are actually required by the hotel.

Delivery note

Figure 48.3 shows a typical delivery note.

The delivery note is prepared by the supplier and forwarded with the goods so that the customer can identify the goods.

```
┌─────────────────────────────────────────────────────────────────────┐
│                          DELIVERY NOTE                              │
│   TO:  The Elite Hotel    TED COLE & CO                             │
│        Norwich             BIRMINGHAM          Date: 22.7.90        │
│            Tel. No. 684572    VAT No. 629457214                     │
├──────────────┬──────────────┬──────────────────┬────────────────────┤
│  Quantity    │   Unit size  │   Description    │     Remarks        │
├──────────────┼──────────────┼──────────────────┼────────────────────┤
│  4 bags      │   10 kg      │   White sugar    │                    │
│  8 bags      │    5 kg      │   Plain flour    │                    │
│  3 bottles   │   850 g      │   Tomato sauce   │ Balance to follow  │
├──────────────┴──────────────┴──────────────────┴────────────────────┤
│   Your Order No. ...6432...        Delivery Note No. ....857A....   │
└─────────────────────────────────────────────────────────────────────┘
```

Fig. 48.3 A delivery note

Invoice

The invoice (fig. 48.4) is an important document and should be treated

```
┌─────────────────────────────────────────────────────────────────────┐
│                             INVOICE                                 │
│   TO:  The Elite Hotel    TED COLE & CO      No: 16259              │
│        Norwich             BIRMINGHAM        Date: 23.7.90          │
│            Tel. No. 684572    VAT No. 629457214                     │
│                                        Delivery Note No. 857A       │
├──────────────┬──────────┬──────────────────┬──────────┬─────────────┤
│  Quantity    │   Size   │   Description    │Unit price│ Total value │
├──────────────┼──────────┼──────────────────┼──────────┼─────────────┤
│  4 bags      │  10 kg   │   White sugar    │   £6     │   £24.00    │
│  8 bags      │   5 kg   │   Plain flour    │   £1.60  │    12.80    │
│  3 bottles   │  850 g   │   Tomato sauce   │   75p    │     2.25    │
├──────────────┴──────────┴──────────────────┼──────────┼─────────────┤
│                                      Total │          │    39.05    │
│                                      VAT   │          │     Nil     │
│                                            │          │   £39.05    │
├────────────────────────────────────────────┴──────────┴─────────────┤
│  Terms: 2½% cash 7 days; otherwise net 30 days   Your Order No. 6432│
└─────────────────────────────────────────────────────────────────────┘
```

Fig. 48.4 An invoice

carefully and not mislaid or lost. It records the amount now owed for the goods supplied, and once it has been checked it is entered into the accounting records of the business.

Statement of account

A statement of account (fig. 48.5) is prepared each month and sent by suppliers to their customers. It shows the transactions that have taken place between them during the month and the amount owed at the end of the month. Debit transactions represent goods supplied to the caterer, and credit transactions represent payments made by the caterer.

	STATEMENT TED COLE & CO BIRMINGHAM			Date 31.7.90
The Elite Hotel *Norwich*	Tel. No. 684572 VAT No. 629457214			
Date	Reference	Debit	Credit	Balance
1 July 3 July 6 July 23 July	*Balance b/f* *Cash* *Invoice 15429* *Invoice 16259*	£60.00 39.05	£100.00	£100.00 60.00 99.05

Fig. 48.5 A statement of account

48.9 Stock control

If a catering business is to be financially efficient and if it is to be sure to have the food required to serve the planned menu to the customers expected, then there has to be a suitable system to control stocks.

There are two aspects to stock control:

- stocks must be available when required, and
- stocks must not be excessive, as this would tie up money that might otherwise be used more efficiently in other parts of the business.

It is important that all staff understand the value and need for stock control systems and follow the procedures laid down, even though there will be many occasions when these may seem to a be a bit of a chore.

Bin cards

The bin card system is widely used in catering stock control. A simple bin card has the format shown in fig. 48.6, and a card like this is prepared for every item of stock kept in the stores.

The bin cards are the responsibility of the storekeeper, who must ensure that they are kept up to date. When goods are received, the storekeeper will make an entry increasing the balance remaining, and when goods are issued an entry that decreases the stock will be made.

Item	Stock No. ....
Unit or size	Maximum stock ....
Supplier	Minimum stock ....

Date	Received	Issued	Balance

Fig. 48.6 A bin card

Assuming that the menus used are fairly standard over a period, it will be possible to establish maximum, minimum, and re-order levels for each commodity:

- The maximum stock is the maximum that should ever need to be kept. By calculating this amount, the business can avoid both the cost of maintaining unnecessarily high stock, with the risk of deterioration, and also the cost of unnecessary storage space.
- The minimum stock is the amount below which the stock level should not be allowed to fall under normal conditions, otherwise some requests for the item will not be met.
- The re-order level is the stock level at which an order should be sent to the suppliers. This must take into account the maximum stock – the order should be for sufficient stock but not excessive – and the length of time the supplier needs to deliver the order, so that the stock does not fall below the minimum stock level. In fixing the maximum stock and the order quantity, any discounts given by the suppliers for purchasing large quantities must be considered.

Purchasing procedure

The procedure for controlling food stocks and purchasing is as follows:

- When the stock reaches the re-order level, the storekeeper will advise the purchase order clerk by means of the daily list of items to be ordered.
- The purchase order (see fig. 48.2) will be prepared by the clerk, checked and signed by a designated manager, and dispatched to the supplier with a copy sent to the accounts office. In the case of orders made by telephone, it may be company policy that these are confirmed in writing.
- In due course the supplier will dispatch the goods, accompanied by a delivery note (see fig. 48.3). The storekeeper will carefully check that the goods received agree with the delivery note – as to both quantity and description – and the customer's copy of the delivery note is then passed to the accounts office. This copy will state the date of receipt, the

suppliers' name, the quantity and type of goods received, and the delivery-note number.
- When the invoice (see fig. 48.4) is received from the supplier, the accounts office will check it with the order and the goods-received advice, to ensure that the goods for which the business is being charged have in fact been received and that the charge is as agreed when the order was placed. In due course a payment will then be made to the supplier for the goods.
- Goods may be withdrawn from the stores only when a signed requisition (fig. 48.7) is presented to the storekeeper.
- Different procedures will be needed to cover fresh foods, such as fish and vegetables, which may be delivered straight to the kitchen, as such items would obviously not be kept in store for a period of time.

Department	Stores Requistion		Number	
			Date	
Quantity	Unit Size	Description	Unit Price	Cost
Signed			Total	

Fig. 48.7 A stores requisition

The procedure outlined above will be adjusted to allow for the differing methods and menus used by various caterers, but the same general principles must always be followed.

The storekeeper is obviously a central figure in any stock-control system and should therefore be selected carefully. The qualities required are honesty, experience in the trade so that the different storage requirements of the various items kept in the store are appreciated, and the ability to keep the necessary records, as well as familiarity with the various departments of the business that will use the stores, the offices with which the stores will be in contact, and the staff authorised to sign requisitions.

In many businesses today, the introduction of computers has meant that some of the procedures discussed above are now dealt with by a central computer rather than by separate sections, but this does not remove the need for proper control of items flowing into and out of the stores and the correct authorisation of invoices for payment. The computer only reduces the amount of clerical work and speeds up certain processes (see section 48.11).

48.10 Food control

Control is needed over all the various aspects of a business if a satisfactory profit is to be made. This means that staff costs, telephone usage, heating costs, etc. must all be planned and controlled. The food used and its cost will also have a major effect on the amount of profit made, so it is important that this cost should be kept as low as possible. 'Food control' is the name given to the task of keeping the food cost to a minimum while still satisfying the customer.

Food control can be considered under seven headings: planning, purchasing, storage, pilferage, portion control, poor preparation and production, and profits.

Planning

Menus must be planned for a considerable period ahead of their actual preparation, so that efficient purchasing can take place and unused food can be recycled to the best advantage. Planning also involves the difficult problem of forecasting customer demand, so that stocks are adequate but not too high and the amount of food cooked is similarly not excessive. Linking with the overall planning will be the preparation of standard recipes (section 48.4), costing sheets (section 48.5), and standard portion sizes.

Satisfactory food control can be achieved only by drawing up comprehensive plans, enforcing these plans, and investigating any variation from the expected results of the plans.

Purchasing

When required, stock must be purchased at the lowest possible price. The suppliers should be reviewed constantly, and quotations should be requested from all parts of the country – not just from local suppliers – to enable the purchaser to buy at the lowest possible price compatible with the required quality. Alternatively, a special fixed price may be negotiated with only one supplier to supply a certain commodity for an agreed period – for example, on a 6 months' contract.

Many organisations operating a number of outlets nominate suppliers from which food commodities must be purchased. These nominated suppliers may cover some or all the commodity requirements of the organisation. Different suppliers and changes in ingredients should be considered where possible, if cheaper.

The buying clerk must work closely with the chef, so that not only is the total weight required obtained but that total weight is also obtained by purchasing items of a size that can be split into the standard portion size most economically – for example, would it be better to purchase 3 large chickens or 8 small ones that have the same total weight? A standard quality of items purchased should also be aimed at.

To obtain a standard quality of supplies, a system of 'purchase specifications' is used. A specification is prepared for each product to be purchased, and this details the factors necessary for the supplier to understand precisely what is being asked for. Such information will cover the grade, weight, degree of preparation, method of delivery, and details such as colour, shape, hygiene requirements, etc.

The advantages of purchase specifications are as follows:

- Quotations from different suppliers may be compared accurately, as the prices quoted should be for identical products.
- The stores staff will know the nature and quality of the goods to be sent to them and will be able to check quickly if those received match the expected standards.
- Costing and control figures can be prepared with greater accuracy, as the precise details of the raw materials to be used will be known.

Storage

Stock control has been discussed earlier, and this is an integral part of the overall food-control procedure. In addition it must be remembered that losses can occur through bad storage, incorrect weighing when the storekeeper splits a large quantity, and above all through pilferage.

Pilferage

A business whose basic raw material is cast iron need have little fear of the stock being stolen. Not only would theft be difficult because of the weight: the rewards to the thief would be small. Unfortunately, foodstuffs are not in the same category as cast iron and can be both stolen easily and sold for a reasonable sum of money. All foodstuffs must therefore be kept secure, with definite routines written down as to the time at which refrigerators etc. will be locked after use, who will be responsible for locking them, and who will check that they are locked. Persons authorised to have keys should be listed, and duplicate keys should not be made unless authorised by senior management. Deviations from laid-down procedures should not be allowed.

The best way to avoid pilferage is

- to have all systems documented and approved by senior management, and
- for spot checks to be made as a matter of routine.

This should provide the deterrence that is needed to stop theft.

Portion control

The standard recipe card states the number of portions that should be served from the standard quantity of ingredients. In any system of food control, it is essential that this standard number of portions is actually served. In addition, portion control also means the control of the total quantity of food served to each customer. The staff serving the food must be aware of how much to give to each customer. As well as obtaining statistics on the food used compared with the meals served, management should make daily checks to see that standards are being maintained.

It should be fairly easy to use particular items of equipment to ensure that the correct size of portion is served. For example, a glass of fruit juice on a menu should mean a certain size of glass to the kitchen, and a portion of soup should immediately indicate a certain size of ladle. The portion size of all cooked dishes should be as stated in the standard recipe. The importance of this can easily be shown.

If the ingredients of a pie cost £8 and this should give 20 portions, the cost per portion should be 40 p. If the pie is cut into only 14 portions, the cost per portion will then be 57 p – an increase of 42½ %. If the selling price had been set at £1 per portion, the income should have been £20, giving a gross profit of £20 – £8 = £12. Because of the error in the portion size, the gross profit has been reduced to £14 – £8 = £6 – that is, the gross profit has been halved.

Where the serving is done by the restaurant staff – from a sweet trolley, for example – the chef must tell them how many portions are expected to be obtained from each dish. Again, management should check this very regularly.

Poor preparation and production

As part of the overall food control, it must be remembered that considerable losses can occur from over- or under-production and from poor preparation. The percentage loss allowed in preparation and cooking must be carefully considered before being fixed. The *actual* loss should be calculated and compared with that expected. Any variation should be thoroughly investigated. Also, the food used must be the quantity laid down by the standard recipe.

The use of computers means that restaurant bills can be coded and the sales can be very quickly compared with the materials used. The ability of computers to store information from one task, such as restaurant billing, and then to use this for a different purpose later makes it much less time-consuming and less costly to check kitchen wastage. In many cases it can now be done as a matter of routine rather than as a special check.

Profits

Targets will be set for the gross profit for each week and/or month, and the failure to achieve this because the cost of food is a higher percentage of sales than expected must be investigated. The variation may be caused by outside factors, such as an increase in the cost of food purchased which has not been passed on through price increases. Similarly, changes in the number and demands of customers will affect the cost of food as a percentage of sales.

Whatever the reason, however, the cause must be found and action must be taken to bring the profit back to the amount expected.

This is the purpose of food control: to attempt to control the cost of food used so that the overall plan for the profit of the business is achieved.

48.11 Computers and food control

Many businesses make use of computers to handle their paperwork. Computers are increasingly applied to aspects of food control, at both operative and management level. The benefits of using a computer are:

- *Speed* Computers can carry out a range of tasks very quickly.
- *Accuracy* Provided that correct data is fed in, the computer can be relied on to perform its tasks accurately.

- *Cost* Staff costs can be reduced.
- *Volume* The computer can handle large volumes of work very quickly, and may in fact be the only way of performing certain tasks.
- *Information* Once data is fed into the computer, it can be used for various purposes.

Computers can help kitchen staff by providing information for

- making up commodity orders for the stores;
- keeping a file of ingredients and prices for quick reference, which should be kept up to date;
- keeping a file of standard recipes, which can be recalled when needed – these may also show the calculated selling price as well as the necessary ingredients.

The use of computers for food control also means that management information can be produced quickly – detailing purchases made, commodities used, sales made, etc. – and this information can be used to show where purchase or usage has been excessive, whether prices paid for materials have been higher than expected, whether the kitchen wastage is acceptable, whether the sales mix is as planned, and so on.

Such information enables management to take any action needed to keep the business running on its planned course so that satisfactory profits may be made.

Figures 48.8 to 48.14 show some examples of print-outs and screen displays from a computer program:

- Figure 48.8 shows the options available in the program.

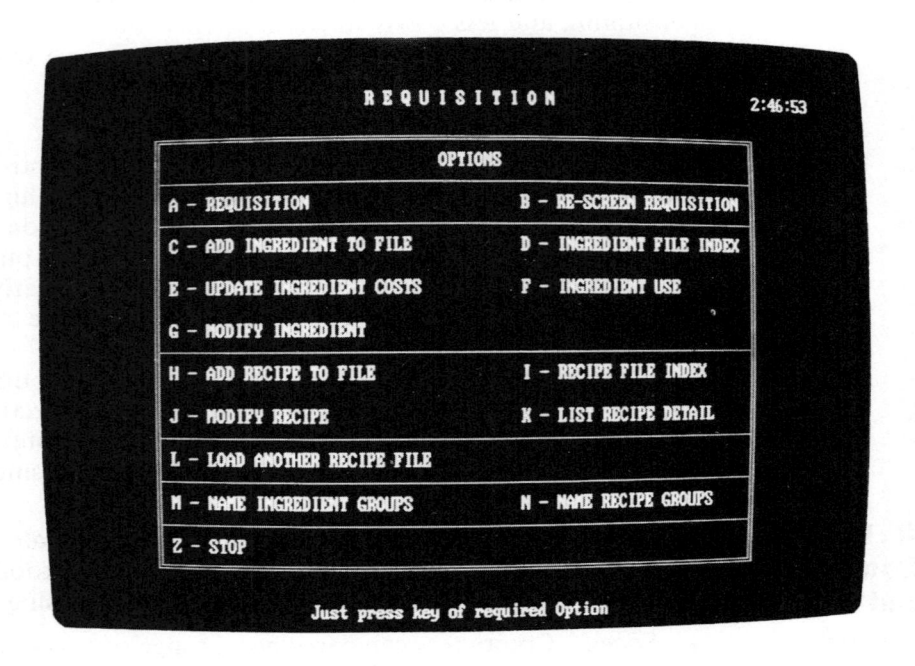

Fig. 48.8 A screen display showing the options available in a computer program

Catering calculations and costing 333

- Figures 48.9 and 48.10 show a requisition for the commodities for one dish for 20 covers. The cost and the selling price based on 66% gross profit and VAT at 15% are also shown. The program allows for these percentages to be altered.

```
RECIPE FILE:CSREC        REQUISITION              2:42:31

        INGREDIENT        QUANTITY       COST £

    GROUP D:DAIRY
    WHIPPING CREAM        1.800 li         3.60
                                    GROUP TOTAL = £  3.60

    GROUP G:GROCERY
    CASTOR SUGAR          600 gms          0.39
    LEAF GELATINE          50 gms          0.54
                                    GROUP TOTAL = £  0.93

    GROUP V:VEGETABLES
    LEMONS                    8            1.12
                                    GROUP TOTAL = £  1.12

                                      TOTAL COST = £  5.65
                      SELLING PRICE (at 66 % profit)= £ 16.62
                                    VAT ( at 15%)=£  2.49
                             TOTAL PRICE incl. VAT=£ 19.11


 Press A to adjust quantities; E to add extra ingredients
 Press F1 for a print-out, or ESC to return to Options_
```

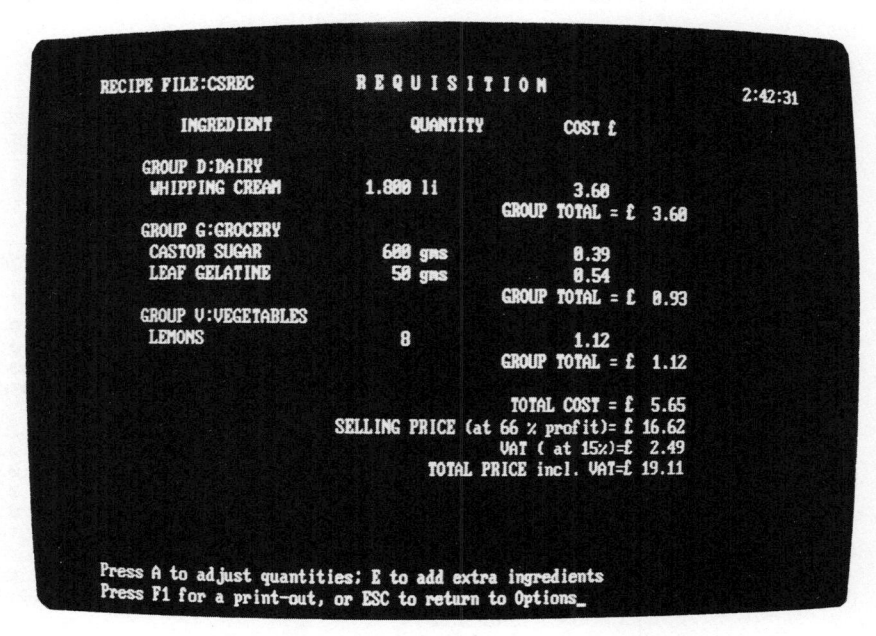

Fig. 48.9 A screen display of a commodities requisition for a single dish

```
                    REQUISITION
   REC.No.        RECIPE NAME                                PORTIONS
   FILE:
     12      LEMON MOUSSE-----------------------------------    20


    INGREDIENT              QUANTITY            COST £

GROUP D:DAIRY
  WHIPPING CREAM          1.800 li              3.60
                                         GROUP TOTAL = £   3.60
GROUP G:GROCERY
  CASTOR SUGAR             600 gms              0.39
  LEAF GELATINE             50 gms              0.54
                                         GROUP TOTAL = £   0.93
GROUP V:VEGETABLES
  LEMONS                      8                 1.12
                                         GROUP TOTAL = £   1.12

                                           TOTAL COST = £   5.65
                         SELLING PRICE (at 66 % profit)= £  16.62
                                         VAT ( at 15%)=£   2.49
                                  TOTAL PRICE incl. VAT=£  19.11
```

Fig. 48.10 A computer print-out of the requisition shown in fig. 48.9

334 *The business of catering*

- Figure 48.11 shows a requisition for the commodities for a complete meal for 20 covers. Notice how the commodities are automatically grouped.

```
                          REQUISITION
     REC.No.           RECIPE NAME                              PORTIONS
     FILE: CSREC
        4      SMOKED SALMON AND MELON SALAD------------------     20
       11      SUPREME OF CHICKEN STUFFED WITH CHEESE & HAM-        20
        8      SHREDDED GREEN CABBAGE WITH CHESTNUTS---------       20
        9      SWEDE PUREE WITH CROUTONS--------------------        20
       10      MINTED NEW POTATOES--------------------------        20
       13      HONEY AND WALNUT TART------------------------        20


          INGREDIENT            QUANTITY              COST £

     GROUP B:BASIC
       FLOUR                    1.500 kg              0.66
       SALT                     78 gms                0.02
       VANILLA ESSENCE          1 ml                  0.01
                                           GROUP TOTAL = £   0.69
     GROUP D:DAIRY
       BUTTER                   1.122 kg              2.47
       MOZARELLA CHEESE         500 gms               2.22
       EGGS                     16                    0.96
       MILK                     200 ml                0.11
       WHIPPING CREAM           428 ml                0.86
                                           GROUP TOTAL = £   6.62
     GROUP F:FISH
       SMOKED SALMON            1.500 kg              0.00
                                           GROUP TOTAL = £   0.00
     GROUP G:GROCERY
       LEAF GELATINE            6 gms                 0.06
       SLICED BROWN BREAD       1                     0.65
       MAYONNAISE               350 ml                0.93
       ASPIC JELLY              50 gms                0.17
       STALE WHITE BREAD        2                     0.70
       PEPPER                   20 gms                0.30
       DRIED CHESTNUTS          223 gms               0.80
       SLICED WHITE BREAD       1                     0.62
       CASTOR SUGAR             200 gms               0.13
       CLEAR HONEY              400 ml                1.12
       WALNUTS                  200 gms               0.96
                                           GROUP TOTAL = £   6.44
     GROUP M:MEAT
       CHICKEN SUPREMES         20                   17.00
       TINNED HAM               500 gms               1.37
                                           GROUP TOTAL = £  18.37
     GROUP V:VEGETABLES
       HONEYDEW MELON           5                     4.80
       TOMATOES                 1.000 kg              1.64
       FRESH MINT               167 gms               0.28
       ORANGES                  4                     0.48
       PARSLEY                  50 gms                0.15
       WATERCRESS               5                     2.25
       POTATOES                 2.000 kg              0.30
       SPRING GREENS            3.111 kg              0.75
       SWEDE                    3.111 kg              1.12
       NEW POTATOES             3.111 kg              1.31
                                           GROUP TOTAL = £  13.08

                                            TOTAL COST = £  45.20
                          SELLING PRICE (at 66 % profit)= £132.94
                                         VAT ( at 15%)=£  19.94
                                TOTAL PRICE incl. VAT=£152.88
```

Fig. 48.11 A computer print-out of a commodities requisition for a complete meal

Catering calculations and costing 335

- Figure 48.12 shows an ingredient list with costs for a group of commodities.

```
GROUP D:DAIRY
        BRIE CHEESE              640 per KG
        BUTTER                   220 per KG
        CAMEMBERT CHEESE         615 per KG
        CHEDDAR CHEESE           240 per KG
        CREAM CHEESE             320 per KG
        CREAM FRAISE             225 per KG
        DANISH BLUE CHEESE       428 per KG
        DOUBLE CREAM             264 per LI
        EDAM CHEESE              320 per KG
        EGGS                       8 per EA
        GRUYERE CHEESE           688 per KG
        KRONA MARGARINE          144 per KG
        LARD                      48 per KG
        MARGARINE                 56 per KG
        MILK                      54 per LI
        MOZZARELLA CHEESE        320 per KG
        PARMESAN CHEESE          800 per KG
```

Fig. 48.12 A computer print-out of an ingredients list, with costs, for a group of commodities

- Figures 48.13 and 48.14 show a list of the recipes included in the program.

```
RECIPE FILE:CSREC        REQUISITION                     2:37:25
                  RECIPE    NAME
                  NO.
        GROUP D:
                  13    HONEY AND WALNUT TART
                  12    LEMON MOUSSE
        GROUP F:
                   1    SEAFOOD TARTLETS WITH SORREL SAUCE
        GROUP H:
                   2    DEEP FRIED MUSHROOM AND CHICKEN PANCAKES
                   4    SMOKED SALMON AND MELON SALAD
        GROUP M:MEAT DISHES
                   5    NORFOLK GAME PIE
                   6    PILLOWS OF ENGLISH LAMB WITH LAYERED VEG.
                   7    SLICES OF VEAL KIDNEY WITH SPINACH MOUSSE
                  11    SUPREME OF CHICKEN STUFFED WITH CHEESE & HAM
        GROUP S:SOUPS
                   3    CUCUMBER SOUP WITH ALMONDS
        GROUP V:
                  10    MINTED NEW POTATOES
                   8    SHREDDED GREEN CABBAGE WITH CHESTNUTS

Press RETURN for next page; ESC to Quit; F1 for a print-out
or Group Letter to start listing at that group
```

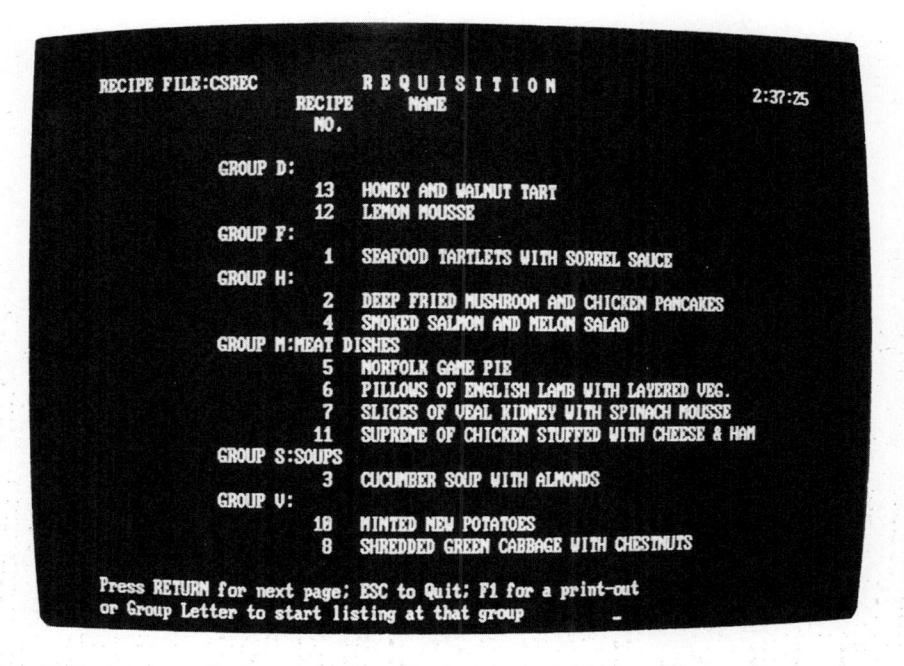

Fig. 48.13 A screen display of the list of recipes included in the program for a particular type of dish

```
INDEX OF RECIPE FILE:

              RECIPE      NAME
                NO.
     GROUP D:
                13      HONEY AND WALNUT TART
                12      LEMON MOUSSE
     GROUP F:
                 1      SEAFOOD TARTLETS WITH SORREL SAUCE
     GROUP H:
                 2      DEEP FRIED MUSHROOM AND CHICKEN PANCAKES
                 4      SMOKED SALMON AND MELON SALAD
     GROUP M:MEAT DISHES
                 5      NORFOLK GAME PIE
                 6      PILLOWS OF ENGLISH LAMB WITH LAYERED VEG.
                 7      SLICES OF VEAL KIDNEY WITH SPINACH MOUSSE
                11      SUPREME OF CHICKEN STUFFED WITH CHEESE & HAM
     GROUP S:SOUPS
                 3      CUCUMBER SOUP WITH ALMONDS
     GROUP V:
                10      MINTED NEW POTATOES
                 8      SHREDDED GREEN CABBAGE WITH CHESTNUTS
                 9      SWEDE PUREE WITH CROUTONS
```

Fig. 48.14 A computer print-out of the list of recipes shown in fig. 48.13

Both the ingredients list and the recipe file can be added to or altered to keep them up to date with price changes and menu changes.

Index

The French names for commodities or cooking techniques likely to be mentioned on a menu are given in *italics* after the English term, followed by '(m)' or '(f)' as appropriate to indicate whether a commodity is masculine or feminine in French.

à l'Orly frying, 216
à l'anglaise frying, 216, 222
à la carte menu, 288, 293, 296, 297, 298
à la française frying, 216
absorption, 139
accelerated freeze drying, 178
accidents, 11–14
acesulfame K, 141
acidity and micro-organisms, 175
additives, 131, 134
aeration, 21, 84, 159
aerobic bacteria, 175
AFD, *see* accelerated freeze drying
afternoon tea, menu, 290
age restrictions, mechanical equipment, 12
air
    and heat transfer, 161, 164
    and micro-organisms, 174
albumen, 81
alcohol, 141, 176
alfabetti, 25
algae, 170
alimentary canal, 138, 139
alkalinity and micro-organisms, 175
almond (*amande* (f)), 115
aluminium, 161, 269
amino acids, 141–2
amoebas, 170
ampere, 167
amylases, 139
anaemia, 149
anaerobic bacteria, 175
antinutritional food components, 155
antiseptics, 186
antivitamins, 155
anus, 138, 139
apple (*pomme* (f)), 111
apricot (*abricot* (m)), 111
aqueous liquid, definition, 193
Arbroath smokies, 73
armed forces, catering for, 5
aromates, 209
arrowroot, 24, 264
artichoke
    globe (*artichaut* (m)), 100
        bottoms (*fonds d'artichaut* (m)), 100
    Jerusalem (*topinambour* (m)), 100

artificial sweeteners, 141
ascorbic acid, *see* vitamin C
asparagus (*asperge* (f)), 100
aspartame, 141
aspic, 84
atmospheric steamers, 213–14
attitudes, professional, 309–10
aubergine (*aubergine* (f)), 100
avocado (*avocat* (m)), 112

bacilli, 171
Bacillus cereus, 171, 179
bacon (*lard* (m)), 54–6
    back, 55
    collar (*collet* (m)), 55
    curing, 54–5
    gammon (*jambon* (m)), 55
    green, 55
    hock (*jarret* (m)), 55
    joints, 55
    purchasing points, 56
    smoked, 55
    streaky (*lard de poitrine* (m)), 55
    storage, 56
    uses, 56
baconers, 51, 54, 57
bacteria, 83, 170–2
    aerobic, 175
    anaerobic, 175
    food poisoning, 179
    multiplication, 172, 174–5
    spores, 172, 173, 194
    uses of, 176
    vegetative state, 172
bactericides, 186
bain-marie
    cooking, 202
    in oven, 227
    hazards, 13
    in hotplate, 285
baking, 226–9
    bacon, 56
    bread, 226–7
    cakes, 226–7
    in combination oven, 255
    effects of, 226
    en croûte, 227
    equipment for, 228–9

Index

baking (cont'd)
  fish, 227
  general points in, 228
  ovens, 229
  pastries, 226–7
  temperatures, 227
  vegetables, 227
baking-sheets, 273
banana (*banana* (f)), 112
banquet menu, 289
barbecue grill, 230, *see also* underfired grill
barding, 240
barley, 22
  flour, 264
basal metabolism, 144, 146
bass (*bar* (m)), 69
batch cooking, 191, 250–6
  equipment used, 251–6
bavarois, 84
beans
  broad (*fève* (f)), 100
  fine (*haricot vert* (m)), 100
  french (*haricot vert* (m)), 100
  mung, 109
  nutritional content, 153
  red kidney, 109, 155, 198
  runner (*haricot d'Espagne* (m)), 101
  soya, 109, 155
beaters, 273
béchamel sauce, 265, 267
bed and breakfast accommodation, 3
beef (*boeuf* (m)), 34–42
  baron, 40
  braising steaks, 40
  braising, 210
  brisket (*poitrine* (f)), 35, 38
  chateaubriand (*chateaubriand* (m)), 39, 41
  chuck rib (*côte du collier* (f)), 35, 38
  clod and sticking (*collier* (m)), 35, 38
  cooking methods, 42
  fillet (*filet* (m)), 35, 37
  fillet mignon (*filet mignon* (m)), 39, 41
  fillet minute steaks (*filet minute* (m)), 39
  fillet steak (*filet* (m)), 39, 41
  fingers/strips, 39
  forequarter, 35, 38–40
  forerib (*côte première* (f)), 35, 38
  grilling, 231
  heart (*coeur de boeuf* (m)), 41
  hindquarter, 35, 36–7
  kidney (*rognon de boeuf* (m)), 41
  leg-of-mutton cut (*talon du collier* (m)), 38
  maturing and tenderising, 34
  middle rib (*côte découverte* (f)), 35, 38
  minute steak (*entrecôte minute* (m)), 39
  neck, 35
  offal, 40–1
  olives (*paupiettes* (f)), 39
  ox liver (*foie de boeuf* (m)), 41
  ox tongue (*langue de boeuf* (f)), 40
  oxtail (*queue de boeuf* (f)), 40
  plate (*plate de côte* (f)), 35, 38
  poêlé cooking, 244
  point steak, 39
  porterhouse steak, 39
  purchasing points, 35
  rib steaks, 40
  roasting, 40, 240
  round/buttock, 40
  rump (*culotte* (f)), 35, 37
  rump steak, 39, 41
  sautéing, 237
  shallow frying, 223
  shank (*jambe* (f)), 35, 38
  shin (*jambe* (f)/*jarret* (m)), 35, 36
  side, 35
  silverside (*gîte a la noix* (m)), 35, 36
  sirloin (*aloyau* (m)), 35, 37
  sirloin steak (*entrecôte* (f)), 39, 41
    double (*entrecôte minute* (m)), 39
  steak tartare (*steak tartare* (m)), 39
  stewing, 206–7
  storage, 36
  striploin (*contrefilet* (m)), 37
  sweetbreads (*ris de boeuf* (m)), 41
  T-bone steak, 39
  thick flank (*tranche grasse* (f)), 35, 36
  thin flank (*bavette d'aloyau* (f)), 35, 37
  top piece, 35, 40
  topside (*tranche tendre* (f)), 36
  tournedos (*tournedos* (m)), 39, 41
  tripes (*tripes* (f)), 41
  wing ribs (*côte d'aloyau* (f)), 35, 37
beetroot (*betterave* (f)), 101
beignets, deep frying, 217
beri-beri, 149
beurre manié, 264
beverage service, 6
beverages non-alcoholic, 118–22
bile, 138, 139
bin cards, 326–7
biocides, 186
biscuits, nutritional content, 153
black-eyed peas, 108
blackberry (*mûre* (f)), 112
blanc, cooking in, 196
blanching
  in boiling water, 195
  deep frying, 215, 216
blanquette, 207
blending, 192
bloaters, 73
blood, 143
  as thickening agent, 266
blood-pressure, high, 144
bobby calves, 34
boiled (*bouillé*) foods, *see* boiling
boiling, 193–201
  bacon, 56
  beef, 42
  in combination oven, 255–6
  convection in, 162
  effects of, 193–4

boiling (*cont'd*)
   eggs, 197
   equipment for, 199–201
   fish, 196–7
   general points, 198–9
   heat transfer in, 163
   lamb, 50
   meat, 197
   pans, 199–200
   pasta, 198
   pork, 54
   poultry, 197
   pulses, 198
   rice, 198
   veal, 45
   vegetables, 193, 194–6
boiling-tables, 200, 201
   hazards, 12
Bombay duck, 73
botarga, 75
bouquet garni, 123
bowl choppers, vertical, 279
bowl cutters, 279–80
bowls, 274
braised (*braisé*) foods, *see* braising
braising, 209–11
   in combination oven, 256
   effects of, 209
   equipment for, 211
   general points in, 210
   lamb, 50
   meat, 209–10
   veal, 45
   vegetables, 210
branding (grilling), 231, 234, 236
Bratt pan, 207–8
brazil nut (*noix du Brésil* (f)), 115
bread
   baking, 226–7
   nutritional content, 153
breakfast menus, 289–90
brill (*barbue* (f)), 69
British Thermal Unit (Btu), 168
broccoli (*brocoli* (m)), 101
brussels sprout (*chou de Bruxelles* (m)), 101
Btu, 163
buckling, 73
budding, yeasts, 173
buffet menu, 289, 296
buildings, standards for, 301
bull beef, 34
bullocks, 34
bummaloe, 73
Business & Technician Education Council (BTEC), 7, 8
business documents, 324–6
butter (*beurre* (m)), 93
   bacteria in production of, 176
   nutritional content, 152
   as thickening agent, 267

cabbage (*chou vert* (m)), 101, 155
   red (*chou rouge* (m)), 102

white/Dutch (*chou pommé* (m)), 102
cakes
   baking, 226–7
   nutritional content, 153
calabrese, 101
calamary (*encomet* (m)/*calmar* (m)), 80
calcium, 143, 145, 155
   in hard water, 194
calorific nutrients, 139, 143, 144
Campylobacter jejuni, 179
canneloni, 25
capacity, units of, 311, 312
capellini, 25
capers, 130
capon (*chapon* (m)), 28
capsicum (*piment* (m)), 105
caramel, 157
caramelisation, 157
carbohydrates
   absorption, 139
   effects of cooking on, 153–4
   energy content, 147
   functions, 140–1
carbonnade, 207
career opportunities, 5–7
   beverage service, 6
   food preparation, 6
   food service, 6
   housekeeping, 6
   reception, 6
carotenes, 81, 145
carp (*carpe* (f)), 71
   young (*carpeau* (m)), 71
carrot (*carotte* (f)), 102
cartouche, 157, 195–6
carveries, 241
cash discounts, 315
cast iron, 270
catering industry, 2–8
   sectors, 2–5
   services provided, 2
cauliflower (*chou-fleur* (m)), 102, 155
caviar (*caviar* (m)), 74–5
celeriac (*céleri-rave* (m)), 102
celery (*céleri* (m)), 102
cells, 137
   yeast, 173
cellulose, 140, *see also* fibre
Celsius temperature, 312, 314
centrigade (Celsius) temperature, 312, 314
centimetre, 312, 313
centralised production systems, 191, 259–62
   work flow, 261–2
cep (*cèpe* (m)), 107
cephalopod molluscs, 76, 79–80
ceramics, 161
cereals, 20–4
   grain, 20
   importance of, 20
   nutritional content, 153
   storage, 24
chalaza, 81

chanterelle (f), 107
charcoal, 169
cheese (*fromage* (m)), 88–93
  bacteria in production of, 176
  British, 90
  classification, 88–9
  cottage, 93
  cream, 93
  curd, 93
  Danish, 92
  Dutch, 91–2
  French, 91
  Italian, 92
  making, 88
  moulds in the production of, 176
  nutritional content, 151
  purchasing, 89
  storing, 89
  Swiss, 92
  uses, 89–90
chef de cuisine, 308
chef de partie, 308
chef's special, 289
chefs, 308
chemical preservation of food, 178
chemicals and food poisoning, 178
cherry (*cerise* (f)), 112
chestnut (*marron* (m)), 115
chick peas, 108
chicken, 27–31, *see also* poultry
  baby/spring (*poussin* (m)), 28
  boiling fowl (*poule* (f)), 28
  breast (*blanc de poulet* (m)), 30
  broiler (*poulet reine* (m)), 28
  drumstick (*pilon de cuisse* (m)), 29
  grades, 28
  preparation for sauté, 28–30
  preparation for suprêmes, 30–1
  roasting, 240, 241
  thigh (*gras de cuisse* (m)), 29
  wing piece (*aileron* (m)), 30
  winglet (*aile* (f)), 30
chicory (*endive* (f)), 102
  red, 105
chillers, 184
Chinese cabbage/leaves, 102
chipped potatoes, frying, 219
cholecalciferol, *see* vitamin D
cholesterol, 142
choppers, vertical bowl, 279
chopping tools, 272–3, 274–6
chutneys, 130
circuit breakers, 168
City and Guilds of London Institute, 7, 8
cleaning
  atmospheric steamers, 214
  boiling pans, 200
  Bratt pans, 208
  combination ovens, 256
  convection ovens, 229
  cooking utensils, 269–71
  deep-fat fryers, 219–20
  general-purpose ovens, 243
  grills, 234–5, 236
  high-pressure steamers, 254
  kitchens, 185–7
  micro-airs, 256
  schedules for, 186
  steam convection ovens, 252
clostridia, 171, 172
Clostridium perfringens, 179
Clostridium welchii, 179
clubs, 4
coalfish (*colin* (m)), 69
cobnut (*noisette* (f)), 115
cocci, 171
cockle (*coque* (f)), 78
cockroaches, 188
cocktail bars, 4
coconut (*noix de coco* (f)), 115
cod (*cabillaud* (m)), 69, 72
cod roe, 72
coffee (*café* (m)), 118, 119–22
  countries of origin, 119
  decaffeinated, 122
  equipment, 120–1
  iced, 122
  instant, 122
  Irish, 122
  preparing, 120–1
  roasting and grinding, 119
  specialities, 122
cold-buffet dishes, decorated, 245
cold preparations, 245–7
  general points on, 247
  nutritional value of, 245
cold-rooms, 184
coley (*colin* (m)), 69
collagen, 153, 159, 193, 206
  in fish, 203
colourings, 131
COMA, 143, 145
commercial catering operations, 3–4
commis chef, 308
Committee on Medical Aspects of Food Policy (COMA), 143, 145
commodities, definition, 19
complementary value of proteins, 142
computers
  and food control, 331–6
  and menu planning, 292
  and purchasing, 328
conchiglie rigate, 25
condiments, 127–9
conduction, 159, 160–2, 163, 164
  in boiling, 194
  in griddle cooking, 162
conductors of heat, 161
coney, *see* rabbit
conference centres, 4
connective tissue, 26, 153, 159, 193, 203, 206, 209
consommé, 84
constipation, 149
contamination, bacterial, 179
  cross-contamination, 180, 182, 271
contract catering, 4, 5
convection, 159, 162–3
  in boiling, 194

convection (cont'd)
  currents, 162, 169
  ovens, 228
convenience foods, 132-3
  nutritional value, 155
  stocks, 263
conversion, metric (SI)/British units, 313
cook-chill operations, 259-61
  advantages, 262
cook-freeze operations, 262
Cookery and Food Association, 8
cooking food, *see also individual methods*
  by heat, 159-63
  reasons for, 156-7, 189
copper, 161, 269
cornflour, 22, 264
corn-salad (*mâche* (f)), 103
cost behaviour, 322
cost of sales, 320-1, 322, 331
costing sheet, 320
costs
  fixed, 322
  food, 292, 318, 319, 322, 329
    convenience foods, 133
  fuel, 167, 168, 169
  labour, 318, 329
    convenience foods, 133
  variable, 322
courgette (*courgette* (f)), 103
court-bouillon, 203
cow beef, 34
crab (*crabe* (m)), 76, 77
  spider crab (*araignée* (f)), 77
crawfish (*langouste* (f)), 77
crayfish (*écrevisse* (f)), 76, 77
cream (*crème* (f)), 87-8, 93
  nutritional content, 151
credit transactions, 326
cress (*cresson* (m)), 103
cross-contamination, 180, 182, 271
crushing, 192
crustaceans, 75, 77-8
cryogenic freezing, 177
cucumber (*concombre* (m)), 103
cupboards, heated, 285
curing, bacon, 54-5
currant (*groseille* (f)), 112
current, electrical, 167-8
Customs & Excise Department, 323, 324
cutting tools, 272-3, 274-6
cuttlefish (*seiche* (f)), 79

date (*datte* (f)), 112
daube, 206
day centres, 4
debit transactions, 326
decorated cold-buffet dishes, 245
deep-fat fryers, 218-20
  hazards, 13
deep frying, 215-20
  coatings for, 215, 216
  convection in, 163
  dessert items, 217
  effects of, 215
  equipment for, 218-20
  fats and oils, 216-17
  fish, 217, 219
  general points in, 218
  meats, 217
  poultry, 217
  presentation of foods, 217
  pressure frying, 216
  vegetables, 217
deep poaching, 203-4
  veal, 45
dehydration, preservation by, 177
delivery notes, 325, 327
design of kitchen, 301-6
detergents, 186
dextrinisation, 158
dextrins, 158
dicing, 192
diet, 146
  balanced, 148-9
dietary fibre, *see* fibre
digestibility, 156-7, 158, 193
digestion, 137, 138-9
dinner menu, 290-1
disaccharides, 141
discounts, 315-16
dishwashers, 283-4
dishwashing, 185-6, 283-4
disinfectants, 186
doughnuts, deep frying, 217
Dover sole (*sole* (f)), 69
draining tools, 272, 273
dripping, 95
dry-heat cooking, 159, 190, 191
drying food, 177-8
  nutritional effects of, 155
duck (*canard* (m)), 31, *see also* poultry
  roasting, 240
  wild (*canard sauvage* (m)), 58, 60
duckling (*caneton* (m)), 31

E numbers, 134
earthenware, 271
earthing, 168
easy peelers, 114
eel (*anguille* (f)), 71, 73
egg plant (*aubergine* (f)), 100
eggs (*oeufs* (m)), 81-5
  baked (*oeufs sur le plat* (m)), 85
  boiled (*oeufs a la coque* (m)), 85
  boiling, 197
  deep-fried (*oeufs frits à la française* (m)), 85
  french-fried (*oeufs frits à la française* (m)), 85
  fried (*oeufs frits* (m)), 85
  grades (EC), 82
  hard-boiled (*oeufs durs* (m)), 85
  in cocotte (*oeufs en cocotte* (m)), 85
  nutritional content, 151
  omelette (*omelette* (m)), 85

eggs (*cont'd*)
  poached (*oeufs pochés* (m)), 85
  poaching, 205
  preservation, 83
  quality points, 81–2
  scrambled (*oeufs brouillés* (m)), 85
  soft-boiled (*oeufs mollets* (m)), 85
  spoilage, 82, 83
  storage, 83
  as thickening agents, 265–6
  uses, 83–4
elastin, 203
electrical food-preparation equipment, 276–82
electricity, 166–8
  cost of, 167
  safety, 167
  unit of, 167, 168
electromagnetic waves, 163, 164
employees' responsibilities, 10
employers' responsibilities, 9–10, 14–15
employment in catering, 5–7
emulsification during digestion, 138
emulsion, 84, 94
en croûte baking, 227
en papillote cooking, 190
endive (*endive frisée* (f)), 103
energy
  foods supplying, 147–8
  needs, 146–7
  units, 146
  use in cooking, 166–9
environmental health officers, 9, 14, 179
enzymes, 34
  digestive, 139
  inactivated by boiling, 195
  spoilage caused by, 176
equipment, *see also individual cooking methods*
  hygiene standards, 181
  layout, 303
  symbols, 303, 304
espagnole sauce, 265, 267
essences, 131
evaporation, 157, 193
extraction rate of flour, 21

faeces, 139
Fahrenheit temperature, 313, 314
farfalle, 25
farfalli, 25
farmhouses, 3
fast-food outlets, 4
fats, 94–6
  absorption, 139
  antispattering agents, 94
  compound, 95–6
  deep frying, 216–17
  deterioration, 94
  effects of cooking on, 154, 158
  energy content, 147
  function in diet, 142–3
  and heat transfer, 164
  mono-unsaturated, 142
  nutritional content, 151–2
  polyunsaturated, 95, 142–3
  rendering, 31, 32, 158
  saturated, 95, 142–3
  for shallow frying, 221
  smoke-point, 94, 158, 216
  unsaturated, 142
  uses, 94
fat-soluble vitamins, 144
fatty acids, 142
fennel, Florence, (*fénouil* (m)), 103
fermentation, 174, 176
fibre, 137, 138, 140, 147
  content of foods, 149
  deficiency, 149
fig (*figue* (f)), 112
filbert (*noisette* (f)), 115
filleting, fish, 192
fines herbes, 123
fire, 15–17
  types of, 16
fire drill, 15
fire extinguishers, 16–17
Fire Precautions Act (1971), 15
fire prevention, 15
fire training, 15
first aid, 14, 181
fish (*poisson* (m)), 63–75 *see also* shellfish and *names of individual fish*
  baking, 227
  boiling, 196–7
  canned, 74
  classification, 63–4
  cuts, 66–8
  darne (*darne* (f)), 66, 68
  deep frying, 217, 219
  deep poaching, 203–4
  délice (*délice* (m)), 66, 67
  dried, 72, 73
  en papillote, 190
  farming, 63
  fillet (*filet* (m)), 66, 67
  fingers, 74
  freshwater, 71–2
  goujon (*goujon* (m)), 66, 67
  grilling, 230, 231
  mousse, 74
  nutritional content, 151
  oily, 63–4
  paste, 74
  pâté, 74
  paupiette (*paupiette* (f)), 66, 67
  pickled, 73–4
  poaching, 203–4
  portion size, 68
  preparation loss, 68
  processed, 74
  purchasing points, 64–5
  quenelles, 74
  saltwater, 69–71
  sautéing, 237
  shallow frying, 221, 222, 223
  shallow poaching, 203
  smoked, 65–6, 72–3

fish (cont'd)
  soused, 74
  steaming, 213
  sticks, 74
  storage, 65–6
  supply, 63
  suprême (*suprême* (m)), 66, 67
  tronçon (*tronçon* (m)), 67, 68
  white, 63–4
fixed costs, 322
flageolets, 100, 108
flambé cooking, 222
flare grill, 230, see also underfired grill
flash-point, 158
flavourings, artificial, 131
fleurons, 203
flexibility, 309
flies, 188
floor hazards, 14
flour, 20–2
  nutritional content, 21–2, 153
fluid ounce, 312, 313
Food Act (1984), 9, 291
food components affected by cooking, 157–9
food composition tables, 147
food control, 329–36
food cost percentage, 319
food costing, 318–22
food costs, 292, 318, 319, 322, 329
Food and Drugs (Control of Premises) Act (1976), 179
Food Hygiene (Markets, Stalls and Delivery Vehicle) Regulations (1966), 179
Food Hygiene Regulations (1970), 9, 10, 179, 180, 181
food mixers, 281–2
food poisoning, 178–9
  prevention, 179–88
food preservation, 177–8
food processors, 278–9
food science, 156–69
food service, 6
food spoilage, 176–8
food storage, 182–3, *see also under individual commodities*
foot, 312, 313
forecasting, 292
freeze-drying, 178
freezers, 184, 185
freezing food, 177
fricassée, 207
fromage blanc/fromage frais, 93
frozen foods
  deep frying, 217
  nutritional value, 155
  regeneration in an oven, 252–3
  thawing, 177
fructose, 140, 141
fruit (*fruit* (m)), 110–14, *see also individual fruits*
  classification, 110
  grades, 110
  nutritional content, 153
  poaching, 204
  preserved, 111
  purchasing points, 110
  shallow frying, 222, 223
  storage, 110–11
  uses, 111–14
fruits de mer, 77, 78, 79
fryers, deep-fat, 218–20
frying, see deep frying and shallow frying
fryplates, 224–5
fuel costs, 167, 168, 169
fungi, 107, 170 see also moulds and yeasts
fuses, 167

gall bladder, 138, 139
gallon, 312, 313
game (*gibier* (m)), 58–62, *see also individual types*
  braising, 210
  hanging, 26, 58
  poêlé cooking, 244
  purchasing points, 58–9
  roasting, 240
  stewing, 206–7
garlic (*ail* (m)), 103
gas, 168–9
  bottled, 169
  cost of, 168
  safety, 169
gelatin, 154, 159, 193, 203, 206
gelatinisation, 157–8, 193, 264
Genoese sponges, 84
germs, see bacteria
gherkins, 103
  pickled, 130
glazes, 263–4
glazing
  meat, 209
  vegetables, 195–6
glucose, 140, 141
  absorption, 139
gluten, 21, 176
goitre, 149, 155
goitrogens, 155
goose (*oie* (f)), 32, *see also* poultry
gooseberry (*groseille verte* (f)), 112
gosling (*oison* (m)), 32
goulash, 207
gram, 311, 313
grape (*raisin* (m)), 112
grapefruit (*pamplemouse* (m)), 112
greengage (*reine-claude* (f)), 113
griddles, 224–5
  conduction in cooking with, 162
grilled (*grillé*) foods, see grilling
grilling, 230–6
  bacon, 56
  beef, 42
  in combination oven, 255
  degree of cooking, 232
  effects of, 230
  fish, 230, 231
  general points on, 233
  lamb, 50

grilling (cont'd)
  meat, 230, 231–2
  pork, 54
  poultry, 230, 232
  veal, 45
  vegetables, 232
grills
  hazards, 13
  types of, 230
  overhead, 230, 233–5
  radiation in, 163
  underfired, 164, 230, 235–6
grinding, 192
gross profit, 319, 322, 331
ground-nuts (*cacahouette* (f)), 115
grouse (*lagopède* (m)) *rouge à l'Écosse*/*poule* (f) *rouge à l'Écosse*), 58, 59
  roasting, 240
guest houses, 3
guinea-fowl (*pintade* (f)/*pintadeau* (m)), 32, *see also* poultry
gullet, 138
gumbo, 105

haddock (*aiglefin* (m)), 69, 73
haemagglutins, 155
haemoglobin, 143
halibut (*flétan* (m)), 70
halls of residence, 5
ham (*jambon* (m)), 57
handtool hazards, 14
hanging meat, 26
hare (*lièvre* (m)), 58, 61
  jugged, 207
  roasting, 240
haricot beans, 100, 108
HASAWA, *see* Health and Safety at Work Act (1974)
hazards in the kitchen, 12–14
hazel nut (*noisette* (f)), 115
health and safety, 9–17
  policies, 10
Health and Safety (First Aid) Regulations (1981), 14
Health and Safety at Work Act (1974), 9
healthy eating, 145, 291
heart, *see under the meat concerned*
heat transfer, 159–63
  substances used, 163–4
heifers, 34
herbs (*herbes* (f)), 123
  uses, 124–5, 126
herring (*hareng* (m)), 70, 73
high-biological-value protein, 63, 141, 150, 151, 153
high-pressure steamers, 253–4
hog meat, 51
holiday camps, 3
hollandaise sauce, 266
honey (*miel* (m)), 117
hors-d'oeuvres, 246
hospital catering, 4

hostels, 5
hot and cold (*cresson* (m)), 103
hotplate hazards, 13
Hotel, Catering and Institutional Management Association, 8
Hotel and Catering Training Board, 7, 8, 9
hotels, 3
hotplates, 284–5
hotpot, 207
housekeeping, 6
humidity, storage, 183
hundredweight, 312, 313
huss (*chien de mer* (m)/*aiguillat* (m)), 70
hygiene, 156, 171
  kitchen, 181–2
  personal, 180–1
  work practices, 181–7

ice-cream, 84
  makers, 185
ice makers, 185
illness, reporting, 11
improvement notices, 9
inch, 312, 313
incomplete protein, 141
induction cooking, 165–6
industrial catering, 5
infra-red grill, 230
infra-red heat, 163
insulators, 161
intestines, 138, 139
invoices, 325–6, 328
iodine, 144
  deficiency, 149, 155
Irish stew, 207
iron, 143, 161
  deficiency, 149
irradiation, 178

jellies, 84
jus-lié, veal, 45, 210

kebabs, grilling, 232
kettles, tilting, 200, 201
kidney, *see under the meat concerned*
kilocalories, 146, 147–8
kilogram, 311, 313
kilojoules, 146, 147–8
kilowatt-hour, 167
kinetic energy, 161
kippers, 73
kitchen
  design of, 301–6
  hygiene, 181
  maintenance and cleaning, 185–7
  organisation, 307–9
kitchen percentage, 319
kiwi fruit, 113
knives, chefs'/cooks', 274–6, 277

Index

labour costs, 318, 329
lactose, 140, 141
lady's fingers, 105
lamb (*agneau* (m)), 46–50
  Barnsley chop, 48
  best end (*carré* (m)), 47, 49
  breast (*poitrine* (f)), 47
  chop (*côte d'agneau* (f)), 48
  chump, 49
    chop, 48
  cooking methods, 50
  crown chop, 48
  cutlet (*côtelette d'agneau* (f)), 48
    double (*côtelette d'agneau double* (f)), 48
  grades (NZ), 46
  grilling, 231
  heart (*coeur d'agneau* (m)), 49
  home-produced, 46
  joints, 47
  kidney (*rognon d'agneau* (m)), 49
  leg (*gigot* (m)), 47, 49
  liver (*foie d'agneau* (m)), 49
  loin chop (*côte d'agneau* (f)), 48
  middle neck (*côte découverte* (f)), 47, 49
  neck and scrag (*cou* (m)), 47
  New Zealand, 46
  noisette (*noisette d'agneau* (f)), 48
  offal, 49
  poêlé cooking, 244
  pré-salé, 46
  purchasing points, 47
  roasting, 240, 241
  rosette (*rosette d'agneau* (f)), 48
  saddle (*selle* (f)), 47, 49
  salt-marsh, 46
  sautéing, 237
  shallow frying, 223
  shoulder (*épaule* (f)), 47, 49
  small cuts, 48
  stewing, 206–7
  storage, 47
  sweetbreads (*ris d'agneau* (m)), 49
  tongue (*langue d'agneau* (f)), 49
lamb's-lettuce (*mâche* (f)), 103
lard, 94
  nutritional content, 152
larding, 240
lasagne, 25
layout of cooking equipment, 303
lecithin, 81, 84
lectins, 155
leek (*poireau* (m)), 103
legislation, 9–10, 291
  fire, 15
  first-aid, 14
  food poisoning, 179
leisure complexes, 4
lemon (*citron* (m)), 113
lemon sole, 69
length, units of, 312
lentils, 108
lettuce (*laitue* (f)), 104
  oak-leaf (*feuille de chêne* (f)), 104

liaison, 84
lighting, 10
lipases, 139
lipids, 137, see also fats and oils
  absorption, 139
  effect of cooking on, 158
  functions, 142–3
Listeria monocytogenes, 174
litre, 311, 313
liver
  human, 138
    bile production, 139
  offal, see under the meat concerned
lobster (*homard* (m)), 76, 77
  Norway (*langoustine* (f)), 77
  red/spiny (*langouste* (m)), 77
low-biological-value protein, 142, 152, 153
low-fat spreads, 96, 152
lunch menus, 290

macaroni, 25
mackerel (*maquereau* (m)), 70, 73
Maillard reaction, 85, 159, 215, 226
maintenance of kitchens, 185–7
maize (*maïs* (m)), 22
maltose, 140, 141
managers, 307, 309
mango (*mangue* (f)), 113
marbling, 35
margarine, 95, 96
  nutritional content, 152
marinades
  braising, 209
  stewing, 206
mark-up, 319
marrow, vegetable (*courge* (f)), 104
mastication, 138
Materials and Articles in Contact with Food Regulations (1978), 308
materials for cooking equipment, 269–71
mayonnaise, 94, 95, 266
measuring equipment, 274
meat (*viande* (m)), 26, see also particular types of meat
  boiling, 197
  braising, 209–10
  deep frying, 217
  grilling, 230, 231–2
  hanging, 26
  nutritional content, 151
  poaching, 204
  roasting, 239–40
  sautéing, 237
  stewing, 206–7
  structure, 26
mechanical equipment
  age restrictions, 12
  hazards, 13–14
melon (*melon* (m)), 113
menus, 288–310
  à la carte, 288, 293, 296, 297, 298
  balance, 292

menus (cont'd)
  banquet, 289
  breakfast, 289-90
  buffet, 289, 296
  compilation, 291-2
  computers in planning, 292
  course content, 289-91
  cyclic, 294, 295
  and design of premises, 301-6
  dinner, 290-1
  fixed, 293-4
  food control, 329
  influences on, 291-2
  language, 300
  lunch, 290
  new dishes, 300-1
  planning work, 191
  presentation, 296, 298-300
  selling, 296, 298-300, 310
  for special functions, 289, 294
  and staffing, 307
  table d'hôte, 288, 293
  tea, 290
merchandising, 310
meringues, 84
metabolism, basal, 144, 146
metals, *see particular types of metal*
  and heat transfer, 161, 164
metre, 312, 313
metric units, 311-12, 313
meunière cooking, 222
mice, 187-8
micro-air, 254-6
microbes *see* micro-organisms
microbiology and hygiene, 170-88
micro-organisms
  conditions for growth, 173-5
  food for, 174
  types of, 171
  uses of, 175-6
microwave cooking, 164-5, 248-9
milk (*lait* (m)), 86-8
  energy content, 147
  fermented, 88
  nutritional content, 150
  puddings, 84
  storage, 87
  types, 86
millet, 24
millilitre, 311, 313
millimetre, 312, 313
milling, flour, 21
mincing, 192
mincing machines, 282-3
minerals
  effects of cooking on, 154
  functions, 143-4
mixes, electric, 281-2
mixing, 192
moist-heat cooking, 159, 190, 191
moisture and micro-organisms, 174
molasses, 116
molluscs, 75, 76, 78-80
monkfish (*baudroie* (f)/*lotte de mer* (f)), 70

monosaccharides, 141
monosodium glutamate (MSG), 128
morel (*morille* (f)), 107
motels, 3
moulds, 170, 172
moulds, 273
  in cheese production, 176
Mucor, 173
mullet
  grey (*muge capiton* (m)), 69
  red (*rouget* (m)), 70
mung beans, 109
mushroom
  common/field (*champignon* (m)), 107
  cultivated (*champignon de couche* (m)), 107
mussel (*moule* (f)), 78
mustard (*moutarde* (f)), 128
mustard and cress (*cresson* (m)), 103
mutton, 46
myoglobin, 143

NACNE, 143, 145
National Advisory Committee on Nutrition Education (NACNE), 143, 145
National Vocational Qualifications, 7
navarin, 207
net profit, 322
new dishes, producing and naming, 300-1
niacin, 144
nicotinic acid, 144
non-commercial catering operations, 4-5
noodles, 25
nutrients
  body's need for, 145-8
  classification, 137, 139-40
  effects of baking on, 226
  effects of boiling on, 194
  effects of braising on, 209
  effects of cooking on, 153-4
  effects of deep frying on, 215
  effects of food service on, 154
  effects of grilling on, 230
  effects of preparation on, 154
  effects of roasting on, 239
  effects of sautéing on, 237
  effects of shallow frying on, 221
  effects of sous-vide cooking on, 257
  effects of steaming on, 212
  effects of stewing on, 206
  effects of storage on, 154
  functions, 139-45
  replacement in white flour, 21-2
nutrition, 137-55
nuts (*noix* (f)), 114-15
  nutritional content, 153

oats, 22-3
octopus (*pievre* (f)/*poulpe* (f)), 79

oesophagus, 138
offal, 26, *see also under the type of meat concerned*
 braising, 210
 grilling, 232
 nutritional content, 151
 shallow frying, 223
Offices, Shops and Railway Premises Act (1963), 9
oil, fuel, 169
oils, 94–5
 deep frying, 216–17
 deterioration, 94
 effect of cooking on, 158
 function in diet, 142
 heat transfer in, 164
 nutritional content, 152
 shallow frying, 221
 uses, 94
okra, 105
olive oil, 95
olives, pickled, 130
omelette (*omelette* (m)), 85
onion (*oignon* (m)), 104
 button, 104
 pickling/pickled, 104, 130
 salad ('spring'), 104
orange (*orange* (f)), 113
orders, purchase, 324–5, 327, 328
organisation, kitchen, 307–9
osmosis, 177–8
ounce, 312, 313
 fluid, 312, 313
ovens
 baking, 229
 combination (micro-air), 254–6
 convection in, 162
 convection types, 228
 general-purpose, 241–3
 hazards, 12
 regenerating frozen food, 252–3
 steam convection, 251–3
 temperatures, 242
overhead expenses, 318
overhead grills, 233–5
oxalic acid, 155
oxtail (*queue de boeuf* (f)), 40
oxygen, and micro-organisms, 175
oyster (*huître* (f)), 78
oyster plant (*salsifis* (m)), 105

palatability, 156, 158
pancreas, 139
pans, 274, 275
papaw (*papaye* (f)), 113
papaya (*papaye* (f)), 113
parsnip (*panais* (m)), 104
partie system, 307, 308–9
partridge (*perdix* (f)), 58, 59
pasta, 24–5
 boiling, 198
pasteurisation, 177
pastries
 baking, 226–7
 nutritional content, 153

pâté
 fish, 74
 game, 59–62
pawpaw (*papaye* (f)), 113
pea
 dried, 108–9
 eat-all (*mange-tout* (m)), 105
 garden (*petit pois* (m)), 104
 mange-tout (m), 105
 nutritional content, 153
 petit pois, 105
 sugar pea (*mange-tout* (m)), 105
peach (*pêche* (f)), 113
peanut (*cacahouette* (f)), 115
pear (*poire* (f)), 113
peeler, potato, 283
peeling, 192
penicillin, 173
Penicillium, 173
pepper
 condiment (*poivre* (m)), 127–8
 vegetable (*piment* (m)), 105
percentages, 314–15
peristalsis, 138
personal hygiene, 179–81
pests, 187–8
 damage to food, 177
pH, 174, 178
pheasant (*faisan* (m)), 58, 59
 roasting, 240, 241
phosphorus, 143
phytic acid, 155
pickles, 130
 for braising, 209
pickling, pork, 54
pies
 bacon, 57
 game, 59–62
 pork, 54
 veal, 45
pigeon (*pigeon* (m)), 60
pike (*brochet* (m)), 72
pilferage, 330
pilgrim shell (*coquille Saint-Jacques* (f)), 79
pimento (*piment* (m)), 105
pineapple (*ananas* (m)), 114
pint, 312, 313
pistachio (*pistache* (f)), 115
plaice (*plie* (f)), 70
planning and food control, 329
plans, kitchen, 304–6
plastics, 161, 271
plat du jour, 288–9
plum (*prune* (f)), 114
poached (*poché*) foods, *see* poaching
poaching, 202–5
 in combination oven, 256
 deep, 203–4
 effects of, 202
 eggs, 205
 equipment for, 205
 fish, 203–4
 fruit, 204
 general points in, 205

poaching (cont'd)
    meats, 204
    poultry, 204
    shallow, 203
    shellfish, 204
poêlé-cooked (*poêlé*) foods, *see* poêlé cooking
poêlé cooking, 244
    beef, 42
    lamb, 50
    veal, 45
poisonous foods, 179
pomegranate (*grenade* (f)), 114
pork (*porc* (m)), 51–4
    belly (*poitrine* (f)), 52
    boar, 51
    carcass, 54
    chop (*côte* (f)), 53
    chump, 52
    cooking methods, 54
    escalope (*escalope* (f)), 53
    escalopine (*escalopine* (f)), 53
    fillet, 54
    forcemeat, 54
    gilt, 51
    grilling, 231
    hand and spring (*épaule* (f)), 52
    head (*tête* (f)), 52, 53
    joints, 52
    kidney (*rognon* (m)), 53
    leg (*cuissot* (m)), 52
    liver (*foie* (m)), 53
    loin (*longe* (f)), 52
        long, 54
        short, 54
    offal, 53
    pies, 54
    porkers, 51
    purchasing, 51
    roasting, 240, 241
    sausages, 54
    sautéing, 237
    shallow frying, 223
    shoulder (*épaule* (f)), 52
    side, 54
    small cuts, 53
    sow, 51
    spare-rib (*basse-côte* (f)), 52
    spare-ribs, barbecue style, 53
    stag, 51
    storage, 52
    suckling pig, 51
    trotter (*pied* (m)), 52, 53
portion control, 318, 330–1
potato
    croquette, 84
    flour, 24, 264
    new (*pomme nouvelle* (m)), 105
    nutritional content, 152
    old (*pomme de terre* (m)), 105
    sautéing, 237
potato peeler, 283
pots, 274, 275
poultry (*volaille* (f)), 27–33, *see also individual types*
    boiling, 197
    braising, 210
    deep frying, 217
    grilling, 230, 232
    poaching, 204
    poêlé cooking, 244
    purchasing points, 27
    roasting, 240, 241
    sautéing, 237
    shallow frying, 223
    steaming, 213
    stewing, 206–7
    thawing frozen, 27
pound, 312, 313
poussin, 28
power electrical, 167–8
prawn
    common (*crevette rose* (f)), 77
    Dublin bay (*langoustine* (f)), 77
    jumbo/Mediterranean (*crevette rouge* (f)), 77
premises
    design of, 301–6
    hygiene standards, 181
preparation loss, 331
    fish, 68
preparatory tasks, basic, 191
Prescribed Dangerous Machines Order (1964), 12
preserves, nutritional content, 152
pressure cooking, 164
pressure frying, 216
professionalism, 5, 309–10
profit, 292, 310, 319, 331
prohibition orders, 9
prosecution notices, 9
proteases, 139
proteins, 141–2
    absorption, 139
    effect of boiling, 193
    effect of cooking on, 154, 158–9
    energy content, 147
    functions, 141–2
    as thickening agents, 265–6
protozoa, 170
public houses, 3
puddings, steaming, 213
pulses
    boiling, 198
    dried, 107–8
purchase orders, 324–5, 327, 328
purchase specifications, 329–30
purchasing
    allowing for wastage, 316–17
    and food control, 329
    procedure, 327–8
puréeing, 192
    vegetables, 195

quail (*caille* (f)), 33, *see also* poultry
qualifications, 7–8
quart, 312, 313
quenelles, fish, 74

râble, 61
rabbit (*lapin* (m)), 58, 61
radiation, 159, 163
radish (*radis* (m)), 105
ragoût, 207
raspberry (*framboise* (f)), 114
rats, 187–8
ravioli, 25
reception, 6
rectum, 138, 139
redicchio, 105
refreshing boiled vegetables, 194, 195
refrigeration, 169, 183–4
refrigerators
  cleaning, 186–7
  types of, 184–5
  use of, 185
refuse disposal, 182
regeneration
  of frozen food, 252–3
  of sous-vide dishes, 257
regulations, 9–10
  disposable containers, 308
  food poisoning, 179
reheating
  in combination oven, 256
  vegetables, 196
rendering, 31, 32, 158
Reporting of Injuries, Diseases and Dangerous Occurrences Regulations 1985 (RIDDOR), 11
residential homes, 4
respiration of micro-organisms, 174, 175
restaurants, 3
retinol, *see* vitamin A
rhubarb (*rhubarbe* (f)), 114, 155
riboflavin, *see* vitamin B2
rice (*riz* (m)), 23
  boiling, 198
  flour, 23, 264
rissoles, 84
roast (*rôti*) foods, *see* roasting
roasting, 239–43
  beef, 42
  chicken, 32
  in combination oven, 255
  effects of, 239
  equipment, 241–3
  game, 59–62
  general points on, 241
  heat transfer in, 163
  lamb, 50
  meat, 239–40
  pork, 54
  poultry, 240, 241
  use of trivet, 240
  turkey, 32
  veal, 45
  vegetables, 241
rock salmon (*chien de mer* (m)/ *aiguillat* (m)), 70
rolls, filled, 247
roughage, 137, *see also* fibre
roux, 158, 264

Royal Institute of Public Health and Hygiene, 7, 8
Royal Society of Health, 7, 8
ruotini, 25
rye, 24

sabayon, 84, 266
saccharin, 141
safety, *see also* health and safety *and* hazards
  committees, 10
  electricity, 167–8
  signs, 11–12
Safety Signs Regulations (1980), 11
sago, 24
salad items, purchasing and storage, 99
salads
  compound, 246
  simple, 246
salamander, 230, 231, 233–5
  hazards, 13
  radiation in, 163
Sale of Goods Act (1979), 291
sales mix, 292
salivary glands, 138, 139
salmon (*saumon* (m)), 72, 73
salmon trout (*truite saumonée* (f)), 72
Salmonella enteriditis, 83
salmonellae, 17, 83, 171, 172, 179
salsify (*salsifis* (m)), 105
salt (*sel* (m)), 127, 144, 194
sandwiches, 247
sardine (*sardine* (f)), 70
sauces, 265, 266, 267–8
  anglaise, 84
  béchamel, 265, 267
  bottled, 129
  espagnole, 265, 267
  fruit, 267
  hollandaise, 266
  mayonnaise, 266
  miscellaneous, 268
  preparation using egg-yolk, 266
  preparation using a roux, 264, 265
  purposes of, 267
  vegetable, 267
  velouté, 265, 267
sauerkraut, 176
sausages, pork, 54
sautéed (*sauté*) foods, *see* sautéing
sautéing, 237–8
  in combination oven, 255
  commodities suitable, 237
  effects of, 237
  game, 59–62
  general points on, 238
  lamb, 50
  pans for, 274, 275
scallop (*coquille Saint-Jacques* (f)), 79
scampi (*langoustine* (f)), 77
school meals service, 5
scollop (*coquille Saint-Jacques* (f)), 79
scurvy, 149

searing, 206
selling, 310
   price, 318–19
semolina, 23–4
service charges, 316
service equipment, 274
setting up, 206, 209
shallot (*échalote* (f)), 106
shallow frying, 221–5
   bacon, 56
   beef, 42
   in combination oven, 255
   conduction in, 161
   effects of, 221
   equipment, 221, 224–5
   fish, 221, 222, 223
   fruit, 223
   general points on, 223–4
   lamb, 50
   meat, 223
   pork, 54
   veal, 45
   vegetables, 223
shallow poaching, 203
shellfish (*coquillage* (m)), 75–80, *see also names of individual types*
   classification, 75
   crustaceans, 75, 77–8
   molluscs, 75, 78–80
   poaching, 204
   purchasing points, 76
   storage, 76
   uses, 75, 76–8
shortening, 94
shredding, 192
shrimp (*crevette grise* (f)), 78
SI units, 311–12, 313
silver, 161
silver plate, 270
simmering, 193
singeing, 206
skate (*raie* (f)), 71
slicing, 192
slicing machines, 280–1
smoke-point, 94, 158, 216
smoking
   bacon, 55
   fish, 72
snail (*escargot* (m)), 80
snipe (*becassine* (f)), 60
sodium, 144
solid fuels, 169
soufflés, 84
sous chef, 308
sous-vide cooking, 257–8
soy sauce, 129
soya beans, 109
spaghetti, 25
specifications
   for purchasing, 329–30
   recipes, *see* standard recipes
spices (*épices* (f)), 123, 124
   uses, 124–5
spinach (*épinard* (m)), 106, 155
spirillae, 171

spoilage of food, 176–8
spores
   bacteria, 172, 173, 194
   mould, 173
sprat (*esprot* (m)/*sprat* (m)), 71, 73
spreading, 192
squid (*encomet* (m)/*calmar* (m)), 80
staffing structures, 307–9
stainless steel, 161, 270
standard recipes, 320, 321, 329, 330–1, 332
Staphylococcus aureus, 171, 172, 179
staphylococci, 171, 180, 181
starches, 141
   effect of boiling, 193
   digestion, 141
   effects of cooking on, 153, 157
   as thickening agents, 265
statements of account, 326
steaks, *see* beef
   frozen, 41
steam convection oven, 251–3
steamer
   hazards, 13
   high-pressure, 253–4
steaming, 212–14
   at atmospheric pressure, 213–14
   convection in, 163
   effects of, 212
   equipment for, 213–14
   fish, 213
   general points in, 213
   high-pressure, 212
   poultry, 213
   puddings, 213
   vegetables, 213
steel
   black/plain, 270
   stainless, 161, 270
steers, 34
sterilisation, 177
stewing, 206–8
   in combination oven, 256
   effects of, 206
   equipment for, 207
   game, 59–62
   general points on, 207
   lamb, 50
   veal, 45
stews (*ragoûts* (m)), 207
still room, 302
stir-frying, 222
stirring, 192, 272, 273
stock control, 326–8, 330
stock levels, 327
stocks, 263
   convenience, 263
   in stewing, 206
   veal, 45
stomach, 138, 139
storage cupboards, hazards, 13
storage of food, 182–3, *see also under individual commodities*
   and food control, 330
   humidity, 183

storage of food (*cont'd*)
  temperature, 182
    cook-chill, 260–1
storekeeper, 327, 328
stores requisition, 328
straining, 192, 272, 273
strawberry (*fraise* (f)), 114
streptococci, 171
Streptococcus lactis, 171
stuffings, 84
sturgeon (*esturgeon* (m)), 73, 74, 75
sucrose, 140, 141
suet, 95
sugar (*sucre* (m)), 116–17
sugars, 140
  double, 141
  effect of cooking on, 157
  nutritional content, 152
  simple, 141
swede (*rutabaga* (m)), 106
sweetbread, *see under the meat concerned*
  braising, 209, 211
sweetcorn (*maïs* (m)), 106
sweeteners, artificial, 141
symbols, equipment, 303, 304
syrup (*sirop* (m)), 117
  corn, 117
  golden (*mélasse raffinée* (f)), 117
  maple, 117

tabasco sauce, 129
table d'hôte menu, 288, 293
tapioca, 24
tea (*thé* (m)), 118
  herb, 118–19
  menus (afternoon tea), 290
temperature
  and micro-organisms, 174
  scales, 160
  storage, 182
  units, 312, 313
textured vegetable protein (TVP), 153
thawing frozen food, 177
therapeutic diets, 291
therm, 168
thermometers, 160
thermostats, 160, 226
thiamin, *see* vitamin B1
thickening agents, 264–7
thyroid gland, 155
thyroxine, 155
tilting kettles, 200
timing operations, 187
tinned foods, nutritional value, 155
tinned ware, 271
tins, 273
tisanes, 118–19
toaster, 163, 230
tofu, 109
tomato (*tomate* (f)), 106
  ketchup, 129
tongue, *see under the meat concerned*
  braising, 211

toxins, 179
Trade Descriptions Act (1968), 291
trade discounts, 315
transport catering, 4
trays, 273
treacle (*mélasse* (f)), 116, 117
trivet, 240
trout (*truite* (f)), 72, 73
  farming, 63
  salmon trout (*truite saumonée* (f)), 72
truffle (*truffe* (f)), 107
trypsin inhibitors, 155
turbot (*turbot* (m)), 71
turkey, *see also* poultry
  cock/stag (*dindon* (m)), 32
  hen (*dinde* (f)), 32
  roasting, 240, 241
turnip (*navet* (m)), 106, 155

underfined grill, 164, 230, 235–6
  radiation in, 163

vacuum-packing, 258
value added tax, 323–4
variable costs, 322
VAT, 323–4
veal (*veau* (m)), 42–5
  best end (*carré* (m)), 43
  brain (*cervelle de veau* (f)), 44
  braising, 210
  breast, (*poitrine* (f)), 43
  chop (*côte de veau* (f)), 44
  chump (*quasi* (m)), 43
  cooking methods, 45
  cushion (*noix* (m)), 43
  cutlet (*côtelette de veau* (f)), 44
  escalope (*escalope de veau* (f)), 44
  escalopine (*escalopine de veau* (f)), 44
  grenadin (*grenadin de veau* (m)), 44
  head (*tête de veau* (f)), 44
  haunch, 43
  joints, 43
  kidney (*rognon de veau* (m)), 44
  knuckle (*jarret* (m)), 43
  leg, 43
  loin (*longe* (f)), 43
  medallion (*médaillon de veau* (m)), 44
  middle neck (*basses côtes* (f)), 43
  neck or scrag (*cou* (m)), 43
  offal, 44
  osso-bucco (*osso-bucco de veau* (m)), 44
  paupiette (*paupiette de veau* (f)), 44
  poêlé cooking, 244
  purchasing points, 42
  roasting, 240
  rump (*quasi* (m)), 43
  sautéing, 237
  shallow frying, 223
  shoulder (*épaule* (f)), 43

veal (cont'd)
  small cuts, 44
  stewing, 206–7
  storage, 43
  sweetbread (*ris de veau* (m)), 44
  thick flank (*noix patissière* (m)), 43
  undercushion (*sous-noux* (m)), 43
vegetables (*légumes* (m)), 97–109, *see also under individual types*
  availability, 98, 100
  baking, 227
  boiling, 193, 194–6
  braising, 210
  classification, 97–8
  cooking in a blanc, 196
  deep frying, 217
  frozen, 99
  glazing, 195–6
  grades (EC), 99
  grilling, 232
  nutritional content, 152
  purchasing points, 98–9
  puréeing, 195
  reheating, 196
  roasting, 241
  shallow frying, 223
  steaming, 213
  storage, 98–9
  uses, 97, 100–7
vegetative bacteria, 172
velouté sauce, 84, 265, 267
venison (*venaison* (f)), 58–9, 62
  braising, 210
  roasting, 240
ventilation, 10
vermicelli, 25
vertical bowl choppers, 279
vibrios, 171
vinaigrette, 95
vinegar (*vinaigre* (m)), 128, 176, 178
viruses, 170
vitamin A, 145, 148
  in fish, 64
  in margarine, 95
vitamin B1, 144, 149
  deficiency, 149
vitamin B2, 144
vitamin C, 143, 144, 149
  effects of boiling, 194, 195
vitamin D, 143, 145, 148
  deficiency, 149
  in fish, 64
  in margarine, 95
vitamins, 144–5
  effects of cooking on, 154
  functions, 144–5
vitreous enamel, 270–1
voltage, 167–8

walnut (*noix* (f)), 115
washing facilities, 10, 180
wastage, 316–17, *see also* preparation loss
water
  in food, effect of cooking on, 157
  and heat transfer, 164
water-soluble vitamins, 144
watercress (*cresson de fontaine* (m)), 103
wattage, 167–8
weight, units of, 311, 312
welfare catering, 4
wheat, 20–2
whelk, 79
whipping, 192
whisks, 262, 263
whitebait (*blanchaille* (f)), 71
whiting (*merlan* (m)), 71
Wine and Spirit Education Trust, 7, 8
wine bars, 4
winkle (*bigorneau* (m)), 79
wood, 161, 271, 274
wood-pigeon (*pigeon* (m)), 60
woodcock (*bécasse* (f)), 60
Worcestershire sauce, 129
work flow, 302–3
  centralised production systems, 261–2
work practices, hygienic, 182–7
work schedules, 310

yard, 312, 313
yeasts, 170, 173
  uses of, 175–6
yield tests, 318
yoghurt (*yaourt* (m)), 88
  bacteria in the production of, 176